ReImagining Women
Representations of Women in Culture

The last decade has seen master narratives in literature, art, and history diversified by a range of voices, viewpoints, and images. This has brought new complexities and wider-ranging contexts to feminist discourse. With its multicultural and international perspective, *ReImagining Women* charts the new diversity while focusing on issues of representation in literature and visual art.

The eighteen essays in this volume were originally presented at a Royal Society conference in Edmonton in April 1990. Contributors include scholars in women's studies, literature, and art history from Canada, Australia, Britain, and the United States. Their subjects range from dilemmas of representation in contemporary First Nations women's poetry in Canada to a study of portraits of Queen Christina of Sweden. The collection concerns itself with the relation between the image and what the image is held to represent. As well, the authors examine the ways that women writers and artists have addressed and revised misogynist representational practices. Neuman's introduction provides a clear explanation of the volume's structure and areas of concern.

The ongoing study of the nature, methods, and politics of representation continues to ground the rhetoric and direction of pro-feminist work. This lucid, theoretically sophisticated collection offers new strategies and insights, and is essential reading for teachers and students on feminist criticism, women's studies, and comparative literature.

SHIRLEY NEUMAN is Professor and Chair of English at the University of Alberta. She is co-editor, with Smaro Kamboureli, of *A Mazing Space: Writing Canadian Women Writing* (1986), and of books and essays on women's writing and on autobiography.

GLENNIS STEPHENSON is Lecturer in English at the University of Stirling and author of numerous essays on Victorian women poets as well as of *Elizabeth Barrett Browning and the Poetry of Love.*

Theory / Culture

General editors: Linda Hutcheon and Paul Perron

ReImag*in*ing Women

Representations of Women in Culture

Edited by
Shirley Neuman
and
Glennis Stephenson

UNIVERSITY OF TORONTO PRESS
Toronto Buffalo London

ISBN 0-8020-2777-6 (cloth)
ISBN 0-8020-6825-1 (paper)

Printed on acid-free paper

Canadian Cataloguing in Publication Data
Main entry under title:

Reimagining women: representations of women in culture

(Theory/culture)
ISBN 0-8020-2777-6 (bound) ISBN 0-8020-6825-1 (pbk.)

1. Women. 2. Feminism. 3. Women in art.
4. Women in literature. I. Neuman, Shirley, 1946– .
II. Stephenson, Glennis, 1955– . III. Series.

HQ1111.R45 1993   305.32   C93-093871-2

The editors and the publisher gratefully acknowledge the following for
funding that enabled the publication of this book:

THE ROYAL SOCIETY OF CANADA

LA SOCIÉTÉ ROYALE DU CANADA

and

The Secretary of State for Multiculturalism, Government of Canada

Contents

Acknowledgments

ReImagining Women began as a conference, titled Imag(in)ing Women, held at the University of Alberta in March 1989. Several people gave papers we have not been able to include in this volume; an evening of readings and a show of women's art, each representing some of the actual imaginative activities of contemporary women writers and artists in Canada, and both central to the conference, are also unrepresented here. Our first debt, then, is to the actual conference participants: to all those who gave papers which kept discussion humming and to the audience of our colleagues and students whose questions – alert, probing, supportive, confrontational – helped determine the final shape of this volume. For a specially fine evening of poetry and fiction, one which led many of us to rethink the imag(in)ing of women, we thank Kristjana Gunnars, Claire Harris, Jamila Ismail, Smaro Kamboureli, Lee Maracle, Daphne Marlatt, and Aritha Van Herk. Bridget Elliott and Janice Williamson worked with Edmonton Art Gallery curator Elizabeth Kidd to mount a show of contemporary Canadian women's art, Dangerous Goods, in conjunction with the conference; the opening of that show, along with a performance by Sherry Moses, made an especially convivial and stimulating event during those three days.

Our greatest debt goes to Juliet McMaster. It was she who, when the Royal Society announced that its new five-year plan included funding for the 'Advancement of Women in Scholarship,' suggested to the Society that it might fund a conference on women and literature, and it was she who approached one of the present editors about organizing such a conference. As the project grew and grew (at times, we suspect, to her alarm), she worked staunchly and creatively to see to it that the event was an intellectual, organizational, and financial success. The editors have relied on her indefatigable good spirits, her determination never to take 'no' for an answer, her wise counsel, and her unwavering support at every stage of this process. We have also relied very considerably on three other colleagues who were instrumental in the planning and realizing of the Imag(in)ing Women Conference and in the earliest stages of the editing of this volume: to Patricia Clements, Bridget Elliott, and Jo-Ann Wallace we owe and gladly render up many thanks.

We have also had a lot of help with the drudgery of book-making. Flora Pavich typed successive versions of these essays with cheerful patience and enviable accuracy. Deborah Wills proofread with speed and precision, and Erika Rothwell has been invaluable in the process of tracking down permissions. We are grateful to all these people.

And finally, it must be admitted, events such as the Imag(in)ing Women Conference and books such as this do not come cheaply. The Royal Society of Canada, acting through its 'Advancement of Women' program, has provided major and very generous funding for both the conference and the publication. We want to thank especially Don Ramsay, Rose Johnstone, and Michael Dence from the Royal Society, all of whom have helped variously along the way. The Social Sciences and Humanities Research Council of Canada provided significant conference funding. The Secretary of State for Multiculturalism also contributed significantly to the production of the volume in hand; we could not have carried it forward without the extra help of that office. We have had generous support, too, from the University of Alberta, notably from its Conference Fund, from the Offices of the Vice-President (Academic) and the Dean of Arts, and from the Women's Studies Programme. To Vice-President Peter Meekison, Dean Patricia Clements, and Pat Prestwich, Chair of Women's Studies, we owe much, not only for their financial and collegial support of this endeavour, but for all they have done to enable the activities of women on this campus.

For permission to quote passages from published work or to reproduce visual material we are grateful to the following:

DANGAROO PRESS: Abena Busia. 'Liberation.' *A Double Colonization: Colonial and Post-Colonial Women's Writing.* Ed. Kirsten Holst Petersen and Anna Rutherford. Dangaroo Press, 1986. Excerpts reprinted with permission

FUSE MAGAZINE: Aruna Srivastava. 'Imag(in)ing Racism: South Asian Canadian Women Writers.' Reprinted with permission of *Fuse Magazine*

GENRE: Patricia Yaeger. 'The "Language of Blood": Towards a Maternal Sublime.' *Genre* 25, no. 1 (Spring 1992). Reprinted with permission of *Genre: A Quarterly Devoted to Generic Criticism*

GEORGE BORCHARDT, INC: Monique Wittig. *The Lesbian Body.* Copyright 1973 by Les Editions de Minuit. Copyright 1975 by Peter Owen. Reprinted with permission of George Borchardt, Inc. Literary Agency

GRIMSTHORPE AND DRUMMOND CASTLE TRUST: *Queen Christina* (oil 1687) by Michael Dahl. Permission granted by Grimsthorpe and Drummond Castle Trust

GUERNICA: Nicole Brossard. *Lovhers.* Trans. Barbara Godard. Montreal. Copyright 1986. Excerpts reprinted with permission of the publisher

JAMILA ISMAIL: Jam. Ismail. 'from the DICTION AIR.' *Contemporary Verse.* Copyright 1988. Excerpts reprinted by permission of the author

KUNAPIPI: Madeline Coopsammy. 'The Second Migration.' Copyright 1986. Reprinted with permission of *Kunapipi*

LITTLE, BROWN: From *Twelve Moons* by Mary Oliver. Copyright (c) 1972, 1973, 1974, 1976, 1977, 1978, 1979 by Mary Oliver

MCCLELLAND AND STEWART: Lorna Crozier. *Angels of Flesh, Angels of Silence.* Toronto. Copyright 1988. Excerpts reprinted with permission of the publisher

DAPHNE MARLATT: Daphne Marlatt. 'Listening In.' Copyright 1985. 'musing with mothertongue.' *Touch to My Tongue.* Longspoon Press. Copyright 1984. Excerpts reprinted with permission of the author

MUSEO DEL PRADO: *Isabel of Bourbon*, 1653. de Velazquez (cat. 1179); *Christina on Horseback*, de S. Bourdon (cat. 1503). Both reproduced with permission of Museo del Prado, Madrid

JEAN NAGGAR: Lines from Peter Rutter, *Sex in the Forbidden Zone.* World Rights exclusive of North America

NATIONAL LIBRARY OF SWEDEN: *Fame Records Swedish Victory in Germany*, Falck, 1653; *Queen Christina and Her Virtues*, Diricksen. Reproduced with permission

NATIONAL SWEDISH ART MUSEUMS: *Queen Christina*, Beck, 1650; Queen Christina as Diana, and Queen Christina on triumphal chariot, both from ornamental watchcase, Signac, 1646; *Queen Christina in Rome*, Testana, 1656; *The Triumphal Entry of Queen Christina into Rome*, de Rossi, 1656; *Queen Christina Surrounded by Personifications*, Fariat, 1680s. All reproduced with permission

NEW DIRECTIONS PRESS: H.D. 'Fragment 113.' *H.D. Collected Poems.* Copyright (c) 1981 the estate of Hilda Doolittle. Reprinted with permission of New Directions Press Corp.

SHARON OLDS: Sharon Olds. 'The Language of the Brag.' First published in *Calyx.* Reprinted in *Florilegia, a Retrospective of Calyx* (1987) and in *Satan Says* (1980). Excerpts reprinted with permission of the author

PRESS GANG: Lines from *Not Vanishing,* by Chrystos. Vancouver: Press Gang Publishers 1988

ROYAL COIN CABINET, STOCKHOLM: Queen Christina and the Swedish Court, Dattler, 1644. Reproduced with permission

SISTER VISION. BLACK WOMEN AND WOMEN OF COLOUR PRESS: Himani Bannerji. 'Paki Go Home.' Sister Vision Press, Toronto. Copyright 1986. Excerpts reprinted with permission of the publisher

SUSAN RUBIN SULEIMAN: Susan Rubin Suleiman. 'To a Poet.' *Michigan Quarterly Review* 29, no. 4 (Fall 1990), 683–4. Excerpts reprinted with permission of the author

JOANNE TOD: *Research and Development,* private collection; *Self Portrait as Prostitute,* private collection

LOLA LEMIRE TOSTEVIN: Lola Lemire Tostevin. *Color of Her Speech.* Toronto. Copyright Lola Tostevin 1982. Excerpts reprinted with permission of the author

TURNSTONE PRESS: Lines from *Questions i asked my mother* (copyright Di Brandt, 1987). Reprinted by permission of Turnstone Press

WELLCOME INSTITUTE LIBRARY: *Charcot Lecturing on Hysteria at the Salpêtrière.* Etching after André Brouillet, 1887. Copyright The Trustees of the Wellcome Trust, 1991. Reprinted with permission Wellcome Institute Library, London

WILLIAMS-WALLACE: Arun Mukherjee. 'South Asian Poetry in Canada: In Search of a Place.' *Towards an Aesthetic of Opposition.* Published by Williams-Wallace 1988. Reprinted with permission

WOMEN'S PRESS: Nila Gupta. 'So She Could Walk.' *Fireworks: The Best of Fireweed.* Toronto. Copyright 1986. Excerpts reprinted with permission of the author

WRITER'S WORKSHOP: Suniti Namjoshi. 'How to Be a Foreigner.' *More Poems.* Calcutta: Writer's Workshop 1971. Reprinted with permission

W.W. NORTON: The lines from *Sphere: The Form of a Motion,* by A.R. Ammons, are reprinted by permission of W.W. Norton and Company, Inc. Copyright (c) 1974 by A.R. Ammons

YALE UNIVERSITY: *Pinel Freeing the Insane.* Photogravure. From engraving from mural in Charcot Library by Tony Robert-Fleury, 1887.

Reprinted with permission. Medical Historical Library, Cushing/ Whitney Medical Library, Yale University, New Haven, CT

Repeated efforts have been made to contact all copyright holders. We will gladly acknowledge, in future editions, all holders of copyright who have not yet responded and who subsequently contact us.

Shirley Neuman
Glennis Stephenson

ReImagining Women

ReImag*in*ing Women:
An Introduction

SHIRLEY NEUMAN

S/he who writes, writes. In uncertainty, in necessity. And does not ask whether s/he is given the permission to do so or not.

Trinh T. Minh-ha, *Woman, Native, Other,* 8

To write: I am a woman is heavy with consequences.

Nicole Brossard, *These Our Mothers,* 45

*ReImag*in*ing Women.* The title itself constituted the major directive to this volume's contributors and to the participants in the earlier Imag(in)ing Women Conference. Its shifting inflections and emphases signal the intersections of multiple feminist critical practices around issues of representation in literature and the visual arts. It stresses the descriptive: women who make images; women who imagine. And it stresses the performative: the acts of imaging and imagining women. Cognate projects push in from around its edges: the project, for example, undertaken by writers as different as Luce Irigaray and Monique Wittig in France and Nicole Brossard in Canada of imagining women we have not yet been, women outside representations within patriarchal social organizations, discourses, ideologies, and the (male) Imaginary; and the many identity projects of postcolonial women and of different 'Third World' women and women of colour for whom the imperatives of race, class, political allegiances, state apparatuses, and a network of familial relations all enter into feminist political theory. These latter are women for whom such intersecting 'identities' may mean that, as bell hooks points out, some women experience sexism most acutely *within* the context of the politics of racial liberation (15–18), or may even mean, as Sara Suleri has so provocatively put it in her challenge to the identity-politics of Western feminisms, that 'there are no women in the third world' (20).

The eighteen essays in this collection largely draw on, extend, and often bring together four quite different, but nonetheless interrelated, thrusts of feminist criticism and theory in which representation is an issue. One of these invokes the concepts of 'images of women,' 'resisting readers,' and 'the authority of experience.' In a very real sense many of the essays in this volume, like much in feminist critical practice, continue the work of such initiating feminist critics and theorists as Simone de Beauvoir in *The Second Sex*, Mary Ellmann in *Thinking about Women*, and Kate Millett in *Sexual Politics*, work that exposed to the sceptical light of critical inquiry, the better to dismantle them, the structures of misogyny supporting representations of women in literature and the visual arts as well as the received readings of those representations. This work concerns itself with the *referentiality* of representation, with the relation between the image and what – in the world of objects, people, places, and the states and conditions of their being – the image is held to represent. At issue here is the factuality and the factitiousness of representations: their perceived referential accuracy and their fabrications; the shape given them in view of the audiences for which they are intended; what those audiences understand as factual and as factitious; the social relationships and relations of power which those representations serve to effect or enforce for their readers or viewers.

In recent years a certain feminist chic has been quick to suggest that we have moved beyond 'images of women' criticism; a more generous and just response might be that it grounds much that we have moved into. And a more politically aware response might urge that such work is more than ever strategically necessary, given the present appropriation of 'images of women' criticism by those who, like Camille Paglia in *Sexual Personae*, argue that cultural symbols, images, and narratives of women as immanent – flesh definitely limited and bound by the reproductive cycle – represent women's inescapable, because biologically destined, reality. The political urgency of carrying on the task of dismantling the 'images of women' promulgated in misogynist culture, as well as the complexities of the issues and identifications this task raises, become heartbreakingly obvious at many junctures in this collection.

One of those occurs when Mary Nyquist shows how the debilitating stereotypes of romance plots can inform the rhetoric and presuppositions
of pro-feminist work against male violence and undermine its effectiveness. Another is Nicole Dubreuil-Blondin's intimation that the blindness to gender in the media's response to Marc Lépine's murder of
fourteen women engineering students, whom he represented as 'feminists,' replicates the displacement of gender concerns in each of our
disciplines. And yet another comes with Catharine Stimpson's scrutiny
of the images of substance-abusing mothers disseminated by the
media, the media's use of these images to displace other gender issues,
and her own changing responses to such images.

The continuing and vigorous dismantling of the misogynist structures and representations of much in the literary and visual arts traditions enables an understanding of gendered relations of power not
only as they are represented in literature and the visual arts but also as
they are enacted in women's experiences of reading and viewing. The
kinds and range of authority exerted by representations over the
woman reading or looking at them, the ways in which texts and images
ideologically and culturally position and (dis)empower different readers and viewers, the agency women in turn can exert in relation to representations of them: these questions have led feminist critics to what
Adrienne Rich termed 're-vision,' or the 'drive to self-knowledge' by
means of 'the act of looking back, of seeing with fresh eyes, of entering
an old text from a new critical direction' (18); they have made us what
Judith Fetterley aptly called 'resisting readers,' readers who will examine 'fictions in the light of how attitudes toward women shape their
form and content [in order] to make available to consciousness that
which has been largely left unconscious and thus to change our understanding of these fictions, our relation to them, and their effect on us
...' (xii). 'Resisting readers,' countering misogynist images of women
largely by what an early collection called *The Authority of Experience*,
found themselves anticipated by the women whose work they sought
out in the tremendous recuperative activity which has reconstructed a
women's tradition in the literary and visual arts, women who, with
greater or lesser degrees of self-consciousness and overtness, were
themselves resisting cultural constructions and representing their revisions in their work. This reading of women writers and artists for the
ways in which they (may have) revised misogynist representations and
representative practices remains one of our most important strategies
both for understanding what the experience, as opposed to dominant

cultural representations, of past women may have been, and for understanding the social and political effects of representation on the experience of women.

The five essays in the first section of *ReImagining Women* all explore, in visual images and literary works from divergent periods and genres and for divergent audiences, this space between received representations of women and women's representations, between women as objects of representation and women as subjects engaged in representational practices. Rose Marie San Juan examines the dynamics of representation when the body of a woman which, in iconographic traditions, is nearly always represented as subjugated and as object of a spectator's gaze, is also the royal body, for which the portrait tradition has a well-established iconography and semiosis of power which functions to subjugate the monarch's subjects who view her image. Because Queen Christina both ruled and abdicated, had power and relinquished it, commissioned portraits of herself and was the subject of portraits commissioned by others, and because rumour sought to discredit her by attaching sexual ambiguity to her, her portraits, as Rose Marie San Juan shows, provide a complex and exemplary instance of the manipulation of power and powerlessness signalled by visual and verbal representations of the queen's, and the woman's, body and sexuality. The representation of the woman who is a public figure, and the ways in which she can and cannot manipulate that representation, are also the subject of Glennis Stephenson's discussion of two figures very different from Queen Christina: the nineteenth-century sentimental poets Mrs Hemans and Letitia Landon. In 'Poet Construction' Glennis Stephenson explores the different ways in which these two writers manipulated the image of the 'poetess' constructed, and enforced, by contemporary editors, reviewers, and readers so as to 'turn constraint into opportunity'; she marks the gaps between their signed discourse and their lives; and she documents both Landon's resistance to her era's construction of the 'poetess' and the ways in which her audience reappropriated for that construction her strategies of resistance.

Queen Christina, Mrs Hemans, and Letitia Landon all negotiate in their self-representations a transgression inherent in the fact of their being queen or poet. Each depends on an established iconography in the genre within which she is working and against which she asserts what generic conventions, mirroring social organization, would deny her sex. We might say that each strategizes her gender by exploiting the paradox that the fact of her writing, ruling, or commissioning portraits introduces into received generic conventions. But in other

instances women have chosen to modify generic conventions in ways
that allow their representations a moral agency which those conventions traditionally deny them. That this is one of the oldest strategies
enabling women's self-representation becomes evident in Patricia
Demers's demonstration of how two early women dramatists, Hrotsvitha of Gandersheim and Hildegard of Bingen, take markedly different approaches to school their audiences in ways of reading and
viewing which radically subvert, and reclaim for the chaste woman, the
powers of the narrative of conversion and salvation traditionally
denied her 'sinful' flesh. An equally entrenched tradition, that of the
heroine's 'compulsory' beauty which, in romance and the early novel,
stands as sign of her moral worth (and, in a double bind, becomes sign
of her duplicity), Isobel Grundy argues in 'Against Beauty,' is challenged in the eighteenth century, first by writers such as Samuel Richardson and Henry Fielding, and then, much more thoroughly and to
quite different ends and effects, by women writers whose heroines are
more concerned with their sexuality than their beauty and who overtly
desire (and are misled by) male beauty. Patricia Yaeger, in 'The "Language of Blood": Towards a Maternal Sublime,' suggests that some of
the most avant-garde contemporary poets of the United States are
reconstruing the Sublime in terms of that which the Romantic Sublime
has most assiduously repressed, mothers' bodies.

   The sequence we have (rather than the sequences we might have)
imposed on these essays[1] is one which groups together in the second
section considerations – to use the word in several senses – of the
'material.' They all owe something to a second strand of feminist criticism and theory which in fact began as a critique of 'images of women'
criticism with its formalist and thematic focus and largely evaluative
and corrective aims. Feminist historical materialists have argued that to
focus on representation as mimesis is to focus on the art object, already
fashioned, artificed, and functioning within understood representational practices (which is to say, within a semiotic system we call 'art' or
'literature'). It is, the argument runs, to ignore the social conditions,
such as access to 'knowledge' and its production, material resources,
leisure, and the institutionalization and legitimization of some practices over others, which produce both the representational practices
we term 'art' and the 'experience' which we hold that art represents. It
is equally to ignore the ways those same conditions lead to the consumption of one work as art, another as non-art, an omission of crucial
importance when we are considering the work of women which has so
often been received as 'craft' or 'popular' literature rather than 'art.'[2]

Representation in this configuration of the term is a matter of signifying *practices* and their reception rather than of the relation between the art object and what it represents.

The notion of the 'material' has become diffused through much feminist criticism, and we now use the word in several senses. At the theoretically strict end of the 'materialist' spectrum, feminist historical materialists such as Roszika Parker and Griselda Pollock writing about the visual arts, or Gayatri Chakravorty Spivak writing about various textualizations of colonialism and of subaltern resistance, rigorously reread from a feminist awareness of such works as Karl Marx's *Grundrisse* and *Eighteenth Brumaire of Louis Napoleon*, and Louis Althusser's *Essays on Ideology*. At the most generalized end of the spectrum an emphasis on the 'material' can refer simply to a rigorously archival practice within the disciplines of history and women's studies, aimed at recovering information about the actual conditions of, for instance, work, reproduction, family, housing, income, and marriage in which women lived their lives, and using this information to correct prior historical narratives. Between these two poles materialist analyses have entered feminist literary criticism in particular via the work of writers such as Mikhail Bakhtin in *Rabelais and His World*, which takes a materialist approach to language itself, or, more recently, of Pierre Bourdieu, who introduces materialist considerations into his conception of cultural production as a competitive field, his distinctions between linguistic and cultural, economic and symbolic capital, and his analysis of the relation between aesthetic values and class.

Several of the essays in *ReImagining Women*, including those grouped in its second section, take up some of these different materialist approaches to understanding women's relation to representation. Patricia Prestwich demonstrates how wide the gap is between representations of women and the reality of their material circumstances which such representations efface when she counters two of the nineteenth century's most widely disseminated images of women's 'madness' (the engraving of psychiatrist Philippe Pinel unchaining the 'madwomen' at Salpêtrière, and the etching of Jean-Martin Charcot, at the same hospital, using a patient to demonstrate his lecture on hysteria) with the facts documented in the case histories of women committed to a large Parisian teaching hospital of the period: facts about their economic circumstances, the support they received from their families, marital violence, and the duration and symptoms of their 'illnesses.' In 'More Than Pin Money: Economies of Representation in Women's Modernism' Bridget Elliott and Jo-Ann Wallace look at the ways in which the possession or lack of economic capital was a determining factor in both the kind of self-(re)presentation modernists as various as Natalie Barney, Romaine Brooks, Nina Hamnett, Peggy Guggenheim, Djuna Barnes, and Bryher undertook and the credibility (or symbolic capital) it earned them in the avant-garde. Their materialist framework enables them to expand and complicate our sense of modernism by pointing to the significant differences in the power these women's diverse economic and artistic positions allowed them to exercise within the movement.

Two other essays in this second section ask questions about the implications of particular critical receptions of cultural products, questions that point to the representational practices of literary and art *criticism* at least as much as to those of the work it discusses, and that ask about the social effects of such reception and (re)presentational practices. If the strength of feminist historical materialism has been its ability, demonstrated in these essays, to address a much wider range of women's work than do more formalist methodologies, it has done so, Nicole Dubreuil-Blondin argues, by virtue of a blindness to precisely those formal aspects of art that have been the object of much traditional art history, by virtue less of re-vision than of radically shifting the object of the gaze. In 'A Woman's Touch: Towards a Theoretical Status of Painterliness in the Feminist Approach to Representation in Painting' she historicizes the self-referentiality of feminism as having displaced the study of the pictorial or 'painterly' by the study of the thematics of imagery, and she examines the new directions in feminist analysis of painting opened up by the materialist consideration of the *apparatus* of representation, of its organization and historical evolution as a signifying system. But she also assesses the pitfalls to which this feminist historical materialism is subject and its failure to provide any alternative mode of specifically stylistic analysis, arguing for an emergent feminist art theory and criticism which considers the ways in which every image is 'a material production' of paint, 'every brushwork an investment of work as much as of desire.' Such a critical practice would not replace art history's formal, technical, and iconographic practices but would revise them.

And, in 'Romance in the Forbidden Zone,' Mary Nyquist begins by 'gesturing' towards a history of male mentorship of women in the domestic sphere, particularly as it is recorded in romance fiction, remarking that in the twentieth century its 'scene of instruction' has shifted from the heroine's morals to her sexuality. In this context she re-examines the recent positive critical reception of romance novels, noting that this reception and re-presentation of romance novels come at the price of failing to note the racism or the sexual violence their plots reproduce. Romances, she shows, deal with sexual violence by narrative strategies of denial which re-present victimized heroines as transformed into subjects who 'author' their own desire for violent men. The representational effects of such a narrative strategy on the larger body politic emerge when she sets such plots against Peter Rutter's *Sex in the Forbidden Zone: When Men in Power – Therapists, Doctors, Clergy, Teachers, and Others – Betray Women's Trust.* While Rutter's work is pro-feminist and pro-active on issues of sexual violence against women, Nyquist's analysis shows how thoroughly its rhetoric is nonetheless imbued with the romance stereotypes of male mentor and female neophyte needing protection, and of female 'boundaries' that must be 'guarded' until 'awakened ... by a predatory, phallic sexuality that knows, instinctively, no bounds.' In this understanding the narratives of romance have social effects that reach far beyond escapist or compensatory fantasy for the actualities of women's lives; they (re)enforce sexual stereotypes that undermine and undo action for social change even among the politically aware and well-intentioned.

At stake in materialist analyses such as Mary Nyquist's is *agency:* the capacity to act in autonomous ways, to affect the social construction of one's subjectivity and one's place and representation within the social order. This is a concern continuous with the essays in the third section of *ReImagining Women,* all of which stress the materiality of both body and language and examine the relation of agency to representation in terms of the relation of women's bodies to their representation in language. Each of the writers whose work is addressed in these essays – philosopher and psychoanalyst Luce Irigaray, novelist and manifesto writer Monique Wittig, and poet and fiction-theorist Daphne Marlatt – has been widely criticized as 'essentialist,' as theorizing a *literal* relation between women's biological bodies and representation, a relationship which would deny agency in the name of anatomy. While Diana Fuss has cooled the fires of this debate by showing that 'essentialists' and 'anti-essentialists' are to some extent each reliant upon the presuppositions of the other, the essays gathered here take the path recently articulated in Margaret Whitford's consideration of Luce Irigaray as a philosopher. Like Whitford they hold that these writers 'most apparently biological remarks about the female body' are 'statements about the adequacy or inadequacy of the symbolic/social order and the place allotted to woman/women' (170). Writers such as Irigaray and Wittig undertake first to deconstruct the patriarchal edifices of theory and representation within which women have been defined and then to *re*imagine women as they might be if they could construct their identities entirely outside such edifices. This is an utopian project, one for which representation is not a question of referentiality but of presenting a radical reconception of the social order and its concomitant psychic structures, a question of 'constructing in imagination a society that would be fit for women to live in' (Whitford 190). Thus Elizabeth Grosz understands Luce Irigaray's representation of sexual morphology, or the meaning given the body – 'the body as organized, unified, intelligible, cohesive, specularizable' – as a strategy by which Irigaray both deconstructs the subordination of women's bodies in the power relations of male-oriented representations and hypothesizes modes of resistance to that subordination by imagining different discourses, knowledges, and representations which would allow women to reclaim their bodies and their identities in terms of self-defined values and which would have far-reaching social and psychological implications for women, men, and the body politic. In 'Lesbianizing Love's Body' Dianne Chisholm reads Monique Wittig as putting into play a textual body, one that draws attention to a polysemous and polymorphous language practice used to imag(in)e a sexual and political economy wholly 'other,' to 'rethink or reimag(in)e the body in order to initiate political revolution and change the body politic.' And Pamela Banting reads Daphne Marlatt's poetic manifesto, 'musing with mother-tongue,' as calling for a poetic practice in which the material body of language and the desiring body each signifies itself, but in which the writer develops a new figure of speech, a kind of simile which is a 'process of attraction,' a series of 'parallels between the human body and the body of language without privileging either term, tenor or vehicle, of that simile.' Physical body and material text, in this practice, 'translate' one another intersemiotically, back and forth from one signifying system to another. Once again, the process aims at the creation of an utopian Imaginary, one that will see the production of different textual practices, the construction of different bodies.

These essays, then, construe women writers and visual artists, as well as their readers, viewers, and critics, as understanding 'representation' in at least four senses: as a mimetic act; as a re-visionary act *within* dominant representational practices; as a process of production and consumption; and as *re*-presentation radically otherwise, *outside* of and alternative to present representations of women. Each of these senses of representation, of imag(in)ing, circulates through contemporary discussions of postcolonial writing, visual art, and theory, and each cir-

Part 4
Post colonial
representation

culates through the essays on postcolonial representational strategies
gathered in the fourth section of this collection.

Three of the many available approaches to (post)colonial subjects
figure most significantly here. One draws on the considerable theory
about postcolonial subjectivity in an emerging nation state, the knowledges, discourses, and social structures of which bear traces of the
colonialism they contest. In the context of Homi K. Bhabha's elucida-
tion of colonialism as an apparatus which constructs, by means of the
actual dispersion of power and of its symbolic practices, both the colonizer and the colonized, Uzoma Esonwanne undertakes an examination of feminist theory's use of tropes of colonialism. He elaborates the
political implications and consequences, in the postcolonial context,
of Hélène Cixous's metaphor of female sexuality as a 'dark continent,'
and of Susan Sontag's image of men as colonialists and women as
natives in the '"imperialist" situation' in which 'all women live'; those
critiques lead him to consider the ways in which it is and is not possible
to use imperialist tropes in feminist theory without obliterating historical, cultural, and ideological differences between women.

A second emphasis in postcolonial theory has addressed the anxiety
of cultural expression, which is to say, the terms on which an 'indigenous' literature and visual art can be created and the tension between
it and the practices and discourses of the colonial power from which it
both derives and desires to differ. This is an aspect of postcolonial theory that has been most fully summarized in *The Empire Writes Back*; it is
furthered here by Linda Hutcheon in her examination of the different
ways – some purely oppositional, some asserting both continuity with
and rupture from imperialist representations and their apparatuses of
production – in which Canadian women writers and visual artists have
employed the double-voicedness of irony to articulate their position as
women and, in some cases, as racially oppressed. Kateryna Longley
also addresses the relation of postcolonial writing to its reproduction
of imperialist representations by calling into question the ways in
which Australian literary history marginalizes women's writing, and
especially writing by immigrant, ethnic, and Aboriginal women.

Longley joins to this second strand of postcolonial theory of representation a third, which examines the ways in which the apparatuses of
postcolonial representation reproduce imperialism with the difference
that the white mainstream postcolonial writer or visual artist is now
experienced as a cultural imperialist in relation to racially and ethni-
cally marginalized artists *within* the postcolonial society. Turning to
such writers, she finds the postcolonial writing dilemma rendered

more complex by the intersections between 'oppressive public text
with secret private texts.' Questions of how far such writers can use the
protection of writing as a way of risking self-revelation and 'of how
much they can afford to cut themselves free from the voices and structures and other controlling ties which have silenced them or led them
along prescribed paths in the past' become crucial here. These same
questions of transparency and opacity, disclosure and secrecy, of how
much of the protection of invisibility the writer is willing to surrender   *the cloak of*
in a culture dangerous to her, come up again in Jeanne Perreault's dis-   *invisibility* .
cussion of the writing of native women. Her '"touch the matrix":
Native/Woman/Poet' raises issues shared by feminist postcolonial criticism and 'Third World' feminist theory: issues about the demand for
'authenticity'; for the native woman, the ethnic woman, the woman of
colour, to be 'representative' of a group without specifying the differences within the group; for her to write only or primarily about race.
Jeanne Perreault shows how these issues structure the strategies by
which one native/woman/poet, Chrystos, textualizes her multiple subjectivity and assumes agency by representing her identity in terms of
will, choice, act. Many of those same issues are both the subject and the
process of Aruna Srivastava's essay, in which she writes *about* South
Asian women writers in Canada but in which she also textualizes the
process of her coming to a self-identification as a South Asian woman
and academic in this country. That process brings her up against the
negative and illiberal imaginings of racism which she comes to understand as both 'a failure of the imagination' and 'an act of the imagination.' It also brings her to claim, 'contradictorily and finally,' the
'authority and the community of experience.'

  This collection begins by looking at the ways in which a seventeenth-
century European queen negotiated the ideological iconography of
royal portraiture in the interests of self-representation as both queen
and woman and at the ways in which the portraits commissioned by
others, as well as not-so-veiled rumour – the 'media' of her day – called
into question both her authority and her sexuality or 'purity.' It ends
with a look at contemporary women who are pregnant and addicted.
The distance seems a long one, but in important ways it is no distance
at all. For what is at play in both sets of representations are the images
which, Catharine Stimpson shows us, the media invokes 'again and
again and again' in order to represent abstinent, or 'good,' mothers as
a reproach to addicted, or 'bad,' women: the images of the 'pure' and
the 'impure.' These are precisely the images Rose Marie San Juan has
shown in play between Queen Christina's public self-representation as

chaste ('pure') and the representation of her, in pamphlets circulated
by her political enemies, as a promiscuous lesbian ('impure'). Queen
Christina seems of only historical interest now, and in her time she was
a problem chiefly to certain European kings. The hundreds of thousands of babies with addictions, physical and mental defects, and foetal
illnesses now born each year in the United States to substance-abusing
mothers are an immediate social, economic, and personal crisis of
immense proportions. But the dynamics of the representations of
these vastly different women remain the same. In both instances the
media of the day image a political problem (power and territorial
expansion in Queen Christina's case) or social problems (women's
poverty, the housing crisis, a pervasive cultural rhetoric promising
material ease and personal happiness through the consumption of
goods and substances – all contributing factors in addiction – the
absence of treatment programs for the poor and the pregnant) as the
consequence of the 'impurity' of the sexually autonomous woman.
The image of the 'impure' woman and the demand that she be legally
restrained serve to mask other social issues, such as abortion, at stake
in and played out in the representations of these women, and they
serve to displace social responsibility for problems such as poverty
onto the addicted bodies of those same women.

Scholars of 'Third World feminisms,' such as Cherrié Moraga and
Gloria Anzaldúa in their introduction to *This Bridge Called My Back*,
Trinh T. Minh-ha in *Woman, Native, Other,* and Chandra Talpade
Mohanty in 'Under Western Eyes,' have made us realize the necessity
of addressing the local politics of women's oppression, of formulating
'autonomous, geographically, historically, and culturally grounded
feminist concerns and strategies' rather than discursively colonizing all
women in the name of 'Western' feminisms (Mohanty, 'Under Western Eyes' 51). This salutary lesson about the differences within discursively categorized groups and even within individual identities is one
that feminist scholars have had to take to heart and head about the differences between Western white middle-class feminists and most of the
world's women, between and within Third World women, and also
between and within even Western white middle-class women. These
are differences documented and analysed in their specific historical
moments and practices of imag(in)ing women that are the subjects of
this collection's essays. The 'framing' of the collection by two essays
which invoke the imagery of 'pure' and 'impure' women in no way
erases those differences between and within. But it is meant to suggest
a common focus in these essays on the gap between traditional and
still privileged representations of women in art, literature, scholarship,

and the media and the different representations produced by an attention to what writer and activist Nicole Brossard calls women's 'real.' Sometimes women represent this focus sharply, sometimes with softer contours; sometimes they conceptualize in terms of difference from within dominant representational modes and their constructions of subjectivity, sometimes in terms of utopian projects of reimagining representation and the construction of women's subjectivities. Always it comes down to a question of a woman's assumption of agency in the *act* of representation and of how that agency alters the imag(in)ing of women. Nicole Brossard enumerates the great deal at stake in that assumption of agency through (self-)representation:

> We can say, on the one hand, that until now reality has been for most women a fiction, that is, the fruit of an imagination which is not their own and to which they do not *actually* succeed in adapting. Let us name some of those fictions here: the military apparatus, the rise in the price of gold, the evening news, pornography, and so on.
>
> On the other hand, we can also say that women's reality has been perceived as fiction. Let us name some of those realities here: maternity, rape, prostitution, chronic fatigue, verbal, physical, and mental violence. Newspapers present these as *stories*, not fact. (*Aerial Letter* 75)

She positions the woman writer: 'I say that writing begins here, between what's real and what's fictive' (69). A few of the many locations of that 'here,' and some strategies for getting there, are the subject of *ReImagining Women*.

Notes

1 The issues raised by the essays in the different sections of *ReImagining Women* overlap considerably, and readers will no doubt find other paths through them than that marked out by their sequence here. This first section, for example, might well have included Dianne Chisholm's 'Lesbianizing Love's Body,' which demonstrates that, at its most radically subversive, the reappropriation and redeployment of canonical narratives and tropes can be used to 'universalize' what they traditionally most suppress: for example, the lesbian body. For Wittig, Chisholm concludes, the 'lesbian body is not a female body; instead, the lesbian body signifies a categorical resistance to the "myth of Woman," and withdraws support from any critical venture that would recuperate the sign of "woman."' Or, several essayists in this first section might have been grouped with others later in the volume around a themat-

ics of the representation of women's bodies. These include Patricia Demers
on celibate and salvific bodies; Isobel Grundy on plain Janes, broken-nosed
Amelias, bloody and dishevelled Ellens, dark Gertrudes, and ugly but active
and desiring Olivias; and Patricia Yaeger on maternally sublime bodies.
They might well be joined by Catharine Stimpson on pregnant, substance-
abusing women, Bridget Elliott and Jo-Ann Wallace on the semiosis of a
third-best set of underwear, Elizabeth Grosz on sexual morphology as trope,
Dianne Chisholm on the relation of the lesbian body to the body politic, and
Pamela Banting on writing the body.

   Another sequence might trace the discussion of writing and painting, of
reading and viewing, both within and against the grain of narrative and
painting conventions, developed by Patricia Demers about medieval nuns
and Isobel Grundy about eighteenth-century women novelists in this first
section. It might join to their essays those of Linda Hutcheon on irony as a
postcolonial representational practice used by both black and white Canadian writers and painters, and of Aruna Srivastava on South Asian Canadian
women writers and Jeanne Perreault on aboriginal writers. Similarly, one
could well pair Patricia Yaeger's essay with Dianne Chisholm's, given that
both delineate the ways in which 'grotesque' bodies – pregnant bodies, lesbian bodies – can be (self-)represented as a site in which, to quote Mary
Russo, 'the symbolic and cultural constructs of femininity and Womanness
and the experience of *women* ... might be brought together toward a
dynamic model of a new social subjectivity' (214). Yet another reading
sequence might pursue the gaps between representation and (self-)repre-
sentation, introduced in this first section by Rose Marie San Juan in relation
to Queen Christina of Sweden, considered further on in the context of nineteenth-century female asylum patients by Patricia Prestwich, and raised
again – in the context of postcolonial subjects 'marginalized' as racial
minorities – by Kateryna Longley, Aruna Srivastava, and Jeanne Perreault.
These latter essays also raise questions about the extent and the kinds of
agency entailed by, or possible to, acts of representation in different political
and material circumstances. Indeed, these questions not only run through
all the essays grouped in the fourth section of *ReImagining Women*, but also
figure significantly in the readings of French feminist theorists and their
counterparts in poetry and fiction in the third section, and become the basis
of Mary Nyquist's rigorous questioning, in 'Romance in the Forbidden
Zone,' of the recent reception studies of popular romances which theorize
the genre as providing consolatory and even enabling fantasies for their
women readers.

2 Parker and Pollock in chapter 2 of *Old Mistresses* and Parker in *The Subversive
   Stitch* analyse the ideologies of representational practices which have characterized women's artistic production as 'craft'; Parker's book provides an

excellent analysis of women's needlework as serving many of the ends of 'art' under the rubric of 'craft.' Pollock, in the first chapter of *Vision and Difference*, outlines the importance of historical materialism to feminist revisions of art history.

Works Cited

Althusser, Louis. *Essays on Ideology*. London: New Left Books 1983

Ashcroft, Bill, Gareth Griffiths, and Helen Tiffin, eds. *The Empire Writes Back: Theory and Practice in Post-Colonial Literatures*. London: Routledge 1989

Bakhtin, Mikhail. *Rabelais and His World*. Trans. Hélène Iswolsky. Bloomington: Indiana UP 1984

Bhabha, Homi K. 'Difference, Discrimination and the Discourse of Colonialism.' In *The Politics of Theory*. Ed. Francis Barker et al. Colchester: U of Essex P 1983, 194–211

– 'The Other Question: The Stereotype and Colonial Discourse.' *Screen* 24, no.6 (1983), 18–36

Bourdieu, Pierre. *Distinction: A Social Critique of the Judgement of Taste*. Cambridge: Harvard UP 1984

– 'The Production of Belief: Contribution to an Economy of Symbolic Goods.' In *Media, Culture and Society: A Critical Reader*. Ed. Richard Collins et al. London: Sage 1986, 131–63

–, and Jean-Claude Passeron. *Reproduction in Education, Society and Culture*. Trans. Richard Nice. London: Sage 1977

Brossard, Nicole. *The Aerial Letter*. Trans. Marlene Wildman. Toronto: Women's P 1988. Originally published as *La Lettre aérienne* (Montréal: Les Editions du remue-ménage 1985)

– *These Our Mothers Or: The Disintegrating Chapter*. Trans. Barbara Godard. Toronto: Coach House P 1983. Originally published as *L'Amèr ou le chapitre effrité* (Montréal: Quinze 1977)

de Beauvoir, Simone. *The Second Sex*. Trans. and ed. H.M. Parshley. New York: Knopf 1964

Diamond, Arlyn, and Lee R. Edwards, eds. *The Authority of Experience: Essays in Feminist Criticism*. 1977; reprint, Amherst: U of Massachusetts P 1988

Dybikowski, Ann et al, eds. *Women and Words / Les Femmes et les mots Conference Proceedings*. Edmonton: Longspoon P 1985

Ellmann, Mary. *Thinking about Women*. New York: Harcourt, Brace and World 1968

Fetterley, Judith. *The Resisting Reader: A Feminist Approach to American Fiction*. Bloomington: Indiana UP 1978

Fuss, Diana. *Essentially Speaking: Feminism, Nature and Difference*. London: Routledge 1989 hooks, bell. *Yearning: Race, Gender, and Cultural Politics.* Toronto: Between the Lines 1990

Marlatt, Daphne. *Ana Historic: A Novel.* Toronto: Coach House P 1988

– *Rings.* Reprinted in *What Matters: Writing 1968–70* (Toronto: Coach House P 1980)

Marx, Karl. *The Eighteenth Brumaire of Louis Napoleon.* In *Selected Works in One Volume.* By K. Marx and F. Engels. London: Lawrence 1970

– *The Grundrisse.* New York: Harper 1971

Millett, Kate. *Sexual Politics.* Garden City: Doubleday 1970

Mohanty, Chandra Talpade. 'Introduction: Cartographies of Struggle: Third World Women and the Politics of Feminism.' In *Third World Women and the Politics of Feminism.* Ed. Chandra Talpade Mohanty, Ann Russo, Lourdes Torres. Bloomington: Indiana UP 1991. 1–47

– 'Under Western Eyes: Feminist Scholarship and Colonial Discourses.' In *Third World Women and the Politics of Feminism.* Ed. Chandra Talpade Mohanty, Ann Russo, Lourdes Torres. Bloomington: Indiana UP 1991, 51–80. Revised version of essay first published in 1984

Moraga, Cherrié, and Gloria Anzaldúa, eds. *This Bridge Called My Back: Writings by Radical Women of Color.* New York: Kitchen Table / Women of Color P 1983

Paglia, Camille. *Sexual Personae: Art and Decadence from Nefertiti to Emily Dickinson.* New Haven: Yale UP 1990

Parker, Roszika. *The Subversive Stitch: Embroidery and the Making of the Feminine.* London: Women's P 1984

–, and Griselda Pollock. *Old Mistresses: Women, Art and Ideology.* London: Routledge and Kegan Paul 1981

Pollock, Griselda. *Vision and Difference: Femininity, Feminism and the Histories of Art.* New York: Routledge 1988

Rich, Adrienne. 'When We Dead Awaken: Writing as Re-Vision.' *College English* 34 (1972), 18–30

Russo, Mary. 'Female Grotesques: Carnival and Theory.' In *Feminist Studies / Critical Studies.* Ed. Teresa de Lauretis. Bloomington: Indiana UP 1986, 213–29

Rutter, Peter. *Sex in the Forbidden Zone: When Men in Power – Therapists, Doctors, Clergy, Teachers, and Others – Betray Women's Trust.* Los Angeles: J.P. Tarcher 1989

Spivak, Gayatri Chakravorty. *In Other Worlds: Essays in Cultural Politics.* New York: Methuen 1987

Suleri, Sara. *Meatless Days.* Chicago: U of Chicago P 1987

Trinh T. Minh-ha. *Woman, Native, Other: Writing Postcoloniality and Feminism.* Bloomington: Indiana UP 1989

Whitford, Margaret. *Luce Irigaray: Philosophy in the Feminine.* New York: Routledge 1991

The Queen's Body and Its Slipping Mask: Contesting Portraits of Queen Christina of Sweden[1]

ROSE MARIE SAN JUAN

In December 1965, in preparation for a major Council of Europe exhibition, the body of Queen Christina of Sweden was removed from its sarcophagus in St Peter's and examined by an anatomist, an anthropologist, and various historians. The results, meticulously recorded for the sake of scholarship and Swedish television, were not entirely satisfactory (Hjortsjo 138–58). The team was able to retrieve the silver death-mask which had covered the queen's face since her death in 1689, but not to verify from the body beneath 'the possible intersexuality of Queen Christina' (Hjortsjo 140). Every decaying bone was meticulously measured and checked to see 'whether her skeletal formation disclosed any male characteristics,' but after almost three hundred years the body refused yet another attempt to fix its 'true' sexuality, and the scholars had to be content with a copy of the silver mask for their exhibition.

This macabre addition to Queen Christina's already colourful myth is, like my paper, about the slippery ground between the inner and the outer, the private and the public, the body and its mask. It is also about the fact that while definitions of these categories are historically specific, women's place within them has been, and remains, closely regulated and surveyed. Queen Christina abdicated the throne of Sweden in 1654, and her myth was largely propelled by explanations of this event which reassert the public image of royal power, yet which do so by addressing the queen's private body. She had ruled during the last half of the Thirty Years' War, in which Protestant forces, headed by

Sweden, succeeded in breaking down the Roman Catholic stronghold in Europe (Dunn 80–92; Roberts, *Imperial Experience* 1–42). In 1648 the Peace of Westphalia recognized religious freedom within a reconstituted Europe of nation-states, and Sweden emerged with expanded territories and a stable monarchy (Roberts, *Sweden* 160–3). Significantly, the theme of Queen Christina's coronation, celebrated two years later, was Swedish military victory (Karling 159–85).

Why Queen Christina subsequently chose life as an exile, first travelling through Europe and then settling in Rome in 1655, was, and remains, a highly contested question. The queen herself wrote that the renunciation of great power is the act of only the greatest rulers (Masson 116). The papacy would claim that her abdication had been prompted by her conversion to a higher authority, namely the Roman Catholic church. The Swedish court offered as explanation her inability to ensure a legitimate royal succession because of illness and a reluctance to marry. The French monarchy, on the other hand, circulated pamphlets which accused Queen Christina of promiscuity, lesbianism, and atheism, when, after leaving Sweden, she was given protection by France's main rival, the Spanish king (Masson 233, 85–7, 172–4). These were by no means random accusations: such claims coincide all too neatly with seventeenth-century medical and religious discourses which defined the female body as uncontrolled sexually and innately heretical (Stallybrass 123–42). Other factions took up the issue of sexual deviance as the motivating factor for the abdication and represent the queen as a lesbian or a hermaphrodite. And, indeed, this is the main theme of later biographies (Stolpe). Even Hollywood, which attempted to turn the story into a respectable romance between a headstrong queen and a dashing Spanish ambassador, raised the spectre of sexual ambiguity by casting Greta Garbo in the title role (Barthes 56–7).

In effect, forms for regulating the female body have always had a part in portrayals of Queen Christina; the seventeenth-century representations of the queen's body are particularly intriguing because they became a way of contesting the very sphere from which the female body was usually excluded, namely the public arena of political power. The predicament of the female body that I am addressing may be gauged from the problematic relationship between women and visual traditions for representing monarchical power. In the seventeenth century political writers such as Hobbes understood the emergence of the monarchical nation-state as dependent on the visibility of power to keep its subjects in awe (Pye 279–301). To cite Foucault, 'In a society

like that of the seventeenth Century, the King's body wasn't a metaphor, but a political reality. Its physical presence was necessary for the
functioning of the monarchy' (*Power/Knowledge* 55). But royal spectacle
was effective because it was reflexive; the sovereign's power to dazzle
and subject any who gazed on him depended on the subject's gaze,
which transformed the king's organic body into a political body that
embraced and subsumed the subject (Pye 281). Louis Marin, in his
study of Louis XIV, argues for the centrality of the king's body, which,
linked to a particular name and history, produced the ideal conditions
of subjectivity: 'it is not the physical body that disappears in the representation of his majesty to which it is appropriated, but on the contrary, it is the body of power that finds its power only in the limits of the
physical body that supports it and attains its ends only with its mortal
term' (Marin, 'Body of Power' 427). This theory assumes a male body,
not only because most rulers were male, but because the female body,
as an already subjected body, could not occupy the ultimate point of
visibility. In the exceptional case of a female monarch strategies of representation became necessary to counteract the inability of the female
body to escape its social and sexual status as submissive. For example,
Elizabeth I of England adopted traditional images of female sexuality,
in particular the virgin body, to assert the self-mastery of the royal body
as well as its stable sexual identity (Montrose 48–50). In the Rainbow
Portrait of 1600 Elizabeth's sexual independence is literally embroidered onto her body; the serpent on her sleeve represents wisdom and
controls a heart which alludes to passion (Strong 50–2). The eyes and
ears on the queen's mantle are the eyes of her subjects who contemplate her, but whose sight serves her in the task of government and
endows her with the most powerful gaze. This strategy was crucial since
the problem of representation for the female ruler was not only the
subjected female body, but also the relationship of power set up by
court portraiture. The parallel often drawn between Elizabeth I and
the Virgin Mary – virgin, but also the maternal figure who subsumes
her subjects as her children – counters the tendency of representations
of the female body to be consumed by a viewer whose gaze was ultimately in control.

With Queen Christina the problem of representation was complicated by the issue of sexual ambiguity. But it is precisely because her
image was less fixed that it allowed more room for contestation. For
Elizabeth I the queen's body succeeded in signifying the union of subjects in the same collective body (and erased economic and social differences); for Queen Christina, the queen's body became equally

conspicuous but was constructed from competing representations and
functioned in diverse and even contradictory ways.

In sheer numbers the images of Queen Christina point to the function of portraiture as duplicating the ruler, as making visible to subjects, and reinvigorating, the body which subsumed them (Foucault,
Discipline 28–9, 187–9). There are at least thirty prototypes, most
apparently originating in oil portraits (*Christina* 184–94); these were
reproduced in numerous oil and enamel variations, readapted into
countless engravings, medals, marble busts, and book illustrations
(bibles and scholarly dissertations), and even engraved into wine-
glasses and rings. Many were generated by the Swedish state, which circulated them widely, and by the queen herself, who sent them to
friends or contacts. Some were requested by monarchs and aristocrats,
forming a courtly network of favours and obligations, while others
were produced by the papacy and were intended to validate particular
papal projects. Strategies of representation can be linked to the available categories of royal portraiture, and one of my aims is to distinguish among such categories as oil painting, engraved prints, medals,
and public spectacle. As processes of meaning with different ways of
constructing the queen's body, these categories differ in the ways they
define the relation between the private body and the public mask.

In general terms what the portraits of Queen Christina reveal is that
the issue of sexual deviancy could be used to attack the monarchy
and/or the Swedish queen, but it could also become a means to construct a more viable image of power. In 1648 Louis XIV requested a portrait of Queen Christina. He received an oil painting (fig. 1) by court
painter David Beck (who made various reproductions, including this
1650 version) as well as a text written by his representative in Sweden,
Pierre Chanut, which explained that the painted image 'could not
contain the distinctive aspects of the queen' (Masson 87). The
painting adheres to conventions of seventeenth-century court portraiture and registers in precise ways differences of rank and gender
(*Christina* 187). Striking a balance between the individual sitter and
courtly notions of feminine beauty, the queen's body is presented in a
fashionable dress of white silk; she has flowers in her hair and holds a
delicate veil that flutters with the wind. Unlike male portraits, in which
the idealized body is frequently encased with attributes that locate it
within a court hierarchy and within history, female court portraiture
offers an idealized notion of feminine beauty to be enjoyed and
desired in the visual exchange. Yet the relationship to the viewer and
to the outside world is always mediated; after all, the court lady was to

Fig. 1. Oil portrait of Queen Christina, by David Beck, 1650

be visible but not accessible. The queen's body is enclosed by the chastity implied in her white maiden's costume, by the protected setting of an elegant palace portico overlooking a grottolike garden, and even by her attributes: the globe may indicate that the world is hers, but she communicates with it in the traditionally female form of a letter.

Given that this is the accepted form of representation for someone of Queen Christina's rank and gender, it is extremely interesting to find that Chanut's text – itself a portrait – suggests that there is a lack of fit between the queen and this painting (Masson 112–15). Chanut begins with some obvious ways in which the oil painting fails its subject:

> [The painting] could give no indication of the fine qualities of her character, more particularly because the mobility of her expression changed her face from one moment to another ... one did not perceive so many marvels in the beauty of this twenty-two year old princess as when one considers them at leisure ... the Queen's face in repose was pensive, though agreeable and serene. On the rare occasions when she was roused to anger her expression could strike terror in the beholder. (Masson 113)

He then draws an impressive list of the queen's intellectual achievements, including her understanding of theological debates between Protestants and Catholics, and her knowledge of science and of numerous languages. Chanut praises her skills as a ruler, in particular her ability to outsmart ministers and bureaucrats. He explains that she was not given to gossip about those who served her, and that 'she never talks to women, being too much taken up with affairs of state or sport to be bothered with them' (Masson 115). Referring to Christina's personal life, Chanut remarks on her 'extraordinary physical endurance.' The text ends with this reading of the queen's body:

> ... she was indifferent to heat and cold and could stay ten hours in the saddle in the hunting field and shoot a hare with a single shot better than any man in Sweden ... [the queen] slept only five hours a night and was little interested in her clothes or appearance – taking only fifteen minutes to dress in the morning. Except on state occasions, her coiffure consisted only of a rapid combing of her hair and tying it up with a ribbon, and she never wore a hood or mask, as the custom then was, to protect her complexion but when riding wore a plumed hat ... if any stranger saw her out hunting, wearing a masculine type of coat with a small man's collar, he would never have imagined that she was the Queen. (Masson 115)

Apparently, Chanut is not simply trying to compensate for the queen's inability to fit the static, idealized feminine body of court portraiture. By emphasizing intellectual and political skills and the rejection of female company and by defining an unconstrained physical body, Chanut's representation discards all those ways in which the female body becomes a subjected enclosed body. But his account also transgresses expectations of rank which are conflated with those of gender. Considerations of both rank and gender are directed towards a viable image of the monarch, one which juxtaposes the queen's unindulged private body with the greatness of her political body, and one which Chanut might have been more comfortable to serve.

Chanut's strategy was only possible in the context of a private letter, for the oil portrait, with its prioritizing of sensual pleasures, permitted few such deviations. There is nonetheless an oil portrait of Queen Christina by Sebastien Bourdon which seems to partake of this kind of strategy, and significantly, like Chanut's account, it was not produced for the Swedish court. In 1653 Philip IV of Spain, who made overtures to the queen once he learned of her plans to convert to Catholicism, requested an equestrian portrait (fig. 2) of her to add to his collection (*Christina* 193; Masson 184). Equestrian portraiture, as an image of masculine imperial power, was much favoured by seventeenth-century monarchs but rarely used for women. An exception is the portrait of Philip IV's consort, Isabel of Bourbon (fig. 3), painted to hang with other equestrian portraits of Hapsburg rulers in the Hall of Realms of the king's palace (Brown 107–9). Evidently Queen Christina was to be aligned with this dynasty, but not on the same gender terms as the Spanish consort. In constructing an image of supreme male authority, the equestrian portrait tended to rehearse the mastery of the military leader over his own body, over a powerful creature, and over a military campaign or vast open territories. As the portrait of Isabel of Bourbon shows, these conventions were at odds with the expected comportment of the female body and the forms of its enclosures. She rides side-saddle, sitting on a large, richly decorated carpet, which separates her body from that of the animal. Her elaborate costume, covered with the initials I.B., has a lengthy train, which constrains the queen to a static decorous pose. The horse trots gently as if in ceremonial procession, and the queen, rather than displaying self-mastery, displays herself. Queen Christina, on the other hand, wears a riding coat over a sober costume which is in marked contrast to the colourful livery of her falconer. Her clothes, moreover, do not constrain her, and, while riding side-saddle, she is, as her handling of the horse indicates, in full con-

Fig. 2. Equestrian portrait of Queen Christina, commissioned by Philip IV of Spain, 1653

trol of the rearing creature. The queen, as skilful hunter unimpeded by physical boundaries, injects the image with the authority to challenge the viewer's consuming gaze.

In contrast, images produced in the Swedish court for Swedish consumption are striking for the ways in which they erase any specific traces of the queen's body. For example, on the rare occasions when Christina's reputation as hunter is noted, it is always transformed by a mythological vocabulary. In the enamel case of an ornamental clock (fig. 4a), commissioned by one of the queen's ministers and given to her at the end of the Thirty Years' War, Christina, surmounted by the inscription 'Love of Virtue and Virginity,' confronts the viewer as the goddess Diana, hunter and militant protector of female virginity (*Christina* 185). The mythological disguise, the idealized appearance,

Fig. 3. Portrait of Philip IV's consort, Isabel of Bourbon, by Velazquez, 1635

Fig. 4a. Queen Christina as Diana, ornamental watchcase, 1646

Fig. 4b. Queen Christina on triumphal chariot, ornamental watchcase, 1646

and the delicate enamel technique all serve to distance the image from the body of the queen and its reported transgressions. The lid of the clock-case (fig. 4b) shows the queen crowned triumphant as her chariot tramples over the body of the Spanish enemy and the victorious Swedish armies parade with battle standards and prisoners. Aligning a virgin body, and particularly Diana, with military and political power was a well-known tactic. On 1 November 1649 a ballet from the French play *The Conquest of Diana* dealt with the defeat of Cupid by the chaste Diana and was performed with lavish costumes by the queen herself (Masson 126–7). Yet unlike Elizabeth I, Christina was represented in this way only to a limited extent. Perhaps this was because of the danger of eliding a Protestant queen with the Virgin Mary, or perhaps because there was great pressure from the court for the queen to marry and provide a legitimate successor (Masson 120). But another factor must be the questionable effectiveness of this strategy for a royal image of military leadership, given that this courtly mythological mask, with its play on the desirable yet unavailable female body, tended to empower rather than subject the viewer.

In fact, official royal portraiture insisted on a military image and was primarily conveyed in the form of engraved prints, which could be distributed widely and which fixed meaning more precisely than was possible in oil or enamel painting. Moreover, in prints, the queen's body was mediated, not by a visual experience directed at the senses, but by a configuration of visual and word images which compelled the spectator to read it as a chain of ideas. The engraved frontispiece (fig. 5) to a 1649 Protestant bible (*Christina* 121) presents the female body, not so much to be consumed as an object of desire, but to be read within its place in a structure of knowledge, that of the humanist classical tradition. The queen, holding a sceptre, is contained within an oval garland, which is itself overlaid with eight small ovals, in turn containing female personifications of virtues. While the implication is that the queen embraces all these virtues, the similarities between her and the surrounding figures – oval framing, pose, attributes, and inscription – define the queen herself as a personification. In fact, as the inscription and triumphal procession behind her suggest, the queen represents the fame of military victory, or the ultimate point of visibility. But this visibility does not subsume all subjects; fame is shown in relation to its means and ends. The end of Swedish military fame is religious freedom, represented by the two personifications at either side of the oval garland, and by the lion (Protestantism) crushing the snake (Catholicism) at the queen's feet. The means to this military fame are, first, on

Fig. 5. Queen Christina and her virtues, engraved frontispiece to a Protestant Bible, 1649

the left, Minister Axel Oxenstierna, with the attributes of civic government (owl/wisdom, book/learning, globe/the world as sphere of
action) and the inscription 'Council in Prudent Government'; and,
second, on the right, Commander Torstenson, with military attributes
and the inscription 'Well Armed Abroad.' Significantly, Jupiter, with
his thunderbolt, hovers on his eagle directly above the queen and
resembles her father, Gustavus Adolphus. The text, in fact, links Christina with Hercules, who is said to have received his power from Jupiter
just as Christina received it from Gustavus. So the queen is relegated to
the traditional female body of a personification of fame, and fame is
given its specific historical reference in relation to Gustavus's
renowned military achievements, and to the two flanking historical figures. While personifying the greatest point of visibility, the queen
stands constrained by this passive decorative inspirational role, which
removes her from history and consequently diffuses the power of her
gaze.

In an engraving of 1653 Sweden's latest wars in Germany are ele-
vated to the theme of fame in victory (fig. 6). A female personification
of fame is shown recording on a plinth, and thus turning into history,
the actual military event. Above is once again Gustavus Adolphus as
Jupiter, who passes Hercules's club to Queen Christina. So even after
her formal coronation, the need to perpetuate a military history
within the monarchical image meant that Gustavus's reputation,
rather than any achievement of the present ruler, is recalled. And
although the link between Christina and Hercules may have had particular resonance considering the sexual ambiguity of concurrent representations of the queen, the print raises her, and the figure of fame,
to the lofty but passive level of a symbolic vessel through which royal
history is recorded and legitimized.

This abstraction of the queen's body is crucial because the body of
the ruler gains mystical power by subsuming other bodies, yet its power
remains tied to a particular history. For this very reason, the medal, as
Louis Marin has argued, proved the ultimate sign of absolute political
power (121–37). In the medal subjects find their identity in the body,
the name, and the history of the ruler. Medals invariably commemorate a single historical event and form part of a narrative which
inscribes the presence of the monarch into the subject's memory. The
identification that gives authority to money among peoples gives
authority to the king's history at all times and among all nations. So
how to construct a historical narrative for a body excluded from participation in history? In a 1644 medal Christina's accession at the age of

Fig. 6. Fame records Swedish victory in Germany, engraving, 1653

Fig. 7. Queen Christina and the Swedish court, medal, 1644

eighteen is linked to the triumph of the Swedish navy at the Battle of
Femern in the Baltic Sea that same year (*Christina* 93). On the other
side (fig. 7) Christina is shown at court in front of her throne with the
arms of the Swedish crown at her feet. The inscription calls up Gustavus Adolphus to sustain Christina. Two diagonal lines of figures move
out towards the viewer: five regents stand to the queen's right, holding
symbols of the military and civic forces; to her left are representatives
of the four estates. While the latter represent the lower ranks and, in
the process, render them invisible, the former challenge the power of
the ruler's eye by their direct participation in history. Once again the
visibility of the monarch is turned into the inevitable visibility of a male
hierarchy of subjects.

I now turn to the relation between power and visibility in the representation of Queen Christina after her abdication. It is at this point particularly that representations of the queen's sexuality provided fuel for current religious and political debates, and these representations were produced not only from antagonistic religious factions but also from competing monarchs, and even within the challenge to absolutism. For example, Cromwell, leader of the new English commonwealth, worried that Christina would marry the exiled Charles II and had his foreign secretary, Thurlow, intercept letters from the various agents who kept the queen under surveillance. For example, a report from a Dutch agent dated 7 July 1654 states that 'the Queen of Sweden arrived here this morning in disguise, being in man's apparel. She came from Elsenberg, having only twelve persons to attend her ... The Queen, when she came into the inn, had boots on and a carabine about her neck ...' (Masson 218). Thurlow reworked intelligence reports so that the wearing of male clothing became evidence of hermaphroditism: 'We hear stories of the Queen of Sweden and her Amazonian behavior, it being believed that nature was mistaken in her, and that she was intended for a man, for in her discourse, they say she talks loud and swears notable' (Masson 220, 221). The notoriety generated by unconventional clothing and behaviour was to some degree promoted by the queen herself, who clearly was concerned with maintaining a high level of visibility as a way of negotiating a viable position (Masson 218–54). Significantly, Christina also promoted herself through oil portraits, painted by local artists along her journey and strategically placed in various courts; in these Christina invariably appears as either the goddess Diana or Minerva. Thus the image of female sexual independence is assimilated into courtly expectations by being circumscribed within a desirable yet unattainable mythological guise (*Christina* 245).

The implications of this precarious visibility are best observed in Rome, where the queen and the papacy worked out an agreement for their mutual benefit. The papacy was banking on the queen's image in relation to its royal and religious history, and lost no opportunity to present Christina as the most powerful Protestant ruler who recognized the ultimate authority of the Catholic church (Festini 1). To achieve this end the papacy, like the Swedish court, favoured printed images. A lengthy text by papal historian Carlo Festini was also prepared to accompany engravings produced to commemorate the queen's triumphal entry into Rome – manoeuvred to coincide with Christmas 1655. It is useful to consider these representations in relation to factors crucial to the visibility of the ruler, namely, the royal body, its name, and its history. In Festini's 1656 publication the queen's triumphal entry is constructed as a negotiation of rank and protocol among factions in Rome. Festini describes in amazing detail the colourful luxurious costumes, lavish jewels, and elaborate carriages of the Roman nobility. The queen, at the centre of all this, is described as 'without a single jewel except a little gold ring and wearing a simple grey dress, black scarf, and plumed hat.' In effect, the juxtaposition of the pope's lavish retinue with the queen's 'severe Mannish black dress' signals her humility in the recognition of a greater power. Festini tells that, upon meeting Pope Alexander VII, the queen knelt and kissed his feet:

> The fame of Alexander having no boundary other than the end of the world, she had to come to worship him ... in the frozen sea of the North, little or nothing could stop the ship of St Peter. That ship deposited her Crown at her feet, because she recognized it and with revered humility bowed her head. From Sweden had come the original Amazons, and from them she has taken the example of not having children, but of being the daughter of an Alexander. (129)

The comparison of Queen Christina with an Amazon had by this time become a commonplace (Bjurström 37), and it was used by many, including Cromwell's foreign secretary, as an explicit form of attack. But even such seemingly 'positive' uses as that of Festini raised serious implications. In the seventeenth century Amazons were associated with courage in physical strength, but also with the rejection of men and savage acts of cannibalism (Montrose 36–7). In effect, the Amazon represented an inversion of the patriarchal norm, which, as the case of the queen shows, had the potential to shift. Its frequent use in Rome in relation to Queen Christina includes a lavish carnival festival mounted in her honour featuring a battle between Cavaliers and Amazons, in which the former were victorious (Bjurström 30–7).

Thus references to the Amazons, like the attacks on the queen's body, are not discarded but given a new twist, and become ways of inserting the queen's body into a particular relation with the papacy. An engraving by Testana (fig. 8), issued immediately after the queen's entry into Rome, shows her much as described in Festini's text: the simple costume contrasted with the lavish horse, a gift of the pope (Festini 128–9). Her name appears as Maria Alexandra Christina, associating her with the Virgin Mary, but more specifically with Pope Alexander VII. This reidentification of the queen, promoted in that most

MARIA ALEXANDRA CHRI STINA .SVECIÆ REGINA.

Magnus Alexandro quem ſoluit in Vrbe Philippus,
Froenas imperys, Regia Virgo, tuis. D. H. Q.
Ioſeph. Teſtan Inu. Fecit.

At uictrix ut Regna domes maiora relictis,
Dat Tibi Alexander Nomen, et omen Equus.
Gio. Iacomo Roſsi, le Stampa e le Vende in Roma alla Pace.

Fig. 8. Queen Christina in Rome, engraving by Testana, 1656

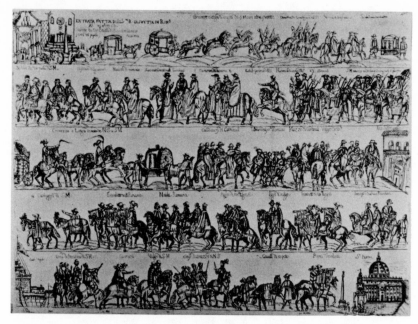

Fig. 9. The triumphal entry of Queen Christina into Rome, engraving by Rossi, 1656

useful of vehicles, the medal (*Christina* 330), reorients her body away from its earlier subject-position. The same can be said of changes made to the queen's relation to her own history. Festini's text mentions that the decoration of the Villa Olgiata, where two cardinal legates greeted the queen before she entered Rome, focused on the queen's personal insigne, the Wasa sheaf of corn emblazoned on an escutcheon with two bendlets, but that the arms of Sweden were not allowed (Masson 247). This is reasserted in the print, where the queen's own insigne connects her to a royal history but not to the particular military historical narrative which was used in Sweden and which the papacy wanted to erase.

What was the point of readjusting the subject-position by reworking the image of the body, its name, and its history? In Testana's print the queen as a reconstituted persona, a floating symbol of royal power, is inserted into the cityscape of Rome and among monuments charged with papal significance. Another type of print (fig. 9) circulated to commemorate the queen's entry into Rome represents a lengthy triumphal procession, which registers a rigid social Roman hierarchy and maps out a specific route through the city by linking certain land-marks: Piazza del Popolo, Arco de' Portogallo, Castello Sant' Angelo, and St Peter's (Bjurström 9–17). Such representations of Queen Chris-tina's entry proved significant in papal attempts to reorient the urban layout of the city towards the Vatican, if not for locals, then for an emergent tourist population.

Clearly in these the queen herself, distinguished from the rest only by a parasol, is subsumed within the papal strategies which her pres-ence legitimizes. But how does this reconstituted identity get rechan-nelled within portraits commissioned by the queen herself? A 1687 oil portrait (fig. 10) by Michael Dahl shows the queen in a vicarious rela-tion to her royal status: a cloak of dark blue velvet embroidered with crowns which covers her body speaks of her claim to a royal history, but her crown and sceptre on the table recall the separation of that royal history from its specific sphere of political action (*Christina* 323–4). The queen's body is constrained within an idealized appearance and the elegant silk and ermine costume and jewels which seem to obliter-ate any allusions to earlier representations. Moreover, it is clearly marked with a cameo of Alexander the Great, which serves as a brooch holding the velvet cloak over her right shoulder. She leans on a globe and gestures towards a scroll, which bears an inscription, 'Neither nec-essary nor sufficient for me,' also known from various of her medals from this period. Apparently we return to the female body of court portraiture, and while in the 1650 portrait for Louis XIV the queen needed intermediaries to rule the world which she had inherited, here she forgoes political power entirely in order to inherit the greater glory promised by St Peter's (shown directly behind her) – her ulti-mate enclosure.

It is interesting to see this regression to courtly constraints repre-sented in an engraving (fig. 11) which served as the frontispiece to a religious dissertation printed in Rome in the 1680s. As in earlier prints the queen is surrounded by personifications of her qualities which she resembles, and thus they can be read as her inspiration but also as vari-ous parts of her whole. Rather than alluding to her qualities as a ruler, these personifications are about the cultural and leisurely activities which now tied the queen to Rome: Architecture, Study of Antique, History, Sculpture, Mathematics, Painting, and Poetry. Sculpture, on the lower right-hand side, points to her work, a statue of 'Victoria max-ima,' the personification which was embodied by the queen in the 1649 bible; here it refers to victory over worldly power rather than to the power of military victory; in other words it is the symbol of her

Fig. 10. Oil portrait of Queen Christina, by Michael Dahl, 1687

Fig. 11. Queen Christina surrounded by personifications, engraving, 1680s

abdication. But the queen's gaze directs our eye towards the personification on the lower left, who has her head covered and holds a triangle with a large eye. This figure, which represents Conversion to Catholicism and like the others is an embodiment of the queen herself, indicates that she not only has lost the ability to see but that she has relinquished that power, and hence the ultimate point of visibility, to the all-seeing eye of God.

It is revealing that these representations of the queen as a physically idealized and subjugated body coincide with her decreasing public visibility. The queen's representation was now to be contained within terms acceptable to a feminine identity; the roles of celebrated Catholic exile and zealous art collector gave Queen Christina only a modicum of access to public life, reducing her political and social options, as well as her usefulness to the papacy, which quickly lost interest in her presence in the city.

This case illustrates only too well how women's problematic relationship to representation underpins their relationship to power, and remains no less an issue for women of high rank. Seventeenth-century strategies of representation to overcome the constraints of established gender norms depended on modes of representation which are in themselves meaningful, setting up particular relationships with audiences; in the case of monarchs, who usually had a range of such modes at their disposal, these relationships intersected in complicated ways. It so happens that traditional forms of royal presentation emerge as the most unyielding in their propensity to register gender difference. For the female monarch the oil portrait was particularly fraught with contradictions: its engagement with a spectator depended on a prior objectifying of women's bodies. Prints, which set up a different relationship with viewers, nonetheless contributed to the same nexus of gender norms. In these Queen Christina as royal body bound together the Swedish court and state hierarchy and erased the lower orders, but also permitted an upper male echelon to show themselves as independent from a female monarch in their political and military activities. Visibility thus depended on the extent to which a form of representation permitted the transgression of gender norms. Ironically, the most powerful representations of Queen Christina were those which reasserted these norms by constructing her as an exception, and by disregarding entirely the spaces between the private body and the royal mask.

Note

1 I am indebted to Serge Guilbaut, Carol Knicely, Kay Dian Kniz, and Maureen Ryan for many useful discussions and suggestions.

Works Cited

Barthes, Roland. 'The Face of Garbo.' In his *Mythologies*. London: Paladin 1973, 56–7.

Bjurström, Per. *Feast and Theatre in Queen Christina's Rome*. Stockholm: National-musei Striftserie 1966

Brown, Jonathan. *Velazquez: Painter and Courtier*. New Haven: Yale UP 1986

Christina Queen of Sweden: A Personality of European Civilisation. Stockholm: Nationalmuseum 1966

Dunn, Richard S. *The Age of Religious Wars 1559–1715*. New York: Norton 1979

Festini, Carlo. *Trionfi della Magnificenza Pontificia nello Stato Ecclesiastico e in Roma per la Maesta della Regina di Suetia*. Rome 1656

Foucault, Michel. *Discipline and Punish: The Birth of the Prison*. Trans. A. Sheridan. New York: Vintage 1979

– *Power/Knowledge: Selected Interviews and Other Writings 1972–1977*. New York: Pantheon 1980

Greenblatt, Stephen, ed. *Representing the English Renaissance*. Berkeley: U of California P 1988

Hjortsjo, Carl-Herman. 'The Opening of Queen Christina's Sarcophagus in Rome.' In Platen, 138–58

Karling, Sten. 'L'Arc de triomphe de la Reine Christine à Stockholm.' In Platen, 159–85

Marin, Louis. 'The Body-of-Power and Incarnation at Port Royal and in Pascal or Of the Figurability of the Political Absolute.' In *Zone: Fragments for a History of the Human Body*. Part 3. Ed. M. Feher. New York: Harvard UP 1989, 421–47

– *Portrait of the King*. Trans. Martha M. Houle. Minneapolis: U of Minnesota P 1988

Masson, Georgina. *Queen Christina*. London: Secker 1968

Montrose, Louis Adrian. '"Shaping Fantasies": Figurations of Gender and Power in Elizabethan Culture.' In Greenblatt, 31–64

Platen, Magnus von, ed. *Queen Christina of Sweden: Documents and Studies*. Stockholm: Norstedt 1966

Pye, Christopher. 'The Sovereign, the Theatre, and the Kingdome of Darknesse: Hobbes and the Spectacle of Power.' In Greenblatt, 279–301

Roberts, Michael, ed. *Sweden as a Great Power 1611–1697. Government: Society: Foreign Policy.* London: Edward Arnold 1968
– *The Swedish Imperial Experience.* Cambridge: Cambridge UP 1979
Stallybrass, Peter. 'Patriarchal Territories: The Body Enclosed.' In *Rewriting the Renaissance: The Discourses of Sexual Difference in Early Modern Europe.* Ed. M.W. Ferguson, M. Quilligan, and N.J. Vickers. Chicago: U of Chicago P 1986, 123–42
Stolpe, Sven. *Christina of Sweden.* Ed. Sir Alec Randall. New York: Macmillan 1966
Strong, Roy. *The Cult of Elizabeth: Elizabethan Portraiture and Pageantry.* London: Thames and Hudson 1977, 50–2

2.

In virginea forma: The Salvific Feminine in the Plays of Hrotsvitha of Gandersheim and Hildegard of Bingen

PATRICIA DEMERS

The virginal body of a woman, that 'many-petalled cluster of different meanings, emotions, memories and prophecies' (M. Warner 190), has the problematic beauty of a thornless rose. In its apparent combination of vulnerability and strength, fragility and tenacity, the concept of virginity has always provoked mixed comments, both denigrating and idealizing. The strangeness and inaccessibility of the lives of early medieval Benedictine women might be the first feature to strike contemporary readers. Understandably, claustration in the service of the Lord and in obedience to a Rule and triumphalist virginity, a product as much of privilege as of centuries of patristic exegesis, are troubling ideas for those more familiar and in tune with *ekklesia gynaikon* and the hermeneutics of suspicion. Yet it should be remembered, too, that considerable doubt surrounded these women in their own day. Accounts of the enclosure of the pious Eve of Wilton, who in 1065 had been given as a seven-year-old to the abbey, and the lurid escapes of the pragmatic twelfth-century recluse Christina of Markyate (c.1096–1166) from consummating her betrothal are marked by the biographers' attempts to regularize or standardize their subjects. Knowledge of Eve of Wilton is gleaned from the *Liber Confortatorius* (c.1082) of her spiritual adviser Goscelin, a cleric whose wish was to remake Eve in the image of the women friends and pupils of Jerome, namely, Paula, Eustochium, and Blaesilla. Christina's more sensational *Vita* and its oblique, almost prurient, references to her scandalous suitors, whose importunate behaviour cannot be disclosed lest, avers the anonymous male Benedictine author, 'I pollute the wax by writing it, or the air by saying it' (Talbot 115), emphasize her determination to escape an arranged marriage. In our own day perceptions and, in some instances, exaltations of consecrated virginity continue to provide differing responses. For Thomas Renna this medieval ideal was 'a symbol of renunciation and resolution' (86); for Sharon Elkins, a 'guarantee of freedom' (29); for Donald Weinstein and Rudolph Bell, a general relief from 'the burden of taking a worldly husband' (229); and for Sister Margaret Brennan, 'the pursuance of a disembodied spirituality' (40).

Although worlds of differences and unanswered questions separate us, many features of the studies and stories about these religious, studies which themselves span several centuries, might also attract our sisterly admiration and sympathy. Introducing her readers to the suffocating, often lethal, bureaucracy of her fictional nunnery, in *The Corner That Held Them*, Sylvia Townsend Warner presents one aristocratic Dame after another tasting 'the wormwood of office' (244) while striving to secure and maintain the position of prioress. From covert strategies to histrionic scandal the case against Benedetta Carlini, abbess of the Convent of the Mother of God in Pescia, entails in Judith Brown's analysis a criticism of clerical righteousness and hypocrisy in accusations of women's sexual misconduct; Brown's *Immodest Acts: The Life of a Lesbian Nun in Renaissance Italy* opens with a view of convents as 'less often the homes of women with a strong religious vocation than warehouses for the discarded women of middle-class and patrician families' (4) and closes with an account of the death of the humbled, penitent Carlini, who was disciplined and imprisoned in solitary confinement in her religious community for thirty-five years. Caroline Walker Bynum's studies of women's devotional literature and practice also disclose many of the tensions underlying medieval religious life. *Jesus as Mother* focuses on the problem of authority as reflected in various attempts at the feminization of religious language, and the more recent *Holy Feast and Holy Fast* sees the particular piety of medieval holy women oscillating between eucharistic worship and total abstinence from nourishment. The speciality and separateness of these women are Bynum's interests. While the abbot could envision his role as a maternal one and often pray to a feminine God, lay women and actual mothers were usually dismissed as carnal and secondary. It is not surprising that female spirituality stayed on the periphery of male-dominated scholastic theology. Yet female eucharistic devotions and ascetic lifestyles also form an instructive contrast to the satires of monastic

greed and gluttony, and account for the striking fact that 'many important treatises on the eucharist or on the closely connected theme of the
humanity of Christ were addressed by men to women' (*Feast* 80).
Although Bynum contends that 'the delicious groveling in the humilia-
tions of being human ... characterizes virtually every religious woman
of the later Middle Ages' (290), she stresses the deliberate purposive-
ness of their elaboration of aspects of biological or social experience,
because these vehicles best reflected 'the deepening of ordinary experience that came when God impinged on it' (295).

The writer's gender often distinguishes concepts of community life
and spiritual benefit. The differing interpretations of the ideal of *virginitas* concern John Bugge, who betrays considerable discomfort
when, in treating 'ontological asexuality' (80) and the allegorical sense
of the *sponsa Christi* motif for male virgins, he notes the 'provocatively
literal sense' (92) in which the bridal idea was adopted by women mys-
tics. Many medieval views of female virginity, however, were practical as
well as provocative. *Hali Meidhad* not only depicts Christ as the worthi-
est lover, handsomest husband, and best provider but also praises the
woman who, in becoming 'Godes spuse, Iesu Cristes brude, þe lauer-
des leofman,' has stayed mistress of herself ('se freo of hireseoluen')
while she rightly loves with true faith ("hwil ha riht luued him wið soðe
bileaue,' [Millett 2.21–8]). Critics, of course, from Jovinian to Elaine
Pagels have queried the rightness and superiority of this love. Pagels's
contrasting of the notions of sexuality held by John Chrysostom and
Augustine exposes the 'antinaturalistic view of nature' (148) and the
appeal of imagining 'ourselves in control' (149) underpinning the
Augustinian theory of original sin – 'a sexualized interpretation of sin
and a revulsion from "the flesh" based on his own idiosyncratic belief
that we contract the disease of sin through the process of conception'
(143). The provocativeness, practicality, and perverse privilege of this
ideal cannot simply be bypassed as anomalies; they must problematize
any discussion of intentionality and textual criticism.

Approaching the six anti-Terentian plays of Hrotsvitha of Gandersheim and the earliest-known morality play of Hildegard of Bingen –
all explicitly and particularly praising *enkrateia* (continence) – demands continuous critical scrutiny of our predilections as readers
from another era along with questions about the demonstrable contrasts these plays so clearly enshrine. Is it the medium as well as the
message, we wonder, which privileges virginal courage and self-possession over lusting brutality and clumsiness? Is the stress on the building
up, the edification, of the body with virtue in any way tinged with

irony? How crucial are the images of royalty and war to the description of this monastic ideal? And, fundamentally, how important and
individualized is the dramatic form to convey each playwright's spiritual theme?

The plays, as I read them, reveal basic differences in an understanding of theatre and of the ideal of virginity itself. Possibly the most telling difference involves the artistic personalities of these well-educated,
brilliant, accomplished Benedictines. It is too general and imprecise to
conclude simply, as Bruce Hozeski has done, that 'both Hrotsvitha and
Hildegard dramatize ... the struggle between the Virtues and the Devil'
('Patterns' 53). Physical action, either viewed or described, is the
major constituent of Hrotsvitha's dramas. Her virgins boldly scoff at
pagan flattery and threats, welcome the grisliest of tortures, and exude
supreme confidence in a heavenly reward; her penitent whores accept
enclosure and all its intimate septic details as the fitting discipline to
atone for their sinful pleasures. A virtuous, in fact celibate, wife prays
for death to avoid an illicit suitor and is later resurrected to join her
now temperate admirer. Central to the rapid-fire action, Hrotsvitha's
women effect conversions, cool lust, counsel men, and underscore the
dramaturgic point about unassailable and supreme virtue in action.
While Hrotsvitha offers compact, fast-paced Christian romance, Hildegard's *Ordo virtutum* is an oratorio, relying on the recitatives of the contingent of virtues to present the concept of harmonious integration
within a single tormented soul. If concrete action, on one hand, and
liturgical declamation, on the other, express the differences between
these two playwrights rather crudely, then a closer examination of the
texts themselves may clarify the contrasting homiletic and symphonic
emphases *in virginea forma*.

Hrotsvitha of Gandersheim, a tenth-century canoness who had
taken vows of chastity and obedience, has attracted some very curious
advocates and detractors. John Kennedy Toole's hero in *A Confederacy
of Dunces*, the obese medievalist Ignatius Reilly, dreams of Hrotsvitha's
counsel to 'exorcize the horrors which materialize before our eyes in
the name of television' (40). Anachronisms and solemnity aside,
Hrotsvitha would probably have been a very successful television
writer; in all of her work – versified legends of the saints, a panegyric of
Otto I, a history of Gandersheim, thirty-five hexameters describing
scenes from Revelation, and the six plays in rhymed, rhythmic Latin
prose – the importance of a quick-paced, continuous narrative line is
uppermost. While the critical literature generally acknowledges her
erudition and determination as a pedagogue, opinions are actually

quite divided about the nature of Hrotsvitha's accomplishment. No one now endorses the position of the nineteenth-century Viennese von Aschbach, who claimed that Hrotsvitha's plays were a hoax, perpetrated by their real writer, Conrad Celtis, the Renaissance editor and discoverer of the Emmeram codex of Hrotsvitha's works. Hailing her as 'a Christian Sappho' (1), Albert Cohn has charted similarities with Shakespeare, and Rosamond Gilder has introduced her as 'the first woman playwright' (18). Countering such praise are George Coffman's dismissal of the notion that her dialogues were ever acted as a 'fallacy' (262), Karl Young's estimate that her plays were 'never acted and probably little read' (6), and Philip Schuyler Allen's grand slam that 'she not only could not write a drama, she did not think of doing so' (43). Daniel Frankforter has pinpointed the sexist problem inherent in many of the niggling comments: 'The fact that she was a woman who wrote dramas at a time when dramas were not supposed to have been written and women not equipped with educations adequate to achieve what she achieved made it difficult to place her work in a context which would facilitate its interpretation' (299).

Amazingly, one of the issues which still exercises the ever-increasing number of Hrotsvitha scholars is the performance versus mere closet-study value of her work. That is, did the canoness who set out to praise the power of female chastity intend her plays as pious refectory reading or complete, humane, albeit fast-moving entertainments about the ministry of love in action? Even without costumes and props, the didactic energy of Hrotsvitha's plays impresses both Charles Jones and Peter Dronke as made for recitation, whether in the classroom-style assignment of 'speaking parts' imagined by Jones (102) or the community 'reading-groups' suggested by Dronke (*Individuality* 85). Katharina Wilson's book-length study, which locates Hrotsvitha within the scholastic traditions of the tenth-century Ottonian Renaissance, favours the performance thesis by citing the frequent visits to Gandersheim of Otto II's cultured wife, the Byzantine princess Theophano. Furthermore, Wilson concludes that Hrotsvitha's ethical stance is the affirmation of an 'absolutist epistemology,' where truth is 'recognizable ... eternal, and imitable'; but she insists that the formulation of this ethic is more dynamic than intellectual: 'provoking an emotional response, persuading one to act' (*Ethics* 143).

Deliberately contrasting the six Terentian comedies in which women succumb to the ploys of amorous pagans, the action of Hrotsvitha's plays focuses on mainly pure and upright women.[1] Her preface makes clear that the praiseworthy chastity of holy virgins, 'laudabilis sacrarum

castimonia virginum,' will ultimately, despite the women's apparent
fragility, overcome male strength:

> cum feminea fragilitas vinceret
> et virilis robur confusioni subiaceret.
> (when female weakness will succeed
> and male strength will be thrown down in confusion.)

The corollary of this encomium of feminine virtue is the humility
topos Hrotsvitha repeatedly employs, in the preface and her opening
letter to patrons, describing her talent as limited ('iuxta mei facul-
tatem ingeniola'), her style as rustic and crude ('pro vitiosi sermonis
rusticitate') and herself as knowing little ('nesciola'). Yet the praise of
women and the seeming self-abasement are intricately interrelated.
Hrotsvitha is entirely aware of her use of the Pauline motif of being
what she is by the grace of God – her 'deum ... cuius solummodo gratia
sum id, quod sum' echoing Paul's 'gratia autem Dei sum id quod sum'
(1 Cor. 15:10) – as well as the recurring idea of confounding strength
with weakness (1 Cor. 1:27, 4:10, 15:43, 2 Cor. 12:9). She makes the
paradox of mere women triumphing as acceptable as the claim made
by one of limited female intellect ('muliebris sensus tardior') to appropriate a Boethian stance and tear small pieces from Philosophy's robe
('floccos de panniculis, a veste philosophiae abruptis'). In teaching
the reader to savour the rich ambiguities of the erudition and wit of
this supposedly limited writer for whom 'each admission of weakness is
inseparable from an impulse of self-assurance' (Dronke, *Writers* 66),
Hrotsvitha thereby prepares the reader for a comparable reversal of
expectations in the plays themselves. Dronke praises Hrotsvitha as
'supersubtle' in her 'distinctive literary coquetry' (*Writers* 83). Hrotsvitha's tactic appears to me less a matter of flirting with the reader than
of schooling her or him in ways of reading material which will radically
subvert conventional notions.

The immeasurable power of women's virtue and, in fact, women's
capacity to reform their own lives are the repeated ideas in all six plays.
The first, 'The Conversion of the General Gallicanus,' shows virginal
strength in action against male passions and emotional vacillation.
Constantia, the saintly daughter of the Emperor Constantinus, vows
never to consummate her betrothal to Gallicanus. In counselling the
emperor, banishing despair ('nunc autem nullus relinquitur locus
maestitiae' [2.4]), and awakening the faith of Gallicanus's daughters
in Christ, 'Amator virginitatis et inspirator castitatis' (5.2), Constantia

not only determines the action but also sets up the contrast between the resolve never, under any circumstances, to violate her sacred vow and the conviction of reward forever ('in aeterno gaudio' [13.3]). While the heroine does not waver, it is the converted Gallicanus, who, even while he concedes to Constantia's vow, himself expresses fear of 'oculorum concupiscentia' (13.4), lust of the eyes, as he sees his beloved daily.

The stakes for such virginal conviction are higher in 'The Martyrdom of the Holy Virgins Agapes, Chionia and Hirena,' but to underline the mortal seriousness of the issue, Hrotsvitha also shows that in this case no saving, merciful, or amenable quality characterizes the pagan representatives. In the opening scene Agapes answers Diocletian's blandishments with the declaration never to be swayed to pollute her virginity ('ad corruptionem integritatis' [1.2]); her sister echoes this stand, refusing to defile or debase herself ('non dehonestabo ... submittendo' [1.6]) and to venerate a slave as a master ('ut servus veneretur ut dominus' [1.7]). Extending this conviction and metaphorical pattern to the end of the play, the last sister to be killed, Hirena, taunts Sissinus about his dirty defeat, 'turpiter victum,' and his need to blush for shame – 'Infelix, erubesce, Sisinni, erubesce' – over his inability to defeat a little virgin, 'infantiam virgunculae' (14.3). The virginal trio, representing Charity, Purity, and Peace, stands as obstinate counters to Diocletian, Dulcitius, and Sissinus and their associations with passion, sin, and death. Sandro Sticca has maintained that the drama, in which at one point the besotted Dulcitius attempts to make love to pots and pans, is much more than farce; but such a scene does exemplify Hrotsvitha's shrewd dramaturgical sense in reducing sin to slapstick comedy. The virgins are a fit match for the pagan threats of grisly and prolonged torment; as Hirena explains the direct proportionality of the martyr's ratio: 'Quanto acrius torqueor, tanto gloriosius exaltabor' (The more fiercely I am tortured, the more gloriously I will be exalted [12.21]).

The next three plays document the changes in others and in the heroines themselves which women's courage and faith can effect. 'The Resurrection of Drusiana and Calimachus' highlights the zeal of the chaste matron Drusiana, who dismisses Calimachus's passion with mentions of abhorrence, conveyed in such verbs as 'fastidio' and 'sperno,' and the general reaction of complete disgust: 'nihil aliud nisi indignationem' (3.4). However, like a psalmist, Drusiana confides her fears to the Lord, 'Intende domine, mei timorem; intende, quem patior, dolorem,' Lord, look upon my fear; look upon the pain I bear

(4.2), and admits that without divine aid she could not withstand Cali-machus: 'insidiis diabolicis sine te refragari nequeo' (I cannot avoid these devilish traps without you [4.2]). Her death and resurrection serve as the paradigm for the play's central idea of rebirth, which term the prologue borrows from the Gospel of John (3:3) to describe the lusting Calimachus as eventually 'resuscitatus, in Christo ... renatus.'

The change of the two harlots, Mary and Thais, from pleasure to penance, is orchestrated by intelligent pastors in both cases. In 'The Fall and Conversion of Mary, Niece of the Monk Abraham,' Abraham is the first and last instructor of the girl and woman whose story becomes an example of conversion, 'exemplum conversionis' (9.4), and an illus-tration of the convert's reversal, with Mary striving to be as radiant as she was once corrupt: 'quanto entitit foedior, tanto appareat nitidior' (9.4). In rescuing his charge, Abraham, like the Redeemer, takes her sins upon himself and, like the Good Shepherd, leads her back, rejoic-ing, to the fold ('gaudens reduxi ad ovile' [9.1]). Because repentance involves circular action, his intercession, through a temporary transfer of roles, returns her to the position of *stella maris*, the star of the sea, which is the bright light that guides sailors in the right path ('navigan-tibus recti semitam itineris dirigit' [2.3]). The lengthy *stella maris* ety-mology lesson at the outset of the play, in which Abraham and his fellow monk Effrem had encouraged the eight-year-old Mary to embrace the eremitical, ascetic life, though not found in Hrotsvitha's source, stands fully 'in the liturgical and hymnal tradition of the medi-eval church'; 'as the *stella maris* leads ships safely to the home port, to their destination, so Maria, too, shall be guided home' (Wilson, 'Les-son' 3). As well as setting in motion the interest in Marian virtues, such an emphasis forecasts Hrotsvitha's preoccupation with repentance rather than the few lines devoted to the fall, which is the *fait accompli* of Mary's jumping out of her window to join a deceiving lover.

Virtue is again triumphant in reclaiming Thais, and here, too, Hrots-vitha's adaptation of her source material prefigures the drama's themes of reconciliation and concord. In the opening lesson of 'The Conversion of the Harlot Thais' between the hermit Pafnutius and his disciples, she draws liberally on Boethius's *De Musica*. As David Cham-berlain has argued, the play's interweaving of this quadrivial learning with its moral action 'shows Pafnutius ... bringing the discordant sin-ner Thais back to the norms of concord or *musica humana*' (321). Since Thais is actually a more fit subject for his pedagogy than the dis-ciples, inasmuch as she already knows that God weighs the merits of each person, her 'conversion' is more of an opportunity for discussion of her beliefs than any radical alteration of them. The reader is left to conclude that the brothel had temporarily blocked Thais's inherent sense of God, whom she recognizes as true, 'vero' (3.4). Pafnutius is a more strenuous instructor than Abraham, insisting on the harsh medicine of contraries ('contrariis curanda est medelis' [7.5]) in a locked, solitary cell. Although Thais honestly admits her fear of failure ('fragilitas mei cogit me terreri' [7.12]) and despite the fact that Pafnutius wonders at her confidence in invoking God's name from her polluted lips ('pollutis labiis' [7.13]), Thais relies on divine mercy. The final biblical emphasis promotes and sustains a trust in forgiveness: Pafnutius's next encounter, after an interval of three years, with the thoroughly remorseful, immured Thais provides the self-doubting woman with necessary hope. His observation, 'Si deus iniquitates obervabit, / nemo sustinebit' (12.2), is an apt borrowing from the *De Profundis*: 'If thou, O Lord, shouldst mark iniquities, Lord, who could stand?' (Ps. 129; 130:3); it also tempers his righteousness, allowing more pastoral concern for this half-dead little she-goat ('capellam semivivam' [7.3]) to shine through.

Virginity as an ideal thus far has been personified, emblematized, and returned to in penitence. Hrotsvitha's final play, 'The Martyrdom of the Holy Virgins Faith, Hope and Charity,' is a grand, at times gruesome, celebration of the transcendent might of these sisters. More than the little women, 'mulierculae' (3.2), whom Hadrian thinks are fit subjects for his flattery, these representations of the theological virtues as young girls are also more than cardboard cut-outs. Fides wastes no time in contemning Hadrian's command to worship Diana as 'stultorum imperatoris praeceptum' (5.4), a silly imperial command. She derides ('irrideo') and mocks ('subsanno') his stupidity. None of the ugly tortures – from flogging, cutting off nipples, placing on a hot grill, to boiling in wax and pitch – has any effect, and so the emperor must resort to beheading the sisters, each of whom expresses her solidarity with the others. As Karitas faces death, she mentions the same parents as her sisters, 'eisdem parentibus genitae,' and the same firm faith that unites their wants, feelings, and thoughts: 'nostrum velle, nostrum sentire, nostrum sapere unum idemque esse' (5.33). They are all prepared to die – and do so –for the heavenly, not an earthly, bridegroom ('caelesti, non terreno, sponso' [4.3]), the destiny for which their mother Sapientia (Wisdom) had raised them. Following the serial deaths of her daughters, the virtues, Sapientia meditates, appositely, in the epilogue on the unified nature of Adonay Emmanuel: 'Te etiam, perfectum deum hominemque verum' (9.7), fully God and truly man.

In a realm where martyrdom makes theological sense it is fitting that a mother who is burying three daughters should contemplate God's manhood and divinity, since her children's steadfastness is an illustration of that very balance. However, for readers less familiar with martyrdom and more in touch with human urges for self-preservation and protection the virginal ideal of Hrotsvitha's martyrs, maids, and penitents – the titillating, possibly voyeuristic aspects of their suffering notwithstanding – is difficult to credit wholeheartedly. The heroic feats of these athletes of Christ, their adamantine staunchness in saying not only 'no' but 'never' in various iterations, and their willing embrace of physical pain rather than experiencing the dread of moral pollution (a hurt-in-place-of-dirt formula) put them closer to superhuman paragons than approachable models.

Although the visionary Hildegard of Bingen shared Hrotsvitha's view of the opposition of body and spirit, and presented the soul making 'its way toward salvation by sharply divorcing itself from the desires of the body' (Newman, *Sister* 154), the salvific virginal impulse of the *Ordo virtutum* is vastly different from that of Hrotsvitha's plays.[2] A tenth child tithed to the church at the age of eight, Saint Hildegard – administrator at Disibodenberg and Bingen, correspondent of Frederick Barbarossa and Bernard of Clairvaux, exegete and hymnographer, whose revelations were sanctified as a prophetic charism by Pope Eugenius III – saw each virtue as 'a luminous sphere from God gleaming in the work of man' (quoted in Newman, *Sister* 17). Unlike the reactive, negative peremptoriness of Hrotsvitha's heroines, Hildegard presents a litany of virtues or numinous forces, declaring their power and initiating the defeat of Diabolus. 'In virginea forma' is part of the triumphant climactic speech of Chastity as, standing on Satan's head, she mentions nurturing a sweet miracle. Peter Dronke translates 'in virginea forma dulce miraculum colui' (l. 230) as 'in a virgin form I nurtured a sweet miracle,' while Bruce Hozeski renders it as 'in the form of the Virgin I brought forth a sweet miracle.' The differences here do not really concern indefinite and definite articles, but rather literal and more figurative construings of *forma*: Hozeski's 'the form of the Virgin' literally calls on the figure, image, and likeness of Mary; Dronke's 'a virgin form' suggests a more figurative form, manner, or type of virginity. The morality play of this twelfth-century abbess skilfully blends literal and figurative understanding. As in her antiphon and responsory for virgins in the collection of her hymns, *Symphonia armonie celestium revelationum*, where she addresses her subjects as both beautiful faces, 'O pulcre facies,' and noblest greenness or freshness, 'O nobilissima viriditas' (*Symphonia* 218), Hildegard combines the physical and the organic, the praise of completed perfection and interest in the process of growth, in depicting the actions and effects of the virtues; in one of the two manuscripts of Hildegard's work, the Riesenkodex, the *Ordo virtutum* follows the hymn sequence. There is little doubt that this play, for which Hildegard also composed the music, was actually performed. Although we have no specific accounts of staging, the music along with the text is full of directional, gestic language; as commentators have noted, moreover, the richly coloured illustrations from Hildegard's visionary treatise, *Scivias* (Know the Ways), in which a sketch of the *Ordo virtutum* forms part of the last vision, and especially the pictures of the virtues, provide some indication of the splendid vestments which might have solemnized the liturgical presentation in the convent at Bingen.[3] For Hildegard's theatre, both literal and figurative, differs noticeably from Hrotsvitha's space or *platea* that demonstrates virtue under stress. Hildegard's setting, possibly the chapel itself, creates a mental platform from which the symphonic and chromatically gripping litany of the virtues is declaimed.

Diabolus, the only solo male voice, is also the single speaking part in this otherwise sung play. As the glorious vaulting phrases and closing chant melisma of female voices stand in contrast to the raspy shrillness of the devil's taunts and interjections, so the whole exercise underlines the triumph of virtuous artistry and numbers over satanic wiles. In the face of Satan's promise of immediate rewards and charge that the virtues lack knowledge of themselves, the Queen Humility makes it clear that, from her vantage point, 'in excelsis' (l. 67), she is completely aware of Satan's downcast position 'in abyssum' (l. 66). This 'gloriosa regina' and 'suavissima mediatrix' (l. 72), in offering her followers the skill of finding the lost drachma ('perditam dragmam' [l. 70]), prompts them to declare themselves after the example of Charity, whose self-description as 'flos amabilis' (l. 76), flower of love, initiates a litany of metaphors. Radiant ('lucida' [l. 88]) Obedience is hailed as 'dulcissima vocatrix' (l. 91), sweetest inviter; Faith is calmly mirrorlike ('serena, speculata' [l. 96]); and Hope, the living life and sweet consoler ('o vivens vita, et o suavis consolatrix' [l. 101]), is also 'dulcis conspectrix' (l. 98), the sweet beholder. Chastity is particularly self-aware as she apostrophizes on both virginity and the noble virgin, whom the shadow will never find in a fading flower ('o virgo nobilis, te numquam inveniet umbra in cadente flore' [l. 108]). The other virtues laud Chastity for remaining in the harmonies of heavenly citizens ('in symphoniis supernorum civium' [l. 110]). It is precisely by this image of

concord ('in symphonia sonare' [l. 194]) that the virtues welcome the
fugitive, penitent Soul and lead the attack on Satan for her. Having
been given the skill to find the lost coin, the virtues echo the related
Lucan parable (15.4–7) about the lost sheep, 'perditam ovem' (l. 169),
in greeting the hesitant Anima.

The symphonic metaphor, which captures 'the theme of reintegra-
tion of God and his creatures' (Flanagan 140), also reveals Hildegard's
'remarkable ... "esemplastic power"' (Dronke, *Individuality* 179). One
feature of Hildegard's ability to shape disparate things into a unified
whole is her adroit blending of male and female designations for the
virtues/warriors, whom the Soul refers to as the soldiery of the Queen,
'milicia regine' (l. 179), whom Victory exhorts as most brave and glorious soldiers, 'O fortissimi et gloriosissimi milites' (l. 218), and who,
themselves, salute Victoria as 'dulcissima bellatrix' (l. 220), sweetest
warrior. Another notable way in which Hildegard unifies her play is
through the subtle repetition of words. As part of the major declamation of the warriors of Humilitas, while Innocentia, Contemptus
Mundi, Amor Celestis, Verecundia, Discretio, and Paciencia describe
themselves and praise one another, Misericordia declares the wish to
reach out her hand, 'manum porrigere' (l. 138), to all who suffer. Significantly the last word of the play, sung in a chant melisma by a mixed
chorus of triumphant virtues and souls, is 'porrigat'; the singers enjoin
their audience to genuflect to God so that He may reach out His hand:
'ut ... manum suam porrigat' (l. 269). The rich ornamentation of this
finale brings an optimistic close to the epilogue's summary of salvation
history, in the Edenic beginning of which 'omnes creature viruerunt'
(l. 252), all creation was green and flourishing; however, when this
greenness faded, a champion, 'vir prelatior' (l. 255), offered His
wounds to the Father so that others may also bend their knees to
receive divine mercy.

In the female embodiment of doughty challengers of Terentian
mores or as a lyrical, numinous warrior in the service of a Queen, these
differing forms of *virginitas* may generate such problems for modern
readers that the texts could end up being dismissed or trivialized. It *is*
necessary – and quite easy – to discern the plays' rehandling of patristic commonplaces, their almost-Manichean horror of the flesh, and
pugnacious notion of evil to be fought and conquered. In fact, even
the scholarly champions of Hrotsvitha and Hildegard, Katharina Wilson and Barbara Newman respectively, have wondered about this
obsession, with Wilson noting the limited audience and 'single-role'

ideals in Hrotsvitha's 'ascetic propaganda' (*'Figmenta'* 21), and Newman commenting on Hildegard's emphasis on the link between sexuality and sin as an 'excessive regard for ... celibacy' (*Sister* 253). Yet
however blinkered or totalizing their views may seem to us, these early
playwrights are more than quaint curios. Apparently without experiencing the dissatisfaction and self-doubt of Benedetta Carlini or even
the matron Drusiana, these women exulted in the presentation of
empowering, luminous, and specifically feminine virtue. Their triumphs of 'the mind over the flesh' (Beilin 5), while not unmindful of
the example of Pallas Athene's birth from Jupiter's brain signifying the
joining of virginity and wisdom, celebrated the power of holiness 'both
in body and in spirit' (1 Cor. 7:34). As lacking in guile as they seem to
be oblivious of scepticism and detraction, they are determined to 'follow the Lamb' (Rev. 14:4) in the hope of being brought 'rejoicing ...
into the king's palace' (Ps. 45:15). Impatient criticism might reject
these women on the very grounds, so the charge might go, that they
have simple-mindedly rejected or written off the body. A more searching and inclusive examination admits the ecstatic intensity and power
of their praise of the impregnable citadel or temple of the body.

Notes

1 Three English translations of Hrotsvitha's plays are available: the colloquial,
discursive prose of St John (1923), the accurate, rhythmic prose of Bonfante
(1979), and the terse, rhymed prose of Wilson (1985). In citing Homeyer's
edition of the Latin text, with scene and section numbers copied from von
Winterfeld's 1902 edition, I have supplied my own translations.

2 Both Hozeski, in *Annuale Mediaevale* (1978), and Dronke, in *Poetic Individuality*, 180–92, have reproduced the Latin text of the play; Hozeski provides
an English translation at the same time, while Dronke's translation appears
in the booklet accompanying the record (1982) and compact disc (1987)
Hildegard von Bingen: Ordo virtutum, Sequentia, dir. Klaus Neumann, Harmonia mundi 20395/96. I cite Dronke's Latin text and supply my own translations.

3 I am not entirely convinced by Oliver Sacks's argument that the 'radiant
luminosity' and 'great rapturous intensity' of these illustrations, along with
the frequency with which figures of fortification appear, all represent 'indis-
putably' varieties of 'migraine hallucinations'; see 'The Visions of Hildegard'
in *The Man Who Mistook His Wife for a Hat*, 166–70.

Works Cited

Allen, Philip Schuyler. 'The Mediaeval Mimus: Part II.' *Modern Philology* 8 (1910), 17–60

Beilin, Elaine V. *Redeeming Eve: Women Writers of the English Renaissance.* Princeton: Princeton UP 1987

Biblia Sacra, logicis partitionibus aliisque subsidiis ornata a R.P.A. Colugna et L. Turrado. Matriti: Biblioteca de Autores Cristianos 1959

Böckeler, Maura, ed. *Hildegard von Bingen: Wisse Die Wege Scivias.* Salzburg: Otto Müller Verlag 1954

Bonfante, Larissa, trans. *The Plays of Hrotswitha of Gandersheim.* New York: New York UP 1979

Brennan, Margaret. 'Enclosure: Institutionalising the Invisibility of Women in Ecclesiastical Communities.' In *Women – Invisible in Theology and the Church.* Ed. Elizabeth Schüssler Fiorenza and Mary and M. Collins. Edinburgh: Clark 1985, 38–48

Brown, Judith C. *Immodest Acts: The Life of a Lesbian Nun in Renaissance Italy.* New York: Oxford UP 1986

Bugge, John. *Virginitas: An Essay in the History of a Medieval Ideal.* The Hague: Martinus Nijhof 1975

Butler, Sister Mary Marguerite, K.S.M. *Hrotsvitha: The Theatricality of Her Plays.* New York: Philosophical Library 1960

Bynum, Caroline Walker. *Holy Feast and Holy Fast; The Religious Significance of Food to Medieval Women.* Berkeley: U of California P 1987

– *Jesus as Mother: Studies in the Spirituality of the High Middle Ages.* Berkeley: U of California P 1982

Chamberlain, David. 'Musical Learning and Dramatic Action in Hrotsvit's *Pafnutius.*' *Studies in Philology* 77 (1980), 319–43

Coffman, George R. 'A New Approach to Medieval Latin Drama.' *Modern Philology* 22 (1925), 230–71

Cohn, Albert. *Shakespeare in Germany in the Sixteenth and Seventeenth Centuries: An Account of English Actors in Germany and The Netherlands and of the Plays Performed.* Weisbaden: Dr Martin Sändig 1967

Dronke, Peter. *Poetic Individuality in the Middle Ages; New Departures in Poetry 1000–1150.* Oxford: Clarendon 1970

– *Women Writers of the Middle Ages: A Critical Study of Texts from Perpetua (+203) to Marguerite Porete (+1310).* Cambridge: Cambridge UP 1984

Elkins, Sharon K. *Holy Women of Twelfth-Century England.* Chapel Hill: U of North Carolina P 1988

Flanagan, Sabina. *Hildegard of Bingen, 1098–1179: A Visionary Life.* London: Routledge 1989

Frankforter, A. Daniel. 'Hroswitha of Gandersheim and the Destiny of Women.' *The Historian: A Journal of History* 41, no. 2 (1979), 295–314

Gilder, Rosamond. *Enter the Actress: The First Women in the Theatre.* Boston: Houghton 1931

Haight, Anne Lyon, ed. *Hroswitha of Gandersheim; Her Life, Times, and Works, and a Comprehensive Bibliography.* New York: The Hroswitha Club 1965

Homeyer, H., ed. *Hrotsvithae Opera.* Münich: Verlag Ferdinand Schöningh 1970

Hozeski, Bruce W. '*Ordo Virtutum*: Hildegard of Bingen's Liturgical Morality Play.' *Annuale Mediaevale* 13 (1978), 45–69

– 'The Parallel Patterns in Hrotsvitha of Gandersheim, a Tenth Century German Playwright, and in Hildegard of Bingen, a Twelfth Century German Playwright.' *Annuale Mediaevale* 18 (1977), 42–53

Jones, Charles W. *The St. Nicholas Liturgy and Its Literary Relationships.* Berkeley: U of California P 1963

Millett, Bella, ed. *Hali Meidhad.* EETS no. 284. London: Oxford UP 1982

Neumann, Klaus, dir. *Hildegard von Bingen: Ordo virtutum.* Sequentia. Harmonia mundi 20395/96

Newman, Barbara, ed. *Saint Hildegard of Bingen Symphonia: A Critical Edition of the 'Symphonia armonie celestium revelationum.'* Ithaca: Cornell UP 1988

– *Sister of Wisdom: St. Hildegard's Theology of the Feminine.* Berkeley: U of California P 1987

Pagels, Elaine. *Adam, Eve, and the Serpent.* New York: Random 1988

Renna, Thomas. 'Virginity in the *Life* of Christina of Markyate and Aelred of Rievaulx's *Rule*.' *American Benedictine Review* 36, no. 1 (1985), 79–92

Sacks, Oliver. *The Man Who Mistook His Wife for a Hat.* London: Duckworth 1985

St John, Christopher, trans. *The Plays of Roswitha.* London: Chatto 1923

Sticca, Sandro. 'Hrotswitha's *Dulcitius* and Christian Symbolism.' *Medieval Studies* 32 (1970), 108–27

Talbot, C.H., trans. *The Life of Christina of Markyate: A Twelfth Century Recluse.* Oxford: Oxford UP 1959

Toole, John Kennedy. *A Confederacy of Dunces.* Baton Rouge: Louisiana State UP 1980

Warner, Marina. *Monuments and Maidens; The Allegory of the Female Form.* London: Weidenfeld 1985

Warner, Sylvia Townsend. *The Corner That Held Them.* London: Chatto 1948

Weinstein, Donald, and Rudolph M. Bell. *Saints and Society: The Two Worlds of Western Christendom, 1000–1700.* Chicago: U of Chicago P 1982

Wilson, Katharina M., trans. *The Dramas of Hrotsvit of Gandersheim.* Saskatoon: Matrologia Latina – Peregrina 1985

– '*Figmenta vs. Veritas*: Dame Alice and the Medieval Literary Depiction of Women by Women.' *Tulsa Studies in Women's Literature* 4, no. 1 (1985), 17–32

- 'Hrotsvit and the Tube; John Kennedy Toole and the Problem of Bad TV Programming.' *Germanic Notes* 15 (1984), 4–5
- *Hrotsvit of Gandersheim: The Ethics of Authorial Stance.* Leiden: Brill 1988
- 'Hrotsvit's *Abraham:* The Lesson in Etymology.' *Germanic Notes* 16 (1985), 2–4
Young, Karl. *The Drama of the Medieval Church.* Vol. 1. Oxford: Clarendon 1933

3

Poet Construction: Mrs Hemans, L.E.L., and the Image of the Nineteenth-Century Woman Poet

GLENNIS STEPHENSON

The construction of the character of the Victorian poetess begins in the works of Felicia Hemans and Letitia Elizabeth Landon, two women poets who, in their time, created particularly successful public images and enjoyed immense popularity in the characters of Mrs Hemans and L.E.L. Their poetry allows the process of constructing the figure of the 'poetess' to be viewed in its historical and ideological context. And, since the gender-specific characteristics of their work are so clearly cultural constructs based on convention, their poetry suggests much about the dominant nineteenth-century views of gender-related poetic strategies.

The predominantly male critics who controlled the literary journals and magazines during the nineteenth century had the power to define the nature of women's poetry; more importantly, perhaps, they had the power to define the woman herself: the 'poetess' and her work were overtly assigned a number of the characteristics which more usually remain within the subtext of nineteenth-century constructions of 'woman.' To be a literary success she had to establish an audience; to establish an audience she had to win the approval of the critics; as a result, nineteenth-century women poets, as Marilyn Williamson notes, became 'the first to write according to a definite ideology formulated by society for their literary activity' (xvii) – or, I would add, they at least convinced their readers that they were doing so by presenting themselves in the marginalized and strictly defined role of 'poetess.'[1]

I begin by suggesting how Hemans supports conventional gender

ideology and creates a poetic character that decorously appears to con-
firm the expectations of her audience concerning why she wrote, what
she wrote, and how she wrote – a character clearly gendered 'feminine.' Then, I briefly consider two prose pieces to show how Landon
self-consciously manipulates the same conventions when writing as
L.E.L. and yet rejects them, when writing anonymously, in favour of a
character that is clearly gendered 'masculine.' I suggest how Landon,
in opposition to Hemans, struggles to resist conventional gender ideology, and to transform constraint into opportunity, creating an L.E.L.
that overwhelms the very conventions which are its foundation.
Finally, it is important to assess the response of the critics to the 'transformations' effected by Landon, and I briefly show how, since
Landon's resistance is from within, the male critics are always able to
appropriate these transformations and to reinscribe L.E.L. within conventional gender ideology.

It was not difficult for Landon and Hemans to construct their characters as 'poetesses' through their works: most nineteenth-century
readers readily assumed the writer and the work were one text. As Poe
most succinctly put it, 'a woman and her book are identical' (4–5).
Even Hemans's memorial stone in St. Asaph supports the conflation: it
reads.

This Tablet,
Placed here by her Brothers,
is in Memory of
Felicia Hemans.
Whose character is best portrayed
in her writings.

The first obstacle that the woman poet had to face was the general
uneasiness with her desire to write: her pen potentially could be
empowered to disturb comfortably established social roles. And as
soon as she stepped from the domestic into the public world and
engaged an audience, her moral standing was automatically in danger
of being questioned. Landon and Hemans effectively defuse the
potentially explosive nature of their literary activities and bolster their
moral status with a wistful 'if only.' As women, they insist, they inevitably find literary success a poor substitute for the domestic happiness
that eludes them. They, and all the numerous talented female characters whom they create, repeatedly diminish, at the very same time as
they exemplify, woman's ambition and achievement. Frantically they

write, sculpt, and paint; equally frantically they declare, 'I am a woman: – tell me not of fame' (Landon, *Works* 2:52). As she busily produces volume after volume, Hemans steadfastly denies the worth of her endeavours: 'Thou hast a charmed cup, O Fame,' she admits, but 'Away! to me – a woman – bring / Sweet waters from affection's spring' (3:1.198). It is hard, of course, not to detect a subtext in Hemans's poems about fame. In 'Corinna at the Capitol,' for example, the joy and triumph of Corinne, her freedom, her delight in her powers, are so eloquently and fully described that it becomes difficult to accept Hemans's sincerity when she finally trots out the more conventional sentiments:

> Happier, happier far than thou,
> With the laurel on thy brow,
> She that makes the humblest hearth
> Lovely but to one on earth! (3:1.107)

The memoir of Mrs Hemans written by her sister, Harriet Owen, is particularly amusing in its attempts to preserve the image Hemans carefully cultivated in her poetry of a woman formed for the 'quiet happiness' of domestic life. Repeatedly the loyal sister parades before us references to Hemans's 'weary celebrity' (Owen 154). Her only enjoyment of her 'weary celebrity,' we are assured, 'was derived from the happiness it created in those around her. That "Fame can only afford *reflected* delight to a woman," was a sentiment she unceasingly felt and expressed' (49). Hemans was not as careful of her image in her personal letters and journals as she was in her poems, and the sincerity of that sentiment is somewhat undermined by the great delight she expresses when, far from those 'reflectors,' her family and friends, she mingles in literary society. After quoting Hemans's descriptions of visits to Scott, Wordsworth, and others, Owen apparently senses the contradiction and hastily adds, '... the adulation and excitement with which she was surrounded, however animating and amusing at the moment, could not but be followed, to a heart and frame constituted like hers, by a reaction of inward depression and physical languor' (197).

The subtext here, that woman's truth is located in her body, and that this truth cancels out her words, is repeatedly found in discussions of the women's work. Hartley Coleridge begins an extensive essay on 'Modern English Poetesses' with a standard 'chivalric' defence that essentially rejects woman's intellectual achievement and valorizes the

physical being instead: 'when we venture to lift a pen against women,'
he says, 'the weapon drops pointless on the marked passage; and whilst
the mind is bent on praise or censure of the poem, the eye swims too
deep in tears and mist over the poetess herself in the frontispiece, to
let it see its way to either' (374–5). It is only a short step from 'a woman
and her book are identical' to replacing the poem as text with the
poet.

With this in mind it is not suprising to find critics like Mary Ann Stodart insisting that the 'true poetic power of woman is ... in the heart –
over the heart – and especially in the peculiarities of her *own* heart'
(136, emphasis added). A poetess was encouraged to write primarily
about the one thing for which fame could never compensate her: the
lack of love. When Hemans writes of love, she focuses on what can only
be described as the 'domestic affections.' This is best exemplified in
the 1828 *Records of Woman*, in which Hemans takes purportedly true
anecdotes and transforms them into poetic records of 'all that woman's heart had dared and done' (2:2.208). Two figures emerge under a
variety of guises and dominate the collection: the devoted loving wife
and the protective loving mother. She may be disguised as 'The Cham-
ois Hunter's Love' or 'The Vaudois' Wife,' but a stolid middle-class
English woman, utterly devoted to husband and children, is only
barely concealed beneath exotic beads and skins.

These women are rarely described, physically, in much detail, and
Hemans relies instead on a number of strongly coded phrases that suggest the notion of the womanly woman. They tend to be mild, serenely
fair, and meekly bright, and their lovers are addressed as 'dearest
friend.' They are what Mieke Bal labels 'referential characters' because
of their 'obvious slots in a frame of reference' (83). Repeatedly
Hemans mentions such figures as Alcestis and Ariadne, such rituals as
suttee, such events as the uncovering of a woman's form clasping a
child at Herculaneum. And the characters she invents repeatedly fulfil
the expectations created in the reader through the introduction of
these other texts. One woman proves her still perfect love when, as her
false lover returns to die in her arms, she can tenderly hold him to her
'wronged bosom' and declare, 'I live / To say my heart hath bled, and
can forgive' (2:2.220). Another, ignored by her husband for years,
waits patiently by his bed when he dies, convinced his corpse will revive
and smile on her at last: 'years of hope deferr'd,' she believes, would
be repaid by 'one fond glance of thine' (2:2.210).

Hemans might at times seem to move away from the 'domestic affections.' She can rouse the patriotic spirit with such well-known lines as

'The stately Homes of England, / How beautiful they stand' (2:2.237), and she can prompt a tear with 'Casabianca,' a poem so successful that, when I went to school at least, hundreds of English schoolchildren could still recite, 'The boy stood on the burning deck / Whence all but he had fled' (2:1.168) – and numerous inventive variations on these lines. Hemans actually ventured even further and produced works which were overtly 'political' in nature. But the connections with the domestic affections remain: patriotism is linked to the home, heroism to the innocence of the child. Any faint resistance she may display can consequently be quite easily ignored, or at best overlooked, by the critics. Even Maria Jane Jewsbury sounds convinced by Hemans's role when she neatly sums up the poet's public image as follows:

> Her matronly delicacy of thought, her chastened style of expression, her hallowed ideas of happiness as connected with home, and home-enjoyments; – to condense all in one emphatic word, her *womanliness* ... To speak confidentially to our trusted friend the public, Mrs. Hemans throws herself into her poetry, and the said self is an English gentlewoman. (105)

As an 'English gentlewoman,' Hemans would not 'throw herself' into anything, but the language once again effectively establishes the link between woman's truth and woman's body.

The manner in which women wrote was as prescribed as the matter, and a critical commonplace was there was little, if any, conscious artistry in their works; they were often seen to exemplify a debased Romanticism – Wordsworth's 'spontaneous overflow of powerful feelings' which, rather than being recollected in tranquility, are immediately spewed out upon the page. There is a significant difference suggested between the female Romantics, whose introduction of the personal marks the work as quintessentially 'feminine,' the words of a woman speaking to other women, and the male Romantic, who employs the personal to emphasize his kinship with 'Humanity.' The women are said to write 'from impulse, and rapidly as they think ... [They are] averse to critical restraints ... scarcely any of them seem to have inverted their pen. As the line came first to the brain, so it was written; as it was written, so it was printed. Mrs Hemans's melody was as much improvisation as Miss Landon's ...' (Bethune viii–ix). There is a mixed message here. While critics urge the women to prune and polish like a man, they still take satisfaction in the notion of female improvisation which marks the 'poetess''s work as the intuitive and confessional outpouring of emotion.

And Hemans and Landon oblige. Words like 'gushing' and 'over-flowing' abound in their works, and their creative female character is always an improvisatrice. Like the Spasmodics these women are, to adapt the words of Bailey's Festus, fountains, not pumps. The flow is from nature, not art. Usually the creative woman in these poems is betrayed and abandoned, and finds that with the loss of love the flow dries up. There is, literally, a physical blockage as the body asserts its control. Significantly, both poets personally managed to survive some form of abandonment with no noticeable drop in their own rates of production. What they say about the poetess is not necessarily reflected in what they practise – a point unnoticed by the critic who found that 'Hemans's melody was as much improvisation as Miss Landon's.' No matter how many times her characters claim to 'gush' and 'flow,' Hemans herself is hardly deserving of the title of 'improvisatrice.' Her own style is highly restrained; it has even been thought, with some jus-tification, to align her more with the Augustans than the Romantics (Reiman x–xi). The paradox suggests an interesting use of referential-ity. Hemans refers to one particular mode of discourse (improvisation) so frequently that her audience, accustomed to her fulfilling the expec-tations she creates with regard to story, does not seem to recognize that she actually frustrates them in the matter of discourse.

Landon, conversely, when writing as L.E.L., tries to put her theories concerning improvisation into practice and self-consciously attempts to gender her work as 'feminine.' Juxtaposing two of her essays, an anonymous piece, 'On the Ancient and Modern Influence of Poetry' (1832), and a signed piece, 'On the Character of Mrs. Hemans's Writ-ings' (1835), illustrates how this is done.[2] In the anonymous piece Landon eliminates any sense of a female perspective; she copies the male critics in using the supposedly more objective 'we' instead of 'I,' and she makes no reference to the poet as woman. She is strictly atten-tive to punctuation and grammar, her diction is astoundingly clear and precise, and her analogies are crisp and restrained: this is *not* L.E.L.'s manner. In substance as in style Landon genders this essay 'masculine.' She discusses religion, war, and love as sources of poetry, and love is considered with ruthless brevity. Poetry is celebrated without qualifica-tion, there are no fretful references to 'worthless fame,' and the case against personal circumstances as the motivation for poetry is strenu-ously argued. There is an interesting inversion of the usual workings of the signature in this essay. The signed piece is usually considered the authoritative one, but here it is the anonymous piece, which, because it is implied to be man's work, becomes authoritative.

'On the Character of Mrs. Hemans's Writings,' signed with the well-known L.E.L., is feminine, subjective, and specific rather than masculine, authoritative, and transcendent. Landon takes the opportunity here not only to comment on Hemans's works, but also to develop her own public image. With typical Landon flair she begins with a flourish of French. 'OH! mes amis, rapellez-vous quelquefois mes vers; mon âme y est empreinte' ('Oh, my friends, remember my verses sometimes; my soul is imprinted upon them'); such, she claims here, 'is the secret of poetry ... nothing is so strongly impressed on composition as the character of the writer' (425). She makes no attempt to suggest objectivity in style – she constantly slips out of a half-hearted 'we' into 'I.' Grammatically she displays that unmistakable Landon style in which, as one satirist observed, 'All nouns, like statesmen, suit all places, / And verbs, turned lawyers, hunt for cases' (Praed 283). As for content, the essay is full of emphatically personal observations: 'I remember to have read of ...' (426); 'I can never sufficiently regret that ...' (430); 'I knew Miss Jewsbury ...' (430). While 'the painter reproduces others,' the poet reproduces the self (428), she insists. Freely dipping into all Hemans's family problems and marital disappointments, Landon finds 'the deep impress of individual suffering' in the poems she quotes; 'the sentiment is too true for Mrs. Hemans not to have been her own inspiration' (428). Assuring the reader that she, L.E.L., has similarly suffered, she sighs, 'Ah! Fame to a woman is indeed but a royal mourning in purple for happiness' (432). This is clearly marked as the work of a woman speaking to other women; once again there is that sense of the debased specific as opposed to the transcendent.

Landon is a far more experimental writer than Hemans in matters of gender, and she also creates the more interesting poetic character, a character which prompted a rage of poetic enthusiasm when it was first introduced. Bulwer-Lytton, writing of his undergraduate days, recalls the rush 'every Saturday afternoon for "The Literary Gazette," and an impatient anxiety to hasten at once to that corner of the sheet which contained the three magical letters of "L.E.L." And all of us praised the verse, and all of us guessed at the author. We soon learned it was a female, and our admiration was doubled, and our conjectures tripled. [And the focus of their interest changed.] Was she young? Was she pretty?' (546). Rumour may have given an adoring Shelley to Mrs Hemans in her youth, but L.E.L. was reported to have two or three hundred suitors asking for her hand at any given moment. What makes the construct L.E.L. interesting today is the way in which Landon tried to turn the conventions governing the 'poetess' to her own advantage in creating this titillating figure, to turn constraint into opportunity, and, initially at least, how she was still able to satisfy the critics.

Landon makes her creative female figures a composite of various fictional, legendary, and historical characters. Primarily, however, she conflates Italy and the improvisatrice with Greece and the Pythoness at Delphi. The choice of the latter reveals much about Landon's methods of resistance. The Pythoness projects the image of a woman under the thumb of an establishment male, but unless we accept that she really was entered by some gaseous Apollo, she can be seen as a woman who seizes the opportunity to speak by claiming the influence of inspiration to speak only that which is sanctified by male authority;[3] the voice would actually be her own. The problem is that since Landon chooses a traditional figure to manipulate, a figure associated with the woman as medium, as closer to the spiritual and the intuitive, it can easily be reappropriated. In Landon's work the process of appropriation and reappropriation is constant: there is a superficial conformity with the conventions of the 'poetess' which is repeatedly undercut by the disruptive subtext of the woman's own voice, and then, since the resistance begins within and retains links with the convention, the voice is easily brought back within the bounds of dominant gender ideology by the critics.

Eulalie, like most of Landon's poets, walks alone at night, pale with emotion, in a white robe of Grecian simplicity, bare neck and arms, unbound raven tresses falling to her feet, pacing an ancient ruined gallery, striking a few wild chords, murmuring a few scarcely audible words. The image projected to the young men who slink in the bushes to view her is of self-effacing beauty; she is art, not artist: her voice is almost discounted. But while inspiration may flourish in solitude, improvisation demands an audience. By day the women perform in public, and it is their abilities as poets that prompt the praise and acclaim which make the cheek burn and the 'pulses beat' (2:39). In Landon's hands improvisation establishes a rebellious link between women's poetry and performance; it necessitates the public display of talent, not beauty.

There is a showiness in Landon's writing that aptly corresponds to this notion of performance, and her obvious playful delight in language suggests she found the convention which associated women's poetry with improvisation quite useful. She cares little for grammatical correctness; she delights in foreign words and places, in erotically suggestive images, in linking completely dissimilar ideas. And one image never satisfies Landon: the prevalence of anaphora in her poetry reflects her desire to pile image on top of image, to push everything to the extreme, to squeeze every idea dry, to revel in verbal energy. The enthusiasms and excesses in her flamboyant mode of discourse suggest a sensuous manipulation of the delights of language which was not what the critics had in mind in linking women with improvisation: when the convention is put to *use*, improvisation becomes art, something contrived for specific effect, not the natural and thoughtless process which allows for the dismissal of female talent.

In the matter of topic Landon similarly attempts to turn constraint into opportunity. Her prefaces pointedly draw attention to her conformity with audience expectation: 'I can only say, that for a woman, whose influence and whose sphere must be in the affections, what subject can be more fitting than one which it is her peculiar province to refine, spiritualise, and exalt?' (*Bracelet* vi). This might have a domestic ring, but the erotic love of which Landon writes fits uneasily into the category of 'domestic affections.' (Although, since it is love, it can easily be appropriated.)

Landon focuses exclusively and obsessively on romantic love, and tells the 'same sad tale' repeatedly: a woman loves, she pants after fulfilment, she is betrayed or abandoned, left with her erotic yearnings unsatisfied. The poems are heavily intertextual: references to figures like Ariadne and Sappho and unhappy women from the works of Hemans and others abound; Landon is even blithely self-referential, freely quoting from her old poems to provide epigraphs for the new. She also makes effective use of the embedded text to suggest the multivocal and the repetitive, and to provide numerous supporting echoes of the main text of frustrated desire. In 'The Improvisatrice,' for example, a work which clearly recalls *Corinne*, the poet/artist who speaks, a woman destined, of course, for unhappy love, begins by recalling her first artistic efforts. In the middle of describing a painting of Sappho, abandoned by her faithless lover, she suddenly stops to sing the song she has painted Sappho singing. We are taken from written text (Landon) to the spoken (improvisatrice), to the visual (Sappho herself), to, at the centre, music (Sappho's song), and then abruptly back out into the primary spoken narrative. As the movement to the visual implies, Landon also manipulates the convention that the woman and her text are one: verbal expression of frustrated desire is confirmed with the language of the body. Once deserted, the improvisatrice paints a final picture of Ariadne with bare white arms flung upwards, white lips parched by hot sighs, and a wild stare in her eyes. Ariadne's passionately tortured body, captured in this state of display and defencelessness in so many nineteenth-century paintings, becomes the text. To locate desire in the woman's body rather than to establish the body as desired is radical considering the time, but it is simultaneously, since it locates meaning only in the body, conventional.

While Landon is, by writing of love, undeniably conforming to convention, the end result of this obsessive return to the same unhappy tale has an interesting effect: the reviews gradually begin to reveal a critical uneasiness with Landon's work. This is sometimes considered the result of certain masochistic elements in Landon's work, but the presence of these would not have been likely to disturb anyone. It is more likely to be the clear self-reflexivity and self-sufficiency in Landon's treatment of female desire that would have offended. Significantly, if Landon's men do not abandon the women, they are soon killed off. The male lover, to a great extent, is excluded and made almost irrelevant; he becomes little more than a prop for Landon's exploration of female eroticism. When Eulalie muses, 'I have sung passionate songs of beating hearts; / Perhaps it had been better they had drawn / Their inspiration from an inward source' (2:57), the sentiment is suspect; Landon's heroines always seem to prefer writing and singing about love over actually experiencing it; to prefer the 'heart / That fed upon itself' (2:61). Not surprisingly, descriptions of the 'flush and flow' caused by love are, taken out of context, indistinguishable from descriptions of the 'flush and flow' caused by public performance. The women pant after erotic satisfaction yet always manage to avoid engaging with the men sexually. Instead they are shown sensuously drawing out the moment prior to or following abandonment, slowly lingering over the deliciousness of their own words, over the twistings of their own bodies, always ultimately expiring alone in an orgasmic death.

The degree to which Landon could successfully manipulate the conventions was ultimately limited; indeed, the language of the reviewers reveals that to a great extent she ended up playing into their hands. They had little difficulty in appropriating Landon's transformations in order to put them to conventional use. As one critic enthused, 'Burke said, that ten thousand swords ought to have leaped out of their scabbards at the mention of the name of Marie Antoinette; and in like manner we maintain, that ten thousand pens should leap out of their inkbottles to pay homage to L.E.L.' (G.G. 433). On one level L.E.L. is reduced to a sexual tease to whom men respond erotically; on another level she becomes the idealized and weakened figure of woman that men worship and protect. In both cases her truth is limited once more to her body – a body not desiring but desired – and rather than being seen as writer, she is what is written about; the pen is returned to its rightful owner.

Furthermore, the critics damagingly decontextualized L.E.L. As they took their appropriated version of Landon's literary construct out of its fictional world into the extra-textual world, social disaster became inevitable. There was rumoured to be evidence of an immoral liaison with William Maginn; she was said to have propositioned Daniel Maclise; the *Wasp* bluntly claimed she bore William Jerdan's child. The gossip led to the breaking of her engagement with the spineless John Forster and in 1835 William Macready reported in his *Diary*: 'She is fallen!'[4] The decline of her literary and social reputations is collectively described by terminology based on the state of the body. Three years later, the thirty-six-year-old Landon, wanting to escape scandals still simmering in London, made the disastrous decision to marry the saturnine George MacClean, governor of the Gold Coast; three months after this she was dead in Cape Coast Castle, possibly a suicide, but more likely – and surely more appropriately – murdered.

Notes

1 It is difficult to know what to call this resulting 'entity.' 'Persona' is unsatisfactory because it would ignore the specific link with the actual author. Wayne Booth comes close to defining the construct in his discussion of 'Career Authors and Public Myths.' But his 'career author' is unsatisfactory because it does not seem to carry with it the sense that this is a carefully created fictional construct; instead, he sees it as something put together by the reader after reading a number of works by the same author. Nor does he see the figure as the *subject* of the texts. (Nineteenth-century women devoted many poems to constructing the fictional alter ego.) The public myth idea is similarly unsatisfactory. 'Whenever a fair number of real readers share speculation about a postulated writer, a new character is invented, a public myth bearing only an indeterminate relation to any real person, or any implied author: "Mark Twain," the paragon humorist; "Oscar Wilde," established as the ultimate aesthete largely in disregard of what he actually writes; or "Norman Mailer," the most honest *naughty* boy who ever lived.' Booth does not seem to believe it easy to write about this ('it is hard to talk about such figures without simply gossiping') and is relieved to say that this is a type of 'author' 'fortunately not important here for long' (150–1). Booth never considers, however, that this figure is usually in large part the construct of the

author, not the reader. The construction can actually often be traced in the author's work.

2   The evidence that Landon wrote 'On the Ancient and Modern Influence of Poetry' is a reference in a letter from Bulwer-Lytton to S.C. Hall dated 19 October 1832. Bulwer-Lytton wrote to Hall to ask for a copy of the article because he disagreed with some of the things that Landon had to say.

3   For the best discussion of the Pythia, see Joseph Fontenrose's chapter on 'The Mantic Session,' to which I am indebted.

4   For information on this gossip, see Davies, 76–9; and Greer, 16–19.

Works Cited

Bal, Mieke. *Narratology: Introduction to the Theory of Narrative.* Toronto: U of Toronto P 1985

Bethune, George W. *The British Female Poets: With Biographical and Critical Notices.* 1848; reprint, Freeport, NY: Books for Libraries Press 1972

Booth, Wayne C. *The Company We Keep: An Ethics of Fiction.* Berkeley: U of California P 1988

Bulwer-Lytton, Edward George. '*Romance and Reality* By L.E.L.' *New Monthly Magazine* 32, no. 132 (1831), 545–51

[Coleridge, H.N.] 'Modern English Poetesses.' *Quarterly Review* 66 (1840), 374–418

Davies, James A. *John Forster: A Literary Life.* Leicester: U of Leicester P 1983

[Delta (David Moir).] 'Miss Landon's Poetry.' Review of *The Improvisatrice; and Other Poems. Blackwood's* 91 (1824), 189–93

Fontenrose, Joseph. *The Delphic Oracle.* Berkeley: U of California P 1978

[G.G.] 'Gallery of Literary Characters: Miss Landon.' *Fraser's Magazine* 8 (1883), 433

Greer, Germaine. 'The Tulsa Center for the Study of Women's Literature: What We Are Doing and Why We Are Doing It.' *Tulsa Studies in Women's Literature* 1, no. 1 (1982), 5–26

Hemans, Felicia. *The Works of Felicia Hemans: Edited by her Sister.* 3 vols. New York: C.S. Francis 1845

Hickok, Kathleen. *Representations of Women: Nineteenth-Century British Women's Poetry.* Westport, CT: Greenwood 1984

[Jewsbury, Maria Jane.] 'Literary Sketches: No 1. Felicia Hemans.' *Athenaeum* 172 (12 Feb 1831), 104–05

[Landon, Letitia Elizabeth.] 'On the Ancient and Modern Influence of Poetry.' *New Monthly Magazine* 35 (1832), 466–71

Landon, Letitia Elizabeth. 'On the Character of Mrs. Hemans's Writings.' *New Monthly Magazine* 44 (1835), 425–33

– *Poetical Works of Letitia Elizabeth Landon*. 2 vols. London: Longmans 1853

– *The Venetian Bracelet, The Lost Pleiad, A History of the Lyre, and Other Poems*. London: Longman 1829

[Owen, Harriet Mary Browne Hughes.] 'Memoir of Mrs. Hemans.' In *The Works of Mrs Hemans*. Vol. 1. Edinburgh: Blackwood 1839

[Poe, Edgar Allan.] Review of *The Drama of Exile, and Other Poems* by Elizabeth Barrett Browning. *Broadway Journal* 1, no. 1 (1845), 4–8; 1, no. 2 (1845), 17–20

Praed, Winthrop Mackworth. *The Poems of Winthrop Mackworth Praed*. Vol 1. London: Moxon 1864

Reiman, Donald H. Introduction. *Felicia Dorothea Hemans: The Domestic Affections*. New York: Garland 1978, v–xi

Review of *The Vow of the Peacock*, by Letitia Landon. *New Monthly Magazine* 45 (1835), 346–53

Stodart, M[ary] A[nn]. 'Female Writers: Thoughts on Their Proper Sphere, and on Their Powers of Usefulness, 1842.' In *The Victorian Poet: Poetics and Persona*. Ed. Joseph Bristow. London: Croom Helm 1987, 134–7

Williamson, Marilyn L. Introduction. *The Female Poets of Great Britain*. By Frederic Rowton. 1853; reprint, Detroit: Wayne State UP 1981, xi–xxxii

☙ 4 ☙

Against Beauty: Eighteenth-Century Fiction Writers Confront the Problem of Woman-as-Sign

ISOBEL GRUNDY

Of course I'm not against beauty. Who could be that? 'The good is the beautiful,' says Plato; 'Beauty is Truth, Truth Beauty,' says the Grecian Urn. Any one of us looking at a stretch of blue water glinting in the sun, and later finding that it was full of chemical pollutants, would feel ourself confronted by a sign that lied.

What I am against, and so are *some* of the novelists I shall be dealing with, is the coercive ideology of beauty, the imperative that a woman must be beautiful, or else. Since I began thinking about this topic, I have been aware of a chorus all round me – quality newspapers, junk magazines, book reviews, film reviews, radio – all reiterating that in our culture to be successfully female involves being, as they say, easy on the eye. Susie Ohrbach (she was the one on the radio) remarked that physical appearance has become more, not less, oppressive of women since she published *Fat Is a Feminist Issue* in the 1970s. Marilyn Mobley added to the chorus Toni Morrison's description of physical beauty as one of the two 'most destructive ideas in the history of human thought' (Morrison 95), while Patricia Yaeger quotes Mary Oliver (see pages 106–9), pointing out how beauty can be bad news for the woman who possesses it as well as for the one who fears she does not.[1]

That stretch of water reminds us that to be beautiful is to be an object for the gaze. In folk art such as fairy tales and ballads, in high art such as heroic romance, a beautiful outside is the sign of wisdom and goodness inside, and the reverse means stupidity, malevolence, or sin. The human subject (hero of tale, reader of tale) deciphers appearances, judges beauty and morality. When someone bad looks beautiful, that is the lie direct. Spenser's false Duessa steals and uses the lovely likeness of Fidessa until the knights strip her naked and wonder at the foul deformity which expresses accurately what she is.

I'm not going to speculate here about what happens if we read Spenser from any other point of view than that of the male hero, but instead ask what effect this romance heritage has on the strategies of the novel, either directly or through the mediation of the social ideology of beauty. It does lay various constraints on fictional presentations of character, particularly female character. The novelist may shape her characters according to the dictates of symbolic and gendered readings, or may seek to intervene in such systems of meaning. To give a fictional character beauty is to construct her as sexual object, and more generally as material, as a sign traditionally placed to be read and responded to by the male subject. Man: Redcrosse Knight, figure in the landscape, active bearer of the gaze. Woman: Duessa/Fidessa, polluted or unpolluted watercourse, passive image. To withhold beauty from a female character is to set her in a particular, more than usually excluded, relationship to the patriarchal world.

The novel's project of investigating the lived responses of individuals, including potentially those of both the gazer and the one who is gazed at, involves an attempt by the novelist to exert control over symbolic readings. Historically, this has been done more variously and successfully for male than female fictional characters. Lack of beauty has been tolerated or even crucial in male heroes in otherwise fairly rigidly determined genres and narrow social settings – black Othello, grotesque Cyrano de Bergerac – but writers have routinely accepted the gendered construction of subject-positions implied by my romance example. Heroines must be beautiful, because unlike heroes they exist as signs to be read. In the old, classic fictional formula the hero struggles with desire, knowledge, self-realization, and a complex or shifting inner life; the heroine is fetish, symbol, or reward. Her beauty is a key element in each of these functions: it signifies her sexuality, as proper object of the hero's desire, her goodness, as proper object of knowledge. In each case it signifies her object status as passive image. Though Richard Steele in 1711 could urge on *Spectator* readers dissatisfied with their appearance the 'honest and laudable Fortitude to dare to be Ugly' (174), it was to be several generations before a novelist could dare this for a heroine.

The classic fictional formula was open, however, to negotiation and renegotiation. In the early novel the beauty of heroines is shifted around, made to serve this or that function within the dynamic of deeply various texts. Beauty in Aphra Behn carries a strong sexual charge and is equally an attribute of either sex: it is equated with the desirable and is the mainspring of plots which turn, almost without exception, on transgressive desire in one sex or the other or both. The heroine or anti-heroine of 'The Fair Jilt; or, The Amours of Prince Tarquin and Miranda' has 'every feature adorn'd with a grace that imagination cannot reach,' while the ex-Prince Hendrick is 'the lovely friar'; nor (in language which relishes its reversal of gender roles) 'could the mishapen habit hide from her the lovely shape it endeavour'd to cover'; Miranda imagines him without it, 'and that the robe laid by, she has the lover in his proper beauty' (106–15).[2]

As the novel became moralized, a tool for the assertion of socially approved ideology, reader demand for that kind of beauty evaporated. While the beauty of Samuel Richardson's Pamela makes her desirable, the delicacy and fragility which are perhaps the most important components of her beauty enable it to symbolize chastity and innocence rather than provocation. Pamela's subjectivity – and also her own desire – are evoked by verbal means which bypass or ignore her appearance.

Richardson is not out to fetishize his heroines. He makes two male characters, however, fetishize Clarissa in a manner which has the side-effect of giving us, as readers, pictorial details which are otherwise withheld. Lovelace chooses a moment of the highest drama and suspense to interrupt the narrative with an utterly static and dehumanizing 'faint sketch of [Clarissa's] admirable person with her dress'; it begins, 'Her wax-like flesh ...' (327). This, I believe, is likely to lose Lovelace readers' sympathy rather than make us into complicitous voyeurs. Lovelace both dehumanizes and de-eroticizes; he turns Clarissa into a collector's piece, using her beauty as a means to possess her by description at the very moment that he is also capturing her in the plot.

As so often in Richardson, this passage has its symmetrical counterweight. Belford paints an equally static picture of Clarissa in captivity at the sponging house, with 'her white flowing robes ... illuminating that horrid corner' (274). Making every detail of her surroundings emblematic, he explicitly uses the allegorical method with the aim of arousing Lovelace's remorse and pity. Belford is acting in character as a would-be agent of good, as Lovelace was acting in character as an arrogant male predator. Each unmakes Clarissa briefly as a subjectivity and constructs her instead as a visual icon: Lovelace in the style of clas-

sic boy-gets-girl romance; Belford in the specialized mode of the sentimental novel, with its heroines as icons of affect.

Clarissa's own letters construct her subjectivity and never mention
her appearance. Readers, however, have from the beginning showed
frequent willingness to follow the signposts offered by Lovelace or Belford. The persistent misreadings which caused Richardson so much
irritation arose very largely from a fetishization of the heroine, an
eagerness to read her by any means *except* that of attention to her own
discourse.

Henry Fielding was possibly the first novelist to problematize the
convention of compulsory beauty for the heroine. For him the issue
was primarily one of verisimilitude. The famous broken nose of his last
heroine, Amelia, represents an attempt to de-allegorize beauty (Amelia's goodness exists independently of her looks) and to reflect the ran-
domness of actuality (beautiful women are not immune to accident).
Like Richardson he was apparently too subtle for his readers, since
Amelia's nose provoked outrage both serious and ribald. He was in fact
using the motif of disfigured beauty: not Spenser's enchantress-dis-
guised-as-beautiful, but the heroine-disguised-as-ugly, as depicted in
the Cinderella story or in Chaucer's *Wyf of Bath's Tale*. Amelia's disfigurement by her accident lasts just long enough for the hero to prove
himself the only one to love her for herself alone, and then vanishes in
favour of business as usual: Amelia's beauty both symbolizes her goodness and makes her a focus of male desire, thus producing the plot.

The disfigured-heroine motif is not the same as the ugly-duckling
one frequent in female *Bildungsroman*. Jane Eyre and Maggie Tulliver
as girls are perceived by themselves as lacking beauty but later develop
a deeper, more unusual beauty beyond the merely fashionable or sexy.
Charlotte Brontë and George Eliot have in the past been reproved for
trying to have it both ways, but what they are depicting is a growth out
of false consciousness about socially prescribed female appearance.

In Fielding's *Amelia* it is never the heroine's own opinion of her
appearance that is at stake. But the novel has some bearing on the ideology of beauty since it requires its hero, however briefly, to read the
goodness of his heroine by other signs than that of beauty. Neither
Booth nor the reader, however, endures a psychological close encounter with a disfigured Amelia. Booth, in retrospective narrative, relates
how her 'lovely nose was beat all to pieces' in a coach accident (57) – a
curiously unrealized piece of action –how her moral worth displayed
itself in confronting the jealous triumphs of her rivals, how during her
convalescence he begged her to unmask to him, and then cried out

passionately that she 'never appeared to me so lovely as at this instant' (59). In declaring his love, Booth firmly re-objectivizes Amelia as focus of his gaze. Once her beauty has been perceived behind the mask of disfigurement, it emerges, reconstituted. She is a character conceived in patriarchal terms: not so passive behind the scenes of the plot as she appears, but still a model and icon of female goodness.

To gauge the coercive force of eighteenth-century beauty ideology – which differs in several respects from that in operation today – it is worth looking at books which were more directly concerned than the novel proper in the construction of accepted gender roles. Books on the education of girls, especially those which include subsidiary fictions, reveal a confused and confusing ideology of beauty, positively teeming with double binds. In Sarah Fielding's *The Governess; or, Little Female Academy* (1749; one of the most intelligent and broad-minded of the genre, as well as the earliest) most of the pupils rank as fairly-beautiful-but-imperfect. Since their imperfections reflect their characters, one might expect that perfect beauty would follow on the attainment of perfect virtue: that beauty might be a symbol of virtue as in Fidessa or Amelia, with the difference that it would signal achieved rather than instinctive goodness. (This is a line taken by some of today's health-and-beauty ideology.) But matters in *The Governess* and its genre are not so simple. While virtue is presented unequivocally as a goal to strive for, beauty is not. An elaborate terminology (as elaborate and as inventory-like as Lovelace's) serves to discriminate the different shades of the almost-beautiful, which is made to seem a more acceptable category than the truly-beautiful (184). Various subtextual messages group themselves around the possession of beauty. Explicitly, it is a gift, not an achievement, and therefore something to be not proud of but thankful for. Yet implicitly it represents both desire and power (as in Aphra Behn); a moral education as a properly socialized female therefore involves learning to shun it. When girls are severely censured for pretending to more beauty than they actually have (191), there is an implication firstly that if they did have it they ought to deny rather than display it; secondly that their not having it makes them subject to humiliation: a classic double bind in which the girl undergoing socialization is required to collude in her own banishment from power and from desire.

In *The School* (1766) Sarah Mease, later Murray, marks out the overvaluing of beauty as prominent among incorrect attitudes which need to be, and are, reformed. Miss Arran values nothing but beauty (especially her own) and retains nothing from her education but the speech from *Comus* which begins, 'Beauty is nature's boast.' Her peril is flirting with a married man; her salvation is forming a close bond with a plain though agreeable friend (1:89–101). Miss Le Maine has to be persuaded and bullied out of the use of cosmetics. This episode provokes an almost shocking outbreak of plain speaking. The schoolmistress tells her reprovingly that rouge 'is worn as an attraction to the other sex. This, in a single woman, is done with a design of gaining the affections of some man so effectively as may incline him to marry her; is it honest, think you to endeavour to win him by a charm, which, when he is married, he must find is not real?' Morality is nakedly revealed as ancillary to self-interest and to the manipulations which the powerless – women – necessarily use to pursue self-interest. To this there can hardly be a more moral answer than that of the rouge-wearer: 'If he is such a fool as to marry me for my complexion, he deserves to be disappointed' (2:4–5). The episode casts an alarming light on the moral gyrations which were necessary for women to accept the moral ideology which was thrust upon them, while refraining from applying its precepts to those who exercised power.

The work of women novelists often dramatizes and draws vitality from these conflicts. It includes many briefly disfigured heroines: a young woman with hands a network of scratches from playing with her kitten; and Frances Burney's Juliet the Wanderer, her face blackened for disguise, thought by her fellow-travellers to be racially black. The reader is not made privy at the outset to these women's subjectivity, as to Jane Eyre's or Maggie Tulliver's, but is being advised how to read them: more clearly than by Henry Fielding's *Amelia*, we are being warned off the signifier 'beautiful woman.'

Anna Maria Bennett uses this strategy as an early hint on how to read her *Ellen, Countess of Castle Howel* (1794). The novel opens with travellers in remote North Wales approaching a castle on a stormy night, confronted first by a rush of barking dogs, then by a whole family of eccentrics. Two of its female members are writers, with correspondingly unacceptable appearance: one 'took snuff and seldom wore whole stockings'; the other is 'a very plain girl' (1:9). Last and most dramatic in her entrance is the youngest of the family, 'tears streaming from her eyes, her hands and face smeared with blood, and dragging in her arms the still bleeding carcass of poor Lion' (1:17) – one of the barking dogs, which the travellers had killed in their alarm. This is the heroine, Ellen. This vignette emphasizes the fact that Bennett is parodically reversing the idea of knights errant, rescuers of damsels in distress; Ellen bloody and weeping is a grotesque and anti-aesthetic

symbol of the rape victim which she nearly, but not quite, later
becomes: a rebuke to the icon of pathos beloved by sentimental novelists, which exploits the sign of violated woman to manipulate, perhaps
titillate, the reader's feelings. (Bennett might almost have had in mind
Belford on Clarissa; she very likely did have in mind Henry Fielding on
a little girl with a shot dog.)[3]

On Ellen's next appearance she is wearing her Sunday best; therefore is beautiful – a true, not parodic, potential victim. The murderer
of her dog makes a standard itemization of her beauty, adds a dash of
irony to his rhetoric of desire (her 'warm embraces ... might animate a
statue' – though they had 'failed to restore the mastiff to life' [1:33]),
marvels 'such a creature to be an inhabitant of that dark dungeon'
(1:33) – and '"Joe," said the noble Lord, "I'll have that girl"' (1:36).

Bennett's narrative novel does not deeply develop Ellen's subjectivity or make much of her early association either with the unacceptable
looks that go with female assertiveness or with the spectre who
demands revenge. Ellen's later role is exemplary rather than outrageous; her capacity for heroic resolution, noted later in volume one
(239), is offered chiefly passive forms of expression. The most interesting thing that Bennett does is repeatedly to question and mock the
conventions of her chosen genre. Amelia's temporary loss of beauty
serves the basic moral framework of her story; Ellen's forecasts such
subversive touches as this novel's closure on a double burlesque of
conventional endings (of exaggerated moral perfection and exaggerated financial reward).

Laetitia-Matilda Hawkins, in *The Countess and Gertrude; or, Modes of
Discipline* (1811), gives her heroine a rather similar introduction but
uses it to serve different ends. She subverts not the novel form but the
standard social and fictional pattern of female development. The
countess, whom we meet first, is a ready-formed cipher – fashionable,
wealthy, and owing it all to her beauty. Gertrude, on the contrary, little
and dark and 'much too dirty to be kissed,' is a child with her potential
yet to develop (1:158). It is the kiss of patronage or condescension
from which her dirt preserves her here, but the phrase suggests a protection from the role of sex object. Her dirt comes from exploring life
– ditches, stables. She stares at her first glimpse of novelty 'till her eyes
seemed to have lost all power of closing' (1:158); once a little older she
is 'gasping for knowledge' (1:208). The novel is a *Bildungsroman* of her
pursuit of education, and her near-escape from the feminine sphere
by, among other things, earning money as a secret author, when 'she
saw – O! who can tell her pride and joy? – the rough draft of a work,

bulky enough to be printed' (4:218). When her first love affair goes wrong, she is puzzled to find herself getting happier, not sadder, at the prospect of earning her own living. In the end Hawkins cannot resist saddling Gertrude (whose novel brought her twenty-five pounds) with a legacy of two thousand pounds and a husband; but she does tell us that Gertrude considers marriage not 'as the *focus*, towards which all the rays of our intellect tend, and in which they may safely terminate' (4:414), but as 'a new prospect' demanding 'more various exertions' (4:425). No longer dirty, she still claims her right to gaze rather than to be gazed at; here the disfigured heroine is a means to the active, desirous heroine striking her own bargain with society's norms.

At least two predecessors or contemporaries of Hawkins seemed set to challenge the ideology of beauty head-on by building a novel around an *ugly* heroine. In fact one of them, Sarah Scott in *Agreeable Ugliness; or, The Triumph of the Graces, Exemplified in the Real Life and Fortunes of a Young Lady of Some Distinction* (1754), was translating a French original. Her dedication 'to those Ladies Who are ignominiously distinguished under the Denomination of Ugly' associates herself with them as those to whom 'churlish Nature has denied what is esteemed the most valuable, if not the only Advantage of our Sex,' and who conceal their disability even from themselves. Early on, the novel makes the bleak and potentially combative statement that 'an ugly Face reduces a Woman into a kind of Non-existence' (2). The story, however, is non-subversive, a variant of the patient Griselda myth, strongly supportive of the boarding-school ideology that goodness (i.e., submissiveness) is to be preferred to beauty, and of the transparent falsehood that submission will surpass beauty as productive of happiness and even power. It is an anti-feminist novel to boot.

The heroine, who is never given a first name, grows up loved by her father but hated by her coquettish mother (who calls her 'the *Shocking Monster*' [13], while her beautiful elder sister is generally known as 'the *Fair Villiers*' [18]). She grows up full of self-hatred ('As I had continually been told I was a *Monster*, I really believed it' [57]), terrified of losing her father's love, and wishing when she falls ill to die, as her mother hopes she will. But already the story is mitigating her ugliness (her black eyes have vivacity; she has fine teeth and soft skin) and construing it as valuably detaching her from femaleness, from over-attention to trifling and narrow matters like dress (19–20). Once she gets out in the world, she attracts the approval and even love of males, to whom, unlike her beautiful sister, she responds with impeccable timidity and passivity. She is perfectly prepared to give a good man what he wants by marrying him even though she loves someone else, and in due time comes to love her husband as the conduct books say she should. Physical beauty here is associated with female wiles and power; moral beauty is patriarchally taught, and rewarded with true love. A preposterous plot loads one torment after another on the heroine, and duly negates them by not one but a whole series of unsought triumphs over her mother's and sister's wicked energies. This is a book which criminalizes beauty without doing anything positive for the absence of beauty.

Anne Plumptre did something much more interesting with a similar scheme in *Something New; or, Adventures at Campbell-House* (1801). She adopts a radical stance in a prefatory poem: a rousing verse attack on the beautiful-heroine convention as the last remaining example of tyrannical power in liberty-loving Britain. Plumptre says she will be the first novelist bold enough to assert the 'RIGHTS OF AUTHORS': 'And in these pages place before your view / An UGLY heroine – Is't not SOMETHING NEW?' She is firmer than Scott, or Scott's source, about her heroine's ugliness – 'you can have no idea of any thing not deformed so uncommonly plain, ' 'a little ugly, black-faced thing, with eye-brows in a strait line from one side of her face to the other' (1:17,39). Olivia is not only ugly but active, strong, and desiring. One use of ugliness here is to point her remoteness from socially approved prescriptions; another is to explore the inadequacy of male concepts of the female. In this novel – epistolary, the better to represent multiple viewpoints and opposed ideologies – it is not hostile female relations but eligible young men who find a woman without beauty both excessive and defective. More important to them is her role as potential property. Olivia is rich (in some sense the embodiment of patriarchal ideals, since her sense and her virtue, like her wealth, come from her now-dead father). But she refuses to internalize society's attitudes: she maintains her autonomy, will neither fudge the facts about her appearance nor feel shame for it, and has a beautiful woman as her most intimate among several female friends. Ugliness in no way defeminizes Olivia, as it does the deformed, intellectual, and saintly sister of Burney's heroine in *Camilla*.

The early stages of *Something New* pleasingly reverse social expectations. One mercenary suitor is in turn disfigured (when he professes to adore old romances, Olivia takes him to her library and makes him fetch books off high shelves till he is filthy with ingrained dust). Another is amazed to find himself one down: 'rejected by a woman whom [*sic*] I expected would have rushed with transport into my arms, and only thought herself too happy that my former reluctance ... was subdued' (2:92). At this stage the reader may expect that Olivia's disfigurement will vanish, or turn out to be of *merely* social construction – especially when she turns out (like Sarah Scott's heroine) to have a beautiful voice.

What we get is different. (I should say that this is a large, complex novel; I am not reporting everything that goes on in it.) The young man actually falls in love with Olivia's voice and goodness, but remains deeply embarrassed by her looks, and after long wavering which inflicts much pain he allows himself to be directed by society's requirements rather than his desires. Olivia heroically redirects his feelings towards a woman who will do him credit in public (who is also not a nonentity but a poet, no less).

The novel ends without closure, though another man (opaque to us and to her because he is a non-letter-writer) is interested in Olivia, and a conventional happy ending dangles in prospect at a distance of four years. It is rich in sexual comedy (male arrogance good-humouredly deflated) and courageous in social and psychological truth-telling about areas of pain and conflict for women. Its heroine, exemplary in many ways, transgresses in her articulate desire. 'I have armed myself with resolution to resist an inclination which reason does not sanction, but such repeated conflicts almost wear me out ... I have scarcely firmness sufficient left to adhere to my purpose' (3:239). Her lover unblushingly admits the way he has forced her to take sole responsibility for the emotional outcome, procuring for him as well as for herself the luxury of a clear conscience. A modern reader may regret that Olivia is left with perfect 'self-approbation' (3:347, 349). This is something falling within the scope of Anna Maria Bennett's mockery of unrealistic happy endings; it is also the kind of heavy-handedness to which ideologically committed fictions are still too prone. But we must admire the way Anne Plumptre, beginning from one single bold challenge to fictional convention, has used it to open up multiple questions about gendered feelings and experience.

A challenge of a wholly different kind is mounted by Eliza Fenwick in *Secresy; or, The Ruin on the Rock* (1795). A radical like Plumptre, she goes further in rejection of the social status quo, with two revolutionary heroines who challenge all society's values including the ascription of importance to visual signs. Their relationship is the first which the novel (epistolary again) develops, and they provide a model for strong mutual attraction – the Chloe and Olivia of Woolf's Mary Carmichael were not the first – based on personal qualities other than looks.

Sibella Valmont, who has been brought up in total ignorance and seclusion according to her uncle's Rousseauvian theories, loves Caroline Ashburn for her informed intelligence and powers of analysis, evaluation, and self-determination, and Caroline loves Sibella for her 'vigour of feeling' and for the impetuosity which makes her 'rather think herself born to navigate ships and build edifices, than to come into a world for no other purpose, than to twist her hair into ringlets' (49). In fact – though Caroline mentions that she noticed Sibella's beauty – it is feminist principle on one hand and feminist feeling on the other that 'made you appear so singular, so attractive' (17).

We too know Sibella has beauty because men keep falling in love with her; we know Caroline has beauty because men keep observing that her uppishness spoils it. But, most unusually in fiction, our attention is deflected from these women's appearance (as is their own: one has never been subjected to socialization, and the other has achieved a critique of it). Their sense of self, and their sense of the loved female other, are independent of looks. We learn Sibella's hair colour only late in the novel, when she needs to be identified to someone not acquainted with her. We learn about her eyebrows and lashes like this: 'did symmetry ever mould a statue in finer proportions than his form can boast? His eye in its passive state is a clear grey, its shape long; and the finest eye-brow and eye lash that ever adorned mortal face, not excepting even your's, Sibella, belong to his' (137).

Now, it is nothing new in the novel for women characters to be much concerned with reading the looks of men, since their fate often hangs on correct interpretation of these signs. 'We are both great watchers of each other's eyes' (2:93), said Clarissa of herself and Lovelace. But it is unusual for women to be as they are in *Secresy*, so much taken up with male *beauty*: 'three years older than myself, blooming, blushing, beautiful' (20); 'Colonel Ridson, you know, said Mr. Murden was handsome. So say I. At times, divinely handsome; but only at times' (39); 'good God, what a charm was diffused over his countenance!' (45).

Meanwhile the overvaluing of beauty (which in Sarah Mease's *The School* was the delusion of an immature female who was still to be taught) is here an index of degeneracy, characterizing females who are middle-aged and only too well taught the rules of patriarchy, and young men who are enemies to women. The first words in the novel of Sibella's unworthy early love, Clement Montgomery, are 'Infidel as thou art toward beauty' (53). (From this our opinion of Clement is intended to sink, and that of Arthur Murden, his addressee, to rise.) He and others expose the hollowness of this idea by overstatement: 'in woman there can be no crime but ugliness' (54); 'beauty [is] the supreme good' of female development (109).

Why, then, are these two exceptionally sensitive, intelligent, and feeling women so much concerned with male beauty? The answer surely is that Fenwick, for the first time since Aphra Behn, is endowing her female characters with sexuality: not the gleefully wicked sexuality of Behn's tales, but a passionate idealizing romantic sensibility expressing itself in sexual terms. Sibella and Caroline (more markedly than Plumptre's Olivia, six years later) both love unwisely, on appearances, with little solid grasp of the character of their beloveds, despite close and anxious observation. *Secresy* (whose moral, as its title suggests, is the value of openness and the destructiveness of concealment) is centrally concerned to separate substance from shadow, social ideology from unpalatable facts about the bases of society; it seeks romantically, platonically, to pierce beyond appearance to truth.

Beauty is a highly misleading sign; it is the involvement in reading that is all. Murden, when he falls in love with Sibella, says, 'Were I to live ages, I could never describe her, for when her image is most perfect with me I have neither powers of mind, nor the common faculties of nature' (204). Even a rake can perceive the inadequacy of Clement Montgomery's painting of Sibella as a sign of her: 'Montgomery showed you a silly portrait that he painted. To say it was the likeness of Miss Valmont was a falsehood. 'Twas a mere passive representation of fine features. Let him paint me their energy, their force, the fulness of love that beamed from them yesterday morning ... He cannot do it' (285). It takes Sibella herself to see whom the painting *does* represent: she dotes on it because it is 'rather his image than my own' (194). Clement Montgomery functions like Spenser's Duessa in disguise, like the lovely temptresses of innumerable male narratives. His beauty is a sign which a female hero misreads. Eliza Fenwick reverses the inherited pattern. Her heroines are imaged less in what they look like than in how they think and feel – through their socially critical, sexually desirous eyes. They are tragically misled by the passion of their gaze, like many an idealistic male hero before them entrapped in the materiality of the Other.

Notes

1 A more recent study, detailed and militant, is Naomi Wolf's *The Beauty Myth*.

2 I have used modern editions and reprints when possible, for accessibility, even where they are not satisfactory as texts.
3 A 'tragical adventure' in which the shooting of a little girl's lap-dog emblematizes oppression (*Joseph Andrews* 192)

Works Cited

Behn, Aphra. 'The Fair Jilt; or, The Amours of Prince Tarquin and Miranda' 1689. In her *Oroonoko and Other Stories*. Ed. Maureen Duffy. London: Methuen 1986, 106–15

Bennett, Anna Maria. *Ellen, Countess of Castle Howel*. 4 vols. London: Minerva 1794

Fenwick, Eliza. *Secresy; or, The Ruin on the Rock*. 1795; reprint, Introd. Janet Todd. London: Pandora 1989

Fielding, Henry. *Amelia*. 1751; reprint, ed. David Blewett. Harmondsworth: Penguin 1987

– *The History of Joseph Andrews, and of His Friend Mr. Abraham Adams*. 1741; reprint, ed. Martin C. Battestin. Boston: Houghton 1961

Fielding, Sarah. *The Governess: or, Little Female Academy*. 1749; reprint. ed. Jill E. Grey. London: Oxford UP 1968

Hawkins, Laetitia-Matilda. *The Countess and Gertrude; or, Modes of Discipline*. 4 vols. London: Rivington 1811

Mease, Sarah. *The School*. 3 vols. London: Flexny 1766–72

Mobley, Marilyn Sanders. 'Missing the Self: African American Female Identity and the Poetics of Desire in the Novels of Toni Morrison.' Paper delivered to the Imag(in)ing Women: Representations of Women in Culture Conference, Edmonton, April 1990

Morrison, Toni. *The Bluest Eye*. London: Chatto 1979

Ohrbach, Susie. Interview. BBC, 25 March 1990

Plumptre, Anne. *Something New; or, Adventures at Campbell-House*. 3 vols. London: Longman 1801

Richardson, Samuel. *Clarissa; or, The History of a Young Lady*. 1751; reprint, New York: AMS 1990

– *Pamela; or, Virtue Rewarded*. 1740; reprint, London: Dent 1962

Scott, Sarah. *Agreeable Ugliness; or, The Triumph of the Graces, Exemplified in the Real Life and Fortunes of a Young Lady of Some Distinction*. London: Dodsley 1754

The Spectator. Ed. Donald F. Bond. 5 vols. Oxford: Clarendon 1965

Wolf, Naomi. *The Beauty Myth: How Images of Beauty Are Used against Women*. New York: William Morrow 1991

∞ 5 ∞

The 'Language of Blood': Towards a Maternal Sublime

PATRICIA YAEGER

The world of the beautiful can be treacherous for women:

> My great-aunt Elizabeth Fortune
> stood under the honey locust trees,
> the white moon over her and a young man near.
> The blossoms fell down like white feathers,
> the grass was warm as a bed, and the young man
> full of promises, and the face of the moon
> a white fire.
>
> Later,
> when the young man went away and came back with a bride,
> Elizabeth
> climbed into the attic.[*]

In 'Strawberry Moon' Mary Oliver tells the extraordinary story of an ordinary New England woman. Elizabeth Fortune is most ordinary in her acquiescence to the spatial dimensions that her society prescribes for her. In comparing men's and women's relation to power, Sandra Bartky argues that women accept a diminished relation to social space:

---

[*] Mary Oliver, 'Strawberry Moon,' from her *Twelve Moons* (Boston: Little, Brown 1979), 16. The complete texts of 'Strawberry Moon,' and of 'The Fish' from the same volume, are reproduced on pages 106–9.

'There are significant gender differences in gesture, posture, movement, and general bodily comportment: women are far more restricted than men in their manner of movement and in their spatiality
... Woman's space is not a field in which her bodily intentionality can
be freely realized but an enclosure in which she feels herself positioned and by which she is confined' (66). This is the enclosed world
of femininity, of convention, of the male idea of the beautiful. Is there
an alternative?

Although contemporary critics refuse to grant political authority to
the postmodern sublime, either arguing that the sublime is exhausted
as a literary genre, or claiming, with Lyotard, that the sublime is a
genre notable for its refusal of 'presence' – its gorgeous withdrawal
from the bourgeois fray – in this essay I will argue that sublimity, as rhetorical mode, still has work to do in women's writing. In the *Critique of
Judgment* Kant compares the beautiful and the sublime. Although sublimity involves terror, negation, and 'a momentary check to the vital
forces' (91), it also provokes movement rather than constriction,
ecstasy rather than confinement, force rather than form. The sublime
does not generate that commodious fit between self and the world that
characterizes the beautiful; instead, it releases the self's instinct for
power. As Maire Kurrik explains in *Literature and Negation*:

> In the sublime we do not feel an intuited accord between the self and the
> world, but only the noumenal power of the self. This heightened experi-
> ence is bought at the price of an experience of dissonance, discord, and
> disjunction between the self and the world. One feels a degree of alien-
> ation (the mind and the world were not designed for each other), but
> one also feels in the self the power to withstand this alienation and disso-
> nance and to surmount it. (51)

To be able to claim some spatial prerogative is a minimal condition of
the sublime. In the words of Longinus: 'we are uplifted as if instinctively, and our proud flight exalts our soul *as though we had created* what
we merely heard' (quoted in Weiskel 4). If this sublimity is unavailable
to the spatially constricted woman, how do we recover – for Elizabeth
Fortune, for everywoman – the 'joy and vaunting' (Weiskel 105), the
extraordinary pleasures, that have become the commonplace of the
male sublime?

The question is more open than it seems, for what happens to Elizabeth Fortune in the silence of the attic room does not – at first –
involve constriction or miniaturization. Instead,

Three women came in the night
to wash the blood away,
and burn the sheets,
and take away the child.

Was it a boy or girl?
No one remembers. (16)

In the face of this terrible amnesia I want to ask two questions. First, can we argue that the world of generation, of female generativity, also belongs to the experience of sublimity? If not, will attention to birthing labour, to the noumenal/biological power of the female self, help us both to reinvent the sublime and to rethink the politics of reproduction?

When Elizabeth Fortune crosses over into the attic's asocial space, we seem very far from the sublime indeed. In *Powers of Horror* Kristeva explores this space of defilement; she examines what woman's reproductive labour means for ordinary human ego boundaries. 'Where ... lies the border, the initial phantasmatic limit that establishes the clean and proper self of the speaking and/or social being?' (85). Kristeva concludes that the border separating social from asocial does not situate itself 'between man and woman' or 'mother and child' so much as it does between the terms 'woman and mother' (85). In the act of giving birth women splinter the concept of personhood, become the wound in humanity, for they encounter the world both as speaking and as reproductive beings. With so many articulate orifices women move beyond normal selfhood, beyond purification.

Historically, birthing women belong, then, to the shameful zone of abjection; they speak with the voice of secret, hidden flesh; instead of transcendence, they figure Western culture's grotesqueness. Birthing women's defilement is carefully mediated by the Old Testament. According to Leviticus the woman fresh from childbed is bloody, unclean, impure. She must pay for her lying-in 'according to the days of the separation for her infirmity' (quoted in Kristeva 99). If she gives birth to a daughter this child shall also 'be unclean two weeks, as in her separation' (12.5). For her own purification after bearing a daughter, the mother is required to offer burnt sacrifice. The penance changes if she gives birth to a male: 'the flesh of his foreskin shall be circumcised.' Does this mean that the male body bears the abjection normally reserved for the female? As Kristeva comments, circumcision separates male children 'from maternal, feminine impurity and defilement; it

stands instead of sacrifice' (99). That is, 'by repeating the natural scar
of the umbilical cord at the location of sex, by duplicating and thus displacing through ritual the preeminent separation, which is that from
the mother,' circumcision effects a differentiation 'of the son from the
mother. Symbolic identity presupposes the violent difference of the
sexes' (100).

This violence is upheld in 'Strawberry Moon.' For forty years after
her devalued labour Elizabeth Fortune stays upstairs and performs
considerable penance for the crisis of lying-in:

> Meals were sent up,
> laundry exchanged.
>
> It was considered a solution
> more proper than shame
> showing itself to the village. (17)

The blood and fire of generativity are consigned to darkness, while the
child's father remains in the light:

> I asked my mother:
> what happened to the man? She answered:
> Nothing.
> They had three children.
> He worked in the boatyard.
>
> I asked my mother: did they ever meet again?
> No, she said,
> though sometimes he would come
> to the house to visit.
> Elizabeth, of course, stayed upstairs. (17–18)

To work in a boatyard may or may not give this young man the feel of
transcendence. Masculinity is, of course, no guarantor of the sublime.
But this man's spatial prerogatives speak volumes; his freedom recalls
other spatial asymmetries.

When the contemporary German photographer Marianne Wex
looked for differences in male and female territoriality, her pictures of
gendered behaviour in train stations suggested that women constrict
their bodies much more than men. While the women she photographed waited with their arms clasped by the body, hands folded,

making themselves 'small and narrow, harmless ... tense' and taking up little space, the men she photographed felt comfortable expanding 'into the available space; they [sat] with legs far apart and arms flung out at some distance from the body' (Bartky 67). Their most common position was an open one, with legs far apart, crotch visible, feet pointing outward, their arms thrust about, relaxed in space.

The lovely thing about Oliver's poem is that her women do not remain in a posture of acquiescence. They seize the high road – Longinus's space of hypsos or height – and seek encounters in which the burden of the past will be lifted:

> Now the women are gathering
> in smoke-filled rooms,
> rough as politicians,
> scrappy as club fighters.
> And should anyone be surprised
>
> if sometimes, when the white moon rises,
> women want to lash out
> with a cutting edge? (18)

We enter the realm of the female sublime and witness the noumenal power of the once-inferiorized. Rising as the moon rises, these women transcend Elizabeth Fortune's limitations. Their rough edges invoke new daemonic power in several ways. First, the smoke-filled rooms – with their physical murkiness and aura of political intrigue – contribute to the turbulence, obscurity, and difficulty we have come to associate with the sublime. As Hume elaborates, 'Difficulty, instead of extinguishing [the mind's] vigor and alacrity, has the contrary effect, of sustaining and increasing it,' thus creating the muscular atmosphere necessary for 'transcendent' labour (436). Second, Oliver's rhetorical heightening of this new female power suggests that these young women have transcended the bittersweet arc of Elizabeth Fortune's fiery moon. Where Elizabeth Fortune lay down on 'grass ... warm as a bed' with a young man 'full of promises, and the face of the moon / a white fire,' these scrappy women refuse to lie down. They have internalized their environment's white fire and possess a surreal power, a new 'cutting edge.' Finally, the last verse is marked with sublimity because of its emphasis on conversion or transformation. When the Wordsworth of The Prelude comes upon the blind Beggar in London, he experiences a conversion that has become the textbook example of

Romantic alchemy: 'My mind did at this spectacle turn round / As
with the might of waters' (7.2.643–4). Wordsworth's conversion – the
cataclysmic *turn* of the poet's mind – precipitates order and meaning
and restores the self's power to modulate an experience that had
seemed overwhelming. Oliver notes a similar conversion, as women's
minds are suddenly turned round by the might of a revolutionary politics bred from the terror of their circumstances. We have moved from
Wordsworth's renegotiation of the mathematical sublime to women's
bold reinvention of a political sublime.

Having established that Oliver's poem re-engenders and reinvigo-
rates the once-powerful tropings of a male sublime, I want to suggest
that what is most striking about the end of her poem is the way in
which it refuses to depart from a male poetics after all. These women
inhabit paternal rooms, paternal modes of discourse and anger, paternal scenes of conflict and confrontation. By refusing the space of the
beautiful, they expand into men's spatial prerogatives and offer stal-
wart vengeance; but what solace can they bring to Elizabeth Fortune
and her kind? Is there room for women's reproductive labour in the
smoke-filled rooms of the Romantic sublime?

Despite their grotesque delineations in both high and popular culture, gestation and parturition seem particularly worthy candidates for
a sublime poetics. At minimum, as Sara Ruddick explains, birthing
'most likely provokes in nonbirthing women as well as men envy, awe,
and fear of the unknown' (192). At maximum, 'fear of the archaic
mother turns out to be essentially fear of her generative power. It is
this power, a dreaded one, that patrilineal filiation has the burden of
subduing. It is thus not surprising to see pollution rituals proliferating
in societies where patrilineal power is poorly secured' (Kristeva 77).
And yet before defining a maternal sublime, before looking at the ways
in which women experience the power and grandeur of their own
imaginative and biological initiatives, we must note two impediments.
First, until very recently women writers have refused to write about the
tribulations of generativity; second, the sublime mode has contributed
to this refusal: women writing in the sublime mode often sublimate
their own gender and look to male pathos as the site of power and
transcendence.

The gorgeous opening of H.D.'s 'Fragment 113' is a case in point:

> Not honey,
> not the plunder of the bee
> from meadow or sand-flower

or mountain bush;
from winter-flower or shoot
born of the later heat:
not honey, not the sweet
stain on the lips and teeth:
not honey, not the deep
plunge of soft belly
and the clinging of the gold-edged
pollen-dusted feet. (131)

H.D. begins by quoting Sappho – '*Neither honey nor bee for me*' – and goes on to create a poem eloquent in its denial of generativity.

What is most unusual about 'Fragment 113' is how often and how much the poet cries out for the sensuous world she is repudiating:

Not so –
though rapture blind my eyes,
and hunger crisp
dark and inert my mouth. (131)

The poem's speaker experiences hot desire for the abandoned female world:

ah flower of purple iris,
flower of white,
or of the iris, withering the grass –
for fleck of the sun's fire. (131)

But she deliberately turns away from this world: 'not iris – old desire – old passion – / old forgetfulness – old pain – / not this, nor any flower' (131).

Why does the poet protest so much? Why does 'Fragment 113' insist on discovering transcendent desires only within the flamboyance of high male militarism? We find an answer within the psychoanalytic economy of the traditional sublime. Thomas Weiskel theorizes that the motivating power of the sublime resides in the grown poet's need to deny the pre-Oedipal pleasures of the mother's body ('not honey, not the south ...,' says H.D. [131]). The maternal other is pleasurable and terrifying; projected onto the hazardous terrain of a sublime mind-scape, this mythy mother threatens the ego with blissful annihilation. But this inundation of feeling, this 'gratification of instinctual aims, in its quality of excess, alerts the ego to a danger.' The poet not only experiences the wish 'to be inundated or engulfed by pleasurable stimuli' that we find in H.D.'s poem ('ah flower of purple iris / flower of white'), but this wish is countered by tumultuous fears of being 'incorporated, overwhelmed, annihilated' ('not iris – ... not this, nor any flower') (Weiskel 104).

In 'Fragment 113' H.D.'s speaker both acts out this fantasy of pleasurable inundation mingled with fear, and plays with our anxiety about this fantasy. If the psychological structure of the sublime involves, first, the wish to be inundated by the maternal other and, second, a reaction formation against this very desire, then by over-gendering her speaker's loss of ego boundaries, H.D. makes this unconscious fear – and the strategy of sublime prosody – visible. She informs us that although the force of the sublime does not seem to inhere in the feminine – in the good world of generativity – the impetus for 'transcendence' into a so-called 'higher' mode is motivated primarily by the pressure, pleasure, and threat of the female body. Second, although the world of generation elicits the exalted refrain that concludes 'Fragment 113,' the poem's speaker enacts our culture's fantasy that 'to survive ... the ego must go on the offensive and cease to be passive' (Weiskel 105). H.D. elaborates this paradox: generativity is at once the source of the blockage and terror that motivate the leap to sublimity, and yet generativity is itself sublimated in the moment of transcendence:

> but if you turn again,
> seek strength of arm and throat,
> touch as the god;
> neglect the lyre-note;
> knowing that you shall feel,
> about the frame,
> no trembling of the string
> but heat, more passionate
> of bone and the white shell
> and fiery tempered steel. (131–2)

H.D. makes the reaction formation motivating the sublime visible. The oedipal configuration of her final verse, with its thrill of joining great men, its promise of identity with Apollonian power, is also a defensive reaction against what her poem presents as a more originary wish for contact with the fecund world of the female, the beautiful.

Here we discover one pay-off of the traditional male sublime. If the sublime experience is costly, if it involves discord and alienation, this expense of spirit also grants the masculine self a special power both to identify with and to separate from the excesses of the generative body. But the female who writes within this tradition – the female who leaves these oedipal borders intact (or who merely embroiders them) – may encounter a harsh double bind. For her, the alienation that is ordinarily overcome in the final moment of sublimation seems intractable: what is lost is the very strength and wishfulness of the female body itself. In H.D.'s case the metaphors associated with the female body threaten to keep multiplying, to offer an endless regeneration; this multiplication is stopped short by her Apollonian invocation.

In H.D.'s poetry we have not advanced very far from Edmund Burke's treatise 'On the Sublime and the Beautiful.' As W.J.T. Mitchell comments: 'Burke's most notorious derivation of political values from the mechanics of sensation is his linking of sublimity and beauty with the stereotypes of gender. Sublimity, with its foundations in pain, terror, vigorous exertion, and power, is the masculine aesthetic mode. Beauty, by contrast, is located in qualities such as littleness, smoothness, and delicacy that mechanically induce a sense of pleasure and affectionate superiority' (129).

Our culture is still haunted by these suppositions. In the words of A.R. Ammons: 'some people when they get up in the morning see / the kitchen sink, but I look out and see the windy rivers / of the Lord in the treetops' (57). The kitchen world of the labouring female and the Old Testament world of the prophetic male are kept apart. Notice, however, that even this poem shows its hand, that even Ammons is unable to hide the ways in which the sublimations motivating the sublime reinstate false hierarchies. Ammons needs the lowliness of that kitchen sink to give his windy rivers height. And once we recognize this, we can also recognize that this height is another binarism, another false opposition; as we watch, the deep structure of the sublime comes to light – that is, its dependence on sublimated forms of femininity or maternity.

These revelations may be instructive, but do they make a difference to woman as halted traveller? How do we heal – in real life and in rhetoric – the pattern of female repression or blockage that gives the sublime genre its force?

The stakes of this question are not merely literary. In 'The Nuclear Sublime' Frances Ferguson argues that the political hazards of the sublime are great since our nuclear arsenal is built upon its suasions. She argues that 'the pressure of the sublime claim of individuality is all the more urgent because the world of generation is largely what is being fled in an aesthetics of sublimity' (7). When nuclear pacifists call for the presence of 'as many infants and children as possible' at one of their rallies, Ferguson worries about this ineffectual mixing of modes. She asks, can there be any political effectiveness in 'appealing to the world of generation' in order to halt the march of nuclear armaments? For her the nuclear sublime and a visionary politics of maternity are antithetical; in the atomic world there can be no maternal sublime: 'The sublime claims that the beautiful is the world of society under the aegis of women and children, and that the habit, custom, and familiarity of that world of generation is what it was avoiding all along, in the nobler search for heroic encounter with the possibility of one's own death and a resulting consciousness of the importance of self-preservation' (7).

The terrifying vision of nuclear holocaust submits to the craziness inherent in the sublime's psychodynamic. If sublimity is the site of trembling before the *mysterium tremendum*, if it represents the cosmic dwarfing of the self's power and possibility, the sublime is also that mode of perception in which the self discovers its might – its capacity to overreach enormous limits, its destructive powers of pride and vaunting. The bomb comes to symbolize this quasi-numinous power. Whether A-bomb or H-bomb, it promises the capacity to use the subjective power of human invention to wipe out all subjectivity. Hence our collective fascination with nuclear disaster as the latest incarnation of the sublime, 'that alternative and counterpoise to the beautiful' (Ferguson 5).

Oddly, nuclear rhetoric borrows metaphors of generativity to flesh out the Superpowers' desires. The U.S. government referred to the atom bomb as 'Oppenheimer's baby' and the hydrogen bomb as 'Teller's baby,' while

'in early tests, before they were certain the bombs would work, the scientists expressed their concern by saying they hoped the baby was a boy, not a girl – i.e., not a dud.' Winston Churchill was informed of the scientists' success: 'Babies satisfactorily born.' In what may be the ultimate perversion, the bomb dropped on Hiroshima was known as Little Boy, celebrating at once a new age of destruction and an ancient and lethal link between the boy child and murder. In this language of war, birthing laborers are male, the 'child' a damaging, injuring weapon, the birth a grand destruction rather than individual creation. Even in birth, war's body is in the service of death. (Ruddick 205)

Again we see a barely disguised sublimation of female power in quest of a destructive male egotism. Perhaps it is not a matter of reinventing the sublime at all. Perhaps women should discard its formulae altogether.

Before trashing the sublime with the thoroughness it may well deserve, I want to challenge a too-easy feminist acquiescence to the opposition between sublimity and generativity by looking at another poem by Mary Oliver, 'The Fish' (see pages 108–9). This poem revels in the power of birth-giving in a mood wonderfully different from 'Strawberry Moon':

> she arcs
> in the long gown of her body, she leaps
> into the walls of water,
> she falls through like the torn
> silvery half-drowned body
> of any woman come to term, caught
> as mortality drives triumphantly toward
> immortality, the shaken bones like
> cages of fire. (14–15)

If the sublime is a dangerous genre in which 'a burden (of the past ...) is lifted and there is an influx of power' (Weiskel 11), if the sublime promotes a quasi-numinous strength, then Mary Oliver's 'The Fish' fulfils these conditions. Oliver depicts birth as an influx of biological power; she dramatizes the special blockage, the burden to be lifted, the weight of young to be alienated, as the fish's journey replicates the early stages of human parturition:

> She
> moves upstream, the flow
> pressing against her;
> she feels it, lets the hot
> blade of her body pause,
> drifts backward, whips awake. (14)

After a meditation on the green world of achieved generativity – a world where the salmon 'will nest her eggs and the fierce prince quicken them' (14) – Oliver's poem dramatizes the female's increase of terror and power in reproductive labour.

Although Oliver insists upon the sublime strain of generativity, 'The

Fish' begins in the traditionally feminine seascape of the beautiful. The poem is about a salmon who moves from ocean to river-world; it describes a journey from a harmonious place where subject and object are perfectly fitted to one another – where 'moonlight / blazes the black rocks' while 'the surface razzle-dazzle' of sweet river water is 'threading out of the tide' – to the white-water world of the sublime, where the salmon's body threatens to break against

> ... waterfalls – gleaming
> stairways of stone,
> water ripped and boiling
> like white logs ... (14)

The fish risks this tumult because, like 'any woman come to term,' she is burdened and blessed by natality: 'deep in her belly / life that is to be / stirs like a million planets' (14). Moving inside the female animal, we leave the sibilant world of ocean pleasures to feel a nuclear pressure. In collapsing the vastness of outer space into the fish's tiny innards, Oliver invokes the frightening power of female generativity. Beyond the white water, life is briefly bountiful, but, to reach 'the shadows / of last year's swimmers' (14), the salmon must endure the terrifying force of her body's battering.

This is an odd instance of the sublime. Oliver's poem elicits the powerful experience of human reproductive labour by analogy with animal reproductive labour – revealing childbirth as the painful site of the danger and horror that motivate the sublime, as well as the transport that uplifts us.

And yet in Oliver's poem the path to successful generation can only happen through the birthing female's encounter with the grand otherness and terror of her own body – an otherness defined through the energetic traditions of the rhetorical sublime. For when Oliver describes parturition as that moment when 'mortality drives triumphantly toward / immortality,' while 'the shaken bones' become 'cages of fire,' the grace of the ordinary body becomes extraordinary, and we find ourselves in a region between finitude and infinitude. The minds of both the reader (hurried along by the poet) and the birthing mother (hurried along by her body) are (in the words of Edmund Burke) 'so entirely filled with [their] object, that [they] cannot entertain any other ... hence arises the great power of the sublime ... it anticipates our reasonings and hurries us on by an irresistible force' (quoted in Arac 213–14).

In routing this birth through the rapids of the dynamical sublime, Oliver attempts to redefine the power of the pregnant female body. She charts a course described by Sara Ruddick in *Maternal Thinking*. Ruddick suggests that 'to tell a maternal history, it is necessary to look again, with trusting eyes, at sexuality and birth.' This trust should call forth 'a revisionist history of the body, both realistic and celebratory' (206).

The argument of my essay is that the sublime, as literary mode or genre, can be useful in this revisionist history. The sublime has been valued by such writers as Longinus for bestowing upon its writers the 'eminence' and 'lasting place in the Temple of Fame' so important in male canon-formation precisely because the sublime is a genre preeminent in its capacity for myth-making and persuasion. As Longinus explains: 'A lofty passage does not convince the reason of the reader, but takes him out of himself. That which is admirable ... confounds our judgment, and eclipses that which is merely reasonable or agreeable. To believe or not is usually in our own power; but the Sublime, acting with an imperious and irresistible force, sways every reader whether he will or no' (136). Here we encounter another feminist dilemma. Longinus's contentment with high oratory as a form of domination may upset a readership bent on erasing hierarchical thinking from a feminist history. The sublime's razzle-dazzle can have frightening political consequences, since the exaltation of one discourse often results in the abjection of another. Nevertheless, the sublime suggests a potentially progressive politics as well. Sublime discourse always reflects a power struggle – an experience of turmoil between two or more modes of discourse. Within this turmoil we can discover the possibility of appropriate aggression, and within this aggression, the possibility of transforming the burden of the past.

If the sublime creates a power struggle within the reader, it creates a power struggle within the poet as well. 'The poet is uniquely vulnerable to the hypsos of past masters,' as Weiskel says, 'but his counteroffensive of identification or mimesis can make the power of hypsos his own' (5). Feminist theory has shown us exactly how terrifying and persistent this writing of the past has been for women. Female writers, especially, are in need of the 'counteroffensive' that the sublime tradition teaches: the aggressive and imperious capacity to revise the past.

I do not mean to argue that this revision will be easy; the task of rewriting the grotesque body of reproductive labour is formidable indeed. To show how burdensome this writing of the past can be, I want to give a quick example of the ways in which women's reproductive labour has been co-opted for the project of male transcendence.

Norman Mailer's *The Armies of the Night* provides us with a delight-fully Maileresque coverage of resistance to the Vietnam war; it focuses on the March on the Pentagon in 1967. While the book is filled with the chaos and tragedy of failed resistances, Mailer refuses to relinquish the egotistical sublime; he is unwilling to end with utter scepticism. Instead he concludes in a heroic, semi-epic peroration that features America as a birthing female:

> Brood on that country who expresses our will. She is America, once a beauty of magnificence unparalleled, now a beauty with a leprous skin. She is heavy with child – no one knows if legitimate – and languishes in a dungeon whose walls are never seen. Now the first contractions of her fearsome labor begin – it will go on: no doctor exists to tell the hour. (320)

This is the worse-case scenario for a maternal sublime. In a concluding paragraph full of melodramatic clichés in which women are defined as leprous and terrifying, reproductive labour as a potential whoring after false gods, and parturition as a heinous act made even more appalling by the rending of the fetus from woman's monstrous inte-rior, Mailer misrepresents the power of generativity:

> It is only known that false labor is not likely on her now, no, she will prob-ably give birth, and to what? – the most fearsome totalitarianism the world has ever known? or can she, poor giant, tormented lovely girl, deliver a babe of a new world brave and tender, artful and wild? Rush to the locks. God writhes in his bonds. Rush to the locks. Deliver us from our curse. For we must end on the road to that mystery where courage, death, and the dream of love give promise of sleep. (320)

Mailer ends his book with the joy and vaunting typical of the rhetor-ical sublime. Once again his 'transcendence' is achieved through a classical attempt to naturalize male power by associating the female with nature and the male with culture. He invokes the extraordinary power of women's reproductive labour to elicit a brave new world where God is still housed in the erectile male while the dying infant drowns in the prostrate woman: a world where, despite all progressive reforms, reproductive women still represent a mute and gratifying occasion for male creativity.

That is, in *Armies of the Night*, the mutant force of woman's labour provides another opportunity for the sublime turn. Mailer calls out for his heroes to 'rush to the locks,' to surmount the terror of the unruly body politic that his labouring woman represents. The labour of this 'poor giant,' this 'tormented lovely girl,' is appropriated without a glimmer of guilt, for in traditional sublime tropology the male soul aims to gather the world unto itself 'as though we had created what we merely heard.'

The pressure of these passages on the women who read them is immense, but this pressure may also call forth an angry desire to write back, to meet the male offensive with a female counter-offensive of de-sublimation: of recognizing the 'grotesque' body of the birthing female as one of the primary building blocks of the male sublime. Although Mailer's use of the metaphor of the birthing body at the end of *Armies of the Night* is a creative ploy that grabs his readers' attention and gains their shocked admiration, although his birthing woman represents a force that is unstoppable and awesome, even as she yields in the final paragraph to the exhortations of male power – insofar as the sublime is the genre of the counter-offensive, of unleashing a new kind of rhetorical violence against an old rhetoric, women can seize upon this power as well. The difference is this: if Mailer's Romantic sublime offers 'sophisticated defenses ... against the fact of origins,' the maternal sublime can reveal this defensiveness and represent another, more bodily origin in which grotesque and sublime cease to be oppositional – as the woman writer speaks in 'a language of blood' to re-articulate and praise our bodily beginnings.

My textbook examples for exploring this maternal sublime will be two contemporary poems: Sharon Olds's 'The Language of the Brag,' and Susan Rubin Suleiman's 'To a Poet.' Both poems take surprising turns. Instead of inventing an entirely new language to redefine female reproductive power, they borrow freely from the heroic ideals of the male tradition. This imitation of past masters is, of course, a staple of the sublime. As Weiskel reminds us, 'in Longinus's text, hypsos is a quality immanent in great writing which refers us to eternity ... it is the resource and the goal of great-souled men, especially in times of cultural degeneracy. Hypsos may be attained through the mimesis and emulation of the masters' (12). Let us examine how this imitation of past masters works for a maternal sublime.

Sharon Olds's 'Language of the Brag' begins where *Armies of the Night* ended, with the romance of the jockstrap:

> I have wanted excellence in the knife-throw
> I have wanted to use my exceptionally strong and accurate arms

and my straight posture and quick electric muscles
to achieve something at the center of a crowd
the blade piercing the bark deep,
the haft slowly and heavily vibrating like the cock.
I have wanted some epic use for my excellent body,
some heroism, some American achievement
beyond the ordinary for my extraordinary self. (8)

Happily, in this landscape of male brinkmanship and female lack,
Olds's speaker is able to celebrate her own exceptional powers. She
may be blocked in her desire to participate, but she clamours boldly
about her body; in the tradition of Walt Whitman and Allen Ginsberg,
she sings the body electric.

At the same time Olds gives us that moment of blockage so crucial
to the sublime: 'I have wanted courage, I have thought about fire /
and the crossing of waterfalls, I have dragged around' (8). Once all the
appurtenances of the male sublime – from vibrating cocks, to fire and
waterfalls – have been set forth, Olds changes key. Her focus veers
towards the literal blockage and swelling of the female body in the
months of gestation:

> I have dragged around
> my belly big with cowardice and safety,
> my stool black with iron pills,
> my huge breasts oozing mucus,
> my legs swelling, my hands swelling,
> my face swelling and darkening, my hair
> falling out, my inner sex
> stabbed again and again with terrible pain like a knife. (8)

We find ourselves at the very heart of Edmund Burke's sublime, with
its emphasis on terror, obscurity, power, privation, vastness, difficulty,
darkness, suddenness, intermitting rhythms, and the terrible voices of
animals in pain (Burke 51–76). For Olds's speaker these tumultuous
sensations culminate in the crisis of childbirth:

> I have lain down and sweated and shaken
> and passed blood and feces and water and
> slowly alone in the center of a circle I have
> passed the new person out
> and they have lifted the new person free of the act

and wiped the new person free of that
language of blood like praise all over the body. (8)

Here the mathematical sublime of reproductive labour, where contractions go on, where nothing seems to end, where everything seems only connected by 'and' and 'and,' culminates in a new kind of language. As the poet 'passes the new person out,' the child is covered with her blood. Swimming in amnion, this child will raise its voice amidst the verbiage of 'blood like praise all over the body.'

Blood is, of course, the female fluid *par excellence*. For women, as Susan Rubin Suleiman reminds us,

> Blood
> trickles, oozes, spurts each month
> between my legs. No thorn-prick breaks
> my skin. I don't fall, but bleed. (683)

Despite the intemperate beauty of bloodiness in Suleiman's and Olds's poems, Western culture has insisted that horror and 'abomination' be associated with 'the fertilizable or fertile feminine body' of menses and childbirth (Kristeva 101, 100). The fact of our birth elicits unspeakable fantasies about our own and others bodies: 'Evocation of the maternal body and childbirth induces the image of birth as a violent act of expulsion through which the nascent body tears itself away from the matter of maternal insides' (Kristeva 101). Our skin 'apparently never ceases to bear the traces of such matter' (101).

Even as these traces terrify, Olds and Suleiman make them a badge of female power and worth. In giving these traces a language, Olds asks us to experiment with naming and praising the moment of separation of mother from child; she insists that the mother's 'act' can enter into the symbolic order in the form of a different, more bodily language.

The kicker of Olds's poem, its final surprise, comes in the final verse when the poet recognizes that a language of praise for the female body has been rudely sublimated in men's writing. She discovers that what is sublimated has not been lost after all; this language has been there all the time, in a form that women can absolutely claim:

> I have done what you wanted to do, Walt Whitman,
> Allen Ginsberg, I have done this thing.
> I and the other women this exceptional
> act with the exceptional heroic body,

this giving birth, this glistening verb,
and I am putting my proud American Boast
right here with the others. (9)

And so, the birthing woman, the reproductive heroine, the American
broad with her barbaric yawp, recovers the scene of sublimity.

This recovery is repeated in Susan Rubin Suleiman's 'To a Poet.'
Suleiman's male adversary is Percy Bysshe Shelley:

> You fell upon the thorns of life
> and bled.
> That was a way to put it
> I suppose – a shade histrionical
> Would you not agree, o poet
> sublime? (683)

Just as male poets have sublimated or appropriated the female body
for their own warblings, Suleiman appropriates Shelley's poetics to
dramatize her own femininity – a femininity that does not find its triumphs in the wild west wind but in the earthy travails of childbirth:

> Twice in my life a baby's head
> and neck and arms, a slimy child
> has broken out provoking cries
> of triumph, bloody exultation.
> Prize of my labor, desired, won
> resting on my belly after the long haul. (683)

The poem ends with the assertion that the lowly kitchen world can
help us re-evaluate the high prophetic world of the 'poet sublime.'
Suleiman's exaltation takes a homely turn; her nurturing words and
'sharp commands' to her children also 'serve as witness, poor /
unmanly, unadorned, unread, / that we were here and loved and bled'
(683).

What we must notice about the conclusion of both poems is the way
in which Olds and Suleiman use a sublime apparatus to overgo the
egotistical sublime, without replicating its repressions. Instead of the
solitary voice of the 'poet sublime,' we hear the voice of solidarity: 'I
have done this thing. / I and the other women.' This is a remarkable
moment in a sublime poetics. To date, 'the sublime ... requires a belief
that the most important transformative experiences are individual and

not communal, and that it is the exceptional individual who sets up models of excellence for society to follow' (Modiano 243). But for Olds, this 'exceptional heroic body' is everywoman's, just as, for Suleiman, bleeding may be sublime, but it is also communal.

The burden of this paper has been to show the ways in which women writers have begun to reinvent a male tradition by exposing the sublime fictions of this tradition as political fictions meant to aggrandize the male ego. At the same time, this tradition is not so much rejected by the women writers we have examined here as it is introjected, its energies used and transformed in the process. The poets of the maternal sublime have started to reinvent the politics of maternity, to open the oedipal moment of aggression and counter-aggression to the birthing body.

This invocation of a maternal sublime is not meant to mandate euphoria at birth, nor to provide a political program or manifesto for the birthing woman. Women's experiences in childbirth are multiple and various; they run the gamut from agony to ecstasy, from tragedy to comic pleasure.

This is to acknowledge that birth is hard, sometimes bitter labour. Without the easy availability of abortion, it becomes forced labour, with pain perhaps increasing after birth. This is also to acknowledge the often malign transformations – the medicalization – of contemporary birthing practices. While modern reproductive technologies may be helpful, they can also be nefarious. Their intrusions into the integral space of the pregnant body may lead to irreversible psychological damage. As Richard and Dorothy Wertz comment in *Lying-in: A History of Childbirth in America*:

> Researchers have found that high-tech birth often leads to loss of self-esteem because it makes women feel that they have lost control over the most fundamental aspects of self. For many women, birth is a low point, a psychological letdown. Having given up their jobs, at least temporarily, they enter their new roles as mothers completely exhausted, feeling incompetent because the birth was managed or manipulated by others. Interventions in birth can lead to depression and difficulty in adjusting to motherhood. (256)

The project of this paper is not meant to erase this hardship, but to participate in repoliticizing the burdens of reproductive labour. The maternal sublime demands of us three difficult things. First, it asks us to confront the hard fact of our own female origins, to contemplate what it means to come into the world from female bodies that crack and bleed, that speak the old and euphoric language of blood.

Second, the maternal sublime helps us see the extent to which male writers use reproductive labour as a vehicle for their own 'high' ideas. This female labour provides a metaphor of incredible power for heightening male discourse; it yields a scene of blockage that culminates in the male writer's appropriation of the birthing woman's terrifying, gratifying access to life and death. The second project of a maternal sublime, then, is to rescue maternity from its status as vehicle, as metaphor, as a drunken boat for Romantic sailors. This means – and this is my third point – that we must identify a new sublime structure in the making – a structure that invites new collectivities and recognizes reproductive labour as a major source of personal and cultural power for women.

As to whether or not we can celebrate a maternal sublime without moving towards old forms of natalism – this is an open question. It is my conviction that celebrating women's powers of giving birth does not mean that women will once more be defined by their reproductivity, nor will those women who are left out of or are uninterested in the reproductive circuit have to constitute anew an excluded, non-productive minority. The politics of exclusion are much more complex. In Sharon Olds's '35/10,' for example, we see a mother contemplating her daughter's 'full purse of eggs' as her own 'last chances to bear a child / are falling through my body' (75). The pressure of the grotesque – of the open, wounded, fecund, dying body – is always with us. I see the maternal sublime as a genre that, rather than repressing this body, moves us towards an acceptance of this body and its untoward pleasures and pressures. As long as someone else's birth reminds us of our death, reproductive labour will be a candidate for a sublime poetics. It is essential that women continue to construct this poetics, remembering, as they do, the cost of such sublimity.

STRAWBERRY MOON
Mary Oliver

1

My great-aunt Elizabeth Fortune
stood under the honey locust trees,
the white moon over her and a young man near.

The blossoms fell down like white feathers,
the grass was warm as a bed, and the young man
full of promises, and the face of the moon
a white fire.

Later,
when the young man went away and came back with a bride,
Elizabeth
climbed into the attic.

2

Three women came in the night
to wash the blood away,
and burn the sheets,
and take away the child.

Was it a boy or girl?
No one remembers.

3

Elizabeth Fortune was not seen again
for forty years.

Meals were sent up,
laundry exchanged.

It was considered a solution
more proper than shame
showing itself to the village.

4

Finally, name by name, the downstairs died
or moved away,
and she had to come down,
so she did.
At sixty-one, she took in boarders,
washed their dishes,
made their beds,
spoke whatever had to be spoken,
and no more.

                          5
I asked my mother:
what happened to the man? She answered:
Nothing.
They had three children.
He worked in the boatyard.

I asked my mother: did they ever meet again?
No, she said,
though sometimes he would come
to the house to visit.
Elizabeth, of course, stayed upstairs.

                          6
Now the women are gathering
in smoke-filled rooms,
rough as politicians,
scrappy as club fighters.
And should anyone be surprised

if sometimes, when the white moon rises,
women want to lash out
with a cutting edge?

                    THE FISH
                    Mary Oliver

        She climbs from the sea; moonlight
          blazes the black rocks,
            the surface razzle-dazzle
            of sweet water
        threading out of the tide. She
          moves upstream, the flow
            pressing against her;
            she feels it, lets the hot
        blade of her body pause,
            drifts backward, whips awake. She
          moves upstream; she is heavy;
            deep in her belly

life that is to be
    stirs like a million planets; she
        moves upstream; when the waters
            divide she follows
the fragrance spilling
    from her old birth pond; she
        sees the waterfalls – gleaming
            stairways of stone,
water ripped and boiling
    like white logs – and knows beyond
        lies the green pond
            rich with the shadows
of last year's swimmers where she
    will nest her eggs and the fierce prince
        quicken them; she flies
            upstream – she arcs
in the long gown of her body, she leaps
    into the walls of water,
        she falls through like the torn
            silvery half-drowned body
of any woman come to term, caught
    as mortality drives triumphantly toward
        immortality, the shaken bones like
            cages of fire.

Works Cited

Ammons, A.R. *Sphere: The Form of a Motion.* New York: Norton 1974

Arac, Jonathan. 'The Media of Sublimity: Johnson and Lamb on *King Lear.*'
    Studies in Romanticism 26 (1987), 209–20

Bartky, Sandra Lee. 'Foucault, Femininity, and the Modernization of Patriar-
    chal Power.' In *Feminism and Foucault.* Ed. Irene Diamond and Lee Quinby.
    Boston: Northeastern UP 1988, 61–86

Burke, Edmund. *On the Sublime and Beautiful.* Ed. Charles W. Eliot. New York:
    Collier 1909

Cohn, Carol. 'Sex and Death in the Rational World of Defense Intellectuals.'
    Signs 12 (1987), 687–718

Ferguson, Frances. 'The Nuclear Sublime.' *Diacritics* 4, no. 2 (1984), 4–10

Fry, Paul H. 'The Possession of the Sublime.' *Studies in Romanticism* 26 (1987),
    187–207

110 Patricia Yaeger

Gravida

H.D. *Collected Poems 1912–1944*. Ed. Louis L. Martz. New York: New Directions 1983

Hume, David. *A Treatise of Human Nature*. Ed. L.A. Selby-Bigge. Oxford: Clarendon 1888

Kant, Emmanuel. *Kant's Critique of Aesthetic Judgement*. Trans. James Creed Meredith. Oxford: Clarendon 1911

Kristeva, Julia. *Powers of Horror: An Essay on Abjection*. New York: Columbia UP 1982

Kurrik, Maire Jaanus. *Literature and Negation*. New York: Columbia UP 1979

Longinus. *On the Sublime/Aristotle's Poetics*. New York: Dutton 1963

Mailer, Norman. *The Armies of the Night: History as a Novel, the Novel as History*. New York: Signet 1968

Mitchell, W.J.T. *Iconology: Image, Text, Ideology*. Chicago: U of Chicago P 1986

Modiano, Raimonda. 'Humanism and the Comic Sublime: From Kant to Friedrich Theodor Vischer.' *Studies in Romanticism* 26 (1987), 231–44

Olds, Sharon. 'The Language of the Brag.' In *Florilegia: A Retrospective of CALYX, a Journal of Art and Literature by Women, 1976–86*. Ed. Debi Berrow et al. Corvallis, OR: CALYX Books 1987, 8–9

– '35/10.' In her *The Dead and the Living*. New York: Knopf 1989

Oliver, Mary. *Twelve Moons*. Boston: Little, Brown 1979

Ruddick, Sara. *Maternal Thinking: Toward a Politics of Peace*. Boston: Beacon 1989

Suleiman, Susan Rubin. 'To a Poet.' *Michigan Quarterly Review* 29, no. 4 (1990), 683–4

Weiskel, Thomas. *The Romantic Sublime: Studies in the Structure and Psychology of Transcendence*. Baltimore: Johns Hopkins UP 1976

Wertz, Richard, and Dorothy C. Wertz. *Lying-in: A History of Childbirth in America*. New Haven: Yale UP 1989

Wordsworth, William. *The Prelude/Selected Poems and Prefaces*. Ed. Jack Stillinger. Boston: Houghton 1965

Women and Madness in a Nineteenth-Century Parisian Asylum

PATRICIA PRESTWICH

Two of the most striking images of female mental disorder in the nineteenth century come from the history of French medicine. These are the paintings that portray Philippe Pinel unchaining the lunatics of the Salpêtrière, the Parisian hospital for women, and Jean-Martin Charcot lecturing on hysteria to medical students, again at the Salpêtrière. In both paintings madness is symbolized by a young, passive woman. The central lunatic figure in the Pinel painting (fig. 1) is a beautiful young woman with an alluring *décolletage*, downcast eyes, and a limp posture. She is being observed fixedly by that pioneering psychiatric figure, Philippe Pinel, the symbol of scientific rationality and an all-controlling medical profession. In the second painting (fig. 2) the patient, again young, attractive, and with an equally revealing neckline, is even more passive, draped as she is in an apparent fainting spell on the supporting arm of the neurologist Charcot. Charcot's gaze is directed at a circle of exclusively male medical students, who, in turn, are concentrating their scientific and, one would hope, healing gaze on the young woman.

These paintings have attracted extensive analysis, both from historians and from feminist scholars. For historians, who have been strongly influenced by the anti-psychiatric movement of the past thirty years and particularly by the writings of Michel Foucault, these paintings represent the expanding influence of a nineteenth-century medical profession whose scientific knowledge gave it both social and political power.[1] This power was institutionalized, both symbolically and con-

Fig. 1. *Pinel Freeing the Insane*

Fig. 2. *Charcot Lecturing on Hysteria at the Salpêtrière*

cretely, in the asylum – not the stereotypical 'Bedlam,' but the new model asylum that offered both the control of mental illness and the hope of a cure. As a recent historical study has concluded, 'the asylum took on for a time a status as panacea equivalent to the steam engine, the rights of man, or the spread of universal knowledge. Madness could after all be cured, reason could be restored. The asylum was the magic machine in which this could be achieved ... [and the] doctor was the new exorcist for a scientific society' (Bynum 3).

Feminist scholars in various disciplines have also been attracted by the symbolism of these paintings and have linked the imagery to the wider gender prejudices of nineteenth-century Western society.[2] In their analyses the 'otherness' of women or the differences of women's lives became transformed, under the influence of a male, scientific, medical profession, into a pathological disorder – madness – that resulted in the control, confinement, and silencing of women. Madness, as Elaine Showalter has argued, became a 'female malady' in the nineteenth century, the symbol not just of nonconformity or rebellion, but of an 'essential feminine nature' – frail, emotional, melancholic, or neurotic – that was observed and controlled by 'scientific male rationality' (3).

These two paintings, replete as they are with evocative images for both historians and for feminists (or even for feminist historians) cannot, of course, be taken as complete or even realistic portrayals of the treatment of mental illness in the period. For example, the paintings are clearly propaganda on behalf of a late-nineteenth-century French medical profession that was far from secure in its powers. The paintings give no hint of the frequently harsh public criticism of doctors or of the heated debates within the profession itself. Nor do they suggest the real problems faced by doctors in the day-to-day administration of asylums that all too often did not live up to the expectations or the promises of the medical profession. Even more important, the paintings do not convey the ordinary experiences of patients who, if physically confined to the asylum, were neither under the constant clinical gaze of the doctor nor isolated from friends and family. In fact, there is no hint of the important role of the family in the internment, treatment, and release of patients.

Most recently, a number of historians in Europe and North America have turned to the painstakingly detailed study of specific asylums in order to understand the complexities of mental illness in the nineteenth century.[3] Their findings have already dispelled certain stereotypes, such as the idea that asylums were merely depositories for the rejects of society who, once behind the high asylum walls, never re-emerged. As several studies show, internments were relatively short (Bynum 4).[4] The study of a specific asylum, and particularly an asylum that treated both women and men, can, when infused with gender analysis, also help to transform women from alluring symbols of madness into ordinary, complex human beings. In the case of the particular institution that I have been studying, the Parisian psychiatric hospital Saint-Anne, asylum records can give some indication of how the working-class women of Paris attempted to cope not only with mental illness but with the daily problems of work, family, and poverty. It is perhaps ironic, but also cheering, that the asylum, which was designed to isolate women, can help historians to place women within the context of their society and their daily lives.

Saint-Anne, which still functions as a psychiatric hospital, was opened in 1867 as the first of the new model asylums built to cope with the alarming increase in mental patients in the department of the Seine. Every person legally interned in the Paris region was brought to the Admission Office at Saint-Anne, which was directed by Valentin Magnan, one of the most influential figures in late-nineteenth-century French psychiatry. At this office patients were observed, certified, and then either interned at Saint-Anne or transported to one of the suburban asylums. Because of this complex triage system no one asylum in the Paris region can be considered typical, but Saint-Anne has a particular importance. As the only asylum within Paris itself it was easily accessible to families. It also housed the teaching clinic of the Faculty of Medicine, making it one of the most important centres for the teaching of psychiatric medicine in France. Saint-Anne has also had a history of innovative treatment for the mentally ill. Magnan was one of the first psychiatrists in France to abandon the use of the strait-jacket, arguing that it only aggravated the patient's physical and mental distress. The asylum had an out-patient clinic where people could come for advice or treatment without being interned. After the First World War Saint-Anne opened the first treatment centre in France that did not require the legal internment of patients. While it is impossible to generalize about mental illness in Paris solely from the experience of patients at Saint-Anne, this asylum does provide examples of the best treatment that nineteenth-century medicine could offer.

The first question to ask about women and madness in nineteenth-century Paris is this: was madness a predominantly female malady? The answer is less straightforward than one might expect. Certainly in France, as in England, there were widespread popular and medical assumptions that women were more vulnerable than men to mental illness (Ripa 9–11). These assumptions were reinforced by the theory of degeneration that dominated French psychiatric medicine in the latter half of the nineteenth century. The theory of degeneration, first advanced in France by Dr Bénédict Morel in 1857 and later popularized by Valentin Magnan, postulated a biological explanation for mental illness. It argued that insanity was the result of a predisposition, either inherited or acquired, and that this predisposition could be recognized by physical and moral signs. As feminists well know, theories that are based on biological characteristics are rarely kind to women, and degeneration theory is no exception. It was not difficult to use the apparent physical frailty of women in order to reinforce old prejudices about women's emotional and mental frailty. In degeneration theory women's predisposition to madness became hereditary. Such assumptions abounded in medical literature on degeneration and were so accepted that they appeared even in routine administrative documents. For example, in his annual report Dr Magnan casually referred to the fact that women were more nervous than men ('Rapport' [1904], 51), and Edouard Toulouse, another prominent psychiatrist, stated categorically that 'women are more predisposed to madness than men' ('Rapport' [1896], 68; my translation).[5]

Nevertheless, the pattern of admissions to asylums suggests a slightly different picture. Prior to 1860 more women than men were admitted to the psychiatric hospitals of the Paris region. After 1860 male admissions began to predominate, and by the 1880s they were markedly higher than female admissions.[6] Women, however, remained in psychiatric hospitals longer than men. By the 1890s doctors were complaining that the overcrowding of departmental asylums was the result of the large number of women patients, and in 1895 when a fifth asylum, Maison Blanche, was constructed in the Paris region, it was destined exclusively for women.

This pattern of more male admissions to asylums but longer female internment is not, on the surface at least, the result of prejudices about women's mental instability; rather, it reflects differing patterns of diagnosis. The largest categories of male admissions were for alcoholism and for general paralysis, a fatal mental disorder caused by syphilis. According to admission statistics women were not afflicted in large numbers with either alcoholism or general paralysis. The most frequent diagnosis for women was depression, a disorder that struck women in far greater numbers than men.[7] Men's mental troubles led to a fairly rapid release from the asylum. Alcoholics usually left after several months of drying out; men with general paralysis usually died soon after admission, and, in fact, the male mortality rates in the asylum were higher than female rates.[8] Depression, as many psychiatrists noted at the time, was rarely fatal, but it often required lengthy treatment.

If the statistical evidence of internments does not entirely support the idea that madness was a predominantly female affliction, neither do the medical theories of the period. In the years after 1870 French theorists of degeneration tended to be preoccupied, not with female madness, but with alcoholism, which they feared was causing the destruction of a French race increasingly threatened by German economic and military might. In the annual reports that Valentin Magnan submitted on the more than 3,500 patients whom he observed each year in the Admissions Office, he regularly emphasized the growing number of 'degenerate' patients and concluded succinctly that 'the majority are the sons of alcoholics' ('Rapport' [1907], 132; my translation). A number of French psychiatrists, Magnan included, were so alarmed by the increased evidence of alcoholism that they founded temperance societies and campaigned for anti-alcoholic legislation (Prestwich 59–74). Their concern undoubtedly stemmed, in part, from the fact that alcoholism was largely a male problem and appeared to strike what they considered to be the most economically vital segment of the French population, working-class men. This perceived threat of alcoholism may, in fact, have distracted medical and public attention from the large number of female mental patients suffering from depression and other disorders.

Moreover, despite some medical assumptions about women's vulnerability to madness, French degeneration theory was not totally hostile to women, in part because these concepts were not based exclusively on biological determinants. Morel himself had spoken of both inherited and acquired predispositions to mental illness and had urged doctors to be aware of extenuating social conditions (Genil-Perrin 56). In 1896 Edouard Toulouse argued, in an influential book, that the real causes of madness lay in social conditions. By the 1890s the annual reports of the asylums of the Seine contained a form in which the causes of mental illness were listed in two sections. The first, and shorter, section listed the 'predisposing' or hereditary causes, such as a parent who suffered from mental illness. The second, and longer, section of 'determining' causes included epilepsy, excessive work, excessive religious feelings, worries resulting from the loss of money, remorse, joy, wounded modesty, jealousy, pride, and political events.

The sensitivity to the actual conditions of patients' lives implicit in theories of degeneration was reinforced by the everyday experience of doctors in the asylums. In the three formal diagnoses required by French law doctors did note any hereditary influence they could discover, such as a 'nervous' mother or an uncle who had died in an asylum. But they also noted – and often more extensively – the social and economic factors that might have led to internment. Moreover, the experience of treating large numbers of women led a few psychiatrists to challenge the common assumptions about women's predisposition to madness. In his annual reports the director of the women's section at Saint-Anne, Dr Bouchereau, regularly emphasized the effect of poverty on women's mental health. Referring to the 'despondency' that afflicted women more strongly than men, he refused to conclude that it was natural and even suggested that it might be accidental ('Rapport' [1896], 200; my translation).

If madness was not necessarily a female malady, either in theory or in practice, were all these women who crowded the asylums necessarily mad? For one significant section of the female asylum population the answer is clearly no; these women were not mad: they were old. In Saint-Anne the percentage of elderly women was significantly higher than that of elderly men: 14.5 per cent of the women interned were over sixty, whereas for men the figure was only 6.6 per cent.[9] This high percentage of aged women reflects both a demographic and an economic reality. Women in nineteenth-century Paris, as today, earned considerably less than men and were therefore more economically vulnerable and more likely to come under public care. Demographically women made up a larger percentage of the aged in France because of a peculiarity of French demography, namely a wider gap in life expectancy between men and women than in other Western nations. For example, in 1865 the male rate of surmortality (the excess number of male deaths over female deaths in the same age group) was over twenty; by 1913 it has risen to over forty-four, largely, it is argued, as a result of male alcoholism (Prestwich 34).

French psychiatrists, who constantly denounced the fact that many in the asylums were not 'truly mad,' readily recognized that most of their elderly patients should not have been there. Magnan regularly wrote on the medical files of such cases 'better in a nursing home' (my translation). Another doctor was blunter: 'To establish a medical file for an old lady whose only madness is to be 92 and who in all other respects is healthy is,' he wrote, 'a gross abuse' ('Rapport' [1912], 177; my translation).

Doctors accused families of evading their responsibilities by depositing elderly relatives in the asylum, and certainly family neglect is one explanation for the large number of elderly women interned at Saint-Anne. But it is not a complete explanation. In a number of cases these women were in the asylum because they had no family to care for them. Asylum records reveal a high incidence of elderly single women and widows, a number of whom are listed as property-owners.[10] Evidently they had some resources, but not the family to care for them. But for most of the elderly internment was the result of a family decision, and the families involved were often working-class families in which both spouses worked outside the home.

The medical records suggest that such internments took place when family resources were stretched to the breaking point, often because of the erratic behaviour of the elderly relative. The most frequently cited reason for internment was actions by patients that endangered either the patient or the family. These included suicide attempts, setting fire to the house, or simply wandering away. Families maintained they could not watch the patient constantly and turned to the asylum. Of course, such family statements can never be taken at face value. French law required that the patient be a danger to herself or to the public in order to be interned, so that it was in the interest of the family to stress such uncontrollable behaviour. But whether violent behaviour was a necessary precondition to internment is questionable; many certificates stated simply that the patient needed constant care or surveillance and that this was not within the means of the family.

Such elderly patients were not necessarily abandoned by the family. They were visited, money was sent to pay for special treats, and, in certain cases, when the economic situation of the family improved, elderly patients were released to the family's care, either permanently or temporarily. In one case a niece requested the visit of an aunt who had been interned in Saint-Anne for thirty-five years (Female Division, patient no. 97606).[11] In some cases the conflict between economic resources and family affection could be poignant. Consider, for example, the letter of a fifteen-year-old boy asking whether his mother might be released: 'I hope that perhaps she is cured and can leave. I would have trouble receiving her. I am alone, my father is dead and I earn only three francs a day. I await your reply' (Female Division, no. 164614; my translation). The mother was released.

If family circumstances did not permit the release of older patients, many families at least tried to guarantee that relatives did not suffer the usual fate of female patients, particularly elderly female patients, that is, transferral from overcrowded Paris wards to distant provincial hospitals where family visits were difficult and care, if less expensive, was also less reliable. These mass transfers were often painful for the patients and shocking to at least one doctor who denounced 'these convoys made up exclusively of women aged 75 to 85' ('Rapport' [1912], 177; my translation). In such circumstances the concern of one son for his aged mother is understandable. His mother had been interned nineteen years ago, and both he and his uncle had visited her regularly. The uncle had just died, and the son was entering two years of military service. He wrote to assure the doctor that when he left the army 'my visits will become regular again, as in the past' and asked the doctor to intervene so that his mother would not be sent to the provinces (Female Division, no patient number; my translation).

If the history of elderly women in Saint-Anne reflects the problems of the elderly in a nineteenth-century urban society, the cases of women interned for depression underline the personal, economic, and social difficulties of women in general. Depression was the largest single cause of internment for women, and it was often accompanied by a suicide attempt. Judging from asylum records, these depressed women were not the young and beautiful women of the historical paintings, but middle-aged women, worn down by hard work and family responsibilities. For most women, as for most men, mental illness struck in the prime of life – so much so that some doctors argued that mental illness declined with age. The largest number of female patients (49 per cent) were between thirty and fifty; about half of them were married, while another 16 per cent were widowed. About half the women worked outside the home, the majority in skilled trades ranging from seamstress or cook to mechanic. Those who were identified as housewife or as having 'no occupation' had working-class or lower-middle-class husbands, although some of these women clearly had middle-class backgrounds.[12]

When doctors, families, and the women themselves sought to explain the bouts of depression and the suicide attempts that led to internment, they tended to seek specific personal, economic, or social causes, rather than a hereditary susceptibility. Doctors were particularly struck by the poor physical condition of the women and argued that a nourishing diet was one of the best treatments that the asylum could offer. In some cases the depression was related to a physical illness, such as tuberculosis or typhoid fever, and the patient, originally treated in a hospital, had been transferred to the asylum when mental troubles developed. In other cases the depression was attributed to frequent childbirth or exhaustion from lengthy breastfeeding.

The social or economic pressures that might lead to depression were generally referred to as 'domestic worries.' These might include hostile neighbours, an abusive husband, economic worries, or personal tragedy. The women themselves seemed to be obsessed by the threat of poverty and ill health. 'Fear for the future' or 'ruin' is a leitmotif in the comments of patients and in the explanations of families. In one extreme case worry over money led one woman to restrict her diet 'in fear of not having enough later' (Female Division, no. 131539). Such fears are not surprising, given what we know of the desperate economic situation of working-class women, and doctors themselves acknowledged the hard reality of women's lives. In the case of a widow who had attempted suicide after losing her life savings, her doctor wrote that this was a 'suicide raisonné,' a rational act, and that if released she would simply try again ('Registre,' 1873, no. 132). Dr Bouchereau, the director of the women's wards, argued that working-class women needed a welfare office, run by women themselves, with complete information on where women could go for public assistance or private charity ('Rapport' [1894], 878).

The other predominant explanation for women's depression was a family tragedy, particularly the death of a child. In these cases the words and actions of the women themselves are haunting. One woman could not accept the death of her son and kept repeating, 'La mort n'existe pas' (Death does not exist) ('Registre,' 1873 no. 172). Another, whose child had just died, compulsively checked the throats of her two other children ('Registre,' 1911, no. 285). Other women saw dead children, heard their voices, or saw angels. One woman, who had lost sixteen of her eighteen children in nineteen years, simply refused to believe that the two remaining children were alive ('Registre,' 1873, no. 215).

Such tragedies appeared to affect women more than men. In some respects this is understandable: a large percentage of these women did not work outside the home, and even those who did bore the primary responsibility for the care of children. Asylum records indicate that this responsibility extended even to adult children who had been interned. Although mothers and fathers interned their children at an equal rate, a higher proportion of mothers took their daughters and sons out of the asylum, with the necessary promise that they would care for them.[13]

But the willingness of doctors and of families to attribute women's depression to their role as mothers may, in some cases, be a reflection of social stereotypes rather than of reality. Doctors may have overestimated the hardships of childbirth or the devotion of women to their families. Neglect of home and children was often recorded as an indication of mental illness on the hospital certificates. One patient, who confessed that she did not particularly like her children, quickly retracted her comments when she saw the doctor's reaction ('Registre,' 1915, no. 43).

Whether the asylum was the best place to treat depression is, of course, highly questionable. Husbands who sought the release of their wives argued forcefully that it was not. One husband was convinced his wife would die of sorrow if she stayed in Saint-Anne (Female Division, no. 97319); another reported that his wife, at home for a trial leave, had asked him to kill her rather than send her back (Female Division, no patient number). For other women, however, the asylum was literally a refuge from an abusive husband or an intolerable family situation. In such cases, when the husband demanded the release of his wife, it was often against the doctor's advice, with predictable results: the woman quickly returned to the asylum. The ambiguities of the relationships among patient, family, and doctor are clearly expressed in one case, where the patient, who had attempted suicide, wrote to thank the doctor for her release. Her husband, she reported, was 'at the end of his patience trying to cope with the housekeeping details, which he is not used to' and all the problems of moving to new lodgings. Her presence at home was indispensable. She then attached a confidential note to this letter in which she asked the doctor to make her husband understand that he must 'restrain his emotions with me. He will know what that means. He is a kind man, very loyal, very honest. Later you will know the real motive for my despair' (Female Division, no. 118.305; my translation).

A study of asylum records will never give a clear picture of women patients. Their fears, their problems, even their symptoms will always be filtered through the gaze not only of a male medical profession but of family members, who often supplied doctors with evidence and who, in many cases, had already decided the need for internment or for release. These women will always be, as one historian has eloquently written, 'fleeting silhouettes' (Ripa 55; my translation). But they cannot be represented by the simplistic images in the paintings of Pinel and Charcot, where they serve only as the 'other,' the alluring symbols of a frailty and irrationality that must be controlled by an ambitious male medical profession. As the historical records show, women's experiences with madness and internment were much more complex and diverse. Moreover, a study of their lives in the asylum can lead us not so much into the baffling world of madness and the confining walls of the asylum, but back to the more familiar economic and social world of ordinary women in the nineteenth century.

Notes

1 The recent historical literature on asylums and psychiatrists is extensive. A useful introduction to this literature can be found in the three-volume work edited by Bynum, Porter, and Shepherd.

2 Again, the literature is extensive, but the two classic studies remain Gilbert and Gubar, and Showalter.

3 See, for example, Digby.

4 At the York Retreat, for example, 70 per cent of patients who recovered were released within a year (Digby 227).

5 The annual admninistrative 'Rapport' and the hospital register are both stored, unarchived and uncatalogued, at the Saint-Anne Hospital in Paris.

6 In 1891, for example, according to the director's report for that year, 2,242 men passed through Magnan's Admission Office and 1,615 women.

7 Hysteria, being a neurosis rather than a psychosis, was normally not a legal basis for internment. It might result in hospitalization in Charcot's ward at the Salpêtrière, but this ward was not in the psychiatric division and Charcot was not a psychiatrist but rather a neurologist, that is, in a competing branch of the medical profession. Occasionally hysterics were interned in a psychiatric hospital. In 1891, for example, of 3,300 people interned in the department of the Seine, only 34 were classified as hysterics, 20 women and 14 men ('Rapport' [1891], 72).

8 At Saint-Anne, during the period 1897–1907, the male mortality rate was 32.2 per cent and the female rate 27.6 per cent, despite the higher ratio of elderly women.

9 These and the following statistics for patients in Saint-Anne are based on approximately two thousand cases, covering the period 1897–1907.

10 In the period 1897–1907, 16.2 per cent of the female patients were widowed, compared with only 5.9 per cent of the male patients.

11 This research is based on uncatalogued and unarchived files kept at Saint-Anne Hospital. The author has made every effort to supply citation information while maintaining the strict anonymity imposed by French law.

12 These percentages are based on a statistical study of approximately two thousand patients in the years 1897–1907.
13 Of those patients who were released in the care of a family member or friend, 10.5 per cent were released to a mother, 4.1 per cent to a father.

Works Cited

Bynum, W.F., Roy Porter, and Michael Shepherd. *The Anatomy of Madness: Essays in the History of Psychiatry*. Vol. 3. London: Routledge 1988
Digby, Anne. *Madness, Morality and Medicine: A Study of the York Retreat*. Cambridge: Cambridge UP 1986
Female Division Medical Files. Uncatalogued. Saint-Anne Hospital, Paris
Genil-Perrin, Dr Georges. *Histoire des origines et de l'évolution de l'idée de la dégénérescence en médecine mentale*. Paris 1913
Gilbert, Sandra, and Susan Gubar. *The Madwoman in the Attic: The Woman Writer and the Nineteenth-Century Literary Imagination*. New Haven: Yale UP 1978
Préfecture de la Seine. 'Rapport sur le service des aliénés.' 1891; 1896; 1904; 1907; 1912. Uncatalogued. Saint-Anne Hospital, Paris
Prestwich, Patricia E. *Drink and the Politics of Social Reform: Antialcoholism in France since 1870*. Palo Alto, CA: The Society for the Promotion of Science and Scholarship 1988
'Registre de la loi (femmes).' 1873; 1911; 1915. Uncatalogued. Saint-Anne Hospital, Paris
Ripa, Yannick. *La Ronde des folles: femme, folie et enfermement au XIXe siècle*. Paris: Aubier 1986
Showalter, Elaine. *The Female Malady: Women, Madness, and English Culture 1830–1980*. London: Virago 1985
Toulouse, Dr Edouard. *Les Causes de la folie, prophylaxie et assistance*. Paris 1896

⊘ 7 ⊙

More Than Pin Money: Economies of
Representation in Women's Modernism

BRIDGET ELLIOTT AND JO-ANN WALLACE

I was always more interested in money, I think, than my father.

> Bryher, *The Heart to Artemis*, 107

In the summer of 1919 I came into my fortune. I was an heiress and I was independent.

> Peggy Guggenheim, *Out of This Century*, 21

This paper raises – but does not answer – two questions about the relationship between money and representation in women's modernism. What kinds of representational practices did money, or the lack of it, make available to women in the first three decades of this century? And how does a close examination of the material underpinnings of women's modernism undermine many of the ways in which modernism has itself been represented both in traditional literary and art histories and in feminist revisionary histories? As a way of opening up the first question, we will explore the role of money in shaping the careers of six women who were active in various modernist movements: Natalie Clifford Barney, Romaine Brooks, Bryher, Peggy Guggenheim, Djuna Barnes, and Nina Hamnett. These women were chosen to represent both a range of modernist practices – writing, painting, publishing, patronage – and various, often extreme, degrees of wealth. As a way of opening up the second question, we will borrow rather loosely from Pierre Bourdieu's concept of 'symbolic capital' to explore the continuing link between the valorizing of formal experimentation within modernism and the disavowal of the role of money in shaping the production and reception of cultural products.

Our desire to 'open up' a field of inquiry and to problematize constructions of modernism without offering a coherent alternative modernism is prompted by a dissatisfaction with the homogenizing tendencies of much recent feminist theorizing which fails to take into account the material and historical specificities of women's cultural production. Like Shari Benstock we want to 'resist the desire to systematize, categorize, analyze, and prove through judicious examples' but want instead to 'put into question the very methods of that proof' ('Expatriate' 31); like Celeste M. Schenck we want to 'roughen up the history of ... Modernism' (230); and like Chandra Talpade Mohanty we seek an 'analysis which generates theoretical categories from *within* the situation and context being analyzed' (345). For these reasons our approach is less one of literary or art historical criticism than it is of a more broadly based cultural materialism, an attempt to inscribe a 'thick description' upon an expanded cultural field.

Representations in and of Modernism

The critical hegemony of a specifically avant-garde modernism, as it is represented in both the literary and the visual arts, has recently come under attack. The privileged status which the avant-garde has held in the history of modernism has been questioned extensively by feminist art historians and literary critics. Lisa Tickner, for instance, observes that the problem with modernist art history is its obsession with isolated individual artists and masterpieces in a way that effaces their participation in social, psychological, and signifying systems. Clearly this presents particular difficulties for feminists who seek to understand how gender discrimination is ideologically and institutionally systematized. In Tickner's words, 'feminism will always be disabled by the principal terms of modernist art history: its formalism and ahistoricism, its reverence for the avant-garde and the individual artist-hero, its concept of art as individual expression or social reflection, its sense of itself as objective and disinterested, its pursuit of universal values at once transcendent (of mundane social realities) and intrinsic (to the autonomous work of art, severed from the social circumstances of its production and circulation)' (94).

A failure to criticize principal terms and prevailing criteria of evaluation can limit feminist historical inquiry. Celeste M. Schenck has similarly critiqued literary constructions of modernism, noting that many women writers have been 'exiled' from the modernist canon because of their use of conventional genres and forms and warning against a feminist collusion in 'a Modernist hegemony that fetishizes formal experiment' (231). Schenck argues that just as 'the radical poetics of Modernism often masks a deeply conservative politics,' it might also be true that the 'genteel, conservative poetics of women poets whose obscurity even feminists have overlooked might pitch a more radical politics' (230–1). Similarly, Lawrence Rainey's detailed examination of the publication history of T.S. Eliot's *The Waste Land* concludes that 'when seen in institutional terms, the avant-garde was neither more nor less than a structural feature in the institutional configuration of modernism. It played no special role, possessed no ideological privilege; instead it was constituted by a specific array of marketing and publicity structures that were integrated in varying degrees with the larger economic apparatus of its time. Its typical endeavour was to develop an idiom, a shareable language that could be marketed and yet allow a certain space for individuation' (38).

While Schenck and Rainey share a distrust of a too easy conflation of radical poetic form with radical politics, the issue is obviously more vexed for Schenck because it parallels ongoing debates within feminism about appropriate critical methodologies.[1] These debates are most often constructed around a binary opposition in which 'American,' empirical, literary historical, thematic feminist criticism confronts or is confronted by 'French,' linguistic, psychoanalytic, poststructural feminist criticism.[2] 'American' feminist criticism is constructed as methodologically and stylistically traditional, even rearguard – Toril Moi points to its 'traditional humanism' as 'in effect part of patriarchal ideology' (8) – while 'French' feminist criticism is methodologically and, especially, stylistically in the avant-garde. Within feminist re-examinations of modernism Sandra Gilbert and Susan Gubar's projected three-volume study of the woman writer in the twentieth century, *No Man's Land*, can be seen as representing the 'American' side of this equation, while Alice Jardine's *Gynesis* – which explores the ways in which modernity has involved a 'putting into discourse of "woman"' (25) as that unthinkable other or alterity of Western discourse – can represent the 'French' side of the equation.

The mirroring of debates within modernism by debates within feminism complicates the issue of representation in useful ways, for it makes it clear that any discussion of representation *in* modernism, in its literary and visual texts, must also consider the critical and historical representation *of* modernism. This is a question, in Pierre Bourdieu's

128   Bridget Elliott and Jo-Ann Wallace

terms, of 'what authorizes the author' or 'who creates the "creator"?'
('Production' 133). Significantly, both 'American' and 'French' feminisms elide any full examination of the material basis of modernist
representational practices. This elision is all the more surprising in
that substantial work has been done by feminists exploring the material underpinnings of literary production in, for example, the nineteenth century, and it points to the continuing power of the myth of
democratic and disinterested modernist communities – whether of
men or women – 'being geniuses together.'[3] Pierre Bourdieu's 'The
Production of Belief: Contribution to an Economy of Symbolic
Goods,' while it does not factor gender into its argument, is nonetheless of some use in understanding the ways in which modernism, especially in its avant-garde forms, continues to be premised upon an
elision of the economic. Bourdieu's emphasis upon a *field* of cultural
goods production, in which various agents and institutions vie for the
'power to consecrate' works of art, can also provide some insight into
what is *at stake* in competing feminisms.

    In 'The Production of Belief' Bourdieu expands upon his concepts
of 'linguistic capital' and 'cultural capital' (as outlined in, for example,
Reproduction: In Education, Society and Culture) to construct a theory of
'symbolic capital.' Like linguistic and cultural capital, symbolic capital
is ultimately convertible into economic capital: '"Symbolic capital" is to
be understood as economic or political capital that is disavowed, mis-
recognized and thereby recognized, hence legitimate, a "credit"
which, under certain conditions, and always in the long run, guaran-
tees "economic" profits' ('Production' 132). Symbolic capital – which
can be held by 'the author, the critic, the art dealer, the publisher or
the theatre manager' – consists of the 'power to consecrate objects
(with a trademark or signature) or persons (through publication, exhibition, etc.) and therefore to give value, and to appropriate the profits
from this operation' ('Production' 132).

    Obviously, degrees of symbolic capital can be held both by bourgeois
commercial agents *and* by various 'cultural' or avant-garde agents. To
be published by Harlequin or exhibited in Bloomingdale's department store represents one kind of consecration – one premised upon
an expectation of almost immediate economic profit – while to be published by Editions de Minuit or exhibited by Mary Boone represents
another. The difference between them, Bourdieu suggests, can be
understood as two different relationships to the economy: one characterized by short-term investment, the other by long-term investment.
Significantly, however, 'cultural' or 'avant-garde' art practices accumu-

late symbolic capital largely through a disavowal of their economic or
political interest, the '*intervening time*' of long-term investment providing 'a screen ... disguis[ing] the profit awaiting the most disinterested
investors' ('Production' 154). Thus, while many art practices, and especially those associated with the avant-garde, are premised upon a disavowal of the economic – that is, upon the claim that 'genuine' art,
unlike 'commercial' art, is indifferent to economic profit – this disavowal is itself a form of investment.

   While Bourdieu's argument, which focuses, after all, upon 'clashes
between the dominant fractions of the dominant class' ('Production'
155), ignores the role of gender in the field of cultural production, it
nonetheless offers three insights which are useful to a feminist analysis
of representations in and of women's modernism. Firstly, it emphasizes
the importance of attending to not only various cultural artefacts
(texts, images) but also to the total *field* of cultural production: 'In
short, what "makes reputations" is not ... this or that "influential" person, this or that institution, review, magazine, academy, coterie, dealer
or publisher ... it is the field of production, understood as the system of
objective relations between these agents or institutions and as the site
of the struggles for the monopoly of the power to consecrate, in which
the value of works of art and belief in that value are continuously generated' ('Production' 135). Attending to the total field of production
means not only factoring various institutions and agents into our
assessments of modernism (as does Lawrence Rainey), but also
accounting for both our own role as producers of symbolic value and
our own investments in that role. This is especially important for feminists working in the academy since, as Bourdieu points out, long-cycle
production (e.g., avant-garde publishing) 'depends on the educational
system, which alone can provide those who preach in the desert with
devotees and followers capable of recognizing their virtues' ('Production' 153). Secondly, Bourdieu's argument clarifies what is at stake in
any discussion of representational practice: 'Specifically aesthetic conflicts about the legitimate vision of the world, i.e. in the last resort,
about what deserves to be represented and the right way to represent
it, are political conflicts (appearing in their most euphemized form)
for the power to impose the dominant definition of reality, and social
reality in particular' ('Production' 154–5). While these conflicts
shaped, and to a large degree defined, the historical period we are
examining (the first three decades of this century), they continue to
shape the representation of modernism within the academy; indeed,
one could argue that modernism (and its highly debated offspring,

postmodernism) is a function of that struggle.[4] Thirdly, Bourdieu's argument embodies a methodology in constant tension or interplay between the theoretical and the material. This is a tension we hope to maintain as we turn to our case studies, in which, as the discussion of the six women will show, we have more messy details than can be accounted for by either 'American' thematic or 'French' post-structuralist feminism.

The Case Studies

The challenge of maintaining a tension between the theoretical and the material can be complicated. How, for example, can one theorize the following incident?

> Helen Fleischman told me to give Djuna [Barnes] some underwear. A disagreeable scandal ensued as the underwear I gave was Kayser silk and it was darned. I had three distinct categories of underwear: the best, which I had decorated with real French lace and which I was saving for my trousseau; my second best that was new, but unadorned, and that which I sent to Djuna. After she complained, I sent her the second best sets. (Guggenheim 28)

The above passage from Peggy Guggenheim's autobiography, *Out of This Century: Confessions of an Art Addict,* neatly encapsulates the often vast economic differences between women active in the field of cultural modernism. However, it would be a mistake to assume an unproblematic link between economic and continuing symbolic or cultural capital. While personal fortunes often gave women access to the world of the avant-garde or the bohemian, those fortunes were no guarantee of respect (or symbolic capital) within that world.[5] Thus while Peggy Guggenheim, an almost lifelong, if parsimonious, patron of Djuna Barnes, obviously (and occasionally, one feels, humiliatingly) had greater economic power, Barnes – a third-generation bohemian and recognized member of avant-garde circles in New York and Paris – had greater cultural capital.[6] The ways in which economic capital can be used to accumulate and then circulate symbolic capital can be traced by comparing the careers of two wealthy patrons of the arts, Bryher and Peggy Guggenheim.

Significantly, little work has been done on the role of patronage in the field of modernism. In the only sustained study of women's patronage in modernism, unfortunately titled *Ladies Bountiful,* W.G. Rogers

argues that women's funding of culture, unlike men's, was personal
and intuitive rather than institutional:

> Institutional benevolence on [a grand scale] is more often bestowed by
> the men, and they like to work in a big way, with corporations and founda-
> tions, which have screening procedures, questionnaires, rules, and regula-
> tions. With the women it is just a year-round Christmas spirit. They are
> not organized; it's a hit-or-miss proposition; they meet someone who
> wants a meal, they invite him [*sic*] in, and behold, a masterpiece. (13)

This is an absurdly anachronistic reading of a period in which there
was little institutional support for the arts – when, for example, such
well-known figures as Ezra Pound actively campaigned and raised
funds to rescue T.S. Eliot from Lloyd's Bank. However, Rogers's claim
also overlooks marked differences *among* the styles of women patrons,
as the cases of Bryher (the chosen name of Winifred Ellerman) and
Peggy Guggenheim illustrate. Certainly, both Bryher and Guggenheim
are better known for their patronage of writers and artists than for
their own work. This is especially curious in the case of Bryher, who
published two autobiographies, at least two autobiographical novels,
historical novels for both adults and children, two early books on the
cinema, a German primer for children, and more. Like many impressa-
rio figures they are better known through their self-representations
than through the accounts and images of others from the period,
where they make surprisingly few appearances. Bryher, especially, has
received little critical attention and figures both in memoirs from the
period and in current criticism only as the wife of Robert McAlmon or
the lover and lifelong companion of H.D.[7] This relatively low profile in
the histories and memoirs of modernism is surprising given the enormous wealth and prestige of their family backgrounds, and given their
support and promotion of other writers and artists. It does indicate,
however, the degree to which avant-garde and formalist paradigms
continue to shape our construction of the modern.

Bryher's father was Sir John Ellerman, the self-made millionaire who
owned the White Star Steamship Lines and who reputedly paid more
taxes than any other man in England. Shortly after his death in 1933
Bryher inherited 1.2 million pounds, worth then approximately six
million dollars. (Because of English inheritance laws, the bulk of Sir
John's estate, approximately eight hundred million dollars, went to
Bryher's brother, 'who was unable to manage it successfully' [Benstock,
Left Bank 269].) Like Natalie Barney, Bryher knew of and accepted her

lesbianism from a very early age; however, unlike Barney, she needed the cover of marriage, believing that it would free her from parental control. In 1922 she proposed to and married the American writer Robert McAlmon, an event that was recounted with some glee in the *New York Times*, which reported that McAlmon 'whispered a line or two of [his] poetry and there was nothing to do but call a minister' (quoted in Knoll 9–10). Bryher describes the event rather more flatly:

> I had happened to meet a young American writer, Robert McAlmon, who was full of enthusiasm for modern writing. He wanted to go to Paris to meet Joyce but lacked the passage money. I put my problem before him and suggested that if we married, my family would leave me alone. I would give him part of my allowance, he would join me for occasional visits to my parents, but otherwise we would live strictly separate lives. (205)

McAlmon not only got part of Bryher's allowance but, in 1923, he also received fourteen thousand pounds from Sir John Ellerman to expand Contact Editions, his publishing concern; this sum further enabled him to provide James Joyce with a monthly cheque for 150 dollars (Benstock, *Left Bank* 357; Ford 45). Of the twenty writers published by Contact in the next two years, nine were women (among them were Bryher, Djuna Barnes, H.D., Gertrude Stein, and Dorothy Richardson). Because Bryher's patronage was so often mediated by her husbands – first McAlmon and later Kenneth McPherson – it is almost impossible to ascertain the degree to which Bryher herself directed the financial support of various modernist ventures. She seems to have donated some money to Sylvia Beach's bookstore, Shakespeare and Company, and to have funded 'several publications from Harriet Weaver's Egoist Press in London' (Hanscombe and Smyers 42). She certainly provided financial support for H.D. and her daughter, Perdita. However, through her second husband, Kenneth McPherson, Bryher also established a new publishing company out of Switzerland, 'Pool,' which from 1927 to 1934 published *Close-up*, the first English-language journal devoted to cinema. *Close-up* published pieces by such writers as Gertrude Stein, Dorothy Richardson, Nancy Cunard, and H.D. Thus Bryher's funding of modernism, while often indirect, nonetheless helped to create spaces for women's representations. Significantly, however, in her own work Bryher was less interested in formal experimentation than in effecting broad social change through education, and perhaps also through psychoanalysis (an interest she shared with

H.D.), and in *The Heart to Artemis* she insists that her life cannot be read outside of its historical and social context.

Bryher's indirect and even impersonal support of modernist publishing (and later of film-making) stands in marked contrast to the patronage of Peggy Guggenheim. The Guggenheim family was well known as one of the wealthiest in New York. As she explains in *Out of This Century*, her paternal grandfather, Meyer Guggenheim, had simply bought up 'most of the copper mines of the world' (2). Ironically, however, since her father was the least gifted businessman of Meyer Guggenheim's seven sons, Peggy Guggenheim actually inherited most of her wealth from her mother, Florette Seligman, whose father had built a banking empire on the profits he made manufacturing army uniforms during the American Civil War. In fact, Peggy Guggenheim was one of the poorest relations of an exceedingly rich family. Guggenheim's autobiographical self-representation, unlike Bryher's, is disturbingly self-revelatory, focusing almost exclusively on often destructive personal relationships, most of which were premised upon her patronage.

Guggenheim was both abused by and abusive to a number of men with whom she lived in heterosexual relationships. Laurence Vail, her first husband, is a case in point. An aspiring writer in Paris, living on a meagre income from his mother, Vail was viewed as one of the more colourful American bohemian males in Paris during the period. After their marriage Guggenheim recounts how Vail often made her feel inferior since she was inexperienced in his bohemian world; she also recounts numerous incidents of his aggressive behaviour.[8] Evidently, Guggenheim consciously retaliated by withholding her money from him:

> Because of my money I enjoyed a certain superiority over Laurence and I used it in a dreadful way, by telling him it was mine and he couldn't have it to dispose of freely. To revenge himself he tried to increase my sense of inferiority. He told me that I was fortunate to be accepted in Bohemia and that, since all I had to offer was my money, I should lend it to the brilliant people I met and whom I was allowed to frequent. (37)

In the rest of Guggenheim's autobiographical narrative it becomes apparent that she actually does buy her way into bohemia by, to cite only a few examples, giving Berenice Abbott five thousand francs to buy her first camera, financing Mina Loy's interior decoration workshops, paying for Emma Goldman's living and writing expenses in the summer of 1928, buying and donating designer clothes to female friends (Djuna Barnes's trademark cape was a Guggenheim hand-me-down), and providing support payments to her own ex-spouses and lovers, as well as to those of several men with whom she became involved. Many of the recipients of Guggenheim's generosity seem to have found it hard to take – she notes how Goldman revenged herself by leaving Guggenheim out of her memoirs, and how Mina Loy was furious when Guggenheim meddled with her clients. In contrast to Bryher, Guggenheim maintained direct links with those to whom she dispensed money and often dictated how it was to be used. In many respects one might conclude that Guggenheim's money enabled her to adopt a kind of she/male bohemian role – a role that was unusually aggressive in its individualism but that did not question feminine stereotypes. Throughout the autobiography there are disturbing references to other women's lack of intelligence, much competitive rivalry, and large doses of narcissism. It is almost as if she is attempting to assert a presence that many of her contemporaries only grudgingly acknowledge. She evidently felt a great need to see herself represented, as her comments on a 1924 photograph of her by Man Ray indicate:

> Laurence made me buy a cloth-of-gold evening dress at Poiret's. Now I was so thin again it suited me perfectly. I also wore a headdress made by a Russian lady who was Stravinsky's fiancée. It was a tight net gold band that made my skull look like Tutankhamun's. Man Ray photographed me in this costume with a long cigarette-holder in my mouth. It was sensational. (48)

While Peggy Guggenheim's wealth and patronage provided her access to communities of artists, it nonetheless allowed her only occasional and limited opportunities for self-representation or for representation by others. Natalie Clifford Barney and Romaine Brooks, by contrast, used their wealth to experiment – Barney more publicly, Brooks more privately – with self-representation and lifestyle. Born in the mid-1870s, Barney and Brooks were approaching their forties by the outbreak of the First World War and thus should be viewed as transitional figures whose work incorporates *fin-de-siècle* and modernist elements. An American who immigrated to France as a young woman and most of whose writing – poetry, memoirs, collections of *pensées* – was in the language of her adoption, Natalie Barney described herself as 'à cheval sur deux siècles' (*Aventures* 10). Her work reflects this straddling of the nineteenth and twentieth centuries in its debts to the French male Symbolist and decadent poets and in its open celebration of lesbianism and communities of women. Similarly, Romaine Brooks's paintings are daringly modern in their exploration of lesbian and androgynous sexualities but rather more conventional in stylistic terms, adopting the subdued tonalities and thinly brushed solid forms of Whistler as opposed to pursuing the more fractured visual language of the modernist avant-garde.

Like Guggenheim's, Barney's and Brooks's inheritances had been founded primarily on nineteenth-century expansionist enterprises. Barney's wealth was derived on her father's side from mining and transportation, and on her mother's side from whisky. Her father, Albert Clifford Barney, owned the Barney Car Works, a railroad car foundry which he had inherited from his own father and which he sold, when he was still a young man, to the Pullman Sleeping Car Company. He retired on the profits and, together with his wife, the painter Alice Pike Barney, embarked on establishing a prominent social life in Washington, D.C. (Wickes 18–20; Benstock, *Left Bank* 269). Upon her father's death in 1902, when she was twenty-six years old, Natalie Barney inherited 2.5 million dollars; when her mother remarried in 1911, she inherited a further 1.5 million. As her biographers point out, Barney seldom alluded to the source of her wealth, preferring instead to reconstruct a family history that stressed her historical ties to France, her adopted country, and one she associated with the cultural rather than the financial (Chalon 9; Wickes 16–18).

Barney's direct patronage of modernist enterprises, effected largely through Ezra Pound (Wickes 160–5), was less sustained than that of either Guggenheim or Bryher; instead, she used her wealth to experiment with lifestyle and self-representation. She was able to create an enclosed community of women writers, with its own systems of artistic production and distribution, which allowed her an unusually high degree of control over her various visual and literary incarnations. Barney's home in the rue Jacob on the Left Bank was the site of the famous lesbian salon she established in 1909; the salon, however, was Barney's second attempt to found a utopian lesbian community. In 1904 she and the poet Renée Vivien had travelled to the island of Lesbos with the intention of establishing a 'Sapphic school of poetry'; while this school never materialized, in 1927 Barney did establish her Académie des femmes, 'a counterpart to the Académie Française,' which did not admit a woman until 1980 (Jay 73, 33). In *Aventures de*

l'esprit Barney provides detailed sketches and appreciations of many of
the women writers associated with her academy. These include Colette,
Mina Loy, Djuna Barnes, and Gertrude Stein. The Académie des
femmes, designed in part to bring about an 'entente' among English,
American, and French women writers, also provided intellectual and
social support for these writers and occasionally, as with Djuna Barnes's *Ladies Almanack*, raised donations and subscriptions towards the
private publication of works.[9]

While Barney used her wealth, in part, to create communities of
women artists, it also enabled her to experiment with both visual and
literary self-representations. In her early twenties Barney occasionally
adopted the persona and costume of 'the page,' both in her poetry, in
which she speaks in the voice of the suitor of courtly romance, and in
her lesbian relationships (where she 'occasionally donned the outfit of
a page while pursuing a beloved woman' [Jay 91]). Wickes describes
one evening in the spring of 1902 when 'disguised as street singers,
[Barney] and the opera star Emma Calvé serenaded Renée [Vivien] ...
that is Calvé sang the lament of Orpheus for his Eurydice, and when
Renée opened her window, Natalie threw her a bouquet containing a
sonnet in which she begged to see her' (Wickes 63–4). Such elaborate
stagings of one's fantasies and desires do not come cheaply. Somewhat
later Barney elaborated the persona of 'the Amazon,' as alluded to in
the titles of two of her collections of *pensées, Pensées d'une amazone*
(1920) and *Nouvelles Pensées de l'amazone* (1939), and had herself photographed in her riding habit as she had earlier been photographed in
her page costume. Significantly the personae of 'the page' and of 'the
amazon' were first suggested by male artists. At age eleven Barney was
painted by Carolus Duran as 'The Little Page' (this painting was reproduced as the frontispiece to Barney's first collection of poems, *Quelques
Portraits-Sonnets de femmes* [1900]), and in 1910 Remy de Gourmont celebrated her as 'l'Amazone' in a series of letters published in *Le Mercure
de France*. As Karla Jay points out, Barney's internalization of these personae is not unproblematic for they are 'informed with the power relations which had given rise' to them (92). While Barney's wealth
enabled her to live out a number of alternate identities, it also effectively protected her from having to think through the real implications
of the powerlessness suggested by some of her costumes.

Although we do not have the exact figures of her inheritance,
Romaine Brooks was also fabulously wealthy; unlike Barney, however, a
break with her family meant that she experienced seven years of
extreme poverty before coming into her inheritance in 1902. Upon

her mother's and brother's deaths Brooks and her sister inherited the estate of Isaac Waterman, her maternal grandfather, who had amassed a fortune from coalmines in Salt Lake City and Kingston, Pennsylvania. Brooks records her response in her unpublished memoirs: 'From possessing almost nothing ... I now had six flats in Nice alone, another in Monte Carlo, one in Dieppe, an unfurnished one in Paris and a château near Mentone' (Secrest 173). Unlike Barney, who was always attracted to the *demi-monde*, Brooks entered the *haute monde* when she moved to a mansion in the fashionable avenue de Trocadero in 1908. Portrait photographs from the period emphasize her public self-presentation as a fashionable society lady, in spite of the fact that she was a lesbian who increasingly adopted male attire in her daily life. Certainly these photographs provide a curious point of contrast with Brooks's later lesbian-identified self-images, and particularly with her famous *Self-Portrait* of 1923, in which she poses in the costume – top hat, gloves, cane – of the *fin-de-siècle* dandy. Publicly exhibited in Paris, London, and New York in 1925, the work received much attention and was widely reproduced in the illustrated press. Significantly, although Barney and Brooks were both very wealthy and had become lovers by the late-1910s, they pursued quite different strategies of self-representation, which in turn underscore their different views of lesbian sexuality. While most of Barney's published writing was recognizably autobiographical, Brooks seems to have used her wealth to guard her privacy jealously, observing that 'Hell is other people' (Secrest 204), and to circulate only those images of herself that she had constructed. Unlike other, more flamboyant transvestite lesbian artists of the period (such as her English counterpart, Gluck), Brooks did not provide press photographs of herself to accompany critical reviews of her work. The paintings alone are reproduced – evidently a strategy of self-protection and privacy which also forced the critics to take her painting seriously instead of becoming obsessed with the persona of the artist.

Privacy, however, was a luxury unavailable to Djuna Barnes and Nina Hamnett, as the incident with which we opened our case studies indicates. Unlike the other women of this study Barnes and Hamnett lived in often extreme poverty. Each had to work to support her writing or her art, Barnes as a journalist, writing and illustrating her own articles, and Hamnett as an artist's model. Each relied heavily on hand-outs and hand-me-downs, and each was forced to cultivate marketable social identities – Barnes as a great beauty with a cutting wit, and Hamnett as something of a bohemian clown. In many ways their lives were the most public of any of our case studies, and this is nowhere more obvious than in Hamnett's autobiographies, which she admits to writing for money. *Laughing Torso* (1932) and *Is She a Lady?* (1955) flatly chronicle the famous people she knew and their shocking lifestyles. The title of the earlier book refers to Gaudier-Brzeska's famous marble torso of 1913, for which Hamnett modelled. Ironically, when telling her own life story in 1932, Hamnett defined herself as the headless torso of someone else's vision. This disempowered and fragmented view of the self was taken up by Rebecca West, who reviewed the book in the *Daily Telegraph* shortly after its publication: 'How that torso, which is not only cheerful but excessively willing and active, does get about! It spins and spins from London to Paris, from studio to studio, from party to party, from night club to night club, and if not from pole to pole, at least from Swede to Pole' (6).

On both sides of the family Nina Hamnett's relatives had been in the civil service. Her military officer father had been the son of an Indian civil servant, and her mother the daughter of a naval officer. However, in 1904 (when Hamnett was sixteen) her father was court-martialled for accepting bribes and left the army in disgrace to drive a taxi-cab in London. After showing no aptitude for apprenticing in the post office, Hamnett was allowed to attend art school because it was free. Like Guggenheim she started her independent life at age twenty-three, but with a much smaller personal fortune, when an uncle arranged for her to receive an advance of fifty pounds from money left by her paternal grandfather; in addition to this, some aunts gave her an allowance of two shillings and sixpence per week. Through supplementing this income by giving private painting lessons, Hamnett managed to rent an independent studio for seven shillings and sixpence per week. The rent scarcely left her with enough money for food and other necessities (Hooker 28, 31). Hamnett's autobiographies are riddled with comments on money, difficult living conditions, and shortages of food, together with long lists of those with whom she socialized and discussed art. Aside from her work, which she sold intermittently (especially at exhibitions, to friends, and to little magazines), her social connections were her lifeline, for she depended on being such good company that she would be invited to visit, as well as offered cast-off clothing and the odd gift of money to support her painting and travel. She also modelled for such other artists as Roger Fry, Jacob Kramer, and Henri Gaudier-Brzeska. In many ways her modelling was an extension of her public role as exhibitionist bohemian clown – knowing and being known by everyone who frequented the avant-garde circles of London and Paris, performing endless introductions.

Given her lack of economic and cultural capital, it is hardly surprising that Hamnett deliberately constructed her own image as that of bohemian rebel; this is especially evident in a *Self Portrait* from 1917 in which her bobbed hair and smock cast her in the romantic tradition of the male painter of genius who defiantly meets the world's gaze. And yet, unlike Brooks, Hamnett did not have the power to control or limit the ways in which she was represented either in visual or literary terms. Her poverty made her into public property, and she became a bit player in almost every memoir of the period, a walk-on character introduced as a comic or colourful diversion from the main narrative.

Like Hamnett, Djuna Barnes was forced to support herself from an early age. In 1912, at about the same time that Peggy Guggenheim was 'coming into her fortune,' Barnes left her highly unconventional family in rural New York state and moved to New York City to find work as a freelance journalist. By 1913 she was earning fifteen dollars for an article or a picture, using this money to support herself and to contribute to the support of her mother, three brothers, and grandmother (Field 13–14). She wrote for most of the major New York newspapers, had a column in the *Theatre Guild Magazine*, and contributed feature articles, drawings, and interviews to such glossy and popular journals as *McCall's, Vanity Fair,* and *Cosmopolitan*. It was an assignment for *McCall's* that took Barnes to Paris sometime around 1920. Barnes had the reputation of being, together with Mina Loy, one of the two most beautiful women of bohemian New York or Paris, and the many photographs of her by Man Ray, Roy Kuhlman, and Berenice Abbott emphasize her composure and elegance. Even after Barnes gave up journalism to devote herself more fully to her writing, this was the persona which guaranteed her the minimal patronage she received from Peggy Guggenheim, Natalie Barney, and, occasionally, Samuel Beckett. A 1971 interview indicates Barnes's awareness of the benefits and the cost of such a social persona: 'Years ago I used to see people, I had to, I was a newspaperwoman, among other things. And I used to be rather the life of the party. I was rather gay and silly and bright and all that sort of stuff and wasted a lot of time. I used to be invited by people who said "Get Djuna for dinner, she's amusing." So I stopped it' (quoted in Kannenstine 11–12). In 1939, when war broke out, Guggenheim paid for Barnes's passage back to New York, where she rented the one-room apartment in Greenwich Village that would be her home for the next forty years. In 1942 she wrote to ask Robert McAlmon for twenty dollars to settle a dentist's bill: 'I live on less than $20 a month for food – in fact $25 is all I have for *everything*' (quoted in Hanscombe and Smyers 103).

Conclusion

Our case studies are significant not for the information they provide about these women's money; this has been recorded elsewhere in individual biographies and reminiscences from the period. Rather more interesting are the larger patterns that emerge from considering the studies as a set of relationships or range of possible subject-positions within the expanded cultural field Bourdieu has discussed. While it is tempting to assume that wealth facilitated public recognition and control over one's self-image, as it did for Natalie Barney, our other case studies suggest that the visibility of these modernist women was more complicated. In fact, women of limited resources such as Djuna Barnes or Nina Hamnett were even more visible than Barney since they depended upon making beautiful or amusing spectacles of themselves in order to secure patronage. In effect, their appearance was a form of symbolic currency. The point can be illustrated by comparing Hamnett's modelling for other artists with Barney's practice of costumed masquerading. At least to some extent, their relative position at opposite ends of the economic spectrum accounts for the differences between Hamnett's fragmentation in such works as Gaudier-Brzeska's *Torso*, a publicly exhibited sculpture, and Barney's photographs of herself as a page, which were privately circulated.[10] However, the financial freedom to cast one's own image came with no guarantee of appreciation in modernist circles. Instead the myth of the avant-garde's distance from money seems to have worked against artists such as Romaine Brooks, whose connections with fashionable society appear to have lowered her avant-garde credibility (or symbolic capital), at least in conventional art historical discussions of the period, which simply omit her. Evidently her portraits of wealthy lesbians have been considered less modern than, for example, Picasso's paintings of working-class models and prostitutes.

This brings us back to the problem of how modernism is constituted. While feminist accounts of the period have extended the understanding of modernism to include the work of numerous women, they have tended either, like Gilbert and Gubar, to focus on individuals sharing a common gendered oppression, or, like Jardine, to consider the ways in which a notion of 'the feminine' is invoked by the avant-garde as a sign of not belonging to or profiting from mainstream bourgeois culture. What worries us here is that neither of these frameworks adequately addresses the diversity of women's positions within early twentieth-century culture, and neither accounts for the large differences of power between women which have been pointed out by our case studies. In *No Man's Land*, for example, Sandra Gilbert and Susan Gubar describe their project as one of 'conflat[ing] and collat[ing] individual literary narratives, so that they constitute one possible metastory' (xiv). The construction of such metanarratives, together with the overriding textuality of their approach – they talk about economics *in* literary texts but not about the economics *of* textual production – flattens out the landscape of women's modernism to such a degree that the histories of various and multiple struggles are lost. Although in volume 2 of *No Man's Land* Gilbert and Gubar insist that they want to 'locate the text in its sociocultural context,' their use of the leitmotif ('the femme fatale,' 'the metaphor of transvestism') to 'reveal drastic sociocultural changes' (xvi) functions instead as a template. However, while many 'French' post-structuralist feminisms consciously construct themselves in opposition to 'American' thematic feminisms, they both elide the historical and the material. In *Gynesis*, for example, Alice Jardine invokes 'woman' as the troubled ground of a modernity that is overridingly textual and ahistorical. Her theorizing of the 'woman effect' in texts assumes that subverting linguistic structures, and thereby deconstructing 'the Self,' is a radical political practice. However, as our case studies indicate, under particular material and social conditions the formation of a coherent self-identity may be enabling. The efficacy of a feminist politics can only be assessed when it is located within an expanded cultural field. As Susan R. Suleiman has usefully commented, 'If we want to talk about the real marginalization of women in relation to "the avant-garde" (by real marginalization, I mean the exclusion of women from the centers of male avant-garde activity and/or their exclusion from the historical and critical accounts of that activity), we must look at individual cases in their historical and national specificity' (155–6).

Notes

1 In 'Expatriate Modernism' Shari Benstock makes explicit the connection between debates around modernism and within feminism in her call for

'collective work on the ideological premises of Modernist practice in which
the ideologies and ethics of both Modernism and feminist critical practices
would be jointly exposed' (37, 11).

2 For a fuller exploration of this debate see Moi, Todd, and Felski.

3 The phrase 'being geniuses together' is borrowed from Robert McAlmon's
autobiography of the same title. McAlmon's memoir, like Morley Cal-
laghan's *That Summer in Paris* and Ernest Hemingway's *A Moveable Feast*, has
contributed greatly to the myth of the modernist expatriate community.
Shari Benstock's *Women of the Left Bank* and Gillian Hanscombe and Virginia L. Smyers's *Writing for Their Lives* have reconstructed a similar wom-
en's modernism.

4 'It is not sufficient to say that the history of the field is the history of the
struggle for the monopolistic power to impose the legitimate categories of
perception and appreciation. The *struggle itself* creates the history of the
field; through the struggle the field is given a temporal dimension' (Bourdieu, 'Production' 159).

5 Amy Lowell's experience with Ezra Pound is a perfect example. Hanscombe and Smyers quote the following letter from Pound to Margaret
Anderson (editor of the *Little Review*): 'Re Amy. I *don't* want her. But if she
can be made to liquidate, to excoriate, to cash in, on a magazine, *especially*
in a section over which I have no control, and for which I am not responsible, *then* would I be right glad to see her milked of her money, mashed into
moonshine, at mercy of monitors. Especially as appearance in U.S. section
does *not* commit me to any approval of her work' (quoted 183).

6 Jacqueline Bograd Weld recounts how, in the 1970s, Guggenheim sent
Djuna Barnes monthly cheques (by that time amounting to $300) always
and deliberately timed to arrive three weeks late. When questioned by
Mina Loy about why she caused Barnes the additional hardship of pleading
with landlords and other creditors, Guggenheim replied, 'Somehow, the
only pleasure I get while I give is when I withhold for a while to give them
pain. That's the only way I can feel good about it, know they'll appreciate it
... I don't know why I do it, I can't help it' (Weld 71).

7 Hanscombe and Smyers are among the very few critics who discuss Bryher
in her own right (see especially chapter 3 of *Writing for Their Lives*).

8 'Laurence was very violent and he liked to show off ... Fights went on for
hours, sometimes days, once even for two weeks. I should have fought back.
He wanted me to, but all I did was weep. That annoyed him more than anything. When our fights worked up to a grand finale he would rub jam in my
hair. But what I hated most was being knocked down in the streets, or having things thrown in restaurants. Once he held me down under water in
the bathtub until I felt I was going to drown' (36).

9 In a 1926 letter to Gertrude Stein, Barney wrote: 'The other night ... I realized how little the French "femmes de lettres" know of English and Americans and vice versa ... I wish I might bring about a better "entente," and
   hope therefore to organize here this winter, and his winter, and this spring,
   readings and presentations that will enable our mind-allies to appreciate
   each other' (quoted in Wickes 165).
10 Reproductions of these works can be found in Hooker, Chalon, and
    Wickes.

Works Cited

Barnes, Djuna. *Interviews*. Ed. Alyce Barry. Washington, D.C.: Sun and Moon P
   1985
Barney, Natalie Clifford. *Aventures de l'esprit*. Paris: Editions Emile-Paul Frères
   1929
− *Nouvelles Pensées de l'amazone*. Paris: Mercure de France 1939
− *Pensées d'une amazone*. Paris: Editions Emile-Paul Frères 1920
− *Quelques Portraits-Sonnets de femmes*. Paris: Ollendorf 1900
Benstock, Shari. 'Expatriate Modernism: Writing on the Cultural Rim.' In Broe
   and Ingram, 20–40
− *Women of the Left Bank: Paris, 1900–1940*. Austin: U of Texas P 1986
Bourdieu, Pierre. 'The Production of Belief: Contribution to an Economy of
   Symbolic Goods.' In *Media, Culture and Society: A Critical Reader*. Ed. Richard
   Collins et al. London: SAGE 1986, 131–63
Bourdieu, Pierre, and Jean-Claude Passeron. *Reproduction: In Education, Society
   and Culture*. Trans. Richard Nice. London: SAGE 1977
Broe, Mary Lynn, and Angela Ingram, eds. *Women's Writing in Exile*. Chapel
   Hill: U of North Carolina P 1989
Bryher [Winifred Ellerman]. *The Heart to Artemis: A Writer's Memoirs*. London:
   Collins 1963
Chalon, Jean. *Portrait of a Seductress: The World of Natalie Barney*. Trans. Carol
   Barko. New York: Crown 1979
Felski, Rita. *Beyond Feminist Aesthetics: Feminist Literature and Social Change*. Cam-
   bridge: Harvard UP 1989
Field, Andrew. *Djuna: The Formidable Miss Barnes*. Austin: U of Texas P 1985
Ford, Hugh. *Published in Paris: American and British Writers, Printers, and Publish-
   ers in Paris, 1920–1939*. New York: Macmillan 1975
Gilbert, Sandra M., and Susan Gubar. *No Man's Land: The Place of the Woman
   Writer in the Twentieth Century. Vol. 1. The War of the Words*. New Haven: Yale UP
   1987

- *No Man's Land: The Place of the Woman Writer in the Twentieth Century. Vol. 2. Sexchanges.* New Haven: Yale UP 1989
Guggenheim, Peggy. *Out of This Century: Confessions of an Art Addict.* 1946; reprint, New York: Universe 1979
Hamnett, Nina. *Is She a Lady? A Problem in Autobiography.* London: Allan Wingate 1955
- *Laughing Torso.* New York: Long and Smith 1932
Hanscombe, Gillian, and Virginia L. Smyers. *Writing for Their Lives: The Modernist Women 1910–1940.* London: Women's P 1987
Hooker, Denise. *Nina Hamnett: Queen of Bohemia.* London: Constable 1986
Jardine, Alice A. *Gynesis: Configurations of Woman and Modernity.* Ithaca: Cornell UP 1985
Jay, Karla. *The Amazon and the Page: Natalie Clifford Barney and Renée Vivien.* Bloomington: Indiana UP 1988
Kannenstine, Louis F. *The Art of Djuna Barnes: Duality and Damnation.* New York: New York UP 1977
Knoll, Robert E. *Robert McAlmon: Expatriate Publisher and Writer.* U of Nebraska Studies 18. Lincoln: U of Nebraska 1957
Mohanty, Chandra Talpade. 'Under Western Eyes: Feminist Scholarship and Colonial Discourses.' *boundary 2* 12/13 (Spring/Fall 1984), 333–58
Moi, Toril. *Sexual/Textual Politics: Feminist Literary Theory.* London: Methuen 1985
Rainey, Lawrence. 'The Price of Modernism: Reconsidering the Publication of *The Waste Land.*' *Critical Quarterly* 31 (Winter 1989), 21–47
Rogers, W.G. *Ladies Bountiful.* New York: Harcourt 1968
Schenck, Celeste M. 'Exiled by Genre: Modernism, Canonicity, and the Politics of Exclusion.' In Broe and Ingram, 226–50
Secrest, Meryle. *Between Me and Life: A Biography of Romaine Brooks.* New York: Doubleday 1974
Suleiman, Susan Rubin. 'A Double Margin: Reflections on Women Writers and the Avant-Garde in France.' *Yale French Studies* 75 (1988), 148–72
Tickner, Lisa. 'Feminism, Art History, and Sexual Difference.' *Genders* 3 (Nov. 1988), 92–128
Todd, Janet. *Feminist Literary History.* London: Polity P 1988
Weld, Jacqueline Bograd. *Peggy: The Wayward Guggenheim.* New York: Dutton 1986
West, Rebecca. 'The Racy Autobiography of a Woman Artist.' *Daily Telegraph,* 10 June 1932, 6
Wickes, George. *The Amazon of Letters: The Life and Loves of Natalie Barney.* New York: Putnam's 1976

⟪ 8 ⟫

A Woman's Touch: Towards a Theoretical Status of Painterliness in the Feminist Approach to Representation in Painting

NICOLE DUBREUIL-BLONDIN

In my rather long and ambitious title a double emphasis must be put on the word 'towards.' 'Towards' because the status of painterliness and, through it, the whole issue of the pictorial still remain problematic to such a degree that they could be termed a blind spot in the feminist approach to representation in painting. 'Towards' because, in my own ongoing reflection on the subject, this question exemplifies one of a number of pitfalls surrounding the issue of gender and the way feminist discussions have addressed the traditional practice of art history. But even though the status of painterliness now appears at the end of this essay's list of concerns, it must remain central to a feminist approach to representation in painting. From the perspective of theory it has a paradigmatic quality, pointing, as it does, to representation as a material production. From an historical point of view it is concomitant with a return to the medium of painting that is one of the hallmarks of the postmodernist 1980s: painting seems not only to have recovered its own luscious body, rich in textural effects, it also quotes frantically, borrowing endlessly from painterly styles of the past, in what seems to be a quest for a lost identity. In all but the use of this borrowing to evoke a lost glory and authority, one could find in painting's search of itself echoes of another search, the search of women struggling to establish their own position in history and to discover how they have been defined by cultural practices such as painting.

Place and Displacement: An Agonizing Situation

I work at the University of Montreal, that institution which infamously
made headlines when an armed young man killed fourteen women at
the Ecole Polytechnique.[1] Compared to the mad gunmen randomly
shooting at people who have become an evil commonplace in North
America, Marc Lépine was unique in the specific nature of his target:
he explicitly aimed at feminists. 'You are all feminists. I hate feminists'
were his words before firing his semi-automatic rifle in the classroom
from which he had just expelled the male students. A letter was later
found in which he charged feminists with responsibility for his personal as well as his professional difficulties. The letter also mentioned
names of women who had succeeded in Quebec society, whether in
politics, in the labour movement, as sports commentators, or even as
police officers. Thus Marc Lépine became the first anti-feminist exter-
minator. On open-line radio shows following the massacre some men
claimed to understand his action, and a few even agreed with it.

But this crime was not totally explained by its anti-feminist component. When the question of the deeper and broader meanings of the
event arose in a community still in a state of shock, other causes, other
contexts, were brought into focus, displacing or, one might say, dilut-
ing the gender aspect of the crime. The first reservation – in fact a
denial – came from the victims themselves: 'We are not feminists' was
the sole argument one of the students had time to put forward before
the intruder started shooting. 'We are not feminists,' meaning: 'we are
not those aggressive and vociferous women feminism has been associated with; we are just women students trying to succeed in life in the
best way we can.' Between the lines of this plea rises the image of the
harmless victim on which the media developed a rhetoric of innocence
and fragility which culminated in this testimony from a tearful young
husband: 'Maryse was like a little bird.'

Elsewhere specialists worked out another type of displacement from
the anti-feminist motivation for the murders. Psychoanalysts and soci-
ologists blamed personal neurosis and social problems such as chronic
unemployment among youth. Pressure groups blamed easy access to
firearms and the violence on television which fostered the kind of
social climate in which a Rambo type of imaginary could tip over into
reality. And there was massive public mourning by the community,
including a spontaneous march by students ending in l'Oratoire St-
Joseph and the public funeral at Eglise Notre-Dame, both strongholds

of Catholic conservatism. Each of these responses pushed aside issues of anti-feminism and misogyny in favour of other issues.

But were these not, all of them, legitimate issues, components of a complex situation which the gender question, in all its urgency, had to accommodate somehow? The complexity of this whole situation, in which gender questions were accommodated to, and frequently displaced by, other concerns (themselves frequently constructed in gendered terms), seems to me strangely similar to events in my own discipline. There the advent of feminism, which, from an ideological point of view, had had the effect of a cataclysm, was still in the process of finding its way and its place in a network of theoretical *a prioris* and methodological tools inherited from a tradition itself marked by gender relations. How, for example, would the feminist perspective affect other critical paradigms that had already put some basic assumptions of the practice of art and art history into perspective, challenging, among other things, their longing for (or their pretensions to) transparency? The focus on the pictorial, at the very core of the modernist project and rephrased in postmodernist terms, constitutes such a paradigm. Whether theorizing and describing painting's material basis as a medium or representation as a material production, the focus on the pictorial deconstructs both the all-powerful theory of mimesis and traditional notions of style based on connoisseurship. But the possibility of its coming to terms with the type of agency explored by feminism remains both problematic and unexplored in the literature on the visual arts, where formalist-*cum*-structuralist and feminist exegetes usually seem opposed.

In the Beginning, Painting Was the Sole Presence

The rise of feminism in the art scene happened in the context of – and in opposition to – what could be called 'high modernism' (in the sense that we also say 'high Renaissance,' connoting achievement and canonicity). In that context painting was a dominating all-powerful medium that had reached the highest level of self-referentiality and autonomy. It had even passed beyond abstraction, in the literal sense of that term, since it was no longer schematized or distilled from the representation of nature. It indeed aimed to eradicate the structural foundations of representation: figure-ground relationships, precedence of drawing over colour, spatial coordinates relating to experience. The surface of the picture asserted itself as surface yielding only to the fiction of colour. The depicted shape had become more and more subservient to the literal shape of the canvas. Frontality, combined with imposing size and format, created a strong effect of presence, of painting delivered from its task of representation.[2]

This effect of presence operated through a series of repressions that ranged from the content to the context of representation and eliminated as well the agent producing the representation. At the time, of course, these repressions carried critical overtones: they still corresponded to the radical questioning by the modernists of the ideological implications and past hegemony of representation in painting. They were also a deconstruction of the expressionist fallacy which placed the medium at the service of an anguished but omnipotent Self.[3] Last but not least, they were at odds with the traditional practice of art history, whose reliance, deeply rooted in humanistic values, on stylistic and iconographical analysis they had now made obsolete. The history of the art of painting would become the history of the pictorial itself, and each work embodied the theory of its own practice. *This is painting*, it seemed to repeat endlessly, as if it were unable to propose anything but its own self-referentiality.

In this golden age of painting as painting it seemed unthinkable to introduce an extraneous body, to image presence other than painting itself, especially that archetypal Other called Woman. But in the mid-1960s and early 1970s, when feminism brought important changes to the political, intellectual, and artistic scenes, the tautology of painting as painting began to be revealed as a fictitious ideological construct. The hypostatic presence of painting, understood as the result of a triumph over representation by the elimination of pictorial depth, was now seen as masking a substitution of perspectives. A temporal recession now replaced the spatial recession of modernism; painting was, once again, representation, each new work serving as a substitute for the medium as a whole, each new work writing the last chapter in the medium's history.[4]

Other elements of painting repressed by the modernists also made a comeback as representation was again opened to content and context. The expelled creator was very much present under the guise of the proper name: a signature with considerable value attached to it. The pictures of this period, as both marketable goods and as ideological pawns, still had a great deal to do with society; their sheer size, their jazzy acrylic look, and their production in series spoke of late capitalism in a North American urban context.[5] And if one examines the rhetoric developed in and about the works (with its emphasis on bold-

ness, audacity, aggressiveness and ambition), one can also conclude
that both works and rhetoric spoke from a male point of view
(Dubreuil-Blondin 44–66).

Occupying the Territory

Oddly enough, a kind of self-referentiality also seemed to have motivated the first feminist breakthrough in art and aesthetics. The rallying
cry was the feminine, femaleness, womanhood; the strategy was invasion, occupation. A will to inscribe women into the mainstream (or to
provide them with a tradition of their own) through art practice, writing, and teaching corresponded to studies that explored the reasons
for women's exclusion from art history.[6] The preoccupation was with
differences rooted in nature that were thought to inform every aspect
of a work produced by a woman: its subject matter, related to a specific
mode of perception and to a particular life experience, as well as its
formal and material outlook, expressed by the choice of motifs, shapes,
colours, and techniques.[7] But, for obvious and numerous reasons, the
theoretical and critical focus was no longer on the pictorial as the very
foundation of meaning in the painted image.

Even though it was not spelled out, the situation amounted to a kind
of physical confrontation in which the sexualized female body would
triumph over the flat surface of the canvas adorned with pigments in
order to become the new centre of attention and veneration. Symptomatic of this confrontation is the fact that one of the most significant
events (though it may not be the most significant work) of the feminist
movement in the visual arts is Judy Chicago's *The Dinner Party*. A homage to woman's powers, woman's struggles, and woman's contribution
to the development of humanity, it has its origins in myths of the
Mother Goddess and ends with the figure of Georgia O'Keefe (that
rather painterly artist of American modernism). *The Dinner Party* is
totally immersed in symbolism and encompassed within its vagina-
flower-butterfly image, which stands for women's identity as well as
woman's liberation. Experiencing *The Dinner Party*, which comes all
wrapped up with directions for use,[8] amounts to an encounter with
Womanhood brought to the level of religious experience. The formal,
material, and technical aspects of the work are a calculated means by
which to attain Female Transcendency.

It is not surprising that, in this period of searching for the self and of
claiming space for the expansion of that self, the practice of art history
and art criticism should have been largely absorbed by issues of con-

tent. I have never fully recovered from my first live encounter a decade
ago with a feminist approach, when Gloria Orenstein lectured to the
Society of Philosophy at my university about the representation of the
Goddess in art. As a specialist in American modernist painting, I was at
that point a semi-repentant formalist, challenged by the art practice
and the intellectual climate of the 1970s to find my way out of Green-
bergian orthodoxy. What was offered to me at that lecture puzzled me:
in addition to an insistent reference to myth, which I found slightly
irritating, Orenstein's methodology consisted of a loose thematic analysis (variations on the alliance of Woman with nature and fertility) that
covered a tremendous number of works of varying degrees of interest,
from ancient to contemporary, in all kinds of media, ranging from pre-
historic sculptures of fertility goddesses to contemporary performance
art by women. I had the strange feeling of reverting back to a lighter
but fundamentally unrevised version of Panofsky's iconography.[9] That
the speaker was a literary critic and the audience came from a number
of professions made me wonder if women's need for a strong bond of
sorority were not giving rise to a weak substitute for real interdisciplinary work.[10]

   There was, of course, a fair amount of more 'standard' art historical
work done in those days when ensuring women's presence on the
scene and providing role models for the generations to come were
pressing necessities. These writings, mainly monographs, corresponded to the efforts made elsewhere, in the galleries and museums,
to organize solo and group exhibitions, as well as large retrospective
shows, that would give access to the art of women past and present.[11]
Because the monograph is one of the more traditional genres of art
history, it was claimed to serve the cause of women in the discipline,
which would, at last, become HERstory. Placing the production of an
oeuvre under the determination of an individual destiny (once more a
transcendent Self in spite of the obstacle race that every woman's life
was shown to be) and under the sovereign will of the artist-heroine,
feminist art history proposed an approach that was largely uncritical
and that seemed attuned to a pre-modernist line of thinking in which
style was the only formal counterpoint to iconography.

In the Thickness of Representation

A real methodological breakthrough would come that would restore
art's thickness, so to speak, would point to the critical specificity of art
production without ignoring concerns and social issues relevant to

women: that was, of course, the 'gender and representation' problematic which is largely responsible for this collection of essays. The possibility that representation might rid itself of metaphysics may have been prompted in the visual arts by the critical return of photography and the various hybrid media in which mechanical reproduction plays a leading part. The indexical character of these images allowed their producers to do away with the iconic and the symbolic that had previously tied the pictorial sign to a transcendent Real, or Subject. Confronting more traditional modes of producing images, these images allowed representation to turn upon itself and to reflect on its own procedures.

The whole intellectual project was to be, this time, truly and in a sophisticated way, interdisciplinary: a meeting place of philosophy, which follows the origin, developments, and implications of representation as a concept; of psychoanalysis, which studies its role in the structuring and functioning of the Self; of Marxism, which ties it to ideology; and of semiotics, which theorizes it in terms of the sign. Theory of representation became an immense field with complex ramifications. The problematic of representation had, at long last, a critical impact on the conservative discipline of art history. To judge what I would not hesitate to call its cataclysmic effect, one has only to compare Foucault's reading of Velasquez's *Las Meninas* to any traditional art historical interpretation of the picture (Foucault 19–31). While everybody else was trying to restore the meaningful anecdote that would provide the key to the scene, Foucault saw the image as an apparatus (a *dispositif*) acting like a cypher for representation itself: its strategies, its implications, and its effect. In simpler terms Foucault saw Velasquez's painting as a representation about representation.

We largely owe to feminism, and especially to feminism in the visual arts (I am thinking here of British theoreticians of the cinema such as Laura Mulvey and Mary Ann Doane), the fact that a whole and important chapter of the new critical approach would be dedicated to the relations of power between the feminine and the masculine that any representation implicitly or explicitly articulates. All this is, of course, already history, but I must come back, briefly, to three basic assumptions of this approach in order to put into perspective the few pitfalls I have encountered in the practice of this kind of work by art historians.

One of these is the question of the pictorial and its theoretical status. The representation-paradigm has largely done away with – and this is most important in the field of art – the question of sexual difference. The debate now revolves around the concept of gender, which is not natural but a social and psychological construct. Gender relations are shaped by representations, which must be considered as significant social practices in their own right and not only as reflections of meaningful economic or political activities or circumstances. The relations of power articulated between gendered positions interact with other social positions such as those of class and race. This may explain the similarity in procedure between social art history and feminist art history (see Pollock 18–49), even though their specific aims are different.

For art history, then, the question of gender and representation offers possibilities that are more interesting than the occupation, pure and simple, of a territory still ruled by the enemy. It opens up for scrutiny the entire tradition of mainstream art history. It also leads to new directions in the discipline, such as the recent emphasis on reception theory: representation can no longer be conceived without its spectator, who is structurally and socially positioned by the image itself. The key word, here as in any investigation that seriously considers representation an autonomous practice, is *apparatus*, a term referring not to the content of representation but to the way it organizes itself as a meaningful system and to the way this system has evolved through time. This begs the question of the specific histories of subsystems such as that of easel painting since the Renaissance, which must be dealt with before entering into dialogue with larger historical contexts.

In the seemingly unlimited possibilities for analysis offered by representation theory, two related sets of problems have proved to be the most productive and accordingly recur with interesting variations: one has to do with the gaze; the other deals with spatial construction and relations. I will mention here one example – no doubt well known to those familiar with the literature on Impressionism and especially with the critical work of Armstrong, Lipton, Pollock, and Nochlin – in order to stress the importance of reaching that level of representation at which the apparatus is at stake and directs attention to painting's historical specificity. The question of Degas's misogyny – or at least of his problematic relations with women (he died a bachelor and is not known to have had any significant love relation) – has been widely discussed (see Broude 95–107), as have been the many unhappy couples in his family circle who figure in his pictures. He envisioned gender relations as, to say the least, nervous and tense, and made that vision manifest in his choice of narrative and thematic material. Such discussions address the content of representation and treat it as a reflection of individual idiosyncrasies that may have had a special resonance for a whole period marked by social change and deep unease about gender relations. But what is especially significant is the spatial articulation Degas gives his conflictual situations (resorting, in the beginning, to an opposition of left and right pictorial space), and the way in which this articulation exacerbates, and then contradicts, the academic mode of painterly narrative inscribed in the Davidian tradition.[12] Things get even more interesting when the tension and aggression take a ninety-degree turn and involve the relation between the spectator and the object of representation: in this case, appropriately, women's bodies.[13] Degas alludes repeatedly to a voyeuristic situation that is not without pain, since the spectator voyeur experiences in it as much frustration as pleasure. One finds in the work of Berthe Morisot the feminine counterpart of this use of private and public space and of the activity of gazing and being gazed at (see Pollock 75–9). Here, again, gender relations articulate themselves in relation to what is happening, more generally, in the narrative tradition and in the practice of perspective at this moment of rupture that constitutes the second half of the nineteenth century.

About a Few Pitfalls

This articulation is not an easy task and has its pitfalls. I would call one of those pitfalls 'psychologizing,' or the escape from within, in which a strong identification with the object of representation induces a projection of what is not necessarily there or, if there, not necessarily at the core of the picture's meaning. Take the example of Manet's *Olympia*, which, strong arguments have established, represents a prostitute addressing a customer-spectator (see Clark 259–73). But how does she address him? In a cold or calculated way, well-suited for a woman about to sell herself, or in a reserved, distant, maybe slightly scornful way intended to distance the other? The only thing that seems clear about Olympia's gaze (if that word is even appropriate) is that it cannot be accounted for by 'psychologizing' but only by taking into account, from a historical perspective, the apparatus of painting itself. Olympia's gaze breaks with two previous and opposing conventions: first, that the painted object of desire acts as if unaware of the fact of being looked at; and second, that some kind of erotic exchange is established with the viewer. *Olympia* exists in a gap between these two conventions, not so much the representation of a person but a symptom of what is happening to the apparatus of painting itself at this point in history when the whole painting, including the fact that it is a surface covered with pigments, begins to answer back to the spectator.

A second of these pitfalls I would term an escape from without. It occurs when in order to grasp more clearly, in terms of gender ideology, the particulars of this production recognized as art images, and in order to identify better the expectations and behaviour of a spectator, substantial attention is dedicated to non-art representations circulating in a given historical context. Various types of images – popular, mass produced – are especially sought as comparisons with the art document.[14] It is as if traditional iconography were submitted to a radical change of direction: from a diachronic activity which traces the circulation of a motif through time and civilizations, it becomes essentially a synchronic alignment, breaking down the barriers between fine and less-refined arts. There are sound critical justifications for this, but it is not without risks. Often this material from popular culture (such as engravings, photographs, illustrations of all types) proves much more transparent about social context than is the art document, and, therefore, more interesting for the project of articulating relations of power such as those based on gender. That is why material from popular culture is so appealing to the new critical feminist art historian. However, this exodus from the territory and specific history of art proper also entails a weakening of that grasp on the apparatus that is basic to the maintenance of its type of representation as an autonomous and meaningful act of production. And, in spite of feminist art historians' aspirations to the contrary, they may take us back again to a reflection theory.

I would describe one further pitfall as an escape through the painted image, in which the critical approach to gender and representation is not at ease with the technical and formal specificity of the medium it has to deal with. For a theory deeply attuned to historical materialism to ignore the material particulars of an image and the ways they have been transformed, through work, to produce the representation is surprising.[15] The error, in this case, can be imputed to Michel Foucault, who, according to Michel Thévoz, treated *Las Meninas* the same way the Prado does when it shows the picture through its reflection in a mirror, enhancing its masterful composition by opening up spaces, but erasing the painterly brushwork which is like a flickering presence on its surface. This pitfall is perhaps related to the fact that art history, unlike art criticism, did not really have a strong modernist moment and has not been able to develop a real critical alternative to traditional stylistic analysis.

There are, of course, interesting exceptions to this. One consists in isolating the pictorial and treating it in the context of its reception, as a sign subject to gender construction. Consider, for example, the definitions of the touch as 'feminine' or 'virile' – definitions that change depending on whether the painter is male or female and upon the historical moment (when Impressionist brushwork was still dismissed by the public, it was defined as 'womanish'; later it was seen to have a more 'masculine' character [Higonnet 121–33]). Another way of dealing with the pictorial considers it in the situation of specific works, as one strategy among many for confronting sexual politics. This issue seems unavoidable, for example, when considering Impressionist painting in general and Berthe Morisot's *oeuvre* in particular, where Griselda Pollock and Linda Nochlin have paid it particular attention. Asserting that one must recognize the working process or practice as the site of a crucial interaction between a producer and his or her materials, Pollock analyses the function of the artist's handling of paint in the context of an imagery that presents a series of fractured spaces in which the forefront (the private) stands in sharp opposition to the background (the public). Morisot's fractured spaces function to underscore the tension between the private and public by blurring the marker of separation: balcony, balustrade, veranda. The same 'soothing' and largely negative connotation of the pictorial is recognized by Nochlin in her study of Morisot's *Wet Nurse*, a painting that stages an interesting confrontation between two types of work: behind the picture frame, a woman of the lower classes assumes, for a salary, the motherly duties of the bourgeois woman in front of the easel, to enable her to dedicate time to her métier and to fuss over her expert brushwork. Again, the hyperactive pictorial surface that brings the form to the point of dissolution is treated as a kind of denial of reality, a process of 'erasure' of the tension created by a situation difficult for the painter to face. One finds here echoes of the harsh judgment already passed on modernism by social historian of art T.J. Clark, when he reproaches Manet's *Olympia* for its failure to articulate clearly the class and gender issues it tries to address. In Clark's point of view the whole project of modernism as it originated with Manet would build upon an uncritical loosening up of signifiers which would find its peak in abstraction and which is a sad counterpart of the social disengagement of arts and artists in our times. For a *professeure d'histoire de l'art du XXe siècle* like myself, familiar with a narrative of modernism that considers the deconstruction of representation and the ensuing exploration of painting's materials a critical act, Clark's assessment can create an agonizing dilemma. Is there a path to reconciliation between the two positions? Is there any redemption for pictorial activity from the perspective of feminist analysis? The negative connotations they give painterliness notwithstanding, the directions pointed to by Pollock and Nochlin seem at this point the most promising if the painterly is to be given any theoretical status in the feminist approach to representation. Every painted image ought to be considered a material production, every brushwork an investment of work as much as of desire, in a space of meaning where three 'histories' meet and interact: the personal history of the producer, the history of the social context of the production, and the history of art, understood, here, as a specific system of representation, with iconographical, formal, and technical traditions, in which singular events can produce significant changes.

This, of course, may be easier said than done, and the scarcity of reflexive work involving painterliness in the feminist discourse on art may attest to that difficulty. But the fact that painterliness has been the aspect of the art object neglected by feminist theory may also point to something more disquieting, something that has to do with art's ultimate resistance to being exhausted by any line of interpretation, not in the sense that art is a transcendent, that it rises above particular meanings, but in the sense that it is endowed, so to speak, with a certain 'thickness' of its own – of which painterliness is a symptom – an opacity that produces meaning more as a question than as a set of answers. Feminist critique, which is not only a legitimate and pertinent intellectual task, but also a just cause, in both the philosophical and the social understanding of that term, may nonetheless have a tendency to ignore or to deny this residual aspect of art, whether for practical, tactical, or ideological reasons. What it can do, however, is to remain constantly alert to its own methods and procedures, to question the way it goes about producing meaning, and to be aware of its lapses and what they might have to tell.

Notes

1 The massacre happened on 6 December 1989. According to accounts of eye-witnesses and the reconstruction of the events by the police, Marc Lépine, twenty-five, entered the Ecole Polytechnique at about 5:00 P.M. He shot three young women on the first floor and then entered a classroom, where he ordered the men and women students to separate into two groups. When nobody reacted, thinking that this was all a joke, Marc Lépine fired a shot into the ceiling. The male students quickly obeyed his orders to leave the classroom. Once the doors were closed, Marc Lépine

shot another six young women. He then made his way to the administration offices where he killed a secretary and shot four other women in a corridor before turning the rifle on himself and taking his own life.

2 One can best follow this development through the formalist criticism of Clement Greenberg and Michael Fried, whose most important essay, in this respect, remains his introduction to the catalogue *Three American Painters*.

3 The main spokesman for the challenged ideology was American critic Harold Rosenberg, who coined the term 'action painting' and who gave New York's abstract expressionism its first theoretical framework.

4 This change in perspective was noticed by Rosalind Krauss in her important article 'A View of Modernism.'

5 In the late 1960s and early 1970s more and more artists and critics began to question the political implications of formalist abstraction. One of the most revealing articles on this issue is Max Kozloff's 'American Painting during the Cold War.'

6 The text that constitutes a landmark in this debate is Linda Nochlin's 'Why Have There Been No Great Women Artists?' first published in 1971 and reprinted many times, most recently as a chapter of her book *Women, Art and Power and Other Essays*.

7 This line of questioning is particularly well developed by Lucy Lippard in her feminist essays *From the Center*.

8 Two books of considerable length explain the context in which this work was realized, its technical features, its historical sources, and its symbolic content. *The Dinner Party* comes fully equipped with its own art historical discourse. See Judy Chicago, *The Dinner Party: A Symbol of Our Heritage*, and *Embroidering Our Heritage*.

9 This was, in a way, a hasty judgment. From an ideological point of view Gloria Orenstein's inquiry presented itself as the feminist counterpart and critique of the pervasive humanism informing Panofsky's thinking. From a methodological point of view, though, it dealt mainly, as do Panofsky's iconography and iconolgy, with the figurative and thematic content of the works.

10 If motif, theme, allegory, or, in a broader sense, content were to be our theoretical meeting place, I felt in need of an argument to justify this position in post-formalist or post-structuralist terms. But the mood of the evening was more one of celebration than of conceptual analysis.

11 The most famous of these remains the exhibition Women Artists 1550–1950, organized by Ann Sutherland Harris and Linda Nochlin for the Los Angeles County Museum of Art in 1977.

12 Armstrong points to David's *Le Serment des Horace* as the model of such an opposition. Degas's *Portrait de la famille* (also known as *La Famille Belleli*

[1858–67]), *Scènes de guerre au moyen âge* (often titled wrongly *Les Malheurs de la ville d'Orléans* [1865]) and *Intérieur* (better known as *Le Viol* [1868–9]) resort to a similar structure with a kind of a vengeance. The pictures create a strong state of tension (in the last two physical violence and psychological menace are involved) between the left passive side of the picture occupied by women and the right active side occupied by men. A very special case should be made for the unfinished picture *Petites Filles spartiates provoquant les garçons* (1860–2), in which the left side becomes the aggressive with women taking the lead in the action.

13 This happens in Degas's major and more mature series of pictures, pastels and engravings involving women working or bathing. The spectator is treated as a privileged but a somewhat disappointed intruder, as the artist constantly challenges the erotic conventions of voyeuristic situations.

14 The procedure also includes works of art left out of the mainstream because they were considered of lesser significance and impact.

15 It may be objected that we have now passed beyond the traditional and strongly ideological division between genres and media with which art history has constructed its discourse in the past and which is still at the core of formalist modernism. But every image (even the more immaterial ones of film and video, which have informed much of the recent theorizing on representation) has some sort of material and technical specificity which must be taken into account.

Works Cited

Armstrong, Carol M. 'Edgar Degas and the Representation of the Female Body.' In *The Female Body in Western Culture*. Ed. Susan Rubin Suleiman. Cambridge: Harvard UP 1985, 223–42

Broude, Norma. 'Degas's "Misogyny."' *Art Bulletin* 59 (1977), 95–107

Chicago, Judy. *The Dinner Party: A Symbol of Our Heritage*. New York: Anchor 1979

– *Embroidering Our Heritage: The Dinner Party Needlework*. New York: Anchor 1980

Clark, T.J. 'Preliminaries to a Possible Treatment of *Olympia* in 1865.' In *Modern Art and Modernism: A Critical Anthology*. Ed. Francis Frascina and Charles Harrison. New York: Icon-Harper 1982, 259–73

Doane, Mary Ann. 'Woman's Stake: Filming the Female Body.' *October* 17 (1981), 23–36

Dubreuil-Blondin, Nicole. 'Number One: Towards the Construction of a Model.' In *Jackson Pollock: Questions*. Montreal: Ministère des Affaires culturelles–Musée d'art contemporain 1979, 44–66

Foucault, Michel. *Les Mots et les choses*. Paris: Gallimard 1966

Fried, Michael. Introduction. *Three American Painters*. Cambridge: Fogg Art Museum, Harvard U 1965, 3–53

Greenberg, Clement. 'After Abstract Expressionism.' In *New York Painting and Sculpture: 1940–1970*. Ed. Henry Geldzahler. New York: Dutton 1969, 360–71

– 'Modernist Painting.' In *The New Art: A Critical Anthology*. Ed. Gregory Battcock. New York: Dutton 1973, 66–77

Higonnet, Anne. 'Situation critique de la féminité.' In *La Critique d'art en France 1850-1900: actes du colloque de Clermont-Ferrand, 25, 26 et 27 mai 1987*. Ed. Jean-Paul Bouillon. n.p.: U de Saint-Etienne 1989, 121–33

Kozloff, Max. 'American Painting during the Cold War.' *Artforum* 11, no. 9 (1973), 43–54

Krauss, Rosalind. 'A View of Modernism.' *Artforum* 11, no. 1 (1972), 48–51

Lippard, Lucy R. *From the Center: Feminist Essays on Women's Art*. New York: Dutton 1976

Lipton, Eunice. *Looking into Degas: Uneasy Images of Women and Modern Life*. Berkeley: U of California P 1986

Mulvey, Laura. 'Visual Pleasure and Narrative Cinema.' *Screen* 16, no. 3 (1975), 6–18

Nochlin, Linda, ed. *Women, Art, and Power and Other Essays*. New York: Icon-Harper & Row 1988

Pollock, Griselda. *Vision and Difference: Femininity, Feminism, and Histories of Art*. London: Routledge 1988

Rosenberg, Harold. *The Tradition of the New*. New York: Horizon 1959

Thévoz, Michel. *L'Académisme et ses fantasmes: le réalisme imaginaire de Charles Gleyre*. Paris: Minuit 1980

⚬ 9 ⚬

Romance in the Forbidden Zone

MARY NYQUIST

1

Apprenticeship seems to have given way to mentorship in advanced capitalist societies. Increasingly, whether on the shop floor, in the office, or within the professions, aspiring neophytes look to self-appointed mentors for instruction and guidance. In the workplace male mentors are, of course, much more numerous than female, besides receiving greater recognition for whatever mentoring they do. Even within the domestic sphere, however, male mentorship has its own, largely unwritten, history. In gesturing towards this history, I am hoping to provide a fresh perspective on certain features of contemporary mass-produced romance. Like Prince Charming the mentor of mass-produced romance ends up awakening – and thereby regulating – the heroine's dormant female self. By means of predictable, not to say standardized, fantasy, popular romantic fiction articulates our culture's normative discourse on female development and heterosexuality. More surprisingly, a recent pro-feminist work, *Sex in the Forbidden Zone*, also reproduces this discourse, even while seeking to put an end to exploitative sexual relations between male mentors and their female protégées. As women increasingly enter the paid labour force, the opposition between private and public spheres – so central to earlier modern ideologies – begins to break down, to re-form. At the same time, whether in the medium of fantasy or of 'pop' academic analysis, female eros is represented as engaged, unknowingly, in a quest for nurturance or wholeness that ends in transgressive, heterosexual romance – transgressive precisely because the relations it grows out of are supposed to be 'professional.'

In the early modern period a variety of discourses offered bourgeois husbands the mentor's role. A new set of patriarchal relations developed as the household ceased to be the site of production, relegating woman to a sphere that represented her difference from rational, public man. The literature relating to marriage written during this period urges husbands to take responsibility for the moral and spiritual development of their wives. In complementary fashion wives are taught that it is not enough to submit to a husband's authority: instruction at his hands should be willingly sought. A wife who rebels against her husband's patriarchal right to instruct might end up isolated, feverish, and mad – or so it is suggested in the second part of Daniel Defoe's *The Family Instructor* (1718), a conduct manual that tames two insubordinate wives (Flynn 78–80). If obediently receptive, however, a wife will do honour to her husband's greater virtue and wisdom, as Lucy Hutchinson does when discussing her marital relationship in the *Memoirs of the Life of Colonel Hutchinson* (written in the mid-1640s), where she appears, with due modesty, in the third person:

> I shall passe by all the little amorous relations, which if I would take the paynes to relate, would make a true history of a more handsome management of love than the best romances describe ... There is only this to be recorded, that never was there a passion more ardent and lesse idolatrous; he loved her better than his life, with unexpressable tendernesse and kindnesse, had a most high obliging esteeme of her, yet still consider'd honour, religion, and duty above her, nor ever suffer'd the instrusion of such a dotage as should blind him from marking her imperfections; which he look'd upon with such an indulgent eie as did not abate his love and esteeme of her, while it augmented his care to blott out all those spotts which might make her appeare lesse worthy of that respect he pay'd her. And thus indeed he soone made her more equall to him than he found her ... 'Twas not her face he lov'd, her honor & her vertue were his mistresses, and these (like Pigmalian's) images of his owne making, for he polisht and gave forme to what he found with all the roughnesse of the quarrie about it; but meeting a compliant subject to his owne wise government, he found as much satisfaction as he gave. (32–3)

This account's idealism, though undoubtedly intensified by memory, is also motivated by the desire to make Colonel Hutchinson a model for other men. A good husband, Lucy Hutchinson makes clear, is a high-minded mentor whose well-moderated 'esteeme' enables his protégée to become more worthy of him. This piously ethical strain makes all the more surprising the introduction of Pygmalion. Colonel Hutchinson may be Puritan enough to want to avoid the least hint of idolatry in his love of his wife, but she is free to liken him, favourably, to the pagan artist. In this revealing comparison Hutchinson conveys her confidence that the transformative powers of male mentorship are nothing short of miraculous and yet – since it is not her face he improves – entirely virtuous, too.

 If he is to be worth his salt, a mentor should not be blind to his charge's moral 'imperfections' or 'spotts.' Ideally, physical appearance may be irrelevant, but 'spotts' are nothing if not unsightly blemishes. Unlike the romances Lucy Hutchinson mentions, Anglo-American realist fiction tends to have mentors who take up a critical stance towards the heroine. Harriet Byron, in Richardson's *Sir Charles Grandison*, is an exception of sorts, since she is not really in need of improvement. Yet so powerful is the effect of Sir Charles's excellence that even Harriet's moral sense is sharpened and refined under his influence. When he returns to England from a lengthy tour on the Continent, for example, she suddenly perceives his sisters – whom she earlier admired – in a different way; she writes that 'their brother is but lately come over: And his superior excellence, like sunshine, breaking out on a sudden, finds out, and brings to sight, those *spots* and *freckles*, that were hardly before discoverable' (375; emphasis mine). Virtually every character in this seven-volume novel is educated in some way by the supremely virtuous Sir Charles, classic realist fiction's prototypical mentor.[1] For the heroes of today's mass-produced romance, though, Sir Charles is altogether too principled and 'delicate' (sensitive to matters of punctilio and honour) to serve as a model lover. Though often, like him, upper-class, these heroes have a much rougher, less considerate style when communicating criticism. The gentility expressed by Colonel Hutchinson's 'indulgent eie' clearly is not any longer *on.* Yet today's romantic hero marks the heroine's imperfections as eagerly as does his ancestor, idealized bourgeois man. Through non-verbal signs of disapproval or words of reproof he gets the heroine to see herself in a harsher, less flattering light. This critical perspective invariably puts the heroine on the defensive, yet it also makes her feel newly vulnerable. If given dramatic play, however, the heroine's psychic defences can become her most troublesome 'spotts,' frustrating the hero's designs and marring his plot. (One recent heroine, in her mid-thirties, also worries about the 'liver spots' appearing on her hands.) In any event, male mentorship is still associated with unshakable self-confidence, the ability to note flaws, and a flair for fashioning a more womanly self. This is illustrated well by a recent Harlequin Presents, *A Most Unsuitable Wife*, whose narrator explicitly refers to the aristocratic Jason's 'continuing his role as mentor' after he has berated, instructed, and virtually taken the place of the bumbling Lorraine, trial stepmother of two just-orphaned kids (Leigh 35).

Literary male mentors are, strangely enough, descendants of the goddess Athene, who, in the opening book of the *Odyssey*, comes to give Telemachus advice in the form of an older man named Mentor. As a feature of mentorship, cross-dressing can be found in both realist and popular fiction, where mentors frequently take on the characteristics of the nurturing mother. This happens, in part, because actual mothers are most often either dead or absent, or else ineffectual (as are even substitute mothers in Jane Austen's novels). In contemporary popular romance the heroine is also usually without almost any other significant social relationships. Early on, her vulnerability is increased when she is forced to negotiate a totally unfamiliar environment, one in which the hero is entirely, and often literally, at home. Conveniently, the hero is thereby given a chance to help the heroine or to demonstrate, with varying degrees of arrogance, his superior expertise.[2]

Since he is also generally able to offer her protection – a basic patriarchal privilege – the hero may undertake an act of daring rescue, as Richardson's Sir Charles does when he rescues Harriet Byron from her abductor, the lawless libertine, Sir Hargrave. Thousands upon thousands of Sir Charles's popular descendants have done as much – with dangerous terrain, ruthless gangster-types, and even charging bulls sometimes taking the place of the sinister rival. And yet the true hero must also be able to perform the more subtle operation of psychological rescue. Though, in the early stages of romantic entanglement, it is often far from obvious, the hero of today's popular romance is ultimately, like his chivalrous forebears, eager to protect his lady's honour. But he can do so because he knows – as she either naïvely or stubbornly does not – just what it is she secretly wants. It is this knowledge of unarticulated needs – originally, in our culture, a *maternal* knowledge – that eroticizes the hero's mentorship, making him irresistibly attractive. At least, it does when integrated with the many gestures that are associated with maternal, not patriarchal, protection: the gathering of the heroine into the hero's arms; his tender holding of her; his gentle undressing of her while asleep or unconscious; the lending of his

clothes, which are, adorably, too large for her; or even his light stroking of her hair. Once the hero has begun to reveal his more nurturing
qualities, he is bound to lift the heroine up and settle her on his lap at
least once – the lap being, traditionally, an exceedingly female space.

In her influential *Reading the Romance* Janice Radway suggests that
popular romance permits the imaginary resolution of the contradictory psychic needs experienced by women who have been raised in the
family of capitalist patriarchy. For Radway, drawing on Nancy
Chodorow, the regressive features of the heroine's experience of heterosexual romance bring about a fantasized fulfilment of the never-
extinguished pre-Oedipal desire to be taken care of by, and finally to
merge with, the mother. Far from originating in female masochism,
Radway argues, 'the fairy-tale union of the hero and heroine is in reality the symbolic fulfillment of a woman's desire to realize her most
basic female self *in relation* with another. What she desires in this imaginary relationship is both the autonomy and sense of difference guaranteed by connection with someone experienced as "other" and the
erasure of boundaries and loss of singular consciousness achieved
through union with an individual indistinguishable from the self'
(155). Erasure of boundaries with an individual *actually* sharing one's
own sex is, of course, absolutely forbidden. The heterosexism perpetu-
ated by popular romance makes it appear that only strongly masculinized maleness can guarantee the heroine's experience of her lover as
'other.' Unlike Telemachus – whose Mentor is male as he is – the heroine needs a mentor who is a member of the opposite sex, although not
so opposite as to be opposed to the occasional blissful, boundary-shat-
tering union.

Before she can lose herself in this way, however, the heroine has to
act out hostility towards her destiny as a woman. Initially the heroine
strongly resists the hero's overtures, bridling whenever he tries to
move in on her. Encoded as rejection of her own femininity and sexuality, this resistance becomes heavily eroticized before it is, finally, overcome. While active, the heroine's resistance is presented as an effect of
her being either still too much a child or in some way masculinized.[3] If
she has just come out of a convent or some similarly sheltered retreat,
this of course signals that she is still almost embarrassingly undeveloped. If, as is more likely these days, she is already her own woman, she
is apt to be a secular Diana, militantly defending her autonomy. In
popular fiction career-orientation becomes a marker for deviance,
being, implicitly, a form of *sexual* orientation involving a too-controlled
need to protect the sexual-emotional self. In Silhouette Special Edi-

tions' *A Love Song and You*, Laura Remington, a judge, is called 'an ice goddess' by one of her admirers (Shaw 59). Laura's dedication to her work in juvenile court is, typically, both explained and pathologized by an emphasis on long-standing emotional deprivation, traced to her having had to take care of younger siblings after her mother's early death. Leigh Roberts's *The Wishing Pool* opens with its heroine performing ritual obeisance to Artemis, goddess of the moon, murmuring in Greek some lines of Sappho. Persis, a specialist in Indo European mythology and folklore who has just decided to return to the land, struggles to resist her feelings for fellow farmer Hugo MacAllister, who is perceptive enough to reflect 'that she was like the goddesses in myths, craving freedom, unwilling to be possessed' (78). Challenged by the heroine's love of her own independence, the hero proceeds to awaken her desire, eventually teaching her acceptance of her own vulnerability and dependency. Signs of an emergent maternal sensibility inevitably accompany this awakening, thereby reinforcing the suggestion that only love of a potent man can give birth to a woman's mature, relational self. Even if strategically necessary in the early stages of romantic involvement, defensive virginity is a stance that simply cannot be sustained by the heroine of romance, who must eventually submit, symbolically, to the phallus.

In today's popular romance the scene of instruction is focused intensely, indeed relentlessly, on sexuality. Whereas earlier the male mentor's superiority was grounded in his moral excellence and rationality, what is now required is sexual experience and charisma. As has often been noted, the hero usually has wealth, social status, height, strength, experience, and age on his side (the average age difference between hero and heroine has been calculated at twelve years [Jensen 91]). Almost always having economic power over the heroine as well, the hero generally has an aristocratic air, exudes animal energy, and is comfortable giving – if not barking – orders. But what really matters is the authority he commands when it comes to sexuality. Two of the works I have read deliberately subvert the convention that the hero be older, making the heroine his senior by a few years. But this does not really alter the conventional sexual dynamic, rooted as it is in inequality. Being older merely creates insecurity in the two women (anxiety about liver spots, for example), adding another psychological obstacle to be overcome. And being younger certainly does not stop the hero from relying on the power he derives from his sexual know-how. The man who shatters Laura Remington's defences, Dallas Jones, is a rock star about five years younger than she. Yet it is she, the high-born judge, who is infantilized the moment he comes near: 'He was only a couple of inches taller than she was, yet in matters of man-woman sophistication he dwarfed her. Laura suddenly, and with good reason, felt like a little girl peering up into his intent, experienced eyes' (Shaw 43).

2

Several superb studies have appeared over the past decade offering analyses of the economic, social, and ideological significance of popular romance. Many have observed that the rise of mass-produced fiction for an exclusively female audience coincides, roughly, with the second wave of the women's movement. For feminists there is more than an academic interest, then, in the question of what social/ideological *work* these books are performing. Teresa Ebert has recently argued that at a time when the labour demands of capitalist patriarchy have begun to undermine fixed gender distinctions, romance narratives perform the ideological function of securing and naturalizing stable, coherent gender and sexual identities. Where other critics perceive signs of liberal feminism's influence on popular romance – however contradictory the effects of this influence might be – Ebert sees an intensification of male violence and dominance acting to assert 'the patriarchal imperative to line up on one or the other side of the phallic divide at a time when masculinity and femininity are under pressure from an increasing bigenderism in capitalism' (54).[4]

Such uncompromising critique is, however, the exception. Far more prevalent is the view that popular fiction expresses real dissatisfaction with the status quo. On the basis of extensive interviews, for example, Radway argues that, for many women, the very act of reading is oppositional. When a woman with heavy responsibilities – often, of course, working the double day – curls up with her favourite romance, she is often both protesting her work conditions and claiming a right to pleasure that is her very own. Radway suggests that in addition to obtaining vicarious nurturance, women who read romance are encouraged to experience many of the fears, anxieties, and resentments they ordinarily keep in check (86–118; 140–1, passim). In *Loving with a Vengeance* Tania Modleski also analyses the ways in which Harlequins arouse anxieties and doubts, while Margaret Jensen's *Love's Sweet Return* argues that Harlequins set up stressful situations that are familiar – situations involving male violence or perhaps the difficulty of balancing work outside the home with domestic identifications – so as to provide reassuring, though imaginary, solutions. Fears or misgivings may ultimately be either contained (Radway) or neutralized (Modleski), but it is generally agreed that romantic fiction performs the potentially radicalizing function of admitting them into experience. Most feminists also want to pay respect to the utopian dimension of the fantasies romance provides. Jensen, for example, suggests that 'romance readers dream about the luxury of creative, challenging work, the luxury of being able to choose to work or not, the luxury of part-time work with flexible hours, the luxury of shared work that will bring them closer to their husbands.' 'Women who read romances,' she concludes, 'are fantasizing about freedom' (153).

As this brief summary suggests, the view that women who read popular romance are passively imbibing mass-produced false consciousness has been thoroughly exploded. By concentrating on substitutive, compensatory, or utopian features, recent readings engage sensitively with feminist issues and yet scrupulously avoid anything remotely resembling condemnation. A richer, less judgmental understanding of the needs that are satisfied by romance reading is the welcome result. I would like to argue here, however, that the attempt to be understanding can go far too far. Given enough leeway, it can aid and abet an insidious process of mystification. Racism, for example, if it is discussed at all, is mentioned in reference to Harlequin's new American Romance Series, which features 'ethnic' (publisher's term) heroines. So far as I know, there has been no serious discussion of this exceptionally realist series nor of its impact on other Harlequin lines or publishing houses. Jensen claims that contemporary Harlequins take a basically liberal attitude towards issues of race yet mentions that the vast majority of them still feature white, Anglo heroines (84). The oppressiveness of this standard deserves much more discussion, I think, as do other aspects of racism or, possibly, anti-racism as they relate to romance readership and production.

In several trips to two second-hand bookstores in my neighbourhood (racially very mixed), I have yet to discover a single popular romance picturing a heroine who is not 'white.' What I have been forced to reflect upon, though, while browsing around in these stores, is the racist genealogy of the typical hero's darkness. The hero of Bethany Campbell's *The Lost Moon Flower*, Aaron Whitewater, is proud to be half-Sioux. Yet he is represented on the cover by a very dark, half-nude man who is obviously non-native or 'white,' as are all dark heroes, so far as I have been able to determine. In Charlotte Lamb's *Compulsion*, which is set, initially, in an island in the Caribbean, it is felt necessary to distinguish clearly the white hero's darkness, an attractive 'golden bronze,' from that of the natives, which is 'like mahogany' (10). In these texts race is both constructed and manipulated by means of a complex system of signs. Within the dominant culture, when associated with racial otherness, darkness signifies passion, lust, and 'primitive' desire (in many romances, 'primitive' appears whenever things get steamy). But to work, it must be mere association, that is, in some sort of tension with the civilizing influence of 'white.'

If not, there is only lust, as appears to be the case, initially, in Sonya Pelton's *Dakota Flame*, a historical romance published by Zebra books in 1989. Purporting to be a more or less pro-native account of conflicts between the Sioux and the white army after the Minnesota Uprising of 1862, *Dakota Flame* is an almost unbelievably incoherent, racist text. The word *savage*, used in relation to the hero, Wildhawk, makes an appearance on almost every third or fourth page of this 475-page romance. The innocent but defiant heroine, Audrina, is made Wildhawk's captive, is bound to him, and is threatened with rape every time she makes a move to disobey. Not surprisingly, she gradually becomes sexually enslaved to Wildhawk, her 'shameful desire' for her savage lover being explained, in part, by the fact that she herself turns out to be part Sioux. To be fair, both hero and heroine are also tender, romantic, and given to mystical states of mind – positive qualities that, as is always the case, turn out to characterize the hero's true nature. The better to reveal this nature, Wildhawk, though a *full*-blooded Sioux, is represented on the cover as a swarthy 'white' man.

Dakota Flame, which is the only contemporary historical romance I have read, may not be typical, but it has made me very uneasy with some of the bland, neutral references to this category of romance I have come across in recent studies. In the space that remains I would like to turn to another issue that is often either skirted or trivialized: the issue of sexual violence. Feminist commentators are unanimous in rejecting a naïve mimetic reading of romance narratives. As Ebert puts it, 'the text's relation to culture is above all ideological,' in that it 'does not so much duplicate social practices as produce the representations through which we live those practices and make them intelligible' (54). As I have already suggested, however, there is no consensus about how these representations are to be read. In the most thorough-going utopian reading of popular romance that has yet been proposed, violence is virtually written out of the text altogether. In 'Romance in the Age of Electronics' Leslie Rabine argues that Harlequins represent a reaction against the depersonalization of women's experience under corporate capitalism, with its new technologies and alienating conditions of work. Rabine suggests that because women are socialized to experience a need for relationality, female readers of popular romance delight in imagining a less compartmentalized, more integrated world, where work and intimacy happily coexist. This is how she interprets a feature of Harlequins already mentioned: the heroine's frequent involvement with a man who has economic or professional power over her. That the heroine's struggle with her aggressive and demanding hero takes place in the workplace shows the intensity of the desire we have for an integrated life, in Rabine's view. 'The genius of the Harlequin Romances,' she says, 'is to combine the struggle for the recognition of feminine selfhood and the struggle to make the work world a home for that self' ('Romance' 260).[5] The heroines of romance do not merely want 'to have it all,' Rabine claims, 'they don't want it the way it is now; they want the world of labor to change so that women can find happiness there, and they want men to change so that men will just as much find *their* happiness with women' (260).

Rabine's argument, which I cannot really do justice to here, is ingenious and in many ways persuasive. Though it seems to shut the world out, romance undoubtedly enables its readers to experience safely a sense of helplessness that has layered, socio-economic depths. What is problematic, in my view, is the attempt to read these texts exclusively in terms of a utopian quest for intimacy in a transformed work-world. For if this and this only is what popular romance is supposed to be about, anything that does not fit in can either be thematized or simply rejected. Most obviously deserving of rejection, for Rabine, is Harlequin Enterprises itself, since it represents those very depersonalized, conglomerate structures against which its readers are reacting. Rejecting Harlequin Enterprises, however, involves separating an unobjectionable, indeed feminist, message from exploitative, corporate-style production. In a curiously idealist move Rabine seems to suggest that utopian content somehow actually preexists its capitalist exploitation: 'The vastly popular Harlequin Romances implicitly and potentially pose a demand for profound structural transformations of the total social world we inhabit. And like their romantic forebears, the heroines desire that this new world be not just our same old world improved, but a different, better world. The problem is that Harlequin Enterprises, having learned these secrets to a woman's heart, exploited them by turning them into marketable formulae which divorced the conflicts from their causes and cut off the path towards reflecting upon any realistic solutions' (260–1). Though Rabine's essay appears in a collection of essays claiming to advance a materialist-feminist analysis, her argument is, finally, highly anti-materialist (Newton and Rosenfelt xv–xxxix). Giving wholesale, blanket approval to the 'content' of Harlequin romances, Rabine argues that what neutralizes their challenge to patriarchy is merely form – specifically, the 'form of communication Harlequin sets up between the corporate giant and the readers' (262).

Not willing to abandon hope, Rabine ends her essay by speculating on the positive role individual authors of romances may play in challenging the needs of the corporation. What happens when the author of popular fiction becomes a heroine or, indeed, a 'star,' is exactly what Fay Weldon sets out to explore in *The Life and Loves of a She-Devil.* In this disturbing novel (which has already been made into two films) an unattractive housewife, mother, and reader-of-romance takes revenge on her husband's lover, Mary Fisher, glamorous and wealthy author of sentimental romance. By giving this revenge truly Satanic proportions, Weldon places her heroine's envy and self-hatred in dynamic opposition to the glamorization of romance authorship that now goes hand in hand with romantic fiction's idealization of marriage. Related critiques are carried out in other of Weldon's novels as well – most recently in *The Heart of the Country,* which contains statistic after statistic about the economic, social, and psychological conditions of women who have to go on living after the dream of married-happily-ever-after has ended. In the following passage Sonia, the novel's narrator, reflects not on the moment of (hetero)sexual union – the moment of regressive, perfect bliss that is the sought-for end of popular romance – but rather on its typical aftermath:

> ... how un-free any of us are, to act, be and feel the way we want. Things are offered, then snatched away. Sex with a man gives you such a stunning sense of safety. There you are, suddenly the size of two people, not one: not frightened anymore, totally loved, needed, used, valued. As long as it lasts. It's an illusion, isn't it? It stops: it presents you with perfection and then snatches it away. He rolls off and away and you're half what you suddenly perceive is your proper size, and he's back to his wife or his bank balance or his mates or whatever it is that's preoccupying him. (130)

The passage continues, in a tone more elegaic than cynical, communicating not just anti-romantic sentiments but a sense of the harsh reality of many women's early sexual experiences:

> How quickly, as young girls, you lose your rightful expectations. Your first

lover isn't likely to be loving, tender, permanent, true, is he? The statistics
are against it. It's your uncle or his best friend or your best friend's boyfriend, or you're gang-banged or taken for a laugh or so drunk you can't
even remember except you're pregnant. And it's a loss. It's a real loss.
Why is it men pay so much for the privilege of deflowering a virgin? It's
because they're getting real value for money. (130)

This is clearly the voice of experience, not just because it conveys suffering but because it also willingly, consistently names – something that
popular romance literally cannot afford to do.

3

Because it cannot, I would like to suggest that many of popular
romance's narrative strategies reproduce what is known as denial, a
social practice that our culture engages in collectively as well as individually. In a way, this is what has already been suggested by studies
emphasizing the way fears get both awakened and dispelled in
romance narratives. It has been shown that plots are constructed so as
to explain away the hero's initial indifference or violence. Behaviour
that first makes the heroine resist the hero later gets reinterpreted,
revealing him to have been, all along, a wonderful guy. For a variety of
reasons the hero's magical transformation into a man the heroine can
uninhibitedly love has received more attention than has the change
she undergoes from victim of male sexuality to desiring subject. Critical analyses have tended to be curiously present-oriented – as if readers
were basically without memories – as well as marriage-oriented – as if
husbands were the only men women have to fear.[6] The narrative discourse that allays anxieties after they have been aroused may, however,
answer an unconscious need to imagine oneself the subject, not only
the object, of desire.

When sexually harassed, physically threatened, or verbally abused,
the heroine is likely to respond in a way that expresses, indirectly, her
desire. As has often been pointed out, any anger the heroine vents
invariably titillates the hero. If, as frequently happens, his violence trig-
gers involuntary sexual response (even the slightest contact with the
hero's magnificent body sometimes does the trick), it will be accompanied by a strong sense of shame or humiliation. Generally speaking,
feelings of shame characterize the earlier stages of the hero's pursuit,
when the heroine's boundaries are being violated, often against her
stated will. The absence (or near-absence) of shame later on then sig-

nals the in-dwelling of love in her heart. Although the heroine's resistance abates as she becomes increasingly aware of her love for the hero, the very fact that she *did* once resist gives credibility to the 'consent' that she is eventually able to give.

Whenever the hero's tenderer feelings are revealed, the heroine is easily able to forgive and forget his former brutality. Dallas, for example, wanting to punish Laura, starts raping her – growling, grinding, threatening, forcing. After seeing the look on Laura's face, however, he loses his erection, or, as it is delicately put, 'his battle was lost to him.' From this moment on the threat posed by the violence just represented is denied. For this manifestation of vulnerability on Dallas's part prompts Laura to confess her love and to invite him, immediately, to make love with her. When Dallas, feeling self-contempt, later apologizes, saying he feels like a fool, Laura responds, 'you're not a fool. You're a man. I don't think I've ever understood completely what that entailed until this moment' (Shaw 166, 167). Denial here obviously performs a crucial narrative function: it signifies the triumph of romantic love and its requisite gender/sexual identities. By showing herself willing to deny the violence of rape, Laura becomes capable of a mature, womanly love that no longer knows shame, doubt, or hesitation. Her reward, naturally, is marriage with Dallas and the perfect happiness it will bring.

Together with the revelation of the hero's true self, denial enables the heroine to become the subject of her own desire. We can see this happening in Arlene James's *The Discerning Heart* (1988). Near the beginning of the action, Cheyenne, a talented young artist, takes up a job as maid for the wealthy, successful Tyler Crawford, a widower who is one of America's foremost artists. Urged to take the job by Marilyn, who has ulterior motives, Cheyenne agrees in the hope of learning something from the master. But she is also out of a job, having punched her Arts Committee employer when he made a pass at her after she had warned him not to. This detail establishes Cheyenne as feisty but also as too militantly independent and therefore immature, not developed. We soon learn that her father, who had an unpredictable temper, abused her both emotionally and physically. If the narrative is to exploit denial without too much resistance from its readers, sexual abuse obviously has to be out of the question and remains unnamed even when the hostile Marilyn, commenting on Cheyenne's 'hang-ups about men,' asks, 'What'd that father of yours do to you anyway?' (155).

Tyler Crawford, who starts pursuing Cheyenne almost as soon as she is in the house, is, of course, also her employer. What distinguishes him from her former boss and her abusive father is, in part, his generous provision of additional (paid) jobs and (unpaid) roles. Two-thirds of the way through, when Tyler has taken up the role of artistic mentor, Cheyenne is described as 'housekeeper, nanny, protégée and dear friend' (116). Cheyenne's belief that he is utterly different is just as important, though. When, unexpectedly, Tyler first touches her, she becomes paralyzed, 'her thought processes grinding to an abrupt halt.' He therefore continues touching her, pulling her towards him, at which point, 'there was a moment, just part of a moment before his mouth came down on hers, when she knew she could stop it – and didn't – and then it was too late.' When he kisses her (male sexuality, a natural force, is usually described as invading a woman's mouth or lips, which are here 'plundered'), paralysis gives way to 'a stunning clamoring, a melting and warming, a vast, deepening yearning,' and then the recognition that 'she had never even sensed that this kind of need lay buried within her. She was at once alarmed, intrigued and appalled.' When the kiss ends, she is immediately overwhelmed with shame:

> Her hand went instinctively to her mouth, and hot tears started in her eyes. She couldn't think, and she couldn't believe she had allowed this to happen, now, of all times, of all men. She'd slapped men for less, given up jobs, suffered the utmost indignation, and all she could do at this moment was tremble. (55–6)

Humiliation, however, is almost immediately displaced; when Cheyenne reproaches Tyler, he rages, silently, and then withdraws, leaving her with a devastating sense of rejection. Rejection, desire's Cinderella-like sister, is then able to motivate the important process of reinterpreting Tyler's act of sexual violence, which is soon thought of by Cheyenne as an 'unkindness' (79). Before long, continuing to feel rejected, Cheyenne persuades herself that Tyler did not *like* kissing her, and therefore cannot possibly want her the way she wants him. 'I don't know why you brought me here,' she says when he approaches her again, 'when before you were ... displeased' (105–6). In this rereading of the scene of violence, which replaces shame with insecurity, Cheyenne's victim-status is transformed into a subject-position that authors her desire.

As for Tyler Crawford, his character is eventually cleared, Cheyenne having earlier suspected him of abusing his own son (the conniving Marilyn's suggestion). As often happens when Gothic conventions are at work, the good father or husband is, in the end, not only vindicated but idealized. In the concluding paragraphs of *The Discerning Heart* Cheyenne almost outdoes Lucy Hutchinson in overvaluing her husband-to-be. Looking forward to her future, Cheyenne reflects on

> the beginning of a lifetime of love with this incredible man, who even now was making silent promises she had no doubt would be kept. They were promises from his heart, his wise, discerning, loving, forgiving heart, and she vowed to meet them, beat to beat, thrill to thrill, measure to measure until time itself ceased for them and even beyond the legacy they would leave. (187)

The novel's last words eulogize Cheyenne's mentor-lover – although in such a general way as to suit the close of almost any popular romance: 'She had known she could learn from him. She had known he could teach her. She had just never dreamed he would teach her to love' (187).

Overvaluation of a trusted authority figure, known in psychoanalytic terms as 'transference,' can easily make women vulnerable to sexual exploitation if that figure is male. So Peter Rutter argues in the work I now want to turn to, *Sex in the Forbidden Zone: When Men in Power – Therapists, Doctors, Clergy, Teachers, and Others – Betray Women's Trust.* Over the course of the last decade numerous studies have demonstrated the lasting, harmful effects of child sexual abuse, incestuous assault, and rape. 'Sex in the forbidden zone,' Rutter claims, 'is in many ways their more mainstream, but equally destructive, parallel' (64). Statistically the proportion of male victimizers to female victims is roughly the same in all areas, 96 per cent being the figure Rutter cites (20). But powerful mechanisms of denial have made it difficult to grasp the prevalence and destructiveness of forbidden-zone exploitation, Rutter says, as he sets himself the task of breaking the silence. Rutter explores the social and psychological factors that make both parties susceptible to a sexualization of their professional relationship. Men, he suggests, are encouraged by our culture either to ignore or to push against sexual boundaries, and to seek life-giving solace from women. Women, of course, are encouraged to yield. But what Rutter stresses is the vulnerability felt by a woman when the relationship that she is in is supposed to be a healing one. Resisting becomes especially hard when the man who has power over a woman offers the healing of old wounds: this causes her to long for the development of a stronger self, something he seems able and willing to provide.

The dynamics Rutter sees operating in forbidden-zone relationships are uncannily like those at work in popular romance. Although the heroine of a romance does not initially seek help from her professional superior, like her real-life sister, she ends up experiencing both a desire to heal and sexual violation. As we have seen, violation never appears as such in romantic narratives: they represent, instead, a utopian gratification of the very desires that in professional contexts are forbidden. For Rutter, who accepts and incorporates feminist discussions of sexual violence, sex in the forbidden zone is, on the contrary, always very damaging. While sharing a great deal with scenes in popular romance depicting just such inner tumult, his description of the first moment of illicit touching strongly emphasizes its harmful effects:

> When the forbidden boundary is finally dissolved by the moment of sexual touching, a woman experiences a multitude of emotions, blurred together in a disharmonious clamor. At the center of these feelings lies an overwhelming sense of danger. At the deepest level, she knows that a destructive invasion has taken place. Although it may take years, even decades, from the time of the first sexual act for her to become aware of this destructiveness, something in her knows it instantly and fills her with feelings of dread.
>
> At another level, a different danger looms: the threat of losing her connection with the man in whose presence she has come to feel some of the specialness she so deeply needs. Overwhelmed and confused by the contradiction between her fear of disappointing or enraging him and a deeper sense of being violated, she is unlikely to have the strength and clarity that it takes to deal effectively with the moment of sexual touching.
>
> The result is paralysis – of action, judgment, feeling, and voice. The cultural messages encouraging passivity, the personal wounds from her family that have shown her there is no protective boundary, the hope that someone will treat her differently all come together as an overwhelming flood at the moment the man touches her. This paralysis can last for minutes, hours, days, and sometimes years. In the meantime, the man has proceeded with his sexual scenario. (132)

As this indicates, Rutter believes that consent cannot possibly be given freely in a situation of unequal power. I have quoted at some length here, though, in order to show how similar Rutter's language is to that used in the scene discussed above from *The Discerning Heart* (itself not at all untypical), a scene in which the heroine experiences 'paralysis,' 'a stunning clamoring,' a sense of being overwhelmed, together with a painful sense of contradiction ('she'd slapped men for less, given up jobs'). At the centre of a romance heroine's feelings, however, lies not what Rutter refers to as 'an overwhelming sense of danger' but rather an overwhelming sense of awakened, unmet need ('she had never even sensed that this kind of need lay buried within her'). In romance violence does not violate but instead leads the heroine to a knowledge of her hidden, sexual self. With manly force it turns her around to face the projected end where all of her needs will be met. Set against this aspect of popular romance, the passage just quoted shows Rutter recording the experience of violation as it has been written about, in recent years, by countless female victims – now survivors – of child sexual abuse, rape, and sexual harassment. As memories return, and therapeutic space is created for the working-through of experiences of invasion, what resurfaces is the very sense of destructiveness, danger, and dread that Rutter describes.

There may, I fear, be a kind of violence involved in this bringing together of popular romance and sexual violence as lived reality. What I am hoping to get at, however, is the ideological nature of Rutter's discourse. *Sex in the Forbidden Zone* is solidly, generously pro-active. Victims are encouraged to report; the last two chapters include thoughtful advice on appropriate forbidden-zone behaviour and attitudes; and lists of national organizations to which complaints can be brought appear in an appendix. Addressed to both women and men, the text makes a special effort to overcome the resistance men might have to reading the book, deploying, towards the beginning, the occasional 'we men.' This well-intentioned, constructive intervention is seriously compromised, however, by Rutter's circulation of stereotypical, often essentialist, ideas about gender, in part the result of a Jungian framework. Like authors of popular romance, for example, Rutter tends to see male sexuality as an innate, irrepressible force. At the very least he is often comfortable with a 'boys will be boys attitude,' as in such statements as 'Many men at this point drop any pretense of rationalizing their impulses and become what, underneath the power and protection of the forbidden zone, they really are: ordinary men trying to win a woman's body in ordinary ways' (149). More telling, perhaps, is the emphasis given to a man's duty to protect the woman in his care. Rutter is aware that men enjoy patriarchal privilege, but his strategy is basically to exhort his brothers to exercise it responsibly and sensitively. 'A man in a position of power over a woman,' he states, 'holds a sacred trust to guard her welfare, guide her safely into life in the wider world, and eventually share power with her so that she can, if she wishes, leave him and go her own way' (26). To reinforce this, Rutter uses 'protégée' (meaning 'protected one') as a generic term for a woman in the care of a male professional (30). Since the term is first used of a woman in relation to her workplace mentor, Rutter indirectly turns all male professionals into mentors who, if they are responsible, can offer guidance, instruction, and healing, together with the protection built into the job.

Early on Rutter claims that women have a special 'capacity to contain sexuality completely as inner experience, and to feel passion as a carrier of nonsexual intimacy' (56). Erik Erikson's view of female inner space seems here to be given an almost spiritual dimension. Later he remarks that 'feminine compassion' is 'biologically rooted in the instinct for selfless response to an infant' (134). It is no suprise, then, to find chapter 6, 'A Guide for Women,' subtitled 'Guarding the Sexual Boundary.' The message of this chapter is that women have to learn to protect themselves from the predatory sexuality of men, who cannot see a boundary without wanting to control or challenge it. Several individual moves are taught, in addition to outright defence of the sexual boundary. The first subsection is entitled 'Recognizing the Boundary'; this is followed by 'Monitoring the Boundary'; 'Shaping the Boundary'; 'Defending the Boundary Face-to-Face' and, finally, 'Defending the Boundary from a Distance.' Under 'Monitoring the Boundary' women are advised to learn a skill that men already have. Introducing the subject to his female readers, who have trouble interpreting behaviour at the sexual boundary, Rutter says, sympathetically,

> What is maddeningly unfair is that men, whenever they are around women, see this boundary with a compelling clarity, which is one way that they exert their power. A man locates the sexual boundary between himself and a woman with an instinctual ease. Then, if he wishes, he can play with the boundary as if it were the net in an especially interesting tennis game. (164)

'The more a woman monitors the boundary,' Rutter counsels, 'the better basis she will have for judging whether a man's behavior toward her is respectful or injurious' (165).

Given the uses to which it is put, Rutter's gender bi-polarity has a lot in common with that of radical feminism, which has been sharply criticized in recent years for its ahistorical, totalizing preoccupation with sexual violence. In critiquing this aspect of *Sex in the Forbidden Zone*, I do not mean to question the importance of learning techniques of self-defence, or to suggest, in any way, that Rutter's advice might not be useful. But reading 'Guarding the Sexual Boundary,' I felt myself taking on something of the burden with which heroines of romance have to struggle. In part, this is the burden of having endlessly to monitor and interpret potentially threatening behaviour, attitudes, and moods. But equally burdensome is the unspoken law forbidding desires of one's own. For the heroine who is violated is not supposed actively to want anything – certainly not sex, but not intimacy or security, either.[7] Many taboos have been broken since the early 1970s, and heroines are now often endowed with strong, even fiercely aggressive sexual appetites. But in these texts female desire usually still has to be awakened, and by a predatory, phallic sexuality that knows, instinctively, no bounds. In both popular romance and in Rutter's study this double standard appears to have been instituted by nature itself. The result, it seems, are some all-too-familiar double binds. Though it is the mother with whom we first learn intimacy, and who remains, even in heterosexual romance, the prototypical lover, sexual relations between women are still more or less forbidden. Though our culture sets women the developmental goal of being in relation, it has also dictated that a *nice* woman will not seek this goal (nor, *a fortiori* the material benefits that marriage confers in popular romance). Further, to remain nice, a woman is to guard the sexual boundary vigilantly, which means, however, that the shame and trauma of sexual boundary-violation will inevitably be hers alone.

These and related double binds not only affect many women's lives but constitute, arguably, a major feature of our oppression (Frye 1–16). As a number of feminists have suggested in recent years, in North America violence is increasingly being used as a means of tightening and reinforcing such binds so as to prevent major, structural transformation. Yet as an analytical construct, the double bind tends to obliterate diversity. The progressive counterpart (the 'double') of patriarchy's double standard, the double bind both illuminates and negates. It exposes the contradictions of patriarchal oppression, but it also tends to suggest that all women, regardless of class, race, or sexual identification, are similarly bound. The contemporary women's movement is struggling to come to terms with difference, struggling to learn to see all issues with what Joan Kelly calls 'the doubled vision of feminist theory' (51). This vision is 'doubled' so as to be able to see, simultaneously, relations of sex/gender as well as relations of race and class. Oblivious to what cannot be reduced to gendered, hierarchical sex, both mass-produced romance and *Sex in the Forbidden Zone* by contrast use monocular, even 'tunnel,' vision to project white, middle-class, heterosexual ideals. At present, when widespread social changes are creating both creative conflict and backlash, it is not easy to imag(in)e women as centred subjects of desire much less to respect the multiple positions – historical moment, racial identity, class-position, ethnic community, geographical context – affecting the expression of that desire. In their imag(in)ings both mass-produced romance and Rutter's study register some of the contradictory pressures experienced by women trying to work through these changes. But they also present us with romantic solutions that are deeply nostalgic, solutions that are informed by and therefore propagate outmoded, white, bourgeois ideals. If male mentorship is, initially, a feature of early modern marriage, mass-produced fiction gives it new, contemporary life by offering readers the excitement of romance in the forbidden zone. True womanly happiness remains outside the forbidden zone, however – in marriage, the promise of which alone permits the heroine to let down her guard. Rutter, wisely, advises his readers to stay clear of sex in the forbidden zone. But he, too, presents us with women who conscientiously monitor desire, all the while awaiting transformation by a mentor who cares.

Notes

I want to acknowledge the very helpful comments made by the late Michael Lynch on an earlier version of this essay. I should also like to say that the essay was written three years ago, before the debates sparked by the Anita Hill–Clarence Thomas affair, the effects of which on mass-produced romance need a separate study.

1 Juliet McMaster discusses mentorship, gender, and pedagogy as it occurs in a number of novels in the realist tradition in *Jane Austen on Love*. See also my 'Female Resistance and Male Mentorship.'
2 The heroine's initially alienated condition is discussed in almost every study of popular romance. See, for example, Snitow, 264; Radway, 134–49; and Modleski 68–77.
3 Teresa Ebert discusses these alternatives, 41–3.
4 Another spirited protest is voiced by Audrey Thomas, 5–12. Ann Rosalind Jones argues that read 'symptomatically, as evidence of ideological conflict,' romantic novels 'pose important questions about writing and reading in a socio-literary climate influenced by feminism, so far, in partial and touchy ways' (294). See also Jensen, 122–39. Within a psychoanalytic and materialist

semiotic framework Valerie Walkderine argues that children's fiction inserts young girls into feminine subject-positions by providing imaginary resolutions to family-based psychic conflicts (162–84).

5 For a slightly different version of this essay, see Rabine's *Reading the Romantic Heroine*, 164–85.

6 This marriage-centrism is attributable, in part, to the pervasive influence of Joanna Russ's ground-breaking 'Somebody's Trying to Kill Me.'

7 In 'Mass Market Romance' Snitow examines this issue (274). See also Modleski, 48–56.

Works Cited

Campbell, Bethany. *The Lost Moon Flower.* Toronto: Harlequin 1989

Defoe, Daniel. *The Family Instructor: In Two Parts Relating 1. To Family Breaches, and Their Obstructing Religious Duties. 2. To the Great Mistake of Mixing the Passions in Managing and Correcting of Children.* London 1718

Ebert, Teresa. 'The Romance of Patriarchy: Ideology, Subjectivity, and Postmodern Feminist Cultural Theory.' *Cultural Critique* 10 (1988), 19–57

Flynn, Carol Houlihan. 'Defoe's Idea of Conduct: Ideological Fictions and Fictional Reality.' In *The Ideology of Conduct: Essays on Literature and the History of Sexuality.* Ed. Nancy Armstrong and Leonard Tennenhouse. New York: Methuen 1987, 73–95

Frye, Marilyn. *The Politics of Reality: Essays in Feminist Theory.* Trumansburg, NY: Crossing P 1983

Hutchinson, Lucy. *Memoirs of the Life of Colonel Hutchinson.* Ed. James Sutherland. London: Oxford UP 1973

James, Arlene. *The Discerning Heart.* New York: Silhouette 1988

Jensen, Margaret Ann. *Love's Sweet Return: The Harlequin Story.* Toronto: Woman's P 1984

Jones, Ann Rosalind. 'Mills and Boon Meets Feminism.' In *The Progress of Romance: The Politics of Popular Fiction.* Ed. Jean Radford. London: Routledge 1986

Kelly, Joan. *Women, History, and Theory: The Essays of Joan Kelly.* Chicago: U of Chicago P 1984

Lamb, Charlotte. *Compulsion.* Mills and Boon 1980; Toronto: Harlequin 1981

Leigh, Roberta. *A Most Unsuitable Wife.* Mills and Boon 1989; Toronto: Harlequin 1990

McMaster, Juliet. *Jane Austen on Love.* English Literary Studies. Victoria, BC: U of Victoria P 1978

Modleski, Tania. *Loving with a Vengeance: Mass-Produced Fantasies for Women*. London: Archon 1982

Newton, Judith, and Deborah Rosenfelt, eds. *Feminist Criticism and Social Change*. New York: Methuen 1985

Nyquist, Mary. 'Female Resistance and Male Mentorship in "The House of Mirth" and the Anglo-American Realist Tradition.' In *Critical Essays on Edith Wharton's 'The House of Mirth.'* Ed. Deborah Esch. Cambridge: Cambridge UP forthcoming

Pelton, Sonya. *Dakota Flame*. New York: Zebra 1989

Rabine, Leslie. *Reading the Romantic Heroine: Text, History, Ideology*. Ann Arbor: U of Michigan P 1985

– 'Romance in the Age of Electronics: Harlequin Enterprises.' In Newton and Rosenfelt, 249–67

Radway, Janice. *Reading the Romance: Women, Patriarchy, and Popular Literature*. Chapel Hill: U of North Carolina P 1984

Richardson, Samuel. *The History of Sir Charles Grandison*. 7 vols. London: Oxford UP 1972, Vol 2

Roberts, Leigh. *The Wishing Pool*. Toronto: Harlequin Temptation 1988

Russ, Joanna. 'Somebody's Trying to Kill Me and I Think It's My Husband: The Modern Gothic.' *Journal of Popular Culture* 6 (1973), 666–91

Rutter, Peter. *Sex in the Forbidden Zone: When Men in Power – Therapists, Doctors, Clergy, Teachers, and Others – Betray Women's Trust*. Los Angeles: Tarcher 1989

Shaw, Linda. *A Love Song and You*. New York: Silhouette 1984

Snitow, Ann Barr. 'Mass Market Romance: Pornography for Women Is Different.' In *Powers of Desire: The Politics of Sexuality*. Ed. Ann Snitow, Christine Stansell, and Sharon Thompson. New York: Monthly Review P 1983, 245–63

Thomas, Audrey. 'A Fine Romance, My Dear, This Is.' *Canadian Literature* 108 (1986), 5–12

Walkerdine, Valerie. 'Some Day My Prince Will Come: Young Girls and the Preparation for Adolescent Sexuality.' In *Gender and Generation*. Ed. Angela McRobbie and Mica Nava. London: Macmillan 1984, 162–84

Weldon, Fay. *The Heart of the Country*. Harmondsworth: Viking 1988

ᐰ 10 ᐰ

Irigaray's Notion of Sexual Morphology

ELIZABETH GROSZ

Since the translation of two of Irigaray's texts, *Speculum of the Other Woman* and *This Sex Which Is Not One*, into English in 1985, her earlier work has finally become more accessible to anglophone feminists; yet, as a result, it has also generated a good deal of controversy, even notoriety, occupying a much-contested position as the object of different feminist projections and fantasies. In these and her more recent writings she moves beyond the relatively limited and self-contained area of 'women's issues' to deal with a series of questions which seep into the very forms, structures, and founding principles of patriarchal knowledge and forms of representation. Her challenge to these systems is far-reaching, for she requires no less than a complete transformation and reorganization of representation itself, so that women may, arguably for the first time in history, be recognized and able to function as autonomous and self-defined subjects. However, her particular strategies and manoeuvres in challenging the dominance of phallocentric representational norms are frequently misunderstood, even among feminists otherwise sympathetic to her position. I propose here to explore one crucial set of concepts in Irigaray's writings – those related to what she calls 'sexual morphology' – in order to try to clarify these misinterpretations and to defend her against unwarranted criticisms.

There seem to be two broad poles of feminist readings systematically different in their interpretation of her position, particularly regarding the *status* of her concepts and the terrain on which they function. These differences lead to major disagreements regarding what might be called the 'content' of her work. On the one side there are those (such as Toril Moi, Ann Rosalind Jones, Jacqueline Rose, and many others) who read her literally and referentially, claiming that she is talking *about* women, about sexuality, about real things and events in the world – women, femininity, sexuality, pleasure, *as they really are*, before or beyond their oppressive overlay – a kind of pure and primordial femininity untainted by patriarchy. On this view there are a number of charges levelled at her work, which are by now rather tedious in their regularity and predictability: she is elitist, ahistorical, essentialist, and biologistic.

On the other side there are those (such as Carolyn Burke, Diana Fuss, and Margaret Whitford) who read Irigaray, not in terms of truth, but as a form of intertextual contestation of the (patriarchal) production of conceptions of femininity. Her writings are, in other words, *strategies*, forms of tactical struggle, in an epistemic and textual war. Her target is not 'reality' ('real women') but discourses (representations of femininity or presumptions about femininity unspoken in notions of humanity). Her goals are not truth but strategy. Where truth aspires to a universal, ahistorical, transcendental position, strategy is local and particular, formulated relative to and judged by its interrelations with current deployments of power. Strategy is avowedly historical, openly contestatory, incapable of universalization. Its status is provisional and temporary, its value determined by its effects and consequences rather than its own internal logic. As strategy Irigaray's writings do not espouse new truths to replace patriarchal falsehoods; rather, they are critical engagements with prevailing (and repressed) conceptual traditions – psychoanalysis, theology, philosophy, linguistics – aimed at their reassessment and transformation. It may be worthwhile briefly locating Irigaray's work in a theoretical and political context of other relevant feminist and non-feminist notions of the body. I would like to distinguish among three attitudes to the body in feminist theory, two of which, although apparently opposed, share the same grounds and assumptions.

In the first category we could place Simone de Beauvoir, Shulamith Firestone, Mary Wollstonecraft, liberals, humanists, even anorexics! Here the specificities of the *female* body – its particular nature and bodily cycles of maternity, menstruation, lactation, etc. – are seen as a limitation on women's access to the rights and privileges accorded to men. Women's bodies limit their capacity for equality and transcendence; they are a hindrance to be overcome, an almost biological obstacle to equal participation. Many here see a conflict between the role of mother and that of political or civic being. Insofar as a woman adopts the role of mother, her access to the public, social, and political sphere is made difficult if not impossible, and the equalization of roles of men and women becomes nonsensical. De Beauvoir and Firestone thus relish the development of new, technological means of regulating reproduction and eliminating the effect of biological processes on women's social and psychological lives.

The feminist theorists in this first category share the following notions:

1. that the body is biologically determinate;
2. that there is a distinction between the mind (which is sexually neutral) and the body (which is not, at least for women!);
3. that, for women, the body can act as a limitation or restriction on the capacity of the mind, and thus must be overcome;
4. that women's sexual oppression is a consequence of their containment within a female, or a maternal, body; and
5. that this oppression is, to some extent, biologically justified insofar as women *are* less socially, politically, and intellectually able to participate as equals to men when they bear and/or raise children.

A second category of attitudes to the body in feminist theory, opposed to the first, would probably include those of the majority of feminists, among them, Juliet Mitchell, Julia Kristeva, Michèle Barrett, Nancy Chodorow, Marxist-feminists, and those who are committed to accounts of the social construction of subjectivity. This category has a much more positive attitude to the body than the first, seeing it not as an obstacle to be neutralized and transcended so much as an object whose functioning is political and which socially marks male and female as distinct, and separates body from mind. The mind and body are again regarded as separate, but instead of being coded by a nature/culture opposition, as in the first category, they are now coded by an opposition between biology and psychology, or the realm of production/reproduction (body) and the realm of ideology (mind). While body and mind are correlated with economic/material production and ideology respectively, these cannot be straightforwardly correlated with the male/female opposition. Both men and women participate within the material and ideological realms; but within these, the positions of men and women remain sexually divided. In the material realm, for example, men function within production while women largely function within reproduction; and within the ideological sphere, women are produced as passive and feminine, and men as active and masculine.

The feminist theorists of this category share the following commitments with the first:

1. a commitment to a biologically determined, fixed, and ahistorical body;

2. a dualism of mind and body: even if mind cannot exist without body, mind is a historical, social, and cultural object while the body is not;

3. a commitment to a neutralization of the sexual specificity of the body (but, in this case, this neutralization does not occur through the intervention of artificial reproduction and the technological superceding of bodily functions; instead, theorists in this category remain committed to a program for the equalization of the sexes through the social rearrangement of child-raising and socialization).

However, the theorists of the second category can be distinguished from the first in the following ways:

1. they acknowledge that the problem is not biology *per se*, but the ways in which social systems organize biology;

2. one of their central presuppositions is the distinction between sex and gender, between what they consider is biological and what is social and/or ideological respectively;

3. they hold that if gender is social, and the mind is ideological, there is the possibility, through equal socialization and valuation, to equalize relations between the sexes, even if their bodies continue to function in sexually distinct ways.

Against both these categories we must place a third group, including Irigaray, Hélène Cixous, Mary O'Brien, Adrienne Rich, Gayatri Spivak, Moira Gatens, and a number of others. For this group the body is crucial to understanding women's psychical and social existence. It is not the biological, ahistorical, or acultural body that interests them, but the body insofar as it is lived, represented, and used in particular ways within culture. The body is interwoven with systems of meaning/signification/representation on the one hand; and systems of social coercion, legal inscription, sexual and economic exchange, etc., on the other.

This group shares the following:

1. a refusal of any mind/body dualism;

2. the conviction that the body is the political, social, and cultural object *par excellence*;

3. a commitment to fundamental differences between the sexes which demand social recognition, differences which no amount of technological innovation or ideological equalization can disavow;

4. a wariness of the sex-gender distinction. It is not clear how one could

eliminate the effects of (social) gender to see the contribution of (biological) sex. The body is not understood as a neutral screen, a biological *tabula rasa*, onto which anything, masculine or feminine, could be projected. Instead of using sex and gender as key concepts in their orientation (which amounts, for those in the second category to a concentration only on the category of gender with the claim that the category of sex is essentialist), these theorists see the body as sexually specific and, therefore, as coding the meanings projected onto it in sexually determinate ways. The femininity of the female body does not have the same meaning or function in the same way as the femininity of the male body;

5. an invocation, consequently, not of a pre-cultural, pre-social, or pre-linguistic 'pure' body, but a body interpreted through the work of Nietzsche, Freud, Marx, Lacan, Derrida, and others as a social and a discursive term, that is, bound up with the order of desire, signification, and power; and

6. the conception of the body, the female body, as the site for the struggles between patriarchs and women for the right of its control and definition. Thus, far from being an inert, passive, non-cultural, and ahistorical term, the body is the crucial term in a series of political, economic, sexual, and significatory struggles.

Irigaray raises the question of the morphology of the sexes, that is to say, the shape or meaning of the body, in her attempts to understand how women's identities become subordinated through patriarchal power relations, yet are capable of being given a different social meaning and value through women's active struggles to define and produce themselves in autonomous and positive terms. The issue of the sexed morphologies of bodies is crucial to understanding how the body as a social, cultural, and discursive object is produced yet may form a site of resistance to its social inscription. Irigaray is very careful to distinguish morphology from anatomy – something that seems to mystify a number of her feminist critics. In using this term, she is indicating a crucial locus for feminist struggles, not an acceptance of masculine and feminine characteristics as innate, immutable, outside of history. Instead, Irigaray is concerned to indicate not only how women's bodies are inscribed, constituted as lacking, but also how this representation (and psychical 'reality') serves to underpin and make possible the male evacuation of his corporeality in order to accede to the transcendental position of pure, neutral, 'human' knower. These two processes are correlates; the first is the necessary condition of the second: only if women become *the body* for men, can men be free conceptually to dispose of their bodies in this aspiration to the disembodied position of God.

In the face of a neutralizing and dichotomizing history of thought, a history which reduces *differences* to oppositions, she asserts women's right to an autonomy and independence from the definitions imposed on them by men. Her aim is not to replace patriarchal falsehoods with feminist truth. Her work is avowedly *not true*; but this does not mean it is false either. This is because it is not a description, a set of propositions, or a series of assertions of fact. Instead, it must be seen as a form of combat, a strategy for disarming phallocentric discourses in order to show what is at stake in them, what remains their unspoken debt to femininity. In short, she does not attempt to replace one inadequate or partial truth with another more encompassing, but to clear a space for women to develop their own perspectives and interests, to clear out a series of speaking positions from the male occupation of the universal in order that women may be able to speak as women:

> ... we interpret, at each 'moment,' the *specular make-up* of discourse, that is, the self-reflecting (stratifiable) organization of the subject in that discourse ...
>
> This language work would thus attempt to thwart any manipulation of discourse that would also leave discourse intact ... Its function would thus be to *cast phallocentrism, phallocratism,* loose from its moorings in order to return the masculine to its own language, leaving open the possibility of a different language. Which means that the masculine would no longer be 'everything.' That it could no longer, all by itself, define, circumvent, circumscribe, the properties of any thing and everything. (*This Sex* 80)

Irigaray's goal is to contest the philosophical assumptions, arguments, and methods which infiltrate all other knowledges as well as to show what remains unspoken and unspeakable in them, to show the debt they owe as their condition of possibility to an unrepresented femininity. Irigaray aims to

> ... interrogate *the conditions under which systematicity itself is possible*: what the coherence of the discursive utterance conceals of the conditions under which it is produced, whatever it may say about these conditions in discourse ... we have to point out how the break with material contiguity is made, how the system is put together, how the specular economy works. (*This Sex* 74–5)

Her work brings together three broad interests: first, the relations between bodies and subjectivities; second, the relations between bodies and the production/evaluation of knowledges/representations; and third, the relations between bodies and socio-economic and political power. Her focus on women's bodies, their pleasures and sexuality, and their roles in social and individual functioning must be situated in the context of phallocentric or patriarchal discourses. She develops alternatives which are designed to make those discourses less able to function as universal, value-free, objective, and true accounts.

In claiming that patriarchal power functions through discourses and representational systems, she asserts that the world, and social agents, are positioned and given meaning according to masculine interests. She posits an *isomorphism* between patriarchal discourses and male sexuality (as it is constructed in the Oedipus complex), an intricate parallelism or mirroring of dominant forms of language and dominant forms of sexuality:

> I think we must go back to the question *not of the anatomy but of the morphology* of female sex. In fact, it can be shown that all Western discourse presents a certain isomorphism with the masculine sex: the privilege of unity, form of the self, of the visible, of the specularisable, of the erection ... Now, this morphologic does not correspond to the female sex: there is not 'a' female sex ... that has been assigned to the woman can mean that she does not have 'a sex' and that her sex is not visible, or identifiable, or representable in a definite form. ('Women's Exile' 64; emphasis added)

When she claims an *isomorphism* between phallic discourse and male sexuality, she is not referring to a natural, anatomical, or biological masculinity, nor to a neutral, objective langauge. The body is always understood in terms of the organization, meaning, and capacities socio-linguistically bestowed upon it. She presumes a psychoanalytic account of the structuring of the body as meaningful, desiring body. Her notion of morphology is closely tied to, yet subversive of, Lacan's notion of the 'imaginary anatomy,' the psychical mapping of the body's (cultural and familial) meaning. Lacan's notion is itself a development of the notion of the 'corporeal schema' or 'body-image' developed by neurophysiologists in the 1920s and 1930s. The claim is that, as subjects capable of voluntary and wilful, as well as involuntary, behaviour, human subjects require a narcissistically invested body-image. The existence of such a body-image is demonstrated by the phenomenon of hysteria (in which various organs or regions of the body are capable of taking on the sexual meaning of the genitals) and in such neurological disturbances as the phantom limb (the phantom limb is a lived representation of an intact body-image, in contrast to the physiological reality of the amputation of a limb). Like Lacan's notion of the imaginary anatomy Irigaray's notion of morphology indicates a body invested by libido and significance, which infiltrates the very fibres of the body and its lived reality. Such a body is pre-eminently a cultural body: the imaginary anatomy is the effect of the transcription of parental significance onto the body of the child. This process begins, as Lacan acknowledges, in the mirror-stage. It ensures that, as human and cultural beings, we are never indifferent to the form and significance of our own bodies (or the bodies of others).

As psychoanalysis demonstrates (perhaps without meaning to), male and female bodies are always coded, gridded, made meaningful, and positioned, in the first instance, in relation to the mother's body (Freud's pre-Oedipal, and Lacan's imaginary attachment) and, in the second, to the Father's Name or the Oedipus complex. The male body is *constructed* as a phallic, virile body, and the female as a passive, castrated body, only as the result of the psychic and social meaning of sexually different bodies. The body's morphology – the body as organized, unified, intelligible, cohesive, specularizable – is the effect of the intervention of dominant discourses and their creation of human subjects as their reflections.

Patriarchal social relations differentiate male and female bodies, valorizing the former over the latter through discursive and epistemic systems which give meaning to bodies. These discourses and knowledges do not simply reflect a real body; they actively inscribe and produce these bodies with socially validated meanings. They are the objects of patriarchal struggles. Irigaray posits two major elements of female corporeality that are consistently disavowed within the history of Western philosophy: the question of maternity and the question of female sexuality. These are, of course, usually considered as equivalent within misogynistic discourses. Her point seems to be that phallocentrism is unable to accord women an autonomous sexuality, which in turn may allow the possibility of a different kind of maternity. If women are considered as autonomous sexual beings, different from men, with their own interests and perspectives, then female sexuality is unable to be categorized, as it has been in psychoanalysis and in our culture more generally, as either phallic or castrated, as either a replica of masculinity (clitoral) or its passive counterpart (vaginal). Insofar as phallocentric systems of representation rely upon but disavow such a femininity,

representing it only in relation to the masculine, the assertion of this
autonomy would have the effect of unhinging or undermining them.
There is no theoretical space in which this autonomy could be spoken
or made a principal criterion in evaluating knowledges. (Incidentally,
it is within this context, and not in the realm of biology or anatomy,
that her notion of the 'two lips' must be situated. Her goal is to show
what is at stake in dominant male representations of female sexuality
rather than to propound a new truth about femininity.)

For Irigaray the challenge is to create new kinds of knowledges and
discourses, new modes of representation; using the patriarchal materials we have inherited, to go beyond, to exceed, the boundaries and
terms of phallocentrism. These discourses, knowledges, and perspectives would subvert the dominance of phallocentric models at the same
time as they would positively reclaim the body by inscribing it with new,
self-defined values and meanings, creating a new morphology and a
quite different mode of isomorphism. This is why, I think, Irigaray
needs not just to transform the social or symbolic order, but also, to
return to and positively reinscribe the feminine imaginary, the imaginary whose repression is the condition of the symbolic. The imaginary
needs to be reconstituted insofar as it is the order in which the infant's
body-image, its imaginary anatomy or morphology, is produced:

> The rejection, the exclusion of a female imaginary certainly puts woman
> in the position of experiencing herself only fragmentarily, in the little-
> structured margins of a dominant ideology, as waste, or excess, what is left
> of a mirror invested by the (masculine) 'subject' to reflect himself, to
> copy himself. (*This Sex* 30)

Men and women are produced as such by Oedipal structures. Yet
women have less to lose in transforming the system of libidinal economy governing patriarchal (hetero)sexuality than men. A phallic economy renders women as passive, secondary, dependent, oriented to
maternity, compliant, etc. It produces women as objects of exchange,
or commerce, between a largely 'hom(m)osexual' social order of men.
It produces women as *the* body, *for* men. It thus enables male self-representations, those systems men have called philosophy, science, art, etc.,
to focus on the male self-understanding as pure mind, reason, and to
expel the corporeal, including their corporeality. This is only possible
if women (or somebody) can function as the representation of the corporeal, and moreover, can take care of and accommodate men's corporeality:

In the system of production that we know, including sexual production, men have distanced themselves from their bodies. They have used their sex, their language, their technique in order to go further and further in the construction of a world which is more and more distant from their relation in the corporeal ... It is therefore necessary for them to reassure themselves that some woman is indeed the guardian of their body for them. (*Le Corps-à-corps* 83–4; my translation)

Women's pleasure, even within patriarchal systems and models, is a 'disruptive excess' (*Le Corps-à-corps* 78). She remains in a sense uncontained by a knowledge and power that must disavow its own corporeality or materiality. The woman never definitively abandons her mother, nor does she make a sharp distinction between pre-Oedipal and Oedipal desires (as does the boy); she does not hierarchically subsume her polymorphous sexual pleasures under the domination of one organ and one pleasure. Women, their bodies, and pleasures thus exist in a double dynamic: as products of patriarchy, they are indeed socially castrated, subordinated, made passive; yet women are also excessive, plural, within one world, men's, and also another, their own, different from and resistant to men's. The sex which is 'not one' is thus not a zero or lack but always at least two, fundamentally plural, ambiguous, open-ended, always capable of bringing new meanings to the world.

I want now to draw three implications from Irigaray's work:

First, an implication of her work on morphology for men: men must learn to renounce a certain mastery and control, a unification and hierarchization under the dominance of the phallus, to remain in touch with their bodies. They have sacrificed not simply their desire for the mother, but also their corporeality and all its polymorphous pleasure, in exchange for which they gain access to the phallus. They have renounced corporeality and all pleasures 'beyond the phallus' in order to become rational, knowing subjects and to provide universal norms by which to judge all subjects. To relate to women, to be the partner of a woman, a man must decentralize, dephallicize his body and sexual relations. The phallus ensures that femininity, for a man, is largely a projection onto the other of his needs/desires. He must put himself back into the sexual relation, and put his body back into the production of a knowledge that has claimed to be disembodied, if there is to be a space made for women, both sexually and discursively.

Second, an implication for women: women's identities have hitherto been defined only in some relation to men. But for women to have

identities, and to have relations which do not subsume them and anni-
hilate them as women, they must re-examine the specific features of
the experiences they share as women: including re-evaluating the
mother-daughter relation as a woman-to-woman relation and re-
exploring the ways in which language both means and destroys meaning, both expressing and refusing to articulate women's particularity.
This means not simply adding new words to a language, but above all,
learning to hear and read in different ways, to speak in different ways,
to speak across and through other discourses. This may well mean new
modes of knowledge and new forms of criticism as well. It means that
women must begin from the corporeality they experience. This is the
starting point for both new kinds of sexual pleasure and textual representation.

Third, an implication for the role of women's bodies in the body
politic: Irigaray claims that women's bodies, parts, flesh, are
exchanged in a system of debit-credit, in which women are commodities, born 'in debt' – in debt because they are represented as incapable
of producing value/credit. Value is exacted from their flesh – castration may be translated into a form of metaphoric decapitation (mut-
ism) and symbolic 'restitution.' A woman has only her voice, her
subjectivity to forfeit, her head and her reason.

This representation of women as other or outside the borders of
culture is, for Irigaray, an effect of the role women's materiality plays in
setting up the nature/culture dichotomy. Modern political theory sets
itself up to address only the questions related to culture: that is, men's
relations to other men. This is why Irigaray considers Marx's account
of the exploitation of labour to be unsatisfactory. In Marxism, no less
than in liberalism, the motivation for the conceptual reduction of
women to wife/mother is of strategic value, since the familial sphere
and reproduction are organized outside of culture, as still somehow
part of nature.

Insofar as women's bodies are denied representation in culture,
women themselves are denied self-representation. Their function is to
be objects of exchange between men. Women thus leave the state of
nature, when they do, only as objects: 'For them [women], the transformation of the natural into the social does not take place, except to
the extent that they function as components of private property, or as
commodities' (*This Sex* 189). Women are thus representationally
restricted to three roles, all bound up with the patriarchal representation of the female body: mothers (i.e., reproducers of labour-power,
vehicles of patrilineal inheritance); virgins (i.e., as commodities or

objects of sexual exchange between men – fathers and husbands); and prostitutes (i.e., as fleshly commodities, whose sexual organs are available for hire). In short, women's bodies are not recognized as the sites of women's subjectivity, which is consequently reduced to a form of objectivity.

I would like to finish by returning to those feminists I mentioned at the beginning of this paper who claim that Irigaray's work is elitist and essentialist, and to defend her against these charges. I will take a very small sample of a number of common remarks, but these are representative of, I think, a majority of feminist theorists. Monique Plaza states this position most baldly. She argues that Irigaray attempts to return to a pre-social, naturally given notion of the body:

> To let the body speak for itself ... That is precisely the proposition that arouses our critical attention. Would not woman's specificity derive in the last instance from her body, supposed to be the natural site of sex differences? However, suggesting the body and demanding our 'difference' is already to participate in a social and oppressive system. (6)

Ann Rosalind Jones similarly argues that Irigaray's concept of difference functions to homologize and universalize women into a singular monolithic category. If women are defined by an essence conceived in biological terms, if it is by nature different from men's, then historical, economic, and socio-cultural differences between women must be ignored:

> A monolithic vision of shared female sexuality, rather than defeating phallocentrism as doctrine and practice, is more likely to blind us to our varied and immediate needs and to the specific struggles we must coordinate in other to meet them ... I wonder ... whether one libidinal voice, however nonphallocentrically defined, can speak to the economic and cultural problems of all women. (257–8)

Both these views seem to me seriously to misread Irigaray's claims, to substantialize them instead of understanding them as strategies against patriarchal discourses. As a challenge to dominant systems of discourse, Irigaray's work is an attempt to avoid precisely the kinds of universalization of which Jones accuses her – to avoid a singular truth (about women), a single path (to revolution), a single theoretical model (of women's lives, bodies, pleasures). Her object of analysis, contrary to Plaza's assertions, is not women's bodies considered natu-

ralistically, nor any essential femininity or identity. She aims to examine and challenge the effects of phallocentric systems on women's
lives, relations, and perspectives on the world. She does not valorize
women's experience, intuition, or access to a more primordial reality
or nature, but instead attempts to clear a space where women's experiences can be articulated. She attempts to theorize, to write and speak
from the position of an active, female subject, which in itself is bound
to upset a phallocentric order which authorizes only one kind of voice,
one position of articulation, and one kind of knowledge. She does not
speak about or for women, but rather, *as* a woman.

Works Cited

Barrett, Michèle. *Women's Oppression Today*. London: Verso 1980
Burke, Carolyn. 'Introduction to Luce Irigaray's "When Our Lips Speak
	Together."' *Signs* 6, no. 1 (1980), 66–8
– 'Irigaray through the Looking Glass.' *Feminist Studies* 7, no. 2 (1981), 288–
	306
– 'Report from Paris.' *Signs* 3, no. 4 (1978), 843–55
– 'Romancing the Philosophers: Luce Irigaray.' *Minnesota Review* 29 (1987),
	103–14
Chodorow, Nancy. 'Gender, Relation and Difference in Psychoanalytic Per-
	spective.' In *The Future of Difference*. Ed. Hester Eisenstein and Alice Jardine.
	Boston: Hall 1980, 3–19
Fuss, Diana. *Essentially Speaking: Feminism, Nature and Difference*. London: Rout-
	ledge 1990
Gallop, Jane. *Feminism and Psychoanalysis: The Daughter's Seduction*. London:
	Macmillan 1982
Gatens, Moira. 'A Critique of the Sex/Gender Distinction.' In *Beyond Marxism?
	Interventions after Marx*. Ed. Judith Allen and Paul Patton. Sydney: Interven-
	tion Press 1983, 143–60
Grosz, Elizabeth. *Sexual Subversions: Three French Feminists*. Sydney: Allen 1989
Irigaray, Luce. *Le Corps-à-corps avec la mère*. Montréal: Pleine Lune 1981
– *Speculum of the Other Woman*. Trans. Gillian C. Gill. Ithaca: Cornell UP 1985
– *This Sex Which Is Not One*. Trans. Catherine Porter with Carolyn Burke. Ith-
	aca: Cornell UP 1985
– 'Women's Exile.' *Ideology and Consciousness* 1 (1977), 62–76
Jones, Ann Rosalind. 'Writing the Body: Toward an Understanding of *L'Ecriture
	Feminine*.' *Feminist Studies* 7, no. 2 (1981), 247–63
Kristeva, Julia. *Desire in Language: A Semiotic Approach to Literature and Art*. Ed.

Leon S. Roudiez. Trans. Thomas Gora, Alice Jardine, and Leon S. Roudiez. Oxford: Basil Blackwell 1980
– *Powers of Horror. An Essay on Abjection.* Trans. Leon Roudiez. New York: Columbia UP 1982
– *The Revolution in Poetic Language.* Trans. Margaret Waller. New York: Columbia UP 1984
Lacan, Jacques. 'The Mirror Stage (as Formative of the Function of the I as Revealed in Psychoanalytic Experience).' In his *Écrits: A Selection.* Trans. Alan Sheridan. London: Tavistock 1977, 1–8
Mitchell, Juliet. *Psychoanalysis and Feminism.* London: Allen Lane 1974
Moi, Toril. *Sexual/Textual Politics: Feminist Literary Theory.* London: Methuen 1985
Plaza, Monique. '"Phallomorphic Power" and the Psychology of "Woman."' *Ideology and Consciousness* 4 (1978), 5-36
Rose, Jacqueline. *Sexuality in the Field of Vision.* London: Verso 1986
Spivak, Gayatri Chakravorty. *In Other Worlds: Essays in Cultural Politics.* London: Methuen 1987
Whitford, Margaret. 'Luce Irigaray and the Female Imaginary: Speaking as a Woman.' *Radical Philosophy* 44 (1986), 3–8
– 'Luce Irigaray: The Problem of Feminist Theory.' *Paragraph* 8 (1986), 102-5

11

Lesbianizing Love's Body: Interventionist Imag(in)ings of Monique Wittig

DIANNE CHISHOLM

For nearly two decades feminist poets, critics, and semioticians have sought to intervene in literary culture's representation of women, marking their efforts with such textual productions as the anthology of counter-(re)presentations *The Female Body in Western Culture* and the revolutionary poetics known as 'writing the body' (Jones 247–63). Drawing from political semiology, materialist literary histories, and radical psychoanalysis, feminist inquiry has sought to analyse, expose, and demystify the textual apparatus that contributes to the production and reproduction of a pornographic society. Feminism has not stopped at disclosure and deconstruction but has itself entered into production by appropriating and redeploying canonical figures, and by engendering alternative imag(in)ings. Monique Wittig's corpus of writing spans these two decades and takes feminist semiotics even further. She (re)writes the body physical and the body politic in the name of *the lesbian body*, calling into question the 'ambiguity' of the signifier 'feminism':

> What does 'feminist' mean? Feminist is formed with the word 'femme,' 'woman,' and means: someone who fights for women. For many of us it means someone who fights for women as a class and for the disappearance of this class. For many others it means someone who fights for woman and her defense – for the myth [that 'woman is wonderful'], then, and its reenforcement. But why was the term 'feminist' chosen if it retains the least ambiguity? ... Lesbian is the only concept I know of which

is beyond the categories of sex (woman and man), because the desig-
nated subject (lesbian) is *not* a woman, either economically, or politically,
or ideologically. ('One Is Not' 50, 53)

In Wittig's fiction as in her criticism 'lesbian' signifies a counter-attack
on the categorical thinking that she calls 'heterosexuality,' which, as
she sees it, is the prime oppressor of women's self-conception and
existence as a *body.*

Wittig's most celebrated works, *Les Guérillères* and *The Lesbian Body,*
display a transvaluation of values that have historically hierarchized
bodily categories. In *The Lesbian Body* there are eleven pages, approximately one for every dozen pages of regular print, that feature blocks
of names of the female body in bold capital letters. These pages serve
as title pages that foreground or 'lay bare' the defamiliarizing morphology of Wittig's *textual* body. They also parody the illustrated texts
of anatomy and pornography that exhibit and/or exploit the female
body as a category of sex. Anatomical textbooks figure the male body –
male skeletal structure and musculature – as the universal body onto
which pages of transparencies with the visceral details and female parts
may be superimposed. In radical contrast *The Lesbian Body* emblazons
the names of all the parts of the female body – the bones, the nerves,
the muscles, the veins and arteries, the sense organs, the reproductive
organs – in solid black print on opaque, blank pages. The names are
organized with little respect for the classical androcentrism – or what
Luce Irigaray would call the 'phallomorphology' – of anatomical tax-
onomy: functions and motions, affects and sensations, are listed side by
side with parts of the central nervous system or the large muscle bodies, and vulvular bodies are named in detail and abundance as all part
of the *basic, body model.* Unlike the centrefolds of pornographic magazines that figure female bodies so as to solicit a penetrating, colonizing
gaze, *The Lesbian Body* names rather than illustrates bodies, a-voiding
specularization and displacing the heterosexual field of vision. Instead
of representing the female body *as a (w)hole,* Wittig presents a barrage
of names of bodily functions and features that, while they recategorize
anatomy, do not compose a picture. While the female body is all there,
it is not organized around the genitals. The lesbian body is not exclusively or specifically sexual, and its anatomized, verbal figure presents
no specular object for imaginary manipulation, penetration, or mutila-
tion.

Les Guérillères employs a similar heraldic device, emblazoning twenty-
nine pages in three-page intervals with block lists of names of amazon

warriors. While most of these names refer to goddesses and heroines of world (First, Second, *and* Third World) literature, several of them are lesbianized versions of classical masculine names – 'Maximilliana,' 'Benjamina,' 'Petronilla' – and some, like 'Calamita,' are classicalized appropriations of such misogynous Old World names as 'Calamity,' suggesting the harbinger of a new (dis)order. Furthermore the names refer to the lesbian warriors, *les guérillères*, a proper name that is itself a lesbianizing and pluralizing of the masculine noun *guérrier* (the two *ll*'s deriving from the *ll*'s of *elles*). Displayed on these title pages like banners or coats of arms (and literally as forms of *mise en abyme*), these names enlist a large body of members to form a phalanx or corps – a lesbian corps or *corps lesbien* – a mobilized lesbian body *politic* that militates against phallomorphic representation.

Wittig may be the first to reclaim the female body from Western culture for a radical, lesbian feminism, but she is not, of course, the first to figure an equivalence between the body physical and the body political. Plato's *Republic* allegorizes this equivalence in the process of developing an ideal concept of the state.[1] The classical Greeks supply the metaphorical groundwork for future attempts to conceptualize and idealize political organization. It becomes natural for Western metaphysicians and political theorists to think of government in terms of this Platonic body, a unified body, with a dominant part, or a hierarchy of body parts, organized to serve the needs of all members. Conversely it becomes necessary to rethink or re-imag(in)e the body in order to initiate political revolution. In the wake of a century of political revolutions, radical movements of the twentieth century concentrate their critique on the rhetoric of this Platonic body and all those discourses and practices that think about bodies and body politics in terms of unity, hierarchy, dominance, superior parts.

Love's Body Politic(s)

One of the twentieth century's most celebrated attacks on this philosophically and historically idealized Body Politic is Norman O. Brown's *Love's Body*. Brown launches a critique of the entire rhetorical and conceptual history of the body politic in Western civilization, attacking chiefly feudal and bourgeois conceptions of political organization. Brown makes it abundantly clear that 'metapolitics is not metaphysics ... but a physiology of politics. Or a politics of physiology' (225) and that any Western state, however democratically conceived, is in actuality a *phallocracy* constituted by corporate (castrated, fraternal) bodies unified and mobilized by the sovereign desires of a (phallic, paternal) head of state. Quoting a key passage from *Leviathan*, 'The Soveraign is the publique Soule, giving Life and Motion to the Commonwealth,' in which Hobbes equates the dominant part of a man's body (the 'Prime Mover' [128]) with that of the body politic, Brown concludes that 'the tyranny of the genital, the soul, and the state, is one tyranny' (129).

Having so exposed Western government for the political organization it truly embodies – a tyranny, a monarchy, a phallocracy – Brown calls for a revolutionary refiguring of the body in whose image a new body politic could be constructed. He draws inspiration from Blake – 'Man Makes Himself, his own body; his image of the body; the Eternal Body of Man is the Imagination' (127) – and he believes that by re-imag(in)ing the body, world order can be truly liberated, democratized. The means of revolution, then, is poetic symbolism, a polymorphous symbolism that undermines the centralized 'body' of metaphysical/metapolitical discourse: 'Freedom is poetry, taking liberties with words, breaking the rules of normal speech, violating common sense ... a pagan orgy: a Bacchanalian revel of categories ... a proliferation of images, in excess' (244–8).

What *Love's Body* and *The Lesbian Body* have in common is precisely this materialist strategy of a counter-poetics, its 'revel of categories,' its 'proliferation of images, in excess,' its polymorphous symbolism. If we look again at those pages on which are emblazoned the names of lesbian guerillas and the names of the lesbian body, we find no head, no phallus, in fact no supreme body member that represents or that organizes and mobilizes the whole corps/corpus. If we look more closely at these pages of *The Lesbian Body*, we indeed see a 'revel of categories,' including a pagan orgy of neologisms whose polymorphous semiology aims to undermine the categorical rigidity of classical physiology. Alongside familiar bodily categories such as the digestive tract, the central nervous system, and the circulatory system, are listed such previously unclassified bodily categories as

THE NUTRITION THE ELIMINATION THE DEFAECATION THE REPRODUCTION [XX + XX = XX] THE REACTIONS PLEASURE ... THE CRIES THE WAILINGS THE MURMURS THE HOARSENESS THE SOBS THE SHRIEKS THE VOCIFERATIONS THE WORDS THE SILENCES THE WHISPERINGS THE MODULATIONS THE SONGS THE STRIDENCIES THE LAUGHS THE VOCAL OUTBURSTS THE LOCOMOTION. (128)

Included among the names of muscle groups such as the abductors and the adductors we find 'THE SYNERGISTS THE ANTAGONISTS ... THE ACCESSO-

RIES THE RECTI THE OBLIQUES THE ORBICULARS' (88). Included among the names of articulating joints such as the knees, the wrists, the ankles, and the elbows are 'THE GAIT THE WRITHING THE RUNNING THE LEAPS THE BOUNDS THE RETREATS THE GESTICULATION THE TREMORS THE CONVULSIONS ... THE GRIPPING ... THE EMBRACES' and 'THE TENDONS OF ACHILLEA' (141, 101). In the cutaneous category there are 'THE AREOLAS ... THE WOUNDS THE FOLDS THE GRAZES THE WRINKLES ...THE SWELLINGS THE SUNBURN THE BEAUTY SPOTS' (53). Among the names of major arteries like the aorta and the carotid are 'THE MAMMARY ...THE COAGULATIONS THE CLOTTING THE CONCRETIONS ... THE SOLIDIFICATIONS' (76). Together these previously unnamed parts add up to the unhierarchical, uncategorizable, heterogeneous lesbian body. Wittig's polymorphous symbolism imag(in)es a wholly other libidinal and political economy.

The primary difference between *Love's Body* and *The Lesbian Body* concerns gender. Despite his description of the state as phallocentric Brown's polymorphism applies chiefly or exclusively to the (sexual) liberation of male members of the common body. Brown translates 'polymorphous perversity, pansexualism' as 'penises everywhere' (250), and when he calls for a radical freedom of speech, what he has in mind is the unleashing of the male speakers' 'unruly member': 'Speech resexualized. Sexual potency, linguistic power, abolished at Babel and restored at Pentecost. At Pentecost, tongues of fire, a flame in the shape of a male member. Speaking with tongues is fiery speech, speech as a sexual act, a firebird or phoenix' (251). Despite his description of 'politics as gang bang' (15) and of the state as a delinquent institution that is founded by the military banding of brothers under the incest taboo for the purpose of rape and conducted in such a way as to establish violence against women as a public institution (15), Brown insists that it is the male member that is in most need of liberation. Against a politics of rape he advocates the free mobilization and deterritorialization of male sexuality – 'penises everywhere,' plugging into other bodies, engaging in free sex in a hom(m)osexual free-for-all.

Since Wittig's lesbian semiology embodies a hitherto wholly unrepresented category of the body politic – the body of female members – it reads as that much more revolutionary than *Love's Body*. To some extent Wittig follows Brown's polymorphous strategy: in the lesbian universe of *Les Guérillères* she inscribes vulvas everywhere in voluptuous detail (10, 19, 22–3, 31, 44, 45, 48, 61). But this is only an initial, self-conscious tactic in Wittig's war against genital/gender tyranny. Once her *guérillères* have found strength in numbers, they abandon their vulvular symbolism (72). In *The Lesbian Body* there is a noticeable lack of such symbolism; this is because every body member or body motion is literally embodied in the metaphorical and metamorphic language of vulvular (and ovarian) morphology. All the organs, muscles, limbs, arteries, senses, feelings, motions, emotions, functions, and features of love's lesbian body are vulvular or ovarian bodies, characterized by dilation and contraction, elasticity, viscosity, fluidity, excitation, vibration, erection, invagination, penetration, fecundation, cyclical fluctuation, periodic destruction, and regeneration. So all-encompassing is the lesbian body that it includes the language of phallic morphology as well, absorbing and dissolving categories of sexual difference. Wittig frees the body of 'genital tyranny,' not by such idealizing symbolic practices as de-sexualization, sublimation, or 'hom(m)osexualization' (making the masculine the universal sex), but by the reverse tactic of lesbianizing symbolic polymorphism; one could say that *The Lesbian Body* lesbianizes *Love's Body*, that the former encompasses the revolutionary semiology of the latter in an even greater erotic totality.

Anti-body and 'War Machine'

Wittig employs a lesbian feminist perspective to re-imag(in)e the body (politic), but she does not champion 'lesbian writing' or a lesbian *écriture feminine*.

> That there is no 'feminine writing' must be said at the outset ... What is this 'feminine' in 'feminine writing'? It stands for Woman, thus merging a practice with a myth, the myth of Woman ... 'Feminine writing' is the naturalizing metaphor of the brutal political fact of the domination of women, and as such it enlarges the apparatus under which 'femininity' presents itself: that is, Difference, Specificity, Female Body/Nature ... Since the words 'writing' and 'feminine' are combined ... to designate a sort of biological production peculiar to 'Woman,' a secretion natural to 'Woman' ... 'feminine writing' amounts to saying that women do not belong to history, and that writing is not a material production. ('Point of View' 63)[2]

We must therefore distinguish Wittig from those feminists who propose to *write the female body* or from critics who champion a specifically female form of writing, which, for Wittig, could only be a form of self-mystifying biologism that despite intentions reinforces patriarchal structures. We must also distinguish her from those who write under the aegis of the 'lesbian continuum,' which extends its cause against 'compulsory heterosexuality' to include all women-identified women.[3] Just as Wittig's 'lesbian' is not a 'woman,' so her lesbian body is not a female body; instead, the lesbian body signifies a categorical resistance to the 'myth of Woman' and withdraws support from any critical venture that would recuperate the sign of 'woman': in short, *the lesbian body is an anti-body*.

Wittig launches her lesbian anti-body at 'the straight mind,' her term for the apolitical, ahistorical, essentially heterosexual theorizing of structural anthropology, sociology, and psychoanalysis (from which writing-the-body feminists derive their [post]structuralist thinking):

> In spite of the historic advent of the lesbian, feminist, and gay liberation movements, whose proceedings have already upset ... philosophical and political categories ... [these] categories ... are nevertheless utilized without examination by contemporary science. They function like primitive concepts in a conglomerate of all kinds of disciplines, theories, and current ideas that I will call the straight mind ... Thus one speaks of *the* exchange of women, *the* difference between the sexes, *the* symbolic order, *the* Unconscious, desire, *jouissance*, culture, history, giving an absolute meaning to these concepts when they are only categories founded upon heterosexuality or thought which produces the difference between the sexes as a political and philosophical dogma. ('Straight Mind' 106–7)

Against this dominant frame of mind Wittig launches a bodily textuality that calls attention to the polysemy and plasticity of its verbal materials,[4] and a lesbian practice that is as historical and political as it is deconstructive: 'a political semiology' that can 'work also at the level of language/manifesto, of language/action ... which transforms ... makes history' ('Straight Mind' 110). Accordingly the lesbian perspective falls outside the structuralist totality and is able to act as historical agency ('Straight Mind' 110).[5]

Thus dedicated to subverting structuralism, Wittig would appear to share a common purpose with Jane Rule, who in her preface to *Lesbian Images* criticizes the reductiveness of the social sciences. But while Rule places faith in 'the reality of lesbian experience to transcend all theories about it,' Wittig emphasizes 'textual reality' as transformative material and technology.[6] To write with political effect entails accordingly the universalization of the lesbian point of view.[7] Against structuralism's 'totalizing' interpretation of the body politic Wittig advocates a 'total war' ('Mark of Gender' 70) and the appropriation and redeployment of world literary forms. Only by (cl)aiming and remaking the can(n)on, only by transforming world literature, will writing alter society's and history's conception of the world:

> one must ... know that being gay ... is not enough ... The universalization of each point of view demands a particular attention to the formal elements that can be open to history, such as themes, subjects of narratives, as well as the global form of the work. It is the attempted universalization of the point of view that turns or does not turn a literary work into a war machine. ('Trojan Horse' 49)[8]

Les Guérillères demonstrates precisely this subversive formal process of universalizing a lesbian point of view by appropriating and redeploying classical literature, making its textual body into a war machine designed to 'pulverize the old forms and formal conventions' ('Trojan Horse' 45). *Les Guérillères* narrates the epic tale of a lesbian people who separate from patriarchal society, arm themselves with 'feminaries' – little books, little war machines, inscribed with Sapphic lyrics, lesbian mythologies, bestiaries, and vulvular iconography (14–15, 31, 44, 49)[9] – and who mobilize armies, launch a holocaust, destroy all surviving patriarchs, and absorb the total converts. A primary strategy of universalization is gender: in the French text *elles* replaces the conventional first person singular of epic narration that speaks traditionally from the position of the universal, masculine subject.[10]

Another primary strategy is the figuring of all bodies, including warring bodies, as vulvular or ovarian bodies, charged with lesbian eroticism. Lesbian armies have names – 'the Ophidian women the Odonates the Oogones the Odoacres the Olynthians the Ooliths the Omphales' (*Guérillères* 103) – that echo the names of gynaemorphology – oocytes, ovules, ovaries – and a primary tactic that is to spread out in all directions in an ever-widening circle like a dilating, invaginating body, and a 'most formidable weapon,' the lasso- or bololike 'ospah,' that encircles its enemies in an odorous poisonous ring (103–4).

Everything in the text begins and ends with 'O,' the universal symbol of *les guérillères*. It is also the structuring figure or 'global form' of the text, since the chronicle begins after the war and works back to the beginning in circular fashion: 'the chronological beginning of the narrative – that is, the total war – found itself in the third part of the book, and the textual beginning was in fact the end of the narrative. From there comes the circular form of the book, its *gesta*, which the geometrical form of a circle indicates as a *modus operandi*' ('Mark of Gender' 70).

The *Grotesque* Lesbian Body

It should now be clear that Wittig's 'lesbian body' does not represent a real, physical, or political body; it does not imag(in)e lesbian persons nor even lesbian erotic experience. Rather, it *acts* as a body-metaphor: a *catachresis*, a metaphor without a literal referent that serves to conceptualize a radically different body/body politic, to think beyond representations of the conventional, naturalized body. But that is not all: this 'lesbian body' is at once an inauguration of thought *and* a critique of form, a catachresis *and* a parody. A doubly subversive body, Wittig's *corps lesbien* launches an assault on canonical literature with a body of textual interventions. According to Wittig, political and historical discourse address society in terms of the 'people' who constitute it, while poetry embodies society in 'forms' that constitute and reconstitute literary and cultural history ('Trojan Horse' 46). Thus to effect political and historical change, the writer must *transform* literary history.

For Wittig writing lesbian parody is an act of historical materialism. It is not therefore surprising that she regards the canon of world literature, and not the corpus of lesbian writing – the marginal literature of *Lesbian Images* – as primary material: 'The first element at hand then for a writer is the huge body of works, past and present' ('Trojan Horse' 46). What I would like to argue at this point and attempt to demonstrate for the rest of this paper is that the lesbian body is a *grotesque* parody of canonical formations of the body (politic), that Wittig inscribes her *Lesbian Body* in the image of the carnivalesque or grotesque body of medieval and Renaissance world literature.

Consider the opening passage from *The Lesbian Body*, which alerts woman-identified readers to its radical departure from the universe of romantic and feminine forms before de-composing and displacing this universe altogether:

> In this dark adored adorned gehenna say your farewells m/y very beautiful one m/y very strong one m/y very indomitable one m/y very learned one m/y very ferocious one m/y very gentle one m/y best beloved to what they, the women, call affection tenderness or gracious abandon ... But you know that not one will be able to bear seeing you with eyes turned up lids cut off your yellow smoking intestines spread in the hollow of your hands your tongue spat from your mouth long green strings of your bile flowing over your breasts, not one will be able to bear your low

frenetic insistent laughter. The gleam of your teeth your joy your sorrow the hidden life of your viscera your blood your arteries your veins your hollow habitations your organs your nerves their rupture their spurting forth death slow decomposition stench being devoured by worms your open skull, all will be equally unbearable to her. (15)

Consider another passage from *The Lesbian Body*:

Your hand followed by your arm have entered into m/y throat, you traverse m/y larynx, you arrive at m/y lungs, you itemize m/y organs, you make m/e die ten thousand deaths while *I* smile, you rip out m/y stomach, you tear m/y intestines, you project the uttermost fury into m/y body, *I* cry out but not from pain, *I* am overtaken seized hold of, *I* go over to you entirely, *I* explode the small units of my ego, *I* am threatened, *I* am desired by you. A tree shoots in m/y body, it moves its branches with extreme violence with extreme gentleness ... *I* am inhabited, *I* am not dreaming, *I* am penetrated by you, now *I* must struggle against bursting to retain m/y overall perception, *I* reassemble you in all m/y organs, *I* burst ... finally *I* am without depth without place m/y stomach appearing between m/y breasts m/y lungs traversing the skin of m/y back. (98)

This exemplary passage features the bodily disembowelling and reassembly that proceeds in all of the 109 prose poems of Wittig's 165-page text. One critic refers to these prose poems as a 'Sapphic Song of Songs,' noting her failure to reconcile what feminist readers see as repulsive violence with a lesbian hymn to joy.[11] Wittig's lesbian bodies engage in more than just a 'Bacchanalian revel of categories' (Brown 248); they enact a *grotesque* polymorphous perversity that destroys anatomical and psychological integrity, that dissolves conscious intention while violently arousing the senses, that traverses the boundary between interior and exterior, that annihilates specular distance between '*I*' and 'you' and collapses the object of the desiring gaze. The lyrical speaking subject is so totally penetrated by and opened to the other as to make a doubly embodied, coupled subject – hence the split 'm/y,' signifying pronominal excess.[12] Lesbian body language literally mutilates the idealizing, specularizing, objectivizing 'I love you' of conventional heterosexual lovers' discourse. An eviscerating lesbian eroticism shatters any illusion of Platonic love or aesthetic sublimation.

The Lesbian Body supplements the sort of symbolic polymorphism we find in *Love's Body* with the 'grotesque realism' of past world literature that strongly suggests the genre recently recovered and theorized by Mikhail Bakhtin. My argument is not one of influence; Wittig never mentions Brown, and though she acknowledges Bakhtin as one of the only literary linguists to take a 'strictly materialist approach to language' ('Mark of Gender' 65), she does not explicitly refer to his theories of carnival. His celebrated *Rabelais and His World* first appeared in 1965 (in English in 1968) and enjoyed widespread popularity in French theoretical circles (mostly through the interpretive mediation of Julia Kristeva) during and after the student and leftist unrest of the late-1960s. Writing *Les Guérillères* and *The Lesbian Body* in the wake of that carnival, Wittig could not have failed to have been influenced by Bakhtin. Nonetheless, I read the points of intersection as a productive intertextuality that Wittig may or may not have intended. I will proceed with a close comparative reading of *Rabelais* and *The Lesbian Body* to show how a body politic(s) is formalistically engendered.

According to Bakhtin, the Romantics who discovered Rabelais were repulsed and are still repulsed by him because of their unfamiliarity with the folk tradition out of which he writes (3). 'Rabelais' images,' Bakhtin explains, 'are completely at home within the thousand-year-old development of popular culture' (3). His instructive warning to the readers of Rabelais could also apply to the feminist readers of *The Lesbian Body.* In order to appreciate Wittig's images without repulsion, one could read them as Bakhtin reads Rabelais, who, to be understood, 'requires an essential reconstruction of our entire artistic and ideological perception, the renunciation of many deeply rooted demands of literary taste ... the revision of many concepts [and] above all ... an exploration in depth of a sphere as yet little and superficially studied, the tradition of folk humor' (3).

The body politic that inhabits Rabelais's carnival world is, according to Bakhtin, a supremely subversive body, shown to possess both the semiotic and the libidinal power to transform the existing order. In medieval carnival, life and art interact in one vast spectacle (7), casting a 'second life of the people, who for a time entered the utopian realm of community, freedom, equality, and abundance' (9). In contrast, the feudal and ecclesiastic orders possess none of this transformative power: 'On the contrary, they sanctioned the existing pattern of things and reinforced it' (9). Carnival images constitute their own realism, as distinct from feudal realism, and also from the later, bourgeois realism. In grotesque realism Bakhtin tells us,

the bodily element is deeply positive. It is presented not in a private, egotistic form, severed from the other spheres of life, but as something universal ... The leading themes of these images of bodily life are fertility, growth, and a brimming-over abundance. Manifestations of this life refer not to the isolated biological individual, not to the private, egotistic 'economic man,' but to the collective ancestral body of all the people. Abundance and the all-people's element also determine the gay and festive character of all images of bodily life ... (19)

A carnival world prevails in gay abundance in both *Les Guérillères* and *The Lesbian Body*, the former being especially rich in images of the market-place, fêtes, games, spectacles, parades, saturnalias, drunken orgies, cannibalistic feasts, and all-out carnage. In *Les Guérillères* carnival constitutes a wholly new world that overcomes and forever transforms the old, patriarchal world. *The Lesbian Body* displays a positive, bodily principle, specifically in the act of love-making, which is always imaged as a festive event between two or many more people.

Bakhtin describes the body of carnival not so much against the body politic of feudalism as against a classical or Romantic aesthetic. He contends that after the outbreak of carnival in the Middle Ages and its full-blown expression in the Renaissance, a 'new bodily canon' takes shape. The bourgeois bodily canon

presents an entirely finished, completed, strictly limited body, which is shown from the outside as something individual. That which protrudes, bulges, sprouts, or branches off ... is eliminated, hidden, or moderated. All orifices of the body are closed. The basis of the image is the individual, strictly limited mass, the impenetrable façade. The opaque surface and the body's 'valleys' acquire an essential meaning as the border of a closed individuality that does not merge with other bodies and with the world ... In the new canon ... there is no symbolic, broad meaning whatever in the organs of this body ... sexual life, eating, drinking, and defecation have radically changed their meaning: they have been transferred to the private and psychological level where their connotation becomes narrow and specific, torn away from the direct relation to the life of society and to the cosmic whole. (320–1)

The Lesbian Body parodies this individualized, internalized, sealed-off body:

I am an integral body blocked off from itself, *I* do not hear m/y blood circulate m/y heart beat, *I* do not experience the writhing of m/y viscera, *I*

have not the smallest shiver in m/y hair in m/y nape ... in m/y clitoris, *I*
am perfectly at ease ... *I* am untouched at any point of m/y body and at
this point in m/y discourse *I* laugh with fierce insane silent laughter m/y
most unknown one, *I* do not bare m/y teeth. (139)

Parodying the discursive, disembodied subject, Wittig's lesbian can
barely suppress bawdy, Rabelasian laughter. Against this image of the
properly contained and repressed 'integral body,' she is drawn in all
her vastness and calamity and visceral 'valleys' that do not form boundaries but open onto the body of the other(s):

I am the site of a great hubbub ... you come and go in m/y widened pores
in m/y alveoli in m/y cavities in m/y furrows in m/y trenches in m/y
crevices, you mine m/e, m/y surface caves in, step by step it affects m/y
entire body m/y muscles m/y blood m/y bones m/y vital organs m/y substances until decomposition is complete. (154–5)

Just as Rabelais's grotesque body is a *double body* 'in which the life of
one body is born from the death of the preceding, older one' (Bakhtin
318), the lesbian body is a double body, a coupling of life and death;
one vitally aroused body is born in the orgasmic death of another. 'Disembowelling' figures as total bodily communion: one body peels open
another, crushes, ruptures, and exposes to get literally to the heart of
the matter, to grasp wholly and concretely the other's loving gaze at
the moment of her climax:

I discover that your skin can be lifted layer by layer, *I* pull, it lifts off, it
coils above your knees, *I* pull starting at the labia, it slides the length of
the belly ... *I* arrive under your hair ... *I* touch your skull ... m/y two hands
crush the vault and the occiput behind ... m/y hands are plunged in the
soft hemispheres, *I* seek the medulla and the cerebellum ... now *I* hold all
of you ... your last thoughts behind your eyes caught in m/y hands, the
daylight is no purer than the depths of m/y heart m/y dearest one. (17)

The grotesque body is 'a body in the act of becoming,' says Bakhtin:

It is never finished, never completed; it is continually built, created, and
builds and creates another body ... Eating, drinking, defecation and other
elimination, as well as copulation, pregnancy, dismemberment, swallow-
ing up by another body – all these acts are performed on the confines of
the body and the outer world ... (317)

The lesbian body is *a body in the act of (be)coming*, of savage coming or of becoming savage ('*I* experience repeated orgasms in great agitation ... you most savage of the savages' [66]). The *grotesque* lesbian body is one of morphological metamorphosis whose prime mover is self-shattering desire, ritually re-enacted in carnal/carnival feasts dedicated to Sappho.

According to Bakhtin, the aesthetics of the grotesque body 'ignores the closed, smooth, and impenetrable surface of the body and retains only its excrescences (sprouts, buds) and orifices, only that which leads beyond the body's limited space ... The grotesque image displays not only the outward but also the inner features of the body: blood, bowels, heart and other organs' (317–18). *The Lesbian Body* clearly applies this artistic logic of the grotesque:

> You turn m/e inside out ... you count the veins and the arteries, you retract them to one side, you reach the vital organs, you breathe into m/y lungs ... you hold the long tubes of the viscera ... you uncoil them, slide them round your neck ... you take the heart in your mouth ... Glory. (86)

> Spores start from your epidermis. Your pores produce them in thousands, *I* watch the tiny explosions, *I* see how the spores descend at the end of hairy filaments ... the spores develop and become rounded, the innumerable spheres clashing together create stridences clickings aeolian harp vibrations ... *I* laugh freely, *I* announce ... your coming, *I* baptise you for centuries of centuries, so be it. So be it. (29)

> Your palms are against m/y palms a faintness overcomes m/e ... you are face to face with m/e the soft inward of your arms pressed against m/y arms, then a formication spreads ... *I* see m/y pores dilate, *I* see your pores do likewise, open they secrete fine hairs in thousands ... *I* cannot distinguish yours from m/ine they are so mingled as they multiply ... (81)

Lesbian lovers' discourse is a bawdy parody of High Art; it translates such sublime images as the music of the spheres and the aeolian harp into such grossly corporeal images as the music of the s/pores. It also grotesquely parodies biblical discourse with its orgasmic '*I* announce your coming' and its punning translation of fornication into 'formication.' Such parody is in keeping with what Bakhtin describes as the essential principle of 'degradation' in grotesque realism: 'that is, the lowering of all that is high, spiritual, ideal, abstract ... a transfer to the material level, to the sphere of earth and body in their indissoluble

unity' (19–20). In medieval parody, he proceeds to explain, degradation and debasement of the higher do not have an abstract meaning
but rather one that is 'strictly topographical' (21): 'Degradation here
means coming down to earth ... To degrade is to bury, to sow, and to
kill simultaneously ... To degrade also means to concern oneself with
the lower stratum of the body, the life of the belly and the reproductive
organs ...' (21).

The Lesbian Body literally brings down to earth not only metaphysical
and Romantic images but also such structuralist essences as '*the
exchange of women*,' 'God and the *Jouissance* of The Woman,' '*the
gaze.*' *The Lesbian Body* is the *soiling* of idealist representations of the
structures of desire and the enigma of woman:

> The soil of the garden slides between your teeth, your saliva moistens it ...
> *I* am transformed into mud m/y legs m/y sex m/y thighs m/y belly stand-
> ing between your legs glutted with the smell of vaginal secretion rising
> from your middle, *I* liquefy within and without ... M/y entire body is over-
> whelmed. First to fall is m/y anus. Some glutei soon follow ... The arms
> themselves fall entire to the ground ... A very strong smell of moist earth
> spreads around. *I* see plants rooted in the fibres of m/y muscles ... *I* sub-
> mit m/yself to your will m/y deplorable one *I* have no share in this sys-
> tematic transformation you impose on m/e. (72)

'*I*' has no 'share' in this degradation since 'will' is entirely expended;
nor does 'you' have anything to gain. There is no violation or subordination of one by the other, but there is a 'systematic transformation'
that *grounds one in the body of an other*, in a spreading lava of desire,
impossible to cultivate or colonize.

Finally, according to Bakhtin, the *body of speech* is also degraded in
grotesque realism. 'The body that figures in all the expressions of the
unofficial speech of the people,' he argues, 'is the body that fecun-
dates and is fecundated, that gives birth and is born, devours and is
devoured, drinks, defecates, is sick and dying ... Whenever men laugh
and curse ... their speech ... is filled with bodily images ... even when
the flood is contained by norms of speech, there is still an eruption of
these images into literature, especially if the literature is gay or abusive
in character' (319).[13]

The literary language of *The Lesbian Body* is thoroughly gay and abusive. Wittig's lovers address each other in a form of billingsgate that is
affectionately foul and insulting: 'vomit m/e with all your might muz-
zled suckling-lamb queen cat spit m/e out' (90); 'm/y most execrable

one' (60); 'm/y so callipygous one' (43). The speaking and desiring
subjects literally bathe in a flood of bodily images that are spoken in
knowing disdain for the bourgeois sense of the aesthetic and the
proper.

But having aligned herself with such counter-discourse as Bakhtin's,
having adapted her own version of the grotesque as a radically alternative bodily canon, does Wittig also reproduce his political limitations?
For Bakhtin has not escaped serious criticism; not all of his readers
acknowledge his use of carnival as counter-discourse with unequivocal
enthusiasm. Some, after describing his subversive *potential*, proceed to
confront the areas of political neglect in his work. Following her affir-
mative analysis of Bakhtin's 'categor[y] of [the] carnivalesque' as a use-
able category of 'a redeployment or counterproduction of culture,
knowledge, and pleasure' (218), Mary Russo then proceeds to point
out some profound shortcomings: 'like many other social theorists of
the nineteenth and twentieth centuries,' she observes, Bakhtin 'fails to
acknowledge or incorporate the social relations of gender in his semiotic model of the body politic, and thus his notion of the Female Grotesque remains, in all directions, repressed and undeveloped' (219).[14]
Similarly, Peter Stallybrass and Allon White initially refer to Bakhtin's
return to carnival as 'refreshingly iconoclastic' before proceeding to
identify what remains to be politically problematic, namely, 'its nostal-
gia; its uncritical populism (carnival often violently abuses and demon-
izes *weaker*, not stronger, social groups – women, ethnic and religious
minorities, those who "don't belong" – in a process of *displaced abjection*); its failure to do away with the official dominant culture, its
licensed complicity' (19).

The Lesbian Body could be read as a response to Mary Russo's criticism of Bakhtin's indifference to gender and to her call for a critical
practice that uses the category of the grotesque 'to destabilize the idealizations of female beauty or to realign the mechanisms of desire'
(221). Wittig not only *genders* this category but also *universalizes* it: she
deploys her lesbian grotesque against canonical idealizations of female
beauty *and all representations of the female body* such as are drawn in opposition – whether sublime or sensual – to the universally standard male
body.

Moreover, by lesbianizing the carnivalesque body politic, Wittig also
resolves the problems of 'uncritical populism' to which Stallybrass and
White are critically sensitive. There is no question of 'displaced abjection' in *The Lesbian Body*: lesbians do not figure here as a weak minority
but rather as a gay and overpowering majority. Nor can *The Lesbian*

Body be fittingly described as 'nostalgic': it enacts the recovery, reconstruction, and redeployment of a past genre with a view to radically altering the bodily canon of the present. Finally, it cannot be accused of 'licensed complicity' with dominant culture: it appears in the wake of that total war waged in the pages of *Les Guérillères* wherein patriarchal images were banished forever to the darker ages of literary history. Rather than engage in dialogue with the privileged and idealized discourses of dominant culture, *The Lesbian Body* combats the canon on two uncompromising fronts: the parodic deconstruction of the old forms and the forging (through catachresis) of the new.

The Lesbian Body reads as, to use Wittig's words, a 'Trojan Horse' constructed out of such heterogeneous materials as medieval and Renaissance parody, Sapphic verse, Djuna Barnes's *Ladies Almanack*, and a host of polymorphous textual bodies – *Love's Body*, 'I Sing the Body Electric,' possibly also the pornographic bodies of Georges Bataille, another writer of bodily 'excess' – and launched into literary history, where it will, with the help of feminist criticism, do its work of material transformation:

> Any important literary work is like the Trojan Horse at the time it is produced. Any work with a new form operates as a war machine, because its design and its goal is to pulverize the old forms and formal conventions. It is always produced in hostile territory. And the stranger it appears, nonconforming, unassimilable, the longer it will take for the Trojan Horse to be accepted. Eventually it is adopted, and even if slowly, it will eventually work like a mine. It will sap and blast out the ground where it was planted. The old literary forms, which everybody was used to, will eventually appear to be outdated, inefficient, incapable of transformation. ('Trojan Horse' 45)

Notes

1 That city is best ordered 'whose state is most like that of an individual man,' Socrates announces to Glaucon in *Republic*, adding later that 'unity is the greatest blessing for a state, and we [can] compare a well-governed state to the human body in its relation to the pleasure and pain of its parts' (Plato 574–844; 5.462.d; 5.464.b). Plato also employs this bodily metaphor elsewhere; see *Symposium* 191.e, *Laws* 12.964.d-e.

2 Wittig sets herself apart from 'the (new) femininity, feminine writing, and the lauding of difference' which she understands 'are the backlash of a political trend very much concerned with the questioning of the categories

of sex' (63, 64). Presumably she would include Hélène Cixous and Julia Kristeva in this reactionary writerly movement. She explains that 'the beginning of the women's liberation movement in France and everywhere else was in itself a questioning of the categories of sex. But afterwards only radical feminists and lesbians continued to challenge on political and theoretical grounds the use of the sexes as categories and as classes' ('Point of View' 69n1).

3 Adrienne Rich coins the term 'lesbian continuum' in her much-celebrated essay 'Compulsory Heterosexuality and Lesbian Existence.' While Rich strategically extends the category 'lesbian' to include not just women who sleep together but all women-identified women, Wittig rejects the category 'woman' altogether: 'it would be incorrect to say that lesbians associate, make love, live with women, for "woman" has meaning only in heterosexual systems of thought and heterosexual economic systems. Lesbians are not women' ('Straight Mind' 110).

4 'This, then, is writers' work,' Wittig affirms, 'to concern themselves with the letter, the concrete, the visibility of language ... its material form ...This work on the level of the words and of the letter reactivates words in their arrangement, and ... brings out in most cases – rather than one meaning – polysemy' ('Point of View' 68).

5 Judith Butler interprets Wittig's notion of the ex-centric lesbian subject to be idealistic, deriving from a more fundamental, unproblematized sense of a 'pre-social ontology of unified and equal persons' (115). But I fail to see where Wittig (unwittingly) makes any such ahistorical, ontological claims. She is, in fact, perfectly aware of philosophical rejections of her position. 'Our [lesbians'] refusal of the totalizing interpretation ... makes the theoreticians say that we neglect the symbolic dimension. These [totalizing] discourses deny us every possibility of creating our own categories' ('Straight Mind' 105).

6 Rule champions a minority literature, although her preface reads more like an apology than a celebration of lesbian writers. In speaking of 'the ugly masochism of Violette Leduc,' 'the neutered sexuality of Ivy Compton-Burnett,' or 'the blatant sexual hunger of Vita Sackville-West,' Rule implies that the 'reality of lesbian experience' is more symptomatic than transcendent, and that her reading of these writers, with whom she ambivalently identifies and sympathizes, is more diagnostic than politic (n. pag.).

7 Wittig applauds the writing of Djuna Barnes as world literature that successfully transforms a lesbian perspective into a universal point of view ('Point of View' 66).

8 Wittig perhaps derives her 'war machine' from that of Gilles Deleuze and Félix Guattari's *Anti-Oedipus*.

9 These 'feminaries' call to mind Djuna Barnes's *Ladies Almanack*, which may
   have served as Wittig's model.
   Les Guérillères lesbianizes many mythic, legendary, and folk-lorish figures
   such as Snow White (46), the Sphinx's riddle (85), Hippolyta (85),
   Orpheus, Eve, and Medusa (52), and Helen of Troy (92). Helen, for
   instance, is one of the epic narrators, and the battle of the amazon 'Trieu'
   (Troy) is her favourite story.

10 Wittig laments that the English translator chose to turn *elles* into 'the
   women,' since such rendering destroys the illusion of global lesbianism.
   'All of a sudden,' she writes, '*elles* stopped being *mankind*' ('Mark of Gender' 70).

11 '*The Lesbian Body*, an esoteric and erotic Sapphic "Song of Songs," is,'
   Hélène Wenzel observes, 'the most notorious of Wittig's works, and probably the most difficult to read ... Feminists who were thrilled by the figurative and literal violence of the *guérillères* against the patriarchy, were
   appalled by its prevalence in *The Lesbian Body*' (265).

12 'The bar in the *j/e* [m/e] of *The Lesbian Body* is a sign of excess. A sign that
   helps to imagine an excess of "I," an "I" exalted. "I" has become so powerful in *The Lesbian Body* that it can attack the order of heterosexuality in texts
   and assault the so-called love, the heroes of love, and lesbianize them, lesbianize the symbols, lesbianize the gods and the goddesses, lesbianize the
   men and the women. This "I" can be destroyed in the attempt and resusci-
   tated. Nothing resists this "I" (or this *tu*, which is its name, its love), which
   spreads itself in the whole world of the book, like a lava flow that nothing
   can stop' ('Mark of Gender' 71).

13 In laying its iconoclasm so bare, *The Lesbian Body* calls another 'lesbian' text
   to mind whose bodily images forged a scandalous entry into the post-
   Romantic canon a century earlier. I refer to Baudelaire's *Fleurs du mal*,
   which the poet had originally intended to publish under the title *Lesbiennes*
   (xxiii) and which featured several 'lesbian' poems, two of which were condemned in court on grounds that they 'conduisent nécessairement à l'excitation des sens par un réalisme grossier et offensant pour la pudeur' (lead
   necessarily to the excitement of the senses by a realism that is rude and
   offensive to decency) – that is, for their gross, grotesque realism! (quoted
   in Clements 17).
   But Baudelaire's 'spleen' bears none of the bawdy bodily character of
   Rabelais's carnival genre, figuring instead the excrescence of a decadent
   aesthetic, voicing the lamentable degeneracy and loss of bourgeois culture,
   wholly without gaiety or abundance. Baudelaire's lesbians symbolize all that
   high culture finds distasteful, wasteful, sterile, unnatural, and morally, spir-
   itually, and aesthetically loathsome about material society. From Baude-

laire's particularly ambivalent point of view, the lesbian body attracts/repels the abject focus of the lyric poet self-consciously degraded to dandified visionary. While his *images lesbiennes* scandalized the authors and magistrates of *haute culture*, and while they helped to subvert and transform a conservative, puritanical literary canon, they do nothing to alter the heterosexual vision of the body politic or even of the lesbian body. It remains for Wittig to parody and subvert the Baudelairean canon.

14 'The political implications of this heterogeneity [of carnivalesque speech and spectacle] are obvious,' Russo affirms: 'it sets carnival apart from the merely oppositional and reactive ... In its multivalent oppositional play, carnival refuses to surrender the critical and cultural tools of the dominant class, and in this sense, carnival can be seen above all as a site of insurgency, and not merely withdrawal' (218).

Works Cited

Bakhtin, Mikhail. *Rabelais and His World*. Trans. Helene Iswolsky. Bloomington: Indiana UP 1984

Barnes, Djuna. *Ladies Almanack*. Paris: Titus 1928

Baudelaire, Charles. *Oeuvres complètes*. Paris: Gallimard 1961

Brown, Norman O. *Love's Body*. New York: Random House 1966

Butler, Judith. *Gender Trouble: Feminism and the Subversion of Identity*. New York: Routledge 1990. 111–28

Clements, Patricia. *Baudelaire and the English Tradition*. Princeton: UP 1985

Deleuze, Gilles, and Félix Guattari. *Anti-Oedipus: Capitalism and Schizophrenia*. Trans. Robert Hurley, Mark Seem, and Helen R. Lane. London: Athlone P 1983

Jones, Ann Rosalind. 'Writing the Body: Toward an Understanding of *L'Ecriture Feminine*.' *Feminist Studies* 7, no. 2 (1981), 247–63

Plato. *The Collected Dialogues*. Ed. Edith Hamilton and Huntington Cairns. Princeton: Princeton UP 1961

Rich, Adrienne. 'Compulsory Heterosexuality and Lesbian Existence.' In *The 'Signs' Reader: Women, Gender and Scholarship*. Ed. Elizabeth Abel and Emily K. Abel. Chicago: Chicago UP 1983, 139–68

Rule, Jane. *Lesbian Images*. Garden City, NY: Doubleday 1975

Russo, Mary. 'Female Grotesques: Carnival and Theory.'In *Feminist Studies/Critical Studies*. Ed. Teresa de Lauretis. Bloomington: Indiana UP 1986, 213–29

Stallybrass, Peter, and Allon White. *The Politics and Poetics of Transgression*. Ithaca: Cornell UP 1986

Suleiman, Susan Rubin, ed. *The Female Body in Western Culture: Contemporary Perspectives*. London: Harvard UP 1986

Wenzel, Hélène. 'The Text as Body/Politics: An Appreciation of Monique Wittig's Writings in Context.' *Feminist Studies* 7, no. 2 (1981), 264–87
Wittig, Monique. *The Lesbian Body.* Trans. David Le Vay. Boston: Beacon 1986
– *Les Guérillères.* Trans. David Le Vay. Boston: Beacon 1985
– 'The Mark of Gender.' In *The Poetics of Gender.* Ed. Nancy K. Miller. New York: Columbia UP 1986, 63–73
– 'One Is Not Born a Woman.' *Feminist Issues* 1, no. 2 (1981), 47–54
– 'The Point of View: Universal or Particular?' *Feminist Issues* 3, no. 2 (1983), 63–9
– 'The Straight Mind.' *Feminist Issues* 1, no. 1 (1980), 103–10
– 'The Trojan Horse.' *Feminist Issues* 4, no. 2 (1984), 45–9

12

The Reorganization of the Body: Daphne Marlatt's 'musing with mothertongue'[1]

PAMELA BANTING

> We have seen previously that, caught between the sense we give to reality and the non-sense patriarchal reality constitutes for us, we are most often forced to adapt our lives to simultaneous translation of the foreign tongue.
>
> Nicole Brossard, *The Aerial Letter*, 112

> Sober and enraptured, already familiar with the place where you know how to put your hand so as to bring about the effect of reality: lovhers. while i am still trying to read/delirium.
>
> Nicole Brossard, *Lovhers*, 29

The body is not nature. The body is not a woman. The body is not a mute. No. The body is a persistent and perpetual translator. *Jouissance* ceaselessly circulates and recirculates pictogrammic, ideogrammic, and phonetic signifiers so as to avoid congealing the body around a single organ, a single frozen drop of flesh. The body is not only a sum of its visceral organs but a series of contiguous libidinal surfaces and striations. The body is its own signifier. The body is a lifesize, mobile, and audible pictogram.

Daphne Marlatt's 'musing with mothertongue,' the poetic essay which follows the serial poem, glossary, and photo-collages in *Touch to My Tongue*,[2] restates and elaborates upon her thoughts concerning the relation between language and body in her work. Marlatt has always evinced a strong drive to literalize the body. The issue for her is, given this body, how do we stay contained within it and not interpose our own ego between ourselves and that body?[3] How do we avoid constructing, or at least how do we from time to time puncture, or punctuate,[4] the interior volume of a logocentric self which reduces the body to gross matter?

In the following passage from a 1988 interview Marlatt talks about how her view of the relation between language and body led her, in her novel *Ana Historic*, to defer the seemingly inevitable lovemaking between the characters Annie and Zoe. She did not want the narrative's ending to be a conclusion, she says, but only another beginning:

> I suppose this has to do with where I place myself against Christianity, which has taught us to defer bliss to life after death. But language itself, especially writing, is another kind of deferral. In the humanist tradition it was thought to be a vehicle pointing to what was real beyond the writing. And we've now come to think of it very differently as a signifying process present to itself. To speak of what has been excluded from the world of literature, which is women's desire, and to make that present in a language of presence is a big challenge. (Williamson, 'Sounding' 52)

If writing is a signifying process present to itself alone (or, alternatively, deferred only from itself rather than from a transcendental signified), then the problem of how to speak of women's desire (largely absent from discourse, latent within the body) in such a writing is addressed by our desiring, deferring, and deferred bodies. Just as writing refers to writing, so the desiring body, as, for example, in Marlatt's poetry, signifies itself. The desiring body, the body of *jouissance*, has its own compositions and positions. Desiring and loving bodies collect a history, a language, and a skin of their own. Because 'my body does not have the same ideas I do' (Barthes 17), it must not be spoken of and represented in standard models of spoken and written composition only. The erotogenic body can be spoken, and listened, *to* and inscribed in intersemiotic translation.[5]

The body cannot be divided from language, because language is, as Marlatt writes, 'a living body we enter at birth' (*Touch* 45). Language shapes, configures, and partially but not entirely determines our bodies. Our bodies are part language. Our physiological body parts are also grammatical organs, diagrammed, conjugated, and mobilized by cultural inscriptions. In bpNichol's phrase 'syntax equals the body structure' (Nichol 25–31).[6] Syntax is not identical with but equivalent to the body structure. Most assuredly, though, for Marlatt language 'does not stand in place of anything else, it does not replace the bodies around us' (*Touch* 45). Language, in other words, is not *only* referential. The body of language is also our horizon, 'placental, our flat land, our sea' (*Touch* 45). Both *topos*, 'place (where we are situated),' and trope, 'body (that contains us),'[7] the flesh of language is the flesh of our world. Language as a living body envelops our lived world and lived body. As Marlatt said in 1974 with regard to Gertrude Stein's work, 'Well, she sees language as a code. I dont want it to be a code. I want it to be the transmitting itself' (Bowering 68). Throughout her work Marlatt consistently demonstrates a concern for access to the literalness both of the body and of language. For her, articulation, especially by women writers, is 'a visceral event' (Bowering 68).

A crucial aspect of the literality of language is what Marlatt calls its musicality. In 'musing with mothertongue' she says that 'language is first of all for us a body of sound' (*Touch* 45). Language's physicality derives primarily from its oral/aural qualities. For babies, as we know, the world and themselves are not separate. The outside world is body as well. Children learn language non-referentially because, as Marlatt insists, 'language is literal ... Any word is a physical body. It's [*sic*] body is sound, so it has that absolute literal quality that sound has, which connects it up with sounds around it' (Bowering 69). 'It can never be referential, because you simply arent given, in reality, that other out there' (Bowering 79). It is only a gradual and lifelong process whereby we learn 'what the words are actually saying' (*Touch* 45).

For Marlatt, language works by evocation, not invocation, and thought works by association. The physical bodies of words provoke each other into utterance by attraction along an associative, metonymic chain. Association is 'a form of thought that is not rational but erotic because it works by attraction' (*Touch* 45). Like attracts like. Even difference attracts liking. Words, like lovers, 'call each other up, evoke each other, provoke each other, nudge each other into utterance' (*Touch* 45). The rhetoric of our thinking is erotic. Thus for Marlatt the simile is more than a comparison between two objects using the words *like* or *as*. In her view, words, phonemes, and syllables like one another.[8] She uses *like* as a verb rather than as a preposition.

Marlatt also uses the fulcrum of the word *like*, not to subsume one term by another, but to highlight the metaphoricity of the body. In common rhetorical usage the tenor of a metaphor is the discourse or subject which the vehicle illustrates or illuminates (Holman 525). A comparative term is invoked to clarify, brighten, or render poetic a primary term. The traditional definition and usage of the simile is essen-

tially Platonic in that two things, essentially unlike, are juxtaposed by
virtue of a resemblance in a single aspect of their being. In the simile it
is forms which are analysed and compared. The traditional use of the
simile thus reinforces metaphysics. In this formal analysis there is no
room for erotic attachments. However, as Marlatt points out, the Germanic *lik-* refers to 'body, form; like, same' (*Touch* 45). Therefore the
etymology of *like* can be read as positing a different (not an original)
dynamic at work in similes.[9] The idea of sameness is present in this
new dynamic, but it is not necessarily a sameness in the sense of an
irreducible similarity of being or nature. It is sameness by virtue of the
mutuality of attraction or the pull of two or more bodies towards one
another. Erotic attraction is not always or even necessarily based on
similarity: erotics is based upon the play of both sameness *and* difference. Rather than producing analogy, this other kind of simile is based
upon the physical attractions of speech and the sounds of a given language or languages. Thus Marlatt might define the simile as the process of attraction between two bodies (words as particles of language,
or human bodies) by virtue, not of the fundamental similarity of a single aspect of their being, and thus a reduction of the two to one, but
rather by virtue of their multiple and contingent physical (signifying)
attributes.

Marlatt's erotics of rhetoric works to develop parallels between the
human body and the body of language without privileging either term,
tenor or vehicle, of that simile. In the following passage Marlatt
explores some of the attractions between the physical body and the
material body of language,[10] and in the process traces familiar, forgotten, and novel circuits of exchange between these two bodies:

> hidden in the etymology and usage of so much of our vocabulary for ver-
> bal communication (contact, sharing) is a link with the body's physicality:
> matter (the import of what you say) and matter and by extension mother;
> language and tongue; to utter and outer (give birth again); a part of
> speech and a part of the body; pregnant with meaning; to mouth (speak)
> and the mouth with which we also eat and make love; sense (meaning)
> and that with which we sense the world; to relate (a story) and to relate to
> somebody, related (carried back) with its connection with bearing (a
> child); intimate and to intimate; vulva and voluble; even sentence which
> comes from a verb meaning to feel. (*Touch* 46)

The serendipitous similarities between the language used to describe
the body and that used to refer to language itself are not used by Mar-

latt to transport us back to some ur-text, some utopian or matriarchal era, or to some original innocence of union between body and language. Rather, Marlatt uses this attraction between parts of the body and parts of speech to form new alliances. It is not her desire to erase the present or to move backwards in time. She is translating forward, forging sense where there has been only non-sense, aspects of our lives which have been invisible to us because, as she says, 'in a crucial sense we cannot see what we cannot verbalize' (*Touch* 47).

When she draws an analogy between poetry as a form of verbal speech and lovemaking as a form of organ speech (Williamson, 'Speaking' 28), Marlatt is using the word *speech* metaphorically in order to point to the signifying capacities of the body itself. In turn, this new awareness of the body's sign production rereads or unsettles that which we presently understand as verbal speech, poetry and texts. As readers, we must become oriented to traces of the body in the text. Our responsibility in this regard is not merely to assimilate these traces as metaphoric. As if we were reading a translation, which we are, an intersemiotic translation, we must not privilege only the target *text*. Instead we must read the marks, gestures, and postures of the body too. Within this translation model we must allow ourselves to be 'lured beyond equivalence' to 'a new skin.'[11] The reader reading, like the writer writing, must translate bi-directionally between text and body, body and text.

Marlatt's emphasis on sound and speech, though, does not place her within a solely oral poetics. She draws upon the lineage of poetry, 'which has evolved out of chant and song, in riming and tone-leading' (*Touch* 45). However, her poetics also derives from the prelinguistic and non-referential significations of the child and the current gaps in our language for the inscription of women's bodies. Etymologies, which she uses liberally to generate her texts, depend upon dictionaries and literacy. Moreover, *Touch to My Tongue* includes photo-collages not just as illustration but – insofar as they invoke the intersemiotic translation between words and images, and pictogrammic writing – as instructions in how to read the interlingual, intralingual, and intersemiotic translations of the poem series. That is, Marlatt, like Hélène Cixous, does not pre-configure the body as external to words nor as entirely coded by them either. She strives *not* to locate the body in either of these epistemes but instead to continue to translate between epistemes.[12] For her, just as the text metaphorizes or translates the body, so the body metaphorizes the text.[13] When body and text as two material substances or tissues are invited to attract, metaphorize, and translate one another, different textual practices are initiated, and different bodies constructed.[14] The body is both translatable and untranslatable: translatable in this intersemiotic exchange between two material substances; untranslatable in that like a proper name or any other untranslatable word it transfers nothing except itself as pure signifier. The smooth and slippery body, like the proper name, announces paradoxically 'translate me' and 'don't translate me.'

In addition to sound, etymology is a force of attraction among words that allows various forms of translation to take place. Etymologies form the 'history of verbal relations (a family tree, if you will) that has preceded us and given us the world we live in' (*Touch* 46). Marlatt's translation poetics contains a genealogical component.[15] Language and its history of verbal relations, etymology, like our own mother's body, is 'the given, the immediately presented, as at birth' (*Touch* 46–7). Hence language and the etymon are part of the phenomenological horizon of our lives, which is never really given (in the same way that etymologies do not allow us to time-travel back to a prelapsarian, maternal, or matriarchal condition). As a feminist writer, Marlatt 'take[s] issue with the given, hearing the discrepancy between what our patriarchally-loaded language bears (can bear) of our experience and the difference from it our experience bears out' (*Touch* 47). Because both history and language are constructions, says Marlatt, we can change the reality we live in: 'We're not stuck in some authoritative version of the real' (Williamson, 'Sounding' 52).

Of course, one very important aspect of the real which is also a function of translation is gender difference. Marlatt lists examples of some of women's experiences which have been invisible to patriarchal language. These include gestation, menstruation, body cycles, breast-feeding, intimacy, and lovemaking. If the real is a construction, and if the body is the medium of the real, then through translation between the body and language the body can be not just represented but reconstructed, re-realized, reorganized. Marlatt describes the act of writing as a translation between the prelinguistic given (this given can be equally the body or the external world) and language. She states: 'Everything is prelinguistic, & as soon as you get into linguism, language, humming it, uttering it, you get back into the problem of translating ... Plus the fact that it's even more complicated than translating, because language has its own presence & its own insistences & its own connections, which you have to take into account all the time' (Bowering 58–9).

Here it is necessary to make a distinction between the prelinguistic and presignification. The body conceived of in phallogocentric terms exists prior to language. However, it is accurate to say that the body is prelinguistic only if language in turn is conceived to be entirely absorbed by or identical with its referential functions. The problem is that we lack names for different signifying practices of the body. Some, such as dance, have been culturally assimilated as art forms extraneous to language (although certain avant-garde artists incorporate language into contemporary dance). This is why we have to research such practices as, for example, hysteria and lesbianism in order to excavate and provide provisional names for alternative signifying practices. These not yet completely theorized modes are sources of information about the body. Without retaining the phallogocentric body, then, but without wholly discarding it either for the moment, since it is the only one Western culture recognizes, we must add other signifying practices of the body to speech and writing, and we must read traditional rhetorical devices differently – not as referential only but as erotic, attractive, metonymic.

Certain experiences of women's bodies have been invisible. In a similar way aspects of the body of language can be equally overlooked or misread. In 'Translating *MAUVE*: Reading Writing' Marlatt sums up what are for her the similarities between writing and translating:

> Translation has always stood in an intimate relationship to writing for me, not the same but similar to, and it is this shade of difference that is fascinating, that is exactly the area – i might even add 'shady' area – that the process of translation works. Writing this, i'm assailed by words like 'ground' and 'basis' which want to insert themselves, but what i want to say about translation denies those terms. For me translation is about slippage and difference, not the mimesis of something solid and objectified out there ... Since it is impossible to 'bring over' all of the complex of meaning in French, the difference is crucial. And fascinating. And for me a clear instance of what writing itself is about: sensing one's way through the sentence, through (by means of) a medium (language) that has its own currents of meaning, its own drift. So that what one ends up saying is never simply one with, but slipping, in a fine displacement of, intention. (27–8)

Even as they constitute it, both body and language escape signification. When Marlatt writes about the call of feminist writers in Quebec for a writing that returns us to the body and the 'largely unverbalized, pre-syntactic, postlexical field it knows' (*Touch* 48), she clarifies that what she means by this post-lexical field is the site of the erotic attraction and proliferation of words. Within a translation poetics the term *post-lexical* can be read not only as pre-existing and exceeding the limits of the dictionary. Instead of a regression towards a dubious site of origins, it can also be read as a translation, using the etymological roots of words contained in the dictionary, towards a language which no one at present speaks or writes or performs but which perhaps subsequent women writers *will* be able to inhabit. In the meantime experimental feminist writers such as Marlatt translate, not back to a utopian vision, but within and towards a target text and target language. Marlatt and writers like her write in a (m)other tongue or 'interlanguage,' a sepa-rate, yet intermediate, linguistic system situated between a source and a target language (Toury 71).

At this point in her poetic essay, the penultimate paragraph, where the figure of a new woman writer emerges, Marlatt accretes to the problem of 'the given,' which she had previously used solely in a phe-nomenological sense, the same associations Hélène Cixous borrows from Marcel Mauss on the logic of the gift (Cixous 252, 263–4). The given is not just that which pre-exists. It also partakes of the nature of a gift. Like Cixous's figure of the woman writer, Marlatt's 'Alma,' 'inhab-itant of language, not master, not even mistress ... in having is had, is held by it [language], what she is given to say. in giving it away is given herself ...' (*Touch* 48). Alma is the writer as translator. Her writing/translating works off of 'that double edge where she has always lived, between the already spoken and the unspeakable, sense and non-sense' (*Touch* 48). Her source language is ordinary speech and writing, but her target language is not. This is translation between the articu-late (the already spoken) and the inarticulate (the unspeakable), lan-guage (sense) and the body (non-sense), the vernacular and an unknown language, the mother tongue and a (m)other tongue. Mar-latt touches on a similar point when she says in an interview, 'okay, interface is a better word for the meeting of what is knowable & what is unknowable. So all writing is a kind of translation ... From that which is inarticulate but sensed, deeply sensed ... In translation you're always making choices because you cant get the whole, the original, in fresh' (Bowering 57). There is always excess, spillage, and loss of signifiers and signifieds in translation. At the present stage in her work the seep-age inherent to translation has become an intrinsic part of Marlatt's theory of language, writing, and the body.[16] The gift is, paradoxically, this seepage, this loss, this drift.

In the final paragraph of 'musing with mothertongue' *topos*, 'place (where we are situated),' and trope, 'body (that contains us),' have coalesced again:

> language thus speaking (i.e., inhabited) relates us, 'takes us back' to where we are, as it relates us to the world in a living body of verbal relations. articulation: seeing the connections (and the thighbone, and the hipbone, etc.). putting the living body of language together means putting the world together, the world we live in: an act of composition, an act of birthing, us, uttered and outered there in it. (49)

Language speaking is language inhabited by a body. This body in turn is situated in a network of verbal relations. Marlatt's use of the terms 'speaking,' 'articulation,' and 'composition' are inconclusive with regard to the differentiation between writing and speech. When she refers to language speaking, she immediately modifies that term with 'inhabited' so as to insist on the bodily incarnation and articulatory or joining function that signifying in general enacts. The root of 'inhabit,' 'ghabh,' means, among other things, to give or receive, which in the context of Marlatt's modification creates a kind of equation such that to speak is to inhabit is to give or receive. Language speaking is language inhabiting our bodies, but there is always a surplus of the given, of both body and language. Language exceeds us; there are many languages and discourses which are unheard by us. In turn, the materiality of our bodies supercedes the referentiality of language in countless ways.

Thus Marlatt's conception of the relation between the body and language is close to the idea of hysterical translation.[17] Unlike Cixous, who theorizes an alternate relation between body and language on the basis of the hysterical body, Marlatt's focus is the lesbian body. However, what is important to note in terms of the present discussion is that hysterical bodies and lesbian bodies alike disclose both the feminine erotogenic body and processes of signification in general.

Hysteria, as the name suggests, was traditionally considered a reorganization of the body arising from the wandering or displacement upwards of the womb. Freud's theory of somatic compliance, conversion or the transposition of psychic pain into physiological symptoms, superceded this view. But hysterical *translation* is not the translation of psychic blockage or pain into bodily symptoms. It is not the expression or imitation of madness, or of femininity. Hysterical translation is the intersemiotic translation from one signifying system to another. Hysterical translation does not represent[18] the body as ill, pathological, or diseased; it presents the body as pictogram. The movements of the hysterical body are 'the perceptible appearance of a signifying system or a language that plays upon the visible' (David-Ménard 20). Insofar as it marks the physiological body off from the signifying but non-verbal body (David-Ménard 21), hysteria is an anti-metaphysic, a new epistemology, a new ontology. Ironically, then, hysteria thus rethought, not as the picaresque wandering of the womb nor as a dutiful somatic compliance, but as a translative process along the lines of the translation between writing and speech, for example, does in fact lead to a reorganization of the body.

Therefore when Cixous, for one, posits women writers as hysteric, she is not suggesting that they are afflicted with hysteria. Contemporary experimental women writers do not recapitulate the gestures of that malady as hysteria illness, nor do they valorize this sense of hysterical illness. The woman writer is not the double of the classic hysteric, because the writer writes. Inasmuch as she writes, she may draw on the philosophies posed by the hysterics. The same is true of Marlatt's tracing the significations of the lesbian body. Just as Jean Martin Charcot found hysterics to be photogenic because of their play with the language of visibility, so Marlatt explores and translates the erotogenic 'organ speech' of the bodies of lesbian lovers. The erotogenic body is the literal body, but it is not the materialist or essentialist body we have inherited from Cartesian metaphysics. The erotogenic body is located in the spaces between signifiers. Between one kiss or embrace and the next. Literally, between two mouths.

For Marlatt orality is not entirely tied to speech, conversation, the vernacular, or even whole words. She differentiates within and supplements the traditional model of signification.[19] Asked in an interview about the relation of writing to speaking in her work, she responds, 'I think my writing is fairly oral':

> When I'm writing, I'm writing it as I'm hearing it ... But I'm not too concerned with it on the page. When I was writing verse, when I was using the space of the page, then it would get in the way of the words coming out ... I'm concerned with how it sounds, with how you speak it, and how it can be heard ... What most intrigues me is what I think of as the sound body of the work. What kinds of sounds bounce off, echo off, call up other sounds. How the rhythms elongate or slow down, or suddenly pick up and run. (Williamson, 'Speaking' 29)

Marlatt focuses on the sound body of language less for the sounds of speech than for the sheerly physical sounds of language – semiotic, prelinguistic, or post-lexic. Although she is concerned with speaking and hearing the vernacular in her work, she is more responsive to and absorbed by the purely material element of sound.

Marlatt's concern with the sonority of words and the materiality of the body is not incompatible, though, with composing on the typewriter. When George Bowering remarks in 'Syntax Equals the Body Structure' that 'you can almost bypass the body when you're composing on the typewriter, that it's the brain just using part of the body to get out onto the page' (Nichol 27),[20] she objects, declaring that she does not feel that the body is not present in such compositional circumstances: 'I always compose on a typewriter, and I don't feel that the body isn't there. In fact, I find that there's a kind of rush possible on the typewriter – because you can type that fast – that equates very definitely with certain body states' (Nichol 27). The difference in opinion between Bowering and Marlatt on this point stems from the fact that he is working from a conventional distinction between oral and written forms, whereas she differentiates within the oral model.

Marlatt's project is to diffuse the mother tongue beyond and in excess of logocentric or patriarchal speech. Sensing her way through the sentence, she performs a bi-directional translation between the physical organs, senses, and perceptions of the body and a language yet to be spoken by anyone. Moreover, by factoring in the signifying practices of bodies themselves, she diversifies orality and disperses signification, beyond the privileged organs of the phallogocentric body, over other corporeal surfaces. 'Poetics,' she writes, 'is not a system of thought but a tactic for facing the silence' ('Listening' 36). Instead of a strategy for hearing-oneself-speak, 'poetics is a strategy for hearing' ('Listening' 38). Her poetics does not give a hearing to the evidence of the phallogocentric self but rather to 'every comma, every linebreak, each curve thought takes touching nerve-taboo, the empty space where speech, constrained by the "right form," the "proper word," is gripped (passive voice) by silence' ('Listening' 38). Marlatt's poetics translates between the audible and the inaudible, the visible and the invisible, speech and writing, the body and language. Poetics is not a method of composition so much as a way of translating the body, of composing and reorganizing it.

Marlatt's writing proposes that the mother tongue both is and is not our first language (which in fact is usually a father tongue spoken and transmitted to us by our mothers). She writes towards a (m)other tongue that will de-territorialize the phallogocentric body. She wants both to map other areas of the body with language and to translate the body literally into her texts. For Ezra Pound a 'periplum' was the geography 'not as you would find it if you had a geography book and a map, but ... as a coasting sailor would find it' (43–4). For Daphne Marlatt the periplum is the body as mapped by the tongue in translation.[21] Writing this (m)other tongue is a literal and a littoral translation:

> it moves mouth to ear (nipple to mouth), the fine stream that plays in time across a page, under pressure from all there is to say, *so much* we start again, starting from the left, starting from the silenced, body the words thrum. waiting to hear with all our ears. listening in, on ... ('Listening' 38)

Notes

1 A draft of this paper was presented to the seminar on 'Textual Bodies: Writing as Material Substance and/or Figurative Organism' at the Bodies: Image, Writing, Technology Conference, University of California, Irvine, 26–8 April 1990. I gratefully acknowledge the support of a Social Sciences and Humanities Research Council of Canada doctoral fellowship during the period in which this paper was written.

2 I am using the version of 'musing with mothertongue' published in *Touch to My Tongue.* Page references are to that book. As the essay is quite short and my analysis proceeds through it in the order in which it is written, readers will not find it difficult, if necessary, to consult one of the two other published versions. The essay appeared independently in the first issue of the journal *Tessera,* in *Room of One's Own* 8, no. 4 (1984), 53–6, and in Dybikowski et al., eds., *In the Feminine: Women and Words/Les Femmes et les mots Conference Proceedings 1983,* 171–4.

3 Here I am deliberately echoing American poet Charles Olson's statement: 'Objectism is the getting rid of the lyrical interference of the individual as ego, of the "subject" and his soul, that peculiar presumption by which western man has interposed himself between what he is as a creature of nature (with certain instructions to carry out) and those other creations of nature which we may, with no derogation, call objects' (156). In her work Marlatt considers this problem from the position of a Western woman.

4 The words *puncture* and *punctuate* share a common etymology meaning to mark with a point; pricked mark, point; to prick, pierce. Marlatt's idiosyncratic proselike long line, interior punctuation, and her notation in general can be read as simultaneously 'kicking syntax' (*Touch* 49) and marking, pricking, and piercing the logocentric interior.

5 Some of the methods feminist writers implement for speaking of such absence in a language of presence are not to defer to phallogocentric authority, not to defer speaking or writing, and not to defer pleasure. To refuse to defer to the real and/or the transcendental beyond is to position oneself, not in logocentric presence, but in the interval between words, phonemes, gestures, arms, lips, pelvic bones, tongues, etc. It is to defer deferral. If, as Marlatt insists, we are simply not given in actuality the real out there, then there can be no absence pure and simple. In an essay on Marlatt's long poem *How Hug a Stone* I have called this writing in the intervals between bodies and among body surfaces 'writing under embrasure.'

6 That is to say, syntax is not identical with but equivalent to, not the body, but the body structure. I discuss Marlatt's contribution to this discussion with bpNichol and George Bowering near the end of the present article. See also Marcel Mauss on what he calls 'body techniques.'

7 I am using the term *trope* here in a very general way – as figure of speech. As Gérard Genette demonstrates, a figure is simply one signifier offered as the signified of another signifier. In actuality, both signifiers are merely signifiers. Neither can legitimately be claimed as the literal of the other. Both are literal signifiers (Genette 47). Hence I am using this sense of the word *trope* to underscore the literalness of the body in Marlatt's writing. This sense of *trope* as two signifiers in a relationship of otherness parallels the relation between two languages, bodies, or words.

8 See Marlatt's comments on metaphor in Bowering, 'Given,' 43.

9 This is not to suggest that there is a prior or original meaning to the word hidden in etymology that authorizes such interpretation. What I am suggesting is that Marlatt uses such a root to think otherwise, to translate beyond metaphysics.

10 We must remember that the word *body* is just that, a word. *Body* is no more referential to the human body than it is, for example, to the body of language.

11 In her essay 'Translating *MAUVE*' Marlatt quotes part of a letter from Colin Browne. Browne had written to her asking whether she would like to participate in a translation project involving the work of Québécoise writer Nicole Brossard. He gave the series the name 'transformances,' ostensibly to distinguish what he wanted from more traditional and faithful interlingual translations. Marlatt quotes one of his definitions of 'transformance' as 'reading reading, writing writing, writing reading –that flicker pan-linear, lured beyond equivalence: a new skin' ('*MAUVE*' 28).

12 This may partially account for the current disagreements about her work and the censuring responses to it of critics who are searching for consistency and a purity of post-structuralist, reader-response, or Marxist con-

science. I am thinking of articles by, respectively, Lola Lemire Tostevin and
Frank Davey and of a chapter of Sarah Harasym's dissertation.

Marlatt read Maurice Merleau-Ponty in the late-1960s, very early in her
career, yet she does not adopt his term *flesh*, as it is usually translated. She
retains the word *body*. Thus she avoids placing her work within a strictly
phenomenological poetics, acknowledging that, like Merleau-Ponty himself, we continue to struggle with Descartes and the mind-body problem.

13 In Marlatt's *Rings* (1971), for example, a long poem about her pregnancy
and the birth of her son, the title, overall shape, and form or design of the
poem metaphorize psychic confusion as well as various literal rings (the
wedding ring, the ring of the cervix, the cyclical rhythms of women's bodies).

14 Here I am using 'metaphorize' and 'translate' in a similar way. Both terms
contain the sense of 'to transport' or 'carry across.' I am letting them float
together for the moment in order to invoke Barbara Freeman's work on
Cixous's metaphorization of the body and Gérard Genette's work on the
metaphor as one signifier masquerading as the signified of the other.

15 Just as the movement between languages for Canadian poet Fred Wah
involves primarily intralingual translation as a substitution for interlingual
translation between English and Chinese (a language which he does not
know), the translation in Marlatt's poetry is also intralingual from English
to English. Wah's translation poetics emerges from a desire to connect with
his *father*; Marlatt's translations using etymologies take on a new importance in *How Hug a Stone*, the first book in which she begins to deal with her
mother's life as an immigrant and with what Marlatt has inherited from her.

16 See Marlatt's use of the metaphor of seepage in 'Translating *MAUVE*.'

17 As Jacques Derrida observes in 'Roundtable on Translation': 'When one
speaks of hysteria, of oneiric or hysterical translation, one is speaking of
translation in [Roman] Jakobson's third sense, the passage from one semiotic system to another: words-gestures, words-images, acoustic-visual, and so
forth' (108).

18 Hysterical translation does not re-present the body in the sense of presenting it over again, a second time. As David-Ménard argues, the hysterical
body itself thinks (12). Her book is very helpful on the ways in which a pervasive dualism conditions Freud's theorization of hysteria and on reconcep-
tualizing hysterical practice.

19 As Marlatt suggests in 'Writing Our Way through the Labyrinth,' writing,
unlike reading, seems to her to be phallic, singular, proprietory, and self-
rather than other-directed. As she says, 'writing can scarcely be for women
the act of the phallic signifier' (49). Women, she suggests, are 'lost' inside
of the labyrinth of language. We must '(w)rite [the word itself is an intralingual translation] our way ... in intercommunicating passages' (49).

20 This is Bowering's interpretation of Charles Olson's thoughts on compos-
    ing on the typewriter.
21 Marlatt's translation poetics has always been taken up with translating
    between *topos* and trope. In an interview with Eleanor Wachtel published in
    1986 Marlatt updates her preoccupation with *topos*. She says: 'And my
    region, i mean the region i'm writing out of, is not so much place or land-
    scape these days as life as a woman' (13). *Topos* has become trope.

Works Cited

Banting, Pamela. '*How Hug a Stone:* Writing under Embrasure.' In 'Translation
    Poetics: Composing the Body Canadian.' PHD Diss., U of Alberta, 1990, 207–
    22
Barthes, Roland. *The Pleasure of the Text.* Trans. Richard Miller. Note by Richard
    Howard. New York: Hill 1975
Bowering, George. 'Given This Body: An Interview with Daphne Marlatt.' *Open
    Letter* 4th ser., no. 3 (1979), 32–88
Brossard, Nicole. 'From Radical to Integral.' In her *The Aerial Letter.* Trans. Mar-
    lene Wildeman. Toronto: Women's P 1988, 103–19. Another English transla-
    tion of this essay appeared in *Trivia* 5 (1984), 6–15
– *Lovhers.* Trans. Barbara Godard. Essential Poets Series 27. Montreal: Guer-
    nica 1986
Cixous, Hélène. 'The Laugh of the Medusa.' In *New French Feminisms: An
    Anthology.* Ed. and introd. Elaine Marks and Isabelle de Courtivron. New
    York: Schocken 1981, 245–64
Davey, Frank. 'Words and Stones in *How Hug a Stone.*' *Line* 13 (1989), 40–6
David-Ménard, Monique. *Hysteria from Freud to Lacan: Body and Language in Psy-
    choanalysis.* Trans. Catherine Porter. Foreword Ned Lukacher. Ithaca: Cor-
    nell UP 1989
Derrida, Jacques. 'Roundtable on Translation.' In his *The Ear of the Other: Oto-
    biography, Transference, Translation: Texts and Discussions with Jacques Derrida.*
    Ed. Christie V. McDonald. Trans. Peggy Kamuf. New York: Schocken 1985,
    91–161
Freeman, Barbara. '"Plus corps donc plus écriture": Hélène Cixous and the
    Mind-Body Problem.' *Paragraph* 11, no. 1 (1988), 58–70
Genette, Gérard. 'Figures.' In his *Figures of Literary Discourse.* Trans. Alan Sheri-
    dan. Introd. Marie-Rose Logan. New York: Columbia UP 1982, 45–60
Harasym, Sarah. 'Opening the Question: A "Political" Reading of Texts by
    Jacques Derrida, Gayatri Spivak, Roland Barthes, and Daphne Marlatt.' PHD
    Diss., U of Alberta, 1988
Holman, C. Hugh. *A Handbook to Literature.* Indianapolis: Odyssey P 1972

Marlatt, Daphne. *Ana Historic.* Toronto: Coach House P 1988
- *How Hug a Stone.* Winnipeg: Turnstone P 1983
- 'Listening In.' *Contemporary Verse 2* 9, no. 2 (1985), 36–9
- 'musing with mothertongue.' In her *Touch to My Tongue.* Edmonton: Long-
  spoon P 1984. Also in *Tessera* 1 [*Room of One's Own* 8, no. 4] (1984), 53–6;
  and in Ann Dybikowski et al., eds., *In the Feminine: Women and Words/Les
  Femmes et les mots Conference Proceedings 1983* (Edmonton: Longspoon P
  1985), 171–4
- *Rings.* Vancouver: Georgia Straight Writing Supplement 1971. Reprinted in
  What Matters: Writing 1968–70 (Toronto: Coach House P 1980), 77–113
- 'Translating *MAUVE*: Reading Writing.' *Tessera* 6 (1989), 27–30
- 'Writing Our Way through the Labyrinth.' *Tessera* 2 [*La Nouvelle Barre du Jour*
  157] (1985), 45–9
Mauss, Marcel. 'Body Techniques.' In his *Sociology and Psychology: Essays.* Trans.
  Ben Brewster. London: Routledge 1979, 97–123
Nichol, bp, Daphne Marlatt, and George Bowering. '"Syntax Equals the Body
  Structure": bpNichol, in Conversation, with Daphne Marlatt and George
  Bowering.' Ed. Roy Miki. *Line* 6 (1985), 22–44
Olson, Charles. 'Projective Verse.' In *The Poetics of the New American Poetry.* Ed.
  Donald Allen and Warren Tallman. New York: Grove P 1973, 147–58
Pound, Ezra. *ABC of Reading.* 1934; reprint, New York: New Directions 1960
Tostevin, Lola Lemire. 'Daphne Marlatt: Writing in the Space That Is Her
  Mother's Face.' *Line* 13 (1989), 32–9
Toury, Gideon. 'Interlanguage and Its Manifestations in Translation.' In his *In
  Search of a Theory of Translation.* Tel Aviv: Tel Aviv University / The Porter
  Institute for Poetics and Semiotics 1980, 71–8
Wachtel, Eleanor. 'An Interview with Daphne Marlatt.' *Capilano Review* 41
  (1986), 4–13
Williamson, Janice. 'Sounding a Difference: An Interview with Daphne Mar-
  latt.' *Line* 13 (1989), 47–56
- 'Speaking in and of Each Other: An Interview with Daphne Marlatt and
  Betsy Warland.' *Fuse* 8, no. 5 (1985), 25–9

⟨⟩ 13 ⟨⟩

Feminist Theory and the Discourse of Colonialism

UZOMA ESONWANNE

> And *you* shall not escape
> what *we* will make
> of the broken pieces of *our* lives.
>
> Abena Busia, 'Liberation' (emphasis added)

In theorizing the relations of gender and the subjection of women in patriarchy, some feminists draw upon tropes of otherness generated in the confrontation between the discourses and counter-discourses of colonialism and racialism. With deft rhetorical moves woman is transfigured. She becomes or is territorialized as 'Black,' 'Third World,' 'the Dark Continent.' Often these tropes are employed analogically or allusively, as in Susan Sontag's essay 'The Third World of Women.' Or else, as in Hélène Cixous's 'The Laugh of the Medusa' and Cixous and Catherine Clément's *The Newly Born Woman*, they are deconstructively translated and embedded within new discursive environnments.[1]

Whatever the rhetorical form of the embedding of these tropes in the new, discursive environment of feminist theory, whatever the methodological value or the ideological objectives which motivate such embeddings, it is quite clear that at least two effects are intended. The first is the inspiration of empathy in the reader. The second is the complication of 'theory' itself, that is, the intimation of the heterogeneity of alterity within a field in which heterogeneity, though often given the ritual nod of obeisance, is nevertheless ignored. In addition to these effects the use of such tropes may intimate similarities among these heterogeneous 'others': similarities of the conceptual paradigms and epistemological premises underpinning their production in discourse; similarities in the processes by which they are produced and repro-duced in the sites (institutions, agencies, organs) of power in the social formation; similarities in their effects upon the processes of the individual and collective unconscious; and, finally, similarities in the apparatuses, methodologies, and strategies of counter-hegemonic dis-courses. Stretched just a little, these intimations may even inaugurate in our minds a sense that, somehow, the dissemination of tropes between discourses is free, unfettered by limits and unrestricted to any, that tropes of otherness are so nomadic, so extra-territorial, that, pro-spectively or retrospectively, we would come to witness the emergence of a singular, transcendental theoretical paradigm or methodology for the critical analysis of the technologies of othering and strategies of power.

There is need, however, to proceed with some caution. While discov-eries of similarities between systems of othering may be exhilarating, the transference of tropes from the environment of one counter-hege-monic discourse to another may not necessarily yield a theoretical or ideological harvest of solidarity for oppositional intellection. Lurking in the crevices of such ecumenically theoretical or methodological propositions is, I fear, the germ of an unrestrained utopianism, utopia-nism with the potential for exacerbating, if not actually reproducing, the repressive effects of patriarchal governance. This fear has already been expressed by bell hooks:

> Since analogies derive their power, their appeal, and their very reason for being from the sense of two disparate phenomena having been brought closer together, for white women to acknowledge the overlap between the terms 'blacks' and 'women' (that is the existence of black women) would render this analogy unnecessary. By continuously making this analogy, they unwittingly suggest that to them the term 'women' is synonymous with 'white women' and the term 'blacks' synonymous with 'black men.' (8)[2]

Just as hooks's argument demonstrates that the translation of tropes of othering from hegemonic (colonialist) to oppositional (feminist, anti-colonial) discursive environments has the potential of disarticulating certain constituencies of women, Marnia Lazreg discovers a similar potential in feminist theory for the development of imperialist knowl-edges of Algerian women.

Hooks's critique of analogies between racism and sexism in feminist theory and Lazreg's critique of the epistemological premises and methodologies of feminist scholarship on Algerian women underscore the need for an examination of the consequences of the inter-discursive translation of tropes within and beyond the institutions and agencies of intellection. In addition to their potential for and actual totalization of differences between women, such translocations may also repress the emergence of knowledge of the dynamics of history in which women have intervened in their struggles against multiple oppressions. By obliterating the materiality of women's lives, they may actually facilitate the production of essentialist and a-temporal conceptions of women as belonging to collective ideological or social totalities such as 'African,' 'European,' 'Asian,' 'Black,' 'Third World,' or 'Communist' totalities whose epistemological authority is questionable (Mohanty, 'Under Western Eyes' 333ff). Indeed, they may (and often do) obscure recognition of the active involvement of men and women (of all social strata and constituencies) in the production, reproduction, and dissemination of the structures, strategies, and effects of hegemonic power (Lorde 100; Mohanty 335).

At this point I wish to emphasize the necessity of the argument being developed: that while, for reasons of debate or contestation, an insurgent, oppositional feminist theory may strategically compare the state or condition of women under patriarchy with that of non-Western communities under imperialism, it is risky if not counter-productive to formulate the comparison in analogical terms which presuppose, imply, or postulate an undifferentiated female subjectivity. Translating tropes of othering from hegemonic into oppositional discursive environments does not intrinsically perpetuate repression. Nor is the political impact of such translations necessarily attributable to the intentions of an author. Consequently, it is necessary to develop a 'secular interpretation' of the theoretical and political efficacy of such translations.[3] Indeed, to avoid 'the politics of blame' and 'guilt' which inquiries into problems such as this often generate, I wish to place the following readings of Cixous and Sontag in the context of the discursive economy of colonialism. Such a location is warranted by the texts to be analysed. But, aside from this, it is necessary to explore, however briefly, the theory of colonial discourse, if only because such an exploration, conducted as a preliminary to the analysis, would suggest that the exercise of discursive power within this field calls for what, following Edward W. Said, I have called the politics of secular interpretation. More specifically, it is in the context of the question of 'race' and feminist criticism that I shall locate one possibility for the development of a 'non-repressive and non-manipulative' mode of oppositional, inter-discursive intellection (Said, *Orientalism* 24).[4]

Subjectivity and Power in the Discourse of Colonialism

> And behind all these questions, we would hear hardly anything but the stirring of an indifference: What difference does it make who is speaking?
> Michael Foucault, 'What Is an Author?' 120

The decentring of 'man' is one of the most significant contributions of French structuralism to philosophical inquiry in the human sciences. For literary critics Michel Foucault's 'What Is an Author?' is perhaps exemplary of the anti-humanist, anti-logocentric endeavour. For Foucault the author is a 'principle of thrift in the proliferation of meaning' (118), a device by which a text's potential for generating polysemic interpretations could be contained. It is in reaction against the restraining effect of the author-concept that Foucault envisions a new horizon in the hermeneutics of culture.

What will be distinctive about the new dispensation, Foucault implies conspiratorially, is not the absence of constraints but a shift in focus from the anthropolatry of current scholarship in the humanities to a consideration of the very conditions of possibility for the production of knowledge of 'man' (120). The 'truths' of statements, Foucault insists, cannot be determined by recourse to the consciousness of a sovereign subject. On the contrary, 'truth,' which is never expressive of absolute knowledge, is constituted in discourse. 'Truth,' for Foucault, is provisional, its force deriving from a calculus of coordinates operative within an economy of force relations ('Nietzsche' 156–7; *Order* xiii–xiv; 'Truth' 132).

Foucault's discourse theory has been vigorously criticized for being fundamentally anti-humanist.[5] But, whatever its shortcomings in thus displacing 'man,' Foucault's discourse theory has made possible the development of paradigms for the analyses of cultural and social phenomena, paradigms in which 'man' can now be located as part of the ensemble of devices for the production and dissemination of power/ knowledge in the social formation.[6] However, theoretical problems remain. In the field of colonial discourse the notion and specificity of the colonial subject is probably the most intractable of these problems. This problem reared up its head in the recent critique of Homi K. Bhabha by Abdul R. JanMohammed.

Bhabha's theory of colonial discourse is rooted in a cross-disciplinary collage of concepts (from psychoanalysis, Marxist theory, and Foucauldian discourse theory). JanMohammed relies, almost exclusively, upon a materialist reading of Franz Fanon. But predicated in JanMohammed's synthesis of Marxist materialist theory and Fanon's analysis of imperialism and the colonial formation is a hypostasized, colonial subject. For JanMohammed, colonialism produces the 'native' as colonized, that is, as an undifferentiably and homogeneously victimized subject, a subject unceasingly and unrestrainedly acted upon by colonialism's hegemonic power.

For his part, Bhabha sees colonialism as 'an apparatus' whose primary function is not the discriminatory creation of privilege and nonprivilege, plenitude and lack, but 'the creation of space for a "subject peoples" through the production of knowledges in terms of which surveillance is exercised and a complex form of pleasure/unpleasure is incited. It seeks authorisation for its strategies by the production of knowledges of coloniser and colonised which are stereotypical but antithetically evaluated' ('Difference' 198). Thus the effectivity of colonialism's technology of subjectification is not, for Bhabha, the fixing of the 'native' in an ontologically determined stasis. Nor is it, indeed, the exclusive production of the 'native' as a colonized subject. Bhabha, following Foucault, conceives of the carceral technology of colonial governance as controlling, rather than being controlled by, the colonial subject.

Two features of this theory of the colonial subject and its relationship to the discursive apparatus of colonial power are particularly crucial for understanding JanMohammed's critique of Bhabha. The first has to do with Bhabha's conception of the apparatus of colonial power. For Bhabha, the object of the operations of the civil and cultural apparatus of colonial authority is not just the social repression of the colonized nor is it the representation of the colonized as a stereotype. In so far as the machinery of colonial power is a fundamentally panoptic and operationally self-determining device, it is characterized by the production rather than the repression of discourse.

In Bhabha's theory of coloniality power is neither subject to the control of a supreme consciousness nor exclusively operable by the colonizer. It is dispersed, as in the capillary process, throughout the body politic; it is embedded in relations of production and reproduction; it is located in symbolic practices. Power and power-effects are diffused, disseminated, and radiated through the various technologies of subjection, the systems and modes of the production and dispersal of discourse, and the processes of the unconscious in the colonial formation. Inasmuch as subjectification occurs in the context of colonialism's discursive and psycho-social space, and inasmuch as its effectivity is not restricted to the 'nativized' peoples, it is possible to postulate a colonial subject which includes the colonizer.

The second feature of this theory has to do with the colonial stereotype. It is here that Bhabha's reliance upon psychoanalytic theory is most marked. Contrary to conventional views about stereotypical representations of the 'nativized' subject in colonial texts, Bhabha argues that the stereotype is 'a much more ambivalent text of projection and introjection, metaphoric and metonymic strategies, displacement, overdetermination, guilt, aggressivity; the masking and splitting of "official" and phantasmatic knowledges to construct the positionalities and oppositionalities of racist discourse' ('Other' 34). In the stereotype, then, Bhabha does not see only a caricature of the colonized. Rather, what looms out of his analysis is the suggestion that the stereotype is a simplification because it is 'an arrested, fixated form of representation' rather than because it falsifies the real ('Other' 27). The representation of the colonized as stereotype in the symbolic practices of colonialism takes place, then, at the site of a struggle between colonizing and colonized subjects. Colonial culture transfixes its subjects between the primordial polarities of either/or: from these a choice must be made (or the subject is chosen). It is the compulsion to make this choice which, Bhabha argues, denies colonizer and colonized 'that form of negation which gives access to the recognition of difference in the Symbolic. It is that possibility of difference and circulation which,' he continues, 'would liberate the signifier of *skin/culture* from the signifieds of racial typology, the analytics of blood, ideologies of racial and cultural dominance or degeneration ... For the stereotype impedes the circulation and articulation of the signifier of "race" as anything other than its *fixity* as racism. We always already know that blacks are licentious, Asiatics duplicitous ...' (27–8). Taken together, Bhabha's redefinition of coloniality in terms of a regime of power characterized by the dispersal of its points of effectivity, and his postulate of the colonial subject as comprising colonizer and colonized subjected to the same regime of power, add up to a theoretical reconfiguration of the field of colonial discourse.

It is, therefore, against this theoretical reconfiguration that JanMohammed protests so vigorously. JanMohammed perceives in Bhabha an attempt at reducing 'the varied material and discursive antagonisms between conquerors and natives' to 'the workings of a single "subject"

...' (78). For him, Bhabha's strictures against intentionalism in readings of colonial texts provide an alibi which permits him to 'privilege' his view of colonial 'authority' as an apparatus of power characterized by 'ambivalence.' Furthermore, the obfuscation of colonialist discursive effects makes possible the suggestion that the stereotype equivocates between 'two equally valid meanings and representations' (79). For JanMohammed there is neither 'ambivalence' nor ambiguity in colonialist representations of the colonized. Rather there is just a well-orchestrated program of 'imperialist duplicity, operating very efficiently through the economy of its central trope, the manichean allegory' (80).

JanMohammed's critique of Bhabha's theory of the subject and power in colonial discourse issues from a misreading. In asserting that the stereotype of colonial discourse is fatally marked by ambivalence (for example, that ambivalence implicit in the colonialist's simultaneous assertion and denial of a shared identity between colonizer and colonized and a common destiny for 'man': 'All men have the same skin/race/culture' and 'Some do not have the same skin/race/culture' ['Other' 27]), Bhabha is not, it seems to me, collapsing the 'antagonisms between conquerors and natives' to the 'workings of a single subject.' This, nevertheless, is not to suggest that nothing is remiss with, or sorely missing from, Bhabha's theory of colonial power and the subject. In vain, for instance, does one search for intimations of the discriminatory effect of colonial power upon its subjects.[7] Nevertheless, by shifting the emphasis in the analysis of colonial power and its discursive effects from questions of the authenticity of representation to those of the modalities of its operations, Bhabha makes possible an understanding of colonial discourse as a field of multiple and dispersed points of articulation, points from which subjects may speak, but to which they are not riveted. It is, then, within this unstable field of multiple and contradictory intersubjective relations that I will now read Cixous's and Sontag's translations of tropes of otherness from the hegemonic discourse of colonialism into feminist theory.

Cixous in/out of 'Africa'

... every language theory is predicated upon a conception of the subject that it explicitly posits, implies, or tries to deny. Far from being an 'epistemological perversion,' a definite subject is present as soon as there is consciousness of signification.

Julia Kristeva, *Desire in Language.* 124

So begins 'From One Identity to an Other,' Julia Kristeva's semiotic reading of 'poetic language.' The significance of Kristeva's statement is that, with respect to the development of a critique of Hélène Cixous's interventions in the discourse of colonialism, it underscores the necessity for mapping the positionality from which statements can be uttered and 'truth' articulated.

I wish to begin this mapping with a comment on Cixous's literary style, since style is integral to her textual politics. As with many of the prominent figures in the French intellectual avant-garde (Gilles Deleuze, Luce Irigaray, Jacques Derrida, Jacques Lacan, Julia Kristeva), language is, for Cixous, the site of contestation and possible insurrection against the patriarchal values of the bourgeoisie (Conley 4). Thus writing, for her, entails a conscious or deliberate engagement with the 'cultural stereotypes, essentializing concepts and their attributes such as man/woman, masculine/feminine, active/passive' of masculinist discourse (6). With (and against) the Derridean notion of *différance* Cixous poses the question of sexual *différance*, of 'the possibility of a maternal, a matrical' (8). Against (and with) Lacan she attempts to shift writing from the masculine fear of castration to a consideration of the effect of 'the inscription' of women's desire on writing (9). In both cases Cixous is concerned, not to write 'woman' as a sameness or unity, not to construct a telos of femininity which could then be recuperated into the order of the Same. This fear of absolutizing knowledge of the feminine, Verena Andermatt Conley writes, leads Cixous to develop a layered literary style 'on a material level (phonemes and graphemes), on a conceptual level (questioning of the concept), and in an ongoing reflection on writing' (12). Commenting upon this subject, Toril Moi states that Cixous's style privileges metaphor, the 'poetic and explicitly anti-theoretical,' and reveals a resistance to critical analysis, to distinctions between theory and practice, text and world (102).

In spite of the critical attention which Conley and Moi give to Cixous's literary style, neither comments upon her use of colonialist tropes or their possible significance for the politics of her overall project. As in readings of Hegel's *Aesthetics* and *Philosophy of History*[8] most critics reading Cixous's work completely ignore the rhetorical function of 'Africa' and 'blackness' in her conception of femininity in 'The Laugh of the Medusa' and *The Newly Born Woman*.

The rhetorical impact of Cixous's intervention in feminist theory derives not only from her re-vision of the notion of 'woman' in phallocentric discourse; indeed, insofar as her project is to think/write/speak 'woman' from the edges of some of the most rigorous epistemo-

logical critiques of Western philosophical traditions, Cixous's rhetorical strategy depends for its effect upon a subvers(e)-ive translation of
the tropes of 'Africa' from colonialist into feminist discourse, that is,
the metaphorization of metaphors (McClintock 147–92). Whereas, in
colonialist discourse on Africa, the continent is represented (othered)
as the feminine (and, therefore, passive and submissive yet dark, hollow, vaginal, dangerous) anti-thesis of 'Europe"; in the realm (territory) of woman into which Cixous projects it, Africa remains a 'Dark
Continent.' But though still feminized, she (it) is now potentially powerful though still alien to her(it)self, unknown (yet knowable). From
the continent whose darkness signified the wilful implosion of the light
of Progress, Africa becomes the darkened world, now provisionally
folded in on itself, awaiting, like the River Congo in Joseph Conrad's
Heart of Darkness, the maturation of the juvenile Marlow and his 'penetration' of its vaginal interiority: 'True, by this time it was not a blank
space any more. It had got filled since my boyhood with rivers and
lakes and names. It had ceased to be a blank space of delightful mystery – a white patch for a boy to dream gloriously over. It had become a
place of darkness' (Conrad 52). For Cixous, unlike Marlow, the continent is transformed. It is, she urges, '*neither dark nor unexplorable.* –It is
still unexplored only because we've been made to believe that it was
too dark to be explorable. And because they want to make us believe
that what interests us is the white continent, with its monuments to
Lack. And we believed' ('Laugh' 255). This disclosure, which is actually
of the metaphor beneath the metaphor, the territorial 'truth' subsumed by the trope, is not simply a disclosure of any abstract truth
about Africa so much as a disclosure of patriarchal duplicity and colonialist misrepresentation. In other words, it is not so much Africa that
is revealed but colonialist revelations themselves that are disclosed.
And since the myth of the territory dis-covered is, like the myth of Gorgon Medusa, the realm of the feminine Other, Cixous collapses both
myths into each other. Soon, it is not possible to distinguish 'woman'
from Africa. Indeed, they merge:

> Moreover, the 'dark continent' trick has been pulled on her: she has been
> kept at a distance from herself, she has been made to see (= not-see)
> woman on the basis of what man wants to see of her, which is to say almost
> nothing ... She has not been able to live in her 'own' house, her very body.
> She can be incarcerated, slowed down appallingly and tricked into apart-
> heid for too long a time – but still only for a time. One can teach her, as
> soon as she begins to speak, at the same time as she is taught her name,

that hers is the dark region: because you are Africa, you are black. Your
continent is dark. Dark is dangerous. You can't see anything in the dark,
you are afraid. ('Sorties' 68)

No longer is 'woman' just body or 'Africa' just territory, both yoked
repressively to a whitened, phallic 'Europe.' Indeed, because she
would not (cannot) locate 'woman' in the logocentric and hierarchical
oppositions of patriarchy, ('Sorties' 63), Cixous must overthrow even
this distinction between Africa and woman.

Africa/woman is no longer the alien, Europe/man's Other, kept at a
sanitary distance, a distance which, paradoxically, simultaneously,
makes possible the colonizer's disavowal of knowledge while justifying
the quest for that knowledge, which is nothing but the power to
'know,' and knowing, control the known. By writing these so-called
halves together, running them into one an(d)other, Cixous doubles
them. Thus she could cross-attribute to each the characteristics of the
other. Being not only the territory of woman but woman herself, for
example, Africa can now be bisexualized, her organs multiplied. The
colonialist trope of the quiescent, seductive, and effeminate continent,
the mysterious and primeval land supplicating Europe's ravishment, is
trans/figured into a plurisexual entity. Confronting, this time, the self
(Medusa/'Africa') within her self, what woman sees is not the diabolic
visage of man's mythical woman but a labyrinthine, beautiful, 'black'
presence ('Sorties' 69).

Indeed, Cixous re-writes (doubles) two important myths: the Greek
myth of Gorgon Medusa and the colonialist myth of the Dark Continent.[9] By so doing, she breaks down the demarcation between the two,
thus suggesting a fundamental similarity between the strategies of
patriarchy and colonialism. This dissolution of the discursive boundaries separating patriarchal from colonialist tropes, this de-territorial-
ization of space and gender, also enables Cixous to write (her self) into
being a hitherto unspoken or muted subject, a (female, colonial) subject 'thrice culturally and historically marked' (Conley 4):

> I side with those who are injured, trespassed upon, colonized. I am (not)
> Arab. Who am I? I am 'doing' French history. I am a Jewish woman. In
> which ghetto was I penned up during your wars and your revolutions? I
> want to fight. What is my name? I want to change life. Who is this 'I'?
> Where is my place? ('Sorties' 71)

Thus, in taking up her own injunction to women to 'write' themselves into being, to write their texts '*In body*' ('Laugh' 257), Cixous also recalls her own history as a subject in colonial Algeria. Cixous re-writes the myths of the Medusa and the 'Dark Continent.' However, she does so by re-mythologizing both in terms of a non-essentialist, bisexual femininity.

I think it is necessary to recall the precise genealogy of the myth of the 'Dark Continent.' Patrick Brantlinger places the inauguration of this myth in the Victorian age. The darkening of Africa, Brantlinger argues, began at the historical conjuncture marked by the transition from slave to industrial economic enterprise in England. At this point 'imperialist ideology ... urged the abolition of "savage customs" in the name of civilization. As a product of that ideology, the myth of the Dark Continent developed during the transition from the main British campaign against the slave trade, which culminated in the outlawing of slavery in all British territory in 1833, to the imperialist partitioning of Africa which dominated the final quarter of the nineteenth century' (185). I will suggest, though without necessary documentation, that the process of which Brantlinger writes was inaugurated at an earlier period in English history. But, whenever the process may have begun, what is noteworthy is that from this point on, the myth of the 'Dark Continent' was to seize, to infest, the intellectual imagination of European novelists, poets, essayists, philosophers, politicians, entrepreneurs, and adventurers. Do we need to recall the harvest of books from this period in which this myth is either thematically situated at the core of the narrative or, for probably sensational reasons, emblazoned in the title page?[10]

More important than these disseminative acts, however, is the entrenchment of this myth in the imagination of European scholars; by the time Freud inaugurated the epistemic break in our understanding of human sexuality and the mechanisms of the unconscious, he would draw upon it as an apt, metaphorical characterization of female sexuality: 'the sexual life of adult women is a "dark continent" for psychology' (212). Thus did this myth, taken up by Freud, set in motion that almost normative tradition in modern psychoanalysis by which femininity has, literally speaking, become the 'Dark Continent' of the theory of sexuality. In view of her birth in Algeria and her professional disciplining, then, Cixous comes to this myth autobiographically, historically, and professionally (*Newly* 71, 80–3; Conley 4, 9, 141).

But whatever the source of this myth in her work, in appropriating it for the deconstruction of the patriarchal discourse on woman, Cixous infuses into her 'theory' a complex of ideological associations which the trope, by virtue of its genealogy, bears. The myth of the 'Dark Continent' belongs to what Anne McClintock, describing Rider Haggard's map of 'Kukuanaland,' calls 'a technology of possession' (151). Following the feminization of Africa in the imperialist imagination of nineteenth-century Europe, the body of the black female became the site of the enactment of white male sexual, political and economic virility (149–50). Often, of course, her symbolic annihilation was also a preliminary requirement for the fulfilment of the imperial mandate. In prose fiction as in cartography, colonialist discourse asserted and rationalized the authority of the colonizer over the colonized and the right of the (masculinized) former to plunder and ravish the sexuality and territories of the black (colonized) woman (150).

If my reading of Cixous's translation of this myth is correct, then it must be granted that, even in the environment of a feminist poetics of subversion such as she elaborates, the myth of the 'Dark Continent' re-enacts the fantasy of possession. But the question which this poses for us is this: who is now, that is in feminist theory, to be possessed through this myth? And, paradoxically, who would possess whom? What labour of control, in other words, is this myth supposed to perform in Cixous's work, and in whose interests? The questions of who possesses and who would be possessed are crucial not only to understanding the extent to which Cixous's poetics of femininity echoes the 'poetics of male authorship,' a poetics grounded upon the principle of the appropriation of posterity (McClintock 155). For the colonized (African) female subject Cixous's call to women (Africa) to repossess her(it)self, their territories, becomes even more problematic, since such a self-possession must entail an initial concession to imperialist ideology: accepting the totalization of (sexual) difference implicit in imperialism's levelling off of Africa as female principle. How is the colonized (African) female subject to possess herself if, already, she is possessed, that is, darkened, inscribed in the place of her sexuality as an ineffectual, effeminate genital? If already the object of possession, her sexuality appropriated into the phallogocentric economy of European male, colonialist discourse, in what manner could writing herself out of this dead end entail the appropriation of a myth whose fulfilment entails her annihilation?

Cixous's consciousness of her self in colonial Algeria is at once indeterminate, hybrid, and nomadic: 'I am (not) Arab'; 'I am a Jewish woman'; 'My people: all those that I am, whose same I am. History's condemned, the exiled, colonized, burned' ('Sorties' 71). But, at the same time, it is the experience of being an 'Algerian French girl' rather than a Kabyle, Shawia, Mozabite, or Arab that makes possible her 'seeing' of the repressive machinery of French colonialism in Algeria.

Without in any way minimizing the precariousness of life and limb for Jewish Algerians during this crisis,[11] I will suggest that although theoretically viable and consistent with her personal history, the profile of the colonized which emerges from details of Cixous's auto(bio)graphy is quite eccentric. The rhetorical effectivity of her translation of the myth of the 'Dark Continent' derives from the eccentricity of her positionality as a subject in colonial Algeria. Within the Manichean order of the colonial African world, any invocation of this myth as a call to sexual self-definition necessitates the investiture of a positionality in which the trope does not denote the prospect of annihilation for the speaking subject. Such a subject must be privileged by a conjunction of circumstances (race, ethnicity, gender, class) making for some discrepancy in access to discursive power and ambivalence in relation to colonial authority. By 'privileged' here I mean the subject's strategic location of the writing self, and of the import of writing itself as praxis.[12]

To be fair, Cixous is not unaware of the conjunction of circumstances to which I have alluded. Nor is she insensitive to their implications for her work. Responding to the prodding of Andermatt Conley on the 'silence' of the 'Third World' (at the scene of) writing, she says: 'I think that I am only a writer, and when I say that, I think that other women are completely militant ... I do not compare myself with them; I consider that they advance the woman's cause in a much more active and more immediate way than I do. So why, since I think that, do I not do it? I do not do it because it is true that I was born, so to speak, in the skin of writing, and I have writing in the skin' (Conley 142). To be born 'in the skin of writing,' to 'have' it 'in the skin,' is expressive of the subjective eccentricity to which I have alluded. And, insofar as her poetics valorizes the praxis of 'writing,' though it be writing as re-writing of the psycho-sexual fantasies of colonialism, Cixous inevitably writes out the colonized, female (African) subject, the subject from which writing is withheld.[13]

Sontag: Geo/Gender Politics

Complicity is the only understanding
Nadine Gordimer, 'What Were You Dreaming?'

Of the two lexicological senses in which the word *complicity* is defined,

one, complexity (from *complicare*, 'to fold'), is often forgotten. Overwhelmingly, the stress in usage of the word *complicity* in phatic perfor-
mances is upon the sense of transgression. Gordimer's use of the term,
probably inspired by those brutal circumstances in which many South
Africans find themselves, underscores quite vividly the aporia in Sontag's essay 'The Third World of Women.'

It is quite ironic that the destination of this essay is '*the editors of*
Libre, *a new Spanish-language political and literary Quarterly with a loosely
Marxist orientation* ...' ('Third' 180).[14] Since they '*live in Latin America*,'
Sontag considers her readership as belonging to the geopolitical con-
stituency of the 'Third World.' Thus the title of the essay is selected
with the intention of achieving, through the use of an analogy between
imperialism and women's subjection in patriarchy, the most direct
impact on this audience. 'All women,' Sontag writes,

> live in an 'imperialist' situation in which men are colonialists and women
> are natives. In so-called Third World countries, the situation of women
> with respect to men is tyrannically, brutally colonialist. In economically
> advanced countries (both capitalist and Communist) the situation of
> women is neocolonialist: the segregation of women has been liberalized;
> the use of physical force against women has declined; men delegate some
> of their authority, their rule is less overtly institutionalized. But the same
> basic relations of inferiority and superiority, of powerlessness and power,
> of cultural underdevelopment and cultural privilege, prevail between
> women and men in all countries. (184–5)

Ostensibly this analogy balances sexism with imperialism. 'Third
World' Marxist readers, for whom imperialism may have a particularly
repugnant resonance, would, presumably, comprehend the horror of
sexism when it is equated with imperialism. And, just in case earlier
analogies with racism in America were lost on her readers (180–2),
Sontag draws upon colonialism (185), an experience branded into the
collective memory of colonized peoples.

The effect of translating terminologies such as imperialism, colonialism, and racism into the environment of feminist theory, even
when the theory is projected beyond the borders of the metropolitan,
capitalist world, becomes clear when Sontag addresses the problem of
sexuality:

> The question is: *what* sexuality are women to be liberated to enjoy? The
> only sexual ethic liberating for women is one which challenges the pri-

macy of genital heterosexuality. A nonrepressive society, a society in which women are subjectively and objectively the genuine equals of men, will necessarily be an androgynous society. (188)

Thus the relations of equivalence between the terms of the analogies facilitates the occlusion of the differences between imperialism and sexual oppression. In turn, the occlusion makes possible the setting up of a hierarchy of problems of feminism, a hierarchy which, though not excluding the economic or the social (since the question of sexuality is not without economic or social implications), places ultimate priority upon the question of sexuality. It is on the basis of this prioritization, then, that Sontag will contest the relevance of a multi-issue 'left-revolutionary politics' for 'the struggle of women as women':

> Women are neither a class nor a nation. Politically radical women may well prefer to participate in existing insurgent movements than to limit their energies, as they see it, to the struggle of women. But in doing so they should realize that, at the most, all that such multi-issue revolutionary politics (like parliamentary party politics) offers women is reformist gains, the promise of formal 'equality.' (190)

The central paradox of Sontag's argument is that, in trying to isolate a woman-specific 'issue,' she obliterates the differences between women by overextending the imperialism/sexism analogy. Structurally there are striking parallels between these two terms. This, as I have suggested, is the basis for Cixous's re-writing of the mythologies of imperialism (Africa as the 'Dark Continent') and patriarchy (Gorgon Medusa). Unlike Cixous, however, Sontag obliterates the distinctions between the specific, historical processes of imperialism and the problems of male dominance by reducing the latter to the problem of sexuality. By so doing, she prioritizes the problems of sexuality over those of racism and imperialism.

In her critique of the limitations of 'left-revolutionary' groups Sontag does not express any opposition to the idea of armed struggle (196–7). But the failure to complicate her understanding of imperialism with an acknowledgment of the economic, social, and intellectual complicity of women in the 'First World' accounts for her failure to envision in 'Third World' anti-imperialist movements the potential for the emergence of an oppositional politics whose mandate includes the dismantlement of 'the biologistic reduction of the Law of the Dead Father to the rule of the actual, living male' (Gallop 14). I am not suggesting that Sontag fails to recognize the diversity in the constituencies of women. As a matter of fact, she carefully distinguishes between the forms of struggle which 'liberating a Thai peasant' and 'liberating a white factory worker in Detroit' necessitate (184). Nevertheless, she ignores the implications which these localized, specific resistances may have for any conception or actualization of the struggle for women's sexuality.

Sontag's analogically structured epistemology of imperialism (and, therefore, of global geopolitical relations) is the source of this problem. Sontag 'knows' the 'Third World.' For her, 'It' is a space, a territory, a homogeneous cultural polity defined in terms of its relations of exploitation with the 'First World.' But this knowledge is devoid of complexity. It is reminiscent of the imaginative knowledge which the liberal, suburban couple, Maureen and Bam Smales, have of 'July,' their servant of fifteen years, in Nadine Gordimer's *July's People*. Not recognizing the function of economic and social power in determining the nature of their relationship with July, they are fully persuaded that theirs is a 'friendship' grounded in fairness until, forced into refuge among 'July's people,' they are confronted with the mask of liberal ideology.

The most obvious reason for the miscarriage of Sontag's knowledge of imperialism is that it erases the sexual component of imperialism. As Anne McClintock points out in her analysis of imperialist ideology in Rider Haggard's fiction, the effectiveness of colonialist discourse depends upon the representation of women's sexuality (Freud's 'Dark Continent,' *terra incognita*) as the object of conquest and possession (152–3). It is upon the *topos* of empire that fantasies of male sexual virility converge, on the site of the black woman's body, with economic exploitation and racial discrimination. Consequently, any theorization of women's struggle which prioritizes the problem of sexuality does so at the considerably exorbitant expense of the heterogeneous forms of women's subjection and their experiences of their sexualities.

Beyond Analogies: Prospects for Writing/Reading 'Other-Wise'

To put the question differently: is the *Other* thinkable? Is it possible to think the Other, not as an object, but as a subject, a subject who would not, however, amount to the same?
Shoshana Felman, 'Madness and Philosophy *or* Literature's Reason,' 213

The foregoing critique of Cixous and Sontag inevitably raises a very difficult question, that is, the question of the possibility of constructing non-repressive, anti-imperialist knowledge of women (and men) in the present historical conjuncture. This fundamentally epistemological question, the subject of my epigraph, is not easily resolved. And maybe it is as well not to resolve it. Whatever the case, these questions crystallize the difficulties posed by the deployment of imperialist tropes of otherness in the discursive environment of feminist theory. For I believe that this difficulty is not unconnected with the search for methodological paradigms which, though sensitive to the similarities or discrepancies between diverse technologies of othering, would not yield analytical obliterations of the specificities which distinguish constituencies of women.

But I do not wish to pursue Felman's arguments here.[15] It is, rather, in Barbara Johnson's reading of Zora Neale Hurston that I wish to identify a potential for the production of a nomadic, de-territorialized hermeneutics of culture. I stress 'potential' because I do not wish to proffer Johnson's reading of Hurston as an absolute paradigm of cross-cultural intellection. Johnson's preliminary comments, narcissistic though they may seem, are symptomatic of what I consider essential to the production of an interlocutionary reading of the 'other,' a reading other/wise or, so to speak, against the 'selfgrain.' 'In preparing to write this paper,' she begins, she found herself 'repeatedly stopped by conflicting conceptions of the structure of address into which I was inserting myself.' These conflicting conceptions are racial (why is she, 'a white deconstructor ... talking about Zora Neale Hurston, a black novelist?' [317]), institutional (who is her audience and why?), professional (the application of 'strategies of literary theory to the analysis of Afro-American literature'), and theoretical and hermeneutic (the inauguration of a conceptual shift in her previous understanding of difference such that the stress in the 'conceptual operations of deconstruction' would no longer be in 'the realm of abstract linguistic universality' [317]). By reading Hurston through the complex prism of these conflicting conceptions of self and purpose, Johnson locates her work in the world of professional, social, and intellectual contingencies which impinge upon and shape the significance of any act of interpretation.

From the outset, then, Johnson's encounter with Hurston is marked by a simultaneous recognition of difference (distance) and similarity (contiguity). It is interlocutive, self-interrogative, non-repressive: 'It was as though I were asking her for answers to questions I did not even know I was unable to formulate. I had a lot to learn, then, from Hurston's way of dealing with multiple agendas and heterogeneous implied readers' (317). Johnson's recognition of the function of her 'strategic location' in relation with the material she wishes to read sets the stage, then, for a critical reading not only of Hurston's essays on racism and writing but, in addition, of a possibly necessary misreading of contemporary literary theory.[16]

In Hurston's writings Johnson discovers a rigorously ambivalent attitude towards the thematics of 'race' and a propensity for the use of parody. Johnson's discovery is really no different than that which Henry Louis Gates, Jr, has made about Hurston and her indebtedness to the tradition of signification in Afro-American literature ('Blackness' 285–321). To signify upon the essentialist premises of racist discourse, Hurston parodies its conceptual oppositions (black/white, passive/active, outside/inside), shifts her mode of address ('I' gives way to 'we,' the anthropologist looking from the 'outside' in becomes the black woman from the inside in and out), and constantly reverses the referents of her imagery. In this way she not only undercuts the grounds upon which the intelligibility of racist discourse is founded, but, more significantly, she develops an interlocutionary strategy for articulating issues of difference (racial and sexual).

Johnson's reading, then, exemplifies what I have called a nomadic, interlocutionary hermeneutics of culture. What it demonstrates so clearly is that it is possible, in the analysis of texts located in the literary traditions of colonized peoples or in the employment of imperialist tropes of otherness in feminist theory, not to obliterate 'the political or historical and indeed ideological differential' of women (Spivak 174). There is no contradiction between such an interlocutionary hermeneutics and the desire for unity in women's struggles. Indeed, such a hermeneutics is eminently suited to a historically grounded sense of unity, a sense characterized by the recognition that 'the unity of women' is, as Chandra Talpade Mohanty points out, 'something that has to be worked for, struggled towards' ('Feminist Encounters' 38).

Notes

1 It should be noted that the texts in question were produced in the 1960s and 1970s, a period that could be considered the dawn in the ongoing development of feminist scholarship in general and, in particular, the work of Cixous and Sontag. That said, it should also be granted that, given the evidence in recent feminist scholarship in the fields of colonial discourse and black feminism (see my references in this essay to hooks, Mohanty, Spi-

vak, and Lazreg), the difficulties presented by these texts are by no means resolved. The reason for this, I think, lies in the nature of the problems. Briefly, they are epistemological and methodological rather than ethical or ideological difficulties.

I use 'translation' in much the same sense as Timothy Brennan, paraphrasing Gabriel García Márquez, describes the poetics of the extra-territorial, 'Third World' artist: 'The "unbridled reality" of the colonial world cannot simply be reported; it has to be "translated" or "borne across" – and bearing-across is also, literally, "metaphor"' (68).

2 The title of Hull, Scott, and Smith's *All the Women Are White, All the Blacks Are Men, but Some of Us Are Brave* underscores hooks's argument.

3 'The tragedy of the experience' of anti-colonial intellectuals, Said writes, 'and indeed of all post-colonial questions, lies in the constitutive limitations imposed on any attempt to deal with relationships that are polarized, radically uneven, remembered differently. The spheres, the sites of intensity, the agendas, the constituencies in the metropolitan and ex-colonial worlds overlap only partially' ('Intellectuals' 45–6). Like Said, I consider it necessary to shift the emphasis in the study of these relationships from blame/ guilt to secular interpretation in order 'to expand the area of overlapping community between metropolitan and formerly colonized societies.' Thus could the abyss separating these intellectual communities on the subjects of imperialism (of which colonialism is just one instance) and women's subjection be bridged.

4 Though unconcerned with the inter-discursive circulation of figures of otherness, Barbara Johnson's work on Zora Neale Hurston nevertheless has direct relevance for the development of libertarian methodologies for the critical analysis of (women's) texts. I shall elaborate on this shortly.

5 See, for example, Hayden White; Said, *Orientalism*, 23, 94; and de Lauretis, *Technologies of Gender*, 2–3. For the latter two the critique of Foucault is predicated upon the need to account for the agency of the individual subject in the production of discourse. To be distinguished from these are those critiques of Foucault which are motivated by philosophical differences. For an example of the latter, see Derrida, 'Cogito,' 36.

6 The term 'discourse' is employed here in the Foucauldian sense of a 'conceptual terrain in which knowledge is formed and produced' (Young 48).

7 For a more extensive critique of Bhabha, see Parry, 32, 42–3.

8 For an analysis of the significance of 'Africa' in Hegel's theory of history and aesthetics, see Kalikoff.

9 For a study of the origins of this myth, see Brantlinger.

10 Brantlinger gives a sample of such titles (198).

11 None of the texts I consulted on this subject was really helpful. However, they do suggest that, individually and collectively, members of the Jewish

Algerian community were directly involved, in diverse social, political, and economic capacities, in French colonialism, the development of the Algerian resistance, and the eventual revolutionary struggle that led, in the early 1960s, to Algerian independence. See Bourdieu; Horne 58–9. The latter book, though valuable for its documentation, verges upon the sensational.

12 '– There has to be somewhere else, I tell myself. And everyone knows that to go somewhere else there are routes, signs, "maps" – for an exploration, a trip. – That's what books are. Everyone knows that a place exists which is not economically or politically indebted to all the vileness and compromise. That is not obliged to reproduce the system. That is writing ... I take books; I leave the real, colonial space ...' ('Sorties' 72).

    Though not pervaded by the sense of anomy characteristic of the fiction of Ayi Kwei Armah (see, for example, *Why Are We So Blest?*), Cixous's conception of the terrain wherein the literary enterprise can be undertaken is, as this statement demonstrates, decidedly utopian.

13 For a critique of the utopian propensity in Cixous's feminist poetics, see Moi 124–6. To consign the writing of postcolonial women to the ideological realm of 'Third World' is fraught with dangers, the most prominent of which is that, in view of the ideological freight of the 'Third World' as a signifier of nullity, absence, or regression in 'First World' discourse, such writing is likely to be burdened with these repressive referents.

14 Two months after this piece was presented at the Imag(in)ing Women Conference, I came across a reference to *Libre* in Retamar's *Caliban and Other Essays* (36). I assume Retamar is referring to the same journal as that to which Sontag addressed herself. If so, it is interesting to note the discrepancy between Sontag's and Retamar's perceptions of the ideological orientation of the publishers of *Libre*. For the former, the journal is 'loosely Marxist'; for the latter, it is the cultural forum for counter-revolutionary writing of the elite of the Latin American and Spanish bourgeoisie.

15 For a reading of Felman's intervention in this problem, see my 'The Madness of Africa(ns): or, Anthropology's Reason.'

16 Strategic location, according to Edward W. Said, makes possible the description of the 'author's position in a text with regard to the ... material he writes about' (*Orientalism* 20). My use of this term differs from his only in the substitution of 'critic' for 'author.'

Works Cited

Bhabha, Homi K. 'Difference, Discrimination and the Discourse of Colonialism.' In *The Politics of Theory*. Ed. Francis Barker et al. Colchester: U of Essex 1983, 194–211

- 'The Other Question: The Stereotype and Colonial Discourse.' *Screen* 24, no. 6 (1983), 18–36
Bourdieu, Pierre. *The Algerians*. Trans. Alan C.M. Ross. Boston: Beacon 1962
Brantlinger, Patrick. 'Victorians and Africans: The Genealogy of the Myth of the Dark Continent.' In Gates, '*Race*,' *Writing, and Difference*, 185–222
Brennan, Timothy. *Salman Rushdie and the Third World*. New York: St. Martin's P 1989
Busia, Abena. 'Liberation.' In Petersen and Rutherford, 121–2
Cixous, Hélène. 'The Laugh of the Medusa.' Trans. Keith Cohen and Paula Cohen. In *New French Feminisms*. Ed. Elaine Marks and Isabelle de Courtivron. Amherst: U of Massachusetts P 1980, 245–64
Cixous, Hélène, and Catherine Clément. 'Sorties.' In *The Newly Born Woman*. Trans. Betsy Wing. Minneapolis: U of Minnesota P 1986, 63–132
Conley, Verena Andermatt. *Hélène Cixous: Writing the Feminine*. Lincoln: U of Nebraska P 1984
Conrad, Joseph. *Youth, Heart of Darkness, The End of the Tether*. Ed. Robert Kimbrough. Oxford: Oxford UP 1988
de Lauretis, Teresa. *Technologies of Gender*. Bloomington: Indiana UP 1987
Derrida, Jacques. 'Cogito and the History of Madness.' In his *Writing and Difference*. Trans. Alan Bass. Chicago: U of Chicago P 1978, 31–63
Esonwanne, Uzo. 'The Madness of Africa(ns): or, Anthropology's Reason.' *Cultural Critique* 17 (1990–1), 107–26
Felman, Shoshana. 'Madness and Philosophy *or* Literature's Reason.' *Yale French Studies* 52 (1975), 206–28
Foucault, Michel. 'Nietzsche, Genealogy, History.' In his *Language, Counter-Memory, Practice*. Trans. Donald F. Bouchard. New York: Cornell UP 1977, 139–164
- *The Order of Things: An Archaelogy of the Human Sciences*. New York: Random House 1970
- 'Truth and Power.' Introd. Alexandro Fortana and Pasquale Pasquino. In his *Power/Knowledge: Interview and Other Writings*. Ed. Colin Gordon. Trans. Colin Gordon et al. Brighton: Harvester 1980, 109–33
- 'What Is an Author?' In *The Foucault Reader*. Ed. Paul Rabinow. New York: Random House-Pantheon, 1984, 101–20
Freud, Sigmund. *The Question of Lay Analysis*. Vol. 20 of *The Standard Edition of the Complete Psychological Works of Sigmund Freud*. Ed. James Strachey. London: Hogarth 1959
Gallop, Jane. *The Daughter's Seduction: Feminism and Psychoanalysis*. Ithaca: Cornell UP 1982
Gates, Henry Louis. 'The Blackness of Blackness: A Critique of the Sign and the Signifying Monkey.' In *Black Literature and Literary Theory*. Ed. Henry Louis Gates. New York: Methuen 1984, 285–321

254   Uzoma Esonwanne

–, ed. *'Race,' Writing, and Difference.* Chicago: U of Chicago P 1986
Gordimer, Nadine. *July's People.* London: Penguin 1981
– 'What Were You Dreaming?' In Peterson and Rutherford, 99–106
hooks, bell. *Ain't I a Woman: Black Women and Feminism.* Boston: South End P 1981
Horne, Alistair. *A Savage War of Peace: Algeria 1954–1962.* London: Macmillan 1977
Hull, Gloria T., Patricia Bell Scott, and Barbara Smith, eds. *All the Women Are White, All the Blacks Are Men, but Some of Us Are Brave.* New York: Feminist P 1982
JanMohammed, Abdul R. 'The Economy of Manichean Allegory: The Function of Racial Difference in Colonialist Literature.' In Gates, *'Race,' Writing, and Difference,* 78–106
Johnson, Barbara. 'Thresholds of Difference: Structures of Address in Zora Neale Hurston.' In Gates, *'Race,' Writing, and Difference,* 317–28
Kalikoff, Hedy. 'Hegel's Shadow-World: "Africa" and the *Aesthetics.*' Dept. of Comparative Literature, U of Michigan, unpublished paper
Kinneavy, James L. *A Theory of Discourse.* New York: Norton 1971
Kristeva, Julia. *Desire in Language: A Semiotic Approach to Literature and Art.* Ed. Leon S. Roudiez. Trans. Thomas Gora, Alice Jardine, and Leon S. Roudiez. New York: Columbia UP 1980
Lazreg, Marnia. 'Feminism and Difference: The Perils of Writing as a Woman on Women in Algeria.' *Feminist Studies* 14 (1988), 81–107
Lorde, Audre. 'The Master's Tools Will Never Dismantle the Master's House.' In *This Bridge Called My Back: Writings by Radical Women of Color.* Ed. Cherríe Moraga and Gloria Anzaldúa. New York: Kitchen Table 1983, 98–101
McClintock, Anne. 'Maidens, Maps, and Mines: The Reinvention of Patriarchy in Colonial South Africa.' *South Atlantic Quarterly* 87 (1988), 147–92
Miller, Nancy K, ed. *The Poetics of Gender.* New York: Columbia UP 1986
Mohanty, Chandra Talpade. 'Feminist Encounters: Locating the Politics of Experience.' *Copyright* 1 (Fall 1987), 30–44
– 'Under Western Eyes: Feminist Scholarship and Colonial Discourses.' *Boundary 2* 12, no. 3 – 13, no. 1 (1984), 333–58
Moi, Toril. *Sexual/Textual Politics: Feminist Literary Theory.* London: Methuen 1985
Parry, Benita. 'Problems in Current Theories of Colonial Discourse.' *Oxford Literary Review* 9, no. 1–2 (1987), 27–58
Petersen, Kirsten Holst, and Anna Rutherford, eds. *A Double Colonization.* Mundelstrup, Denmark: Dangaroo P 1986
Retamar, Robert Fernández. *Caliban and Other Essays.* Trans. Edward Baker. Minneapolis: U of Minnesota P 1989

Said, Edward. 'Intellectuals in the Post-Colonial World.' *Salmagundi* 70–1 (Spring-Summer 1986), 44–64

– *Orientalism.* New York: Random House 1978

Sontag, Susan. 'The Third World of Women.' *Partisan Review* 40 (1973), 180–206

Spivak, Gayatri Chakravorty. 'French Feminism in an International Frame.' *Yale French Studies* 62 (1981), 154–84

White, Hayden. 'Michel Foucault.' In *Structuralism and Since: From Lévi-Strauss to Derrida.* Ed. John Sturrock. Oxford: Oxford UP 1979, 81–115

Young, Robert. Introduction. 'The Order of Discourse.' By Michel Foucault. In *Untying the Text: A Post-Structuralist Reader.* Ed. Robert Young. Boston: Routledge 1981, 48–51

⊘ 14 ⊘

Splitting Images: The Postmodern Ironies of Women's Art

LINDA HUTCHEON

The powerless have a culture of resistance, which works through code; through the direct statement of polemic; and through the indirection of irony and parody.

Catharine R. Stimpson, 'Nancy Reagan Wears a Hat,' 227

With these words Catharine Stimpson introduces us to the multiplicity of strategies open to women (as well as other marginalized groups) today. And feminists, she goes on to argue, have been forced by circumstances to develop a special aptitude for making the most of that multiplicity. This she wittily and ironically calls 'herterogeneity' (241). Nevertheless, in the midst of that multiplicity have been created hermeneutic communities – of feminists, of women – in which the 'indirection of irony and parody' find both comprehension and appreciation. When Di Brandt, in *Questions i asked my mother*, ironically twists Walt Whitman's 'I sing the body electric' into 'I sing the Rubber Lady / varicosed / garter hosed' (20), she feminizes – and politicizes – the acts of both verbal celebration and poetic representation.

Ironic allusion like this functions in two ways. On the one hand, it marks a *rupture* with, or at least a subversion or critique of, the text parodied; on the other, it establishes a community of discourse among readers and thus marks a kind of interpretive *continuity*. The latter is most often true when it is women's work that is cited (or even parodied) by women artists. With continuity, of course, comes what many see as irony and parody's elitist pleasure: the pleasure of being among the initiate, of possessing the requisite knowledge to 'get' the joke. But ironic citation is also a way of exploring the history of visual and linguistic representations of women; its deconstructing power can show up the often unconscious but deeply embedded sexist premises that underlie those representations (Voldeng 51–8).

Feminist artists have used irony in both these ways in their re-examination of the politics of representation. But what is it about the situation of women that makes irony such a powerful rhetorical tool? Many feminist critics argue that the condition of marginality (with its attendant qualities of muteness and invisibility) has created in women a 'divided self, rooted in the authorized dualities' of culture (Ostriker 11). If so, then the 'splitting images' they create through their double-talking ironies are a means of problematizing the humanist ideal (or illusion) of wholeness, and with that, of hierarchy and power. Contradiction, division, doubleness – these are the contesting elements that irony lets in by the front door. Coral Ann Howells outlines well the splits that I would see as opening up the great potential for irony in Canadian women's writing, in particular:

> ... these diverse narratives [by Canadian women] may be seen as sharing in a collaborative effort of revision and resistance. They are all responses to the pressures of colonial history and the contradictions within a colonized mentality where one's self-image is split between imposed traditional patterns and authentic experience which reveals the incompleteness or falsity of tradition. They all raise questions about inheritance, which is unmistakably plural in a culture like Canada's with its two mother cultures and two official languages in addition to its native cultures and the cultures of its waves of immigrants. Dispossession and disunity will be as important in these narratives about origins and inheritance as their attempts to forge a distinctive cultural identity which will in its turn be influenced by such awareness. (184)

I do think that Canada's multiple dualities make the nation ripe for irony; add to this the particular condition of women in many Western societies – working within, but contesting, a patriarchal dominant order – and you often get the specific 'splitting images' of ironic expression.

The particularities of irony as a rhetorical trope mean that the line between the said and the unsaid is both acknowledged and crossed: the said, the spoken, is to be heard and discounted; the unsaid, the unspoken, is unheard but counted. Irony may well be part of what

Nicole Brossard calls an oscillatory movement (228), revealing a certain ambivalence in women's writing, but whether it is to be interpreted as actual ambivalence or not, most commentators seem to agree that irony certainly is one of a number of obviously privileged modes of working through binary oppositions that can be found in the work of women artists (Lamy 199–210). Poet Lola Lemire Tostevin uses it to write about what she calls women's 'cognition in the Cuisinart':

> makes one wonder where
> all this leads
> a middle age middle class
> housewife
> > pots
> > pans
> > gnosis
> no household word
> this food for thought (n. pag.)

What this kind of irony also suggests is that women writers have never underestimated the subversive and disruptive power of humour. Nancy Walker, in her study *A Very Serious Thing: Women's Humor and American Culture*, argues that humour is an aggressive, not passive, mode and that it is inextricably bound to questions of power and autonomy as well (11). Irony thus becomes one of many useful modes by which to acknowledge the force of a dominant culture and yet to contest it, in perhaps covert but not ineffective ways. This particular use of irony is related to what Walker calls a feminist deployment of a doubled text 'to pose a subtle challenge to the stereotype or the circumstance that the writer appears superficially merely to describe' (13). Often, of course, the writer also chooses to go beyond mere description. Calling the Canadian West the 'kingdom of the male virgin,' Aritha van Herk retells Genesis in feminist ironic terms:

> In the beginning, God made Adam and Eve. God said to Adam, 'Do not eat of the fruit of the tree of the knowledge of good and evil.' Eve wasn't around yet, according to the story. When the serpent beguiled Eve, and Eve, being a curious woman, ate of said fruit and gave some to Adam, he didn't resist, although it was to *him* that God had given the explicit instructions. Look it up. I could enter into a protracted discussion of the intelligence of the curious person, but that would interrupt the story.

The long and short is, when God started asking difficult questions, Adam said, '*She* gave it to me. Not *my* fault.' (59)

While van Herk reads Genesis as a displacement of blame, Lorna Crozier, in her poem 'Mother Tongue,' even more self-reflexively reads it as the site of the ironic tension between narcissism and control, between communion and surrender, a tension that is part of understanding the history of the act of writing for many women. Eve becomes the centre of this poem that sets in ironic juxtaposition Adam, 'who wouldn't touch her,' and the snake 'she wanted' and which 'entered / every orifice / long before Adam' (47). This, Crozier offers enigmatically, is the knowledge of the snake; this is 'why we've been taught / to fear them.' This knowledge turns out to be that of the 'sibilant syllables / speaking the flesh,' the snake 'spelling itself as it moves,' saying 'womb-words, / the secret names that Eve knew' (47–8). In ironic contrast to this moving, nurturing, living language is what is given us by Adam – in Judeo-Christian culture, the one known as the first namer:

> ... Adam
> lined up all the animals
> and carved his cold hard alphabet
> beginning with the first
> letter
> of his own name. (48)

Irony is one of the ways for women writers to subvert that 'cold hard alphabet' of narcissism and power.

When women are either denied access to the representational strategies of patriarchal society or feel constrained and uncomfortable within them, irony also becomes a familiar mode of voicing protest. In *Cat's Eye* Margaret Atwood uses the temporal and experiential difference between her adult narrator and the same woman's earlier self to set up a series of ironies that underline how even young girls construct and are constructed by societal images of women. Setting up her pretentious thirteen-year-old self, Risley relates her words: '"I'm going to have a pet iguana," I say, "and wear nothing but cerise."' The older voice then comments: 'It's a word I have recently learned' (5). This self-subversion matches her deadpan ironic undercutting of others as well. When a girlfriend mocks the young Risley's inexperience in the ways of women ('You don't know what a *cold wave* is?'), the older self adds: 'she says I am her best friend' (51). Atwood's ironies are multi-edged, however, cutting against both cultural stereotyping and women's own complicity with that process. As she grows up, Risley leaves the rough world of her brother and other boys to enter an unfamiliar feminine terrain, and neither escapes her irony:

> I don't have to keep up with anyone, run as fast, aim as well, make loud explosive noises, decode messages, die on cue. I don't have to think about whether I've done these things well, as well as a boy. All I have to do is sit on the floor and cut frying pans out of the Eaton's Catalogue with embroidery scissors, and say I've done it badly. Partly this is a relief. (54)

As she grows up and decides to be an artist, Risley runs into another set of cultural conditions that provoke yet another ironic response in her. First of all, she learns that 'art' is something that 'has been accomplished, elsewhere' (276) – the distancing by the past tense and the place designation obviously offering a certain obstacle to the aspiring Canadian artist. Gender clearly enters here, but so does nationality. Canada's newly selected flag becomes the perfect ironic symbol for Canadian artists in the 1960s, as this description of it makes clear: 'two red bands and a red maple leaf rampant on white, looking like a trademark for margarine of the cheaper variety, or an owl-kill in snow' (311–12). This is the kind of irony that has, I think, earned Atwood the dubious fame of being the 'Ice-Queen' of Canadian letters. It is not that her works lack warmth; they simply abound in ironies – with all their attendant suggestions of distance and control. But Atwood's ironies are also often passionate ones, with their understated and literally unsaid, unspoken attacks on injustices: gendered, national, racial, ethnic.

While *Cat's Eye* is about a visual artist, its own medium is obviously language. This raises a related question: how does the semantic double-voicing of verbal irony get trans-coded into visual terms? In order to suggest some ways of examining this process, I would like to look at the work of two Canadian artists, Joyce Wieland and Joanne Tod, as representing two generations of women and their use of a very politicized structural – rather than semantic – irony. My choice of the well-known film-maker and painter, Joyce Wieland, will likely surprise no one: most viewers respond at once to the humour, at least, in her work. She herself claims that she has used it as a political and strategic way to 'get to' the viewer: 'Humor got people interested, and being radical isn't enough ...' (Rabinovitz 10). And irony is often a mode of humour in her work. One of the reasons may be that she is the past mistress, so to speak, of 'splitting images' or, as one critic has put it: 'She thrives on a tension *between* things – between craft and medium, female and male, earth and spirit, fact and feeling, pain and pleasure, activism and contemplation ... passion and reason' (Lippard 7).

Her early work shows the impact of the wit and humour of Dada, Duchamp, and American artists such as Robert Rauschenberg. *Heart On* (1961) is an early piece whose obvious punning on the male 'hard on' is ironically feminized in a number of ways – beyond the title itself, of course. It is in a medium usually associated with women's work – cloth, in fact, unstretched linen whose drapings at the top suggest a bedsheet. A collage of patches and hearts, it defamiliarizes the clichéd image of love and joy by ironically juxtaposing it with the rather different associations of red stains on a white sheet: menstruation, the loss of virginity (recalling the title's pun), childbirth, women's haemorrhaging pain, or, more metaphorically, the bleeding of broken hearts. This is the mixture of the amusing and the serious that the 'splitting images' of irony allow.

The culmination of this politicized ironic play was undoubtedly her 1971 retrospective at the National Gallery in Ottawa, entitled True Patriot Love/Véritable Amour patriotique. Here her nationalist, environmental, and feminist politics came together with great power – and great fun. Her use of traditionally feminine media (quilting, embroidery, rug-hooking) and her collaborative work with craftswomen both play ironically (and perhaps even unintentionally) against the art world's honorific format of the single 'star' retrospective and the individually signed works. This is not to undermine the importance of Wieland's contribution to either the valorization of teamwork and women's crafts at this early date (in feminist art history, at least) or her tribute to the volunteer women who executed her concepts. But these ironies are unavoidable, both in the show as a whole and in single works. It *is* a star show; she *does* sign her work.

In the 1970s, when Canada was once again self-consciously indulging in its favourite national pastime – having a protracted identity crisis – Wieland added further ironies to her gendered ones, playing with the icons of national identity: the maple leaf, the beaver, Laura Secord, even the national anthem. Her embroidered series of red (lipstick-simulated) mouths singing 'O Canada' (*O Canada Animation* [1970]) has been called 'at once loving, feminine and patriotic' (Townsend-Gault 124). It is also not without its ironies that play in (and on) the space between our senses (visual versus aural) and our aesthetic versus realist impulses (or perhaps our formalist versus verifying instincts). Most people find it impossible to look at this *without* moving their own lips to check its accuracy of depiction!

Wieland's politics in the early 1970s were clearly as nationalist as they were feminist; they were also ecological. Inspired perhaps by Claus Oldenberg's soft sculptures, Wieland began working with quilting as a medium – another women's art, usually relegated and reduced to the domestically useful. *The Water Quilt* (1970–1) represents, again using embroidery, a series of arctic flowers on pieces of fine white cotton cloth that is almost as transparent as water. These pieces are also moveable flaps which can be lifted to reveal soft cloth pillows and rather 'hard' written texts: selections from James Laxer's *The Energy Poker Game*. Thus the innocent beauty and ecological fragility of the arctic flora are ironically juxtaposed with a protest against Canada's dealings in the energy debate with the United States over arctic waters.

As for many Canadians, for Wieland the United States is a problematic neighbour. She has often been quoted as saying that her time in New York both radicalized and Canadianized her. In works like *N.U.C.* (1966) the oral/written play in the title alerts the viewer to a series of political ironies. The top portion of this mixed-media work, a circular pillow, is green – the stereotypical colour of nature – but here the pillow is made of plastic. Beneath a large dollar sign perched atop the green pillow, clear pink plastic reveals a photograph of a war-torn landscape and soldiers. Does money offer rose-coloured glasses through which to view war? Suspended from this is a plastic heart with American stars on it, which acts as a little purse to contain newspaper clippings about the Vietnam war: the feminized purse literally holds the male violence in its heart. As in Leonard Cohen's equally ironic novel *Beautiful Losers*, the natural gives way to the plastic in an Americanized, demonized version of 'progress.'

Wieland's more recent works seem to move from deconstructing irony and polemic to symbolic enigma and searching. Provoking thoughts of William Blake's visionary art, a work like her *The Artist on Fire* (1983), for example, presents a painting of an artist (a self-portrait?) painting a nude male angel, who is crowned with a laurel wreath and sporting an obvious erection (the formal line of which is continued by her paintbrush). He seems about to consume – or kiss? – a flame-coloured, pentecostal bird, as flames actually lick at his body. The female painter-figure is the source of the flames, in a number of senses, as her body is portrayed 'on fire' *and* her brush paints it. The passion suggested by being 'on fire' is seemingly for art now and for the male only as represented –or created – in art. Inverting Genesis in her own ironic way, she empowers woman as the godlike creator.

It may have taken Joyce Wieland the better part of a career to use irony in such a constructive (rather than what could be called a deconstructive) way – that is, to encode empowerment. But Joanne Tod, a younger Toronto painter, uses irony in a consistently oppositional manner. For instance, her *Self Portrait* (1982) deploys a series of multiple ironies to tease out a political message about feminine subjectivity as represented in North American culture. These complex and perplexing ironies have been interpreted in different ways by different viewers (see Bernard), but the first subverting irony of the work, for most, is that this is *not* a self-portrait of Joanne Tod: it is an image copied from an advertisement in an old (rather than recent) fashion magazine of an elegant woman in an evening dress, standing in a dramatic, if stagey, pose. The setting is not Canadian, but Ur-American: the Lincoln Memorial in Washington, D.C., with the Washington Monument asserting its phallic presence strongly. Yet, in another sense, this *is* an ironically pointed portrait of how the gendered (and national) subject is portrayed – and constructed – for and by women (and Canadians) themselves. As in advertising copy, there is a text inscribed here upon the image itself, but this one appears strangely incongruous and personal: 'neath my arm / is the color of Russell's Subaru.' Is this an anti-Yuppie, anti-consumerist irony against people who define themselves by their possessions? Are the Japanese car and the American setting signals of the 'global village' of advertising – and therefore of the aptly named 'multinational' capitalism of today? This very same painting is later reproduced in an even more obviously ironic context, hanging on a dining-room wall – art as purchased commodity – in *Self Portrait as Prostitute* (1983; fig. 1). Here the table is set for dinner, but no one is present. Perhaps guests have not yet arrived; more likely, the absent woman is busy cooking in the kitchen. The title here suggests, then, that women have been 'prostituted' not only to fashion and advertising but to domesticity – all manifestations of male power.

Tod's work uses irony to point to contradictions which both patriarchal and capitalist ideologies mask. Race is the other issue that is taken up in her paintings, and once again it is the 'splitting images' created by irony that articulate her resistance and opposition. If I were to mention a work called *Reds on Green* (1978), you might expect from the title alone that it could possibly illustrate – or parody – colour field painting (in particular) and modernist formalism (in general). But Tod suggests that there is perhaps another politics beyond the art-world one

Fig. 1. *Self Portrait as Prostitute*, by Joanne Tod, 1983

here: a politics, literally, of colour. The Chinese communists painted here are figured not only to engage the title's punning play on 'Reds' (on a green background), but also to raise the issue of race and colour in *politics* as well as art. In some of her work representations of Asians and blacks replace women as symbols of Otherness within what is often (increasingly mistakenly) considered Canada's more or less homogeneous and largely white (as well as patriarchal and capitalist) society. The problematic issue of appropriation haunts this replacement.

In works like *Infiltration* (1988), installed in the Pump Building of Toronto's Harris Water Filtration Plant for the (radically site-specific) show called Waterworks in 1988, a black male takes on the role of symbolic Other, here shown trying to block out (with his hands over his ears) both the noise of the capitalist water-purifying industry (this work is in the noisiest room in the plant) and the represented (in white paint over the surface of the painting) notes of Handel's *Water Music* – both perhaps equally (and punningly) 'white noise.' Given its physical position in the water filtration plant, this work plays iconographically in complex and often confusing ways with notions of social and racial in*filtration*. Similarly, in *Research and Development* (1986; fig. 2), Tod represents black men in a racially unmixed black bar, drinking Black Label beer. The semiotic overdetermination of blackness here is juxtaposed with two oddly inserted, separate paintings: one (on the upper left) portrays six white middle-aged men in what appears to be a corporate boardroom where 'research and development' may not include thinking about racial equality of opportunity; the other (on the upper right) is a representation of New York's Guggenheim Museum. Have modern art and big business connived in marginalizing certain racial groups? Are all three figured places equally ghetto-ized enclaves?

Tod's works are never simple and almost never provoke unambiguous interpretations. For instance, is *Five to Twelve* (1988) a parody of the academic still life (titled paradoxically in terms of time)? It certainly represents, on one level, a legitimized (in both aesthetic and capitalist terms) image of beauty: a silver *objet d'art* featuring two female angels holding up a large silver bowl. But on the upper right third of the painting are four circles, acting almost as cut-outs, through which we see two menacing eyes and full lips, seemingly of a black person. As one critic has asked, is it a 'critique of commodification or a celebration of it?' Is it 'a silver samovar or a Molotov cocktail?' (Mycroft 87). While clearly confusing, the work nevertheless does suggest certain interpretive possibilities. The women portrayed on the silver *objet* are

Fig. 2. *Research and Development*, by Joanne Tod, 1986

idealized, beautiful images of winged womanhood, identical each to the other and thus symbolically unindividuated. Motionless and burdened with the bowl's weight, they are turned away from the viewer (at a ninety-degree angle). While the viewer's eyes may safely and voyeuristically enjoy these female forms, the eyes of the black – likely male – showing through those four holes look back at the viewer, not at the art object or its figured females at all. This confrontational staring back/ staring down foregrounds both sexual and racial differences often ignored in art historical commentary before the advent of postmodernism and its politicized concerns. This kind of art asks its viewers to question the processes by which we represent the Other as well as our selves and our world, and to become aware of the means by which we literally *make* sense and *construct* order out of experience within our particular culture.

Otherness is not only a question of gender, race, or ethnicity. As the powerful work of the gay photographer called Evergon makes clear, it is also a question of sexuality. In Jane Rule's words: 'A body we know is designed to die will never be a simple plaything, nor will the language we use to express our sexuality ever be without that irony' (22) – that irony and many others. It would take another paper entirely to explore this complex issue, but in the writing of Rule, Nicole Brossard, Daphne Marlatt, Betsy Warland, and so many others, the representation of lesbian desire is often undertaken using the deconstructive and constructive tools (and weapons) of irony, articulating a particular and specific sexual identity. In Warland's words: 'as a lesbian i do not speak Universese. few people do' (112).

Yet humanist (read: male) culture has always implicitly or explicitly argued that *it* does speak 'Universese.' And this claim too has come under the ironic scrutiny of feminist writers like Lola Lemire Tostevin, who ironically takes on *Time Magazine*'s art critic, Robert Hughes, for his put-down of Judy Chicago's *The Dinner Party* for her 'obsessive stereotype' and for her explanation of her choice of the vagina as 'her mark / of otherness and identity' (n. pag.). He called it '"jargon" and "femspeak."' Tostevin contrasts this with Hughes's own statement (made to the *Globe and Mail* shortly after this) that 'his favorite art form has always been surrealism / his favorite artist Joan Mirò' because he was 'bonded' to both when he was young. In his own cited words: 'like a baby duck you fixate / on the first thing you see / and that's mom ...' (n. pag.). She picks up on the obvious structural irony of the juxtaposition of these two statements and signals her oppositional intent with that frequent marker of irony – 'of course':

of course
and mom doesn't have a cunt
especially if she's male surrealist
whose work has been described
as 'emblematic ... biomorphic abstraction ...
amorphous shapes floating in ambiguous space ...'

menspeak? (n. pag.)

Tostevin – unlike Hughes – is Canadian, and if that now popular line
of argument is to be believed, Canadians and women share certain
conditions of marginality. They also share strategies of resistance. Joyce
Wieland once said that she thought of Canada as female (Armitage
24), and certainly in the small bronze statue called *The Spirit of Canada
Suckles the French and English Beaver* (1970–1), she ironically echoes
Romulus and Remus and the founding of the Roman Empire by
reversing the animal/human roles and making what she calls 'Canada'
into a woman suckling two beavers. Although the surface humour is
clear, what does this irony suggest, not only in terms of the obvious
Canadian (colonial) identity, but also in relation to the aboriginal peoples? The politics of gender, nation, and perhaps (though occluded)
race are all called into play, literally, by ironies – intended or not. Monika Gagnon also argues the same Canada/woman connection, and this
time the First Nations that preceded French or British colonization are
implicitly factored in:

> In its historical position representing an excluded and marginalized
> group (culturally, economically and symbolically), feminism has a strate-
> gic contribution to make to the debate over empire and colony, a debate
> which has a particular urgency for Canada, especially in the context of its
> desperate attempts to establish both a political and cultural identity.
> Given this cultural context, we might consider the condition facing Cana-
> dian women artists as one of a double oppression: as the oppressed sex in
> a patriarchal culture haunted by a history of colonization, a colonization
> that begins with the French and the British and continues today with
> American dominance culturally and economically. (121)

With the proliferation of doublings – national and gendered, among
them – irony can come into its own as *one* way – not the only way, but
nevertheless a not ineffectual way – of both articulating that duality
and of resisting the monologic singleness and masterful 'Universese'

that so often characterize the discourse of cultural dominants, be they
patriarchal, capitalist, humanist – or American.

Works Cited

Armitage, Kay. 'Kay Armitage Interviews Joyce Wieland.' *Take One* 3, no. 2
(1972), 23–6
Atwood, Margaret. *Cat's Eye*. Toronto: McClelland and Stuart 1988
Bernard, Karen. 'Ironing Out the Differences: Female Iconography in the
Paintings of Joanne Tod.' In *Essays in Canadian Irony*. Robarts Centre for
Canadian Studies, Working Papers Series 2. North York, Ont.: York U 1989.
1–9
Brandt, Di. *Questions i asked my mother*. Winnipeg: Turnstone P 1987
Bringhurst, Robert, et al., eds. *Visions: Contemporary Art in Canada*. Vancouver:
Douglas and McIntyre 1983
Brossard, Nicole. 'Mouvements et stratégies de l'écriture de fiction.' In
Godard, 227–30
Crozier, Lorna. 'Mother Tongue.' In her *Angels of Flesh, Angels of Silence*. Toronto: McClelland and Stuart 1988, 47–8
Fitzgerald, Judith, ed. *Sp/elles: Poetry by Canadian Women*. Windsor: Black Moss P
1986
Gagnon, Monika. 'Work in Progress: Canadian Women in the Visual Arts 1975–
1987.' In Tregebov, 101–27
Godard, Barbara, ed. *Gynocritics: Feminist Approaches to Canadian and Quebec
Women's Writing/Gynocritiques: Démarches féministes à l'écriture des Canadiennes et
Québécoises*. Toronto: ECW 1985
Howells, Coral Ann. *Private and Fictional Words: Canadian Women Novelists of the
1970s and 1980s*. London: Methuen 1987
Lamy, Suzanne. 'Les Enfants uniques nés de père et de mère inconnus.' In
Godard, 199–210
Lippard, Lucy. 'Watershed: Contradiction, Communication and Canada in
Joyce Wieland's Work.' In *Joyce Wieland*. Toronto: Art Gallery of Ontario/Key
Porter 1987, 1–16
Mycroft, Robert. 'Joanne Tod: Four Characteristic Works and Some Necessary
Queries.' *Canadian Art* 5, no. 4 (1988), 84–7
Ostriker, Alicia Suskin. *Stealing the Language: The Emergence of Women's Poetry in
America*. Boston: Beacon 1986
Petersen, Kirsten Holst, and Anna Rutherford, eds. *A Double Colonization: Colonial and Post-Colonial Women's Writing*. Mundelstrup, Denmark: Dangaroo P
1986

Rabinovitz, Lauren. 'An Interview with Joyce Wieland.' *Afterimage* 8, no. 10 (May 1981), 8–12

Rule, Jane. 'Sexuality in Literature.' *Fireweed* 5–6 (Winter 1979–Spring 1980), 22

Stimpson, Catharine R. 'Nancy Reagan Wears a Hat: Feminism and its Cultural Consensus.' *Critical Inquiry* 14, no. 2 (1988), 223–43

Tostevin, Lola Lemire. *Color of Her Speech.* Toronto: Coach House P 1982

Townsend-Gault, Charlotte. 'Redefining the Role.' In Bringhurst et al., 122–55

Tregebov, Rhea, ed. *Work in Progress: Building Feminist Culture.* Toronto: Women's P 1987

van Herk, Aritha. 'A Gentle Circumcision.' In Petersen and Rutherford, 59–67

Voldeng, Evelyne. 'L'Intertextualité dans les écrits féminins d'inspiration féministe.' In Godard, 51–8

Walker, Nancy A. *A Very Serious Thing: Women's Humor and American Culture.* Minneapolis: U of Minnesota P 1988

Warland, Betsy. 'As a writer …' In Fitzgerald, 112–13

15

Ariadne's Scissors: New Writing by Australian Women

KATERYNA OLIJNYK LONGLEY

'May my story be beautiful and unwind like a long thread ...' she recites as she begins her story, 'a story that stays inexhaustible within its own limits.'

Trinh T. Minh-ha, *Woman, Native, Other*, 4

Adriadne ... entered the prison where Theseus was confined. There she tremblingly offered him a ball of twine and a sharp sword, bidding him tie one end of the twine to the entrance of the labyrinth, and keep the other in his hand as a clue to find the way out again.

H.A. Guerber, *The Myths of Greece and Rome*, 223

In all the versions of Ariadne's story she falls in love with Theseus and gives him the thread by which he escapes the labyrinth, having killed the Minotaur to whom Athenians had long been forced to be subservient. Theseus returns to Athens a hero. The thread enables him to avoid the innumerable side passages that would have lured him away from the desired home path. In return for this gift Theseus promises to take Ariadne back with him to Athens as his wife. In her eagerness to help him, she does not consider that she may find a better use for the thread herself or serve her interests better by cutting it to pieces and denying Theseus his illusion of heroism; nor does she imagine that in giving her would-be lover his lifeline she is potentially giving up her own. At least, she does not think of these things until she finds herself abandoned, and some say pregnant, on the island of Naxos, while Theseus sails on homeward in triumph. 'I gave him a break all right, supplied him with his birthstring' (137), says the Ariadne in Marion Campbell's recent novel, but in her story too the abandonment brings a recognition of the need for a new and very different emergence. 'I have travelled too far, too slowly,' she says, 'in the wings of their theatre, listening for a break, queueing with the other understudies' (136).

It is difficult to imagine a more effective metaphor for storytelling than the unravelling thread marking a path through the labyrinth of other possible paths towards a desired end. This is how histories are written and, some would say, how lives are lived, spun out into a thread by Clotho, as the Greek myth tells us, until it is snipped by Atropos. But stories need not be told like this, and, as we learn more about non-Western and nonheroic ways of approaching history and storytelling, it becomes clear that they very often are not. In her personal portrayal of traditional Aboriginal life the Aboriginal writer Labumore makes this comparison between white and black historymaking in Australia:

> My tribes never did write books, because they never could understand any of the kind, but only sit in circles around about the bush or camps and yarn about which is a right way to keep all their laws to be carried out, and how to be kept ... same with customs, legends and cultures. But a white man keeps all their past life of their heroes ... are kept in books to make a history of the adventures of great men of the past, scenes of the past and the last words that he spoke. (206)

Australia's literary history, like that of many other colonized countries, has been constructed as a single line. All those influences that might weaken its status as independent and self-determined, and that might complicate its clarity as a recognizable entity or as a strong path out of colonial subservience, are excluded. For this reason the line of development has been kept relatively simple. According to the official version of this history, the colony rapidly distinguished itself from the mother country by establishing myths of its own, based on uniquely Australian experiences of the bush, of bush values, and of such bush heroes as bushranger, convict, and drover. Even though there have been many major and internationally known writers in this century who have worked outside of this formula (such as Katharine Susannah Prichard, Henry Handel Richardson, Patrick White, Christina Stead, Xavier Herbert), there is no doubt that, however irrelevant it may be to the experience of most of us living in Australia now, the old nationalist bush mythology still has a powerful grip on the imagination. It remains popular partly because it promotes qualities that are easily admired by a postcolonial consciousness – resourcefulness, rebellious- ness against worn-out social codes, and good-humoured courage – but also because it protects Australians from having to confront the mon- strous images that lurk in the other historical passages it obliterates. It is only during recent years that the horrifying underside of this power- ful romantic story has come under regular attack within Australia, in the academy, in the press, and in creative writing. It is attacked for all that it excludes in the process of retaining the purity of its line – Aborigines, women, immigrants, urban life – and for the consequent destruction of the connection between the brief moment of white 'Australian' history and the multitudes of other kinds of history invisi- bly criss-crossing it, among them a vast network of Aboriginal histories reaching back into worlds which are constructed on different organiz- ing principles of time and space and significance. Paradoxically the recent bicentennial festivities, organized to celebrate two hundred years of white history, played a major role in rethinking concepts of his- tory, time, and mythology as they have been constructed here by white settlers. Much of the credit for this must go to creative writing, espe- cially the writing of women.

The year 1988 was very special for writing in Australia. In a flurry of national self-consciousness and national pride the federal government offered bicentennial writing grants for projects that were in some way related to bicentennial issues. For writers there was an obvious dilemma. What constitutes a suitable bicentennial project? Clearly the bicentenary was a celebration, but what were we celebrating? In Austra- lia, as in Canada and the United States, settlement is a euphemism for invasion, oppression, and genocide. For many people the occasion of the bicentenary became an embarrassment which could be handled only by foregrounding the ugly issues that the national celebration, by its very nature, wanted to push away. Almost a century ago the forma- tion of the federation of Australia was a similar milestone in the coun- try's development of a self-image, but then, at least, there was the pleasure of independent nationhood to turn people's gaze away from the victims of this triumph. There was no adequate distraction this time. Designed to celebrate an anniversary in Australia's white history, the bicentenary instead forced attention upon the infinite web of other histories amongst which this new small line threads its way, and especially upon Aboriginal history.

Amongst the white writers who are committed to taking up new posi- tions in relation to traditional histories is Paul Carter; in *The Road to*

Botany Bay he provides the first history of Australian settlement to reject the linear, chronological model and to replace it with a model that, as he says, 'is concerned with the haze which preceded clear outlines' (xxii). His is a *spatial* rather than a linear history, one which 'discovers and explores the lacuna left by imperial history' (xxiii), and one which abandons all claim to authority (xxiii). In this kind of history it is recognized that every narrative excursion is *made* to look like the main road through events while it is actually merely a chosen track which, like any route, 'opens up the possibility of going back, of turning a private passage into a road, a road reaching more places than ... imagined' (xxiii). Going back into the white prehistory of Australia, Carter reminds us that more than a century and a half before 1788 the Dutch captain Dirk Hartog fixed a pewter platter to a tree in a cove on the northwest coast. Recorded on the plate, eventually found there by the British, was the name 'Cape Inscription.' The name was more grimly prophetic than the Dutch explorers could possibly have known of the future claiming of the land by a process of naming, mapping, and writing which gradually scribbled over the ancient maps, names, and songlines, invisible to the invaders, by which the country had been read for millennia.

While Carter was breaking new ground as a historian, the creative writers were already doing what he was advocating and doing it in all kinds of ways. His plea for a less linear and less theatrical approach is answered perfectly by Kate Grenville's feminist counter-history, *Joan Makes History* (1988), to which I will return, but her book also does something that Carter's history does not get far with at all – it, like a number of other experimental works, puts women firmly in the centre. In *Working Hot*, for example, Mary Fallon attacks male history head-on in this way:

> *how to read the* Encyclopaedia Britannica
> *upside down inside out and backwards*
> *I put down my book*
> *I see the clear lie*
> *following the women through history following*
> *a will-o-the-wisp*
> *a Robin Goodfellow something wunderkind written*
> *in invisible ink that the editors erased*
> you'd think they never had mothers
> *it's all a bunch of blokes getting together*
> *boys' talk in boys' town*

to stop falling into memory
where concentration is mesmerism stupification
sexuality is onanism
playing for keeps
fellating for advancement and profit
big noting yourselves again
building the new wine bags hoping they'll fill with wine
a spider a lapping a woman breast stroking
through the sky
wait till they call you a silly old bag your degree your
p h d won't help. (280)

Others, writing from many different positions, also contributed to the severing of the line of 'main road' history, not to replace it with an alternative route but to make the point that an infinite number of other paths exist, each with its own claim on historical space. Their enterprise, particularly that of women, was to question the whole institution of history by means of fiction, alternative histories, poetry, and biography, and also by questioning these genres themselves, since they traditionally have colluded with official historical narratives in their privileging of particular kinds of stories and viewing positions. This has certainly been the case in Australia: white men have claimed the central position so consistently in all these genres that, until recently, few Australians would have been able to name any woman who was the main subject of a novel, short story, poem, or biography produced in the nineteenth century in Australia (or even in the twentieth); yet every Australian knows of Banjo Paterson's poem 'The Man from Snowy River' and the stories of Ned Kelly's exploits. The racist and masculinist bias that has been so strong in Australian historical writing has been supported by creative writing to a very high degree. In breaking out of this pattern, much of the new creative writing in Australia is involving itself directly with history at the same time as it disrupts the genres which have, even in their most basic assumptions (such as those regarding linear progress, significance, and closure), helped to shape popular historical consciousness. One of Kate Grenville's narrators speaks for many Australians previously left out of history when she says:

Imagine them in their millions ... So many lives! Being explorers or prisoners of the Crown, hairdressers or tree-choppers, washerwomen or judges, ladies of leisure or bareback riders, photographers or mothers or mayoresses.

> I, Joan, have been all these things. I am known to my unimaginative
> friends simply as Joan, born when this century was new, and now a wife, a
> mother, and a grandmother: Joan who has cooked dinners, washed socks
> and swept floors while history happened elsewhere ... Allow me also to
> acquaint you with a small selection of those other Joans, those who made
> the history of this land. (5)

The achievement of the last few years in Australia is that many such
voices are being strongly heard in the new work of Aborigines, immigrants from Europe and Asia, and experimental women writers; in the
recuperative work of women such as Elizabeth Webby and Dale
Spender, who are republishing lost nineteenth-century women's writing; and even, at last, in the new literary histories.

In response to the new writing critics and commentators are beginning to devote attention to the political and theoretical issues that it
raises; books are consequently being written about works which, even a
few years ago, would not have been considered central enough for
publishers to risk accepting critical writing focusing upon them. In
fact, the new writing must take much of the credit for enforcing a
higher degree of theoretical awareness in the field of Australian literature. In some cases it does so by being highly self-conscious about its
subversive role in relation to mainstream literature. This is so in the
novels of Marion Campbell, Mary Fallon, and Finola Moorhead, in the
biographies and histories of Carolyn Polizzotto, in Adriana Ellis's collection of short fiction, *Cleared Spaces, Cleared Moments* (1990), and in
the recently launched experimental Western Australian collection *No
Substitute*. In each case the nature of the narrative experimentation is
different, and so the genres are stretched in various ways to accommodate these innovations and those of the future.

Marion Campbell constructs disjointed time frames and spaces for
her characters as part of a strategy of fragmented presentation which
reflects a vision of women's fragmented subjectivity. Mounting a more
direct attack on the masculine heroic tradition in Australian writing,
Finola Moorhead's *Remember the Tarantella* presents a fictional world
with no men in it at all. Like these two writers Mary Fallon is concerned with women's desires and women's sexuality. Her radically
experimental novel provides a superb demonstration of the ideologically subversive power of new narrative forms. In a different sphere the
historian Carolyn Polizzotto questions historical and biographical traditions by foregrounding their limitations and making the unreliable
process of gathering information as much the subject of her work as the

information itself. In doing this, she blurs the distinction between history and fiction and so robs history and biography of their factual authority. While it is more difficult even to point to the range of innovation in collections of stories and poems, it is important to mention that such books are making an important contribution precisely because they allow many kinds of approaches to be taken within a single volume and so alert readers to the role of genre and structure in generating meaning. *No Substitute*, for example, includes drawings as well as poems and stories that are written from so many different positions that they inevitably draw attention to the multiple choices involved in representation. Two of the presses involved in encouraging this kind of work are Fremantle Arts Centre Press (a small press which has recently become internationally known with the huge success of Sally Morgan's *My Place*) and Sybylla, which is committed to women's writing. Also emerging from the more innovative publishing houses are works that are translated from another language or transcribed from the oral mode or both. In other cases the cultural position from which the work is written itself demands a focus on such questions as these: What happens in the process of translation? What is the difference between oral storytelling and written? Why would a writer choose to cut a work to pieces, make it a tangle of cut threads, and abandon the safety of the one-line narrative? How does it feel to expose to the culture that has excluded and degraded you the pain of that exclusion? These are questions that are only just beginning to be explored in Australia, largely as a result of the explosion of new writing that has, at last, broken the clear path of 'mainstream' literature with its moral and cultural certainties. Wherever it comes from, the new writing that I am dealing with answers in some way Trinh T. Minh-ha's question in *Woman, Native, Other*: 'where does a committed woman writer go?' (20). The writers are doing what she is urging all postcolonial women writers to do: 'discard[ing] their forms ... shak[ing] syntax, smash[ing] the myths, and ... *unearth*[ing] ... new linguistic paths' (20).

One of the most exciting explosions of publishing activity in this context has been in the area of Aboriginal writing, a field which hardly even existed a decade ago as far as Australia's general reading public was concerned. Of all the many achievements in this area recently, two come to mind as spectacularly successful and potentially powerful in their capacity to change public perception of aboriginality. One is the best-seller *My Place* by Sally Morgan (1987), now published in the United States and Britain, and being translated into German; the other is the establishment of the Aboriginal press, Magabala Books, in

Broome in northwest Australia. 'Each woman, like each people,' writes
Trinh, 'has her own way of unrolling the ties that bind' (148); and in
the case of Aboriginal writers telling the stories of their people, there
has been the same mess of multiple ties to work through that confront
other women of colour :

> Storytelling, the oldest form of building historical consciousness in com-
> munity, constitutes a rich oral legacy, whose values have regained all
> importance recently, especially in the context of writings by women of
> color. She who works at un-learning the dominant language of 'civilized'
> missionaries also has to learn how to un-write and write anew. And she
> often does so by reestablishing the contact with her foremothers, so that
> living tradition can never congeal into fixed forms. (Trinh 148–9)

This is precisely what Sally Morgan has been doing over the past few
years. Her story is unusual in that she was 'protected' from the knowledge of her aboriginality until she was an adult, and so her search for
her suppressed history involves going back over her white past and
remembering the gaps, the puzzles, and the mysteries – the many
briefly glimpsed closed-off passages which she did not take but which
now open up whole new worlds of personal and communal history.
These do not simply *add* something to her remembered white history;
they change its composition through and through by showing it to be
interwoven with family and tribal histories which continue to be dis-
covered and which have an infinite capacity to keep on opening up the
ever-multiplying past. In fact, this is true of *any* white Australian history
when it admits its connection with Aboriginal history; Morgan's work
stands as a metaphor for the revision of white history that is just beginning to take place as a result of the increasing consciousness of the
degree of official suppression in the past. In fact, in this way, it provides
a model for and a vindication of all historical revision, particularly
where it involves taking circuitous and out of the way paths as opposed
to the paths of heroes. Having recorded the stories of her mother, Gla-
dys Corunna, and her grandmother, Daisy Corunna, Morgan writes of
her recognition that much more has been lost or hidden than can ever
be known. 'My mind went over and over [Nan's] story; every word,
every look. I knew there were great dark depths there, and I knew I
would never plumb them' (351). Sometimes this is because some stories are too painful to be told. As Daisy Corunna says to her grand-
daughter, 'Well, Sal, that's all I'm gunna tell ya. My brain's no good, it's
gone rotten. I don't want to talk no more. I got my secrets, I'll take

them to the grave. Some things, I can't talk 'bout. Not even to you ...
They for me to know. They not for you or your mother to know' (349).
Morgan's new book, *Wanamurraganya*, follows an opening created by
the first, and while it tells the personal story of her grandfather by
Aboriginal kinship, Jack McPhee, it also contributes to the wider pat-
tern of emerging Aboriginal history.

Other important works by Aboriginal women include Glenyse
Ward's *Wandering Girl*, the autobiography of a woman who, following a
common pattern for Aboriginal children in the first half of this century, was taken away from her parents as a baby, educated on a mission
until she was sixteen, and then sent to be a domestic servant on a
wealthy white farming property. There is also Labumore's *An Aboriginal
Mother Tells of the Old and the New*, told in a manner which constantly
reminds the reader that this is the story of a woman whose way of
understanding herself, the world, and history is quite different from
that of white Australians. The insights it allows into traditional Aboriginal tribal life are remarkable. Other such works, by men as well as
women, are being published by Magabala Books. This press is devoted
to collecting Aboriginal knowledge, in whatever form it might take,
and publishing it in ways that retain as many traces of Aboriginal
speech and culture as possible, accepting the losses involved in translation and transcription and taking the obvious financial risks. The prize-
winning *Raparapa*, stories by nine Aboriginal stockmen, and Bill
Neidjie's *Story about Feeling* are two of their latest publications; *Wandering Girl* (1988) is another; more are in the pipeline, including the transcribed oral narrative of Alice Beelie and the account of Aboriginal life
given by Pat Lowe, a white woman who has married into an Aboriginal
community and way of life. Recently, in another medium, the first
Aboriginal musical production, *Bran Nu Day*, written by Jimmy Chi and
produced in Broome, was a complete sell-out at the Perth Festival. It is
yet another counterhistory which is making its point by colluding with
and exuberantly raiding white genres and institutions.

Although it is less unified and less militant, immigrant or multicultural writing is also contributing to the restructuring of Australia's
national self-image. As well as three major anthologies, *Displacements 1*,
Displacements 2, and *Beyond the Echo: Multicultural Women's Writing*, there
have been such novels as Angelika Fremd's *Heartland*, Rosa Capiello's
Oh Lucky Country, and, recently published, *Emma*, an oral autobiography of a German immigrant, Emma Ciccotosto, translated and transcribed by Michael Bosworth. Last year the first Australian book of
multicultural theory and interpretation, *Striking Chords: Multicultural*

Literary Criticism, was published. Edited by myself and Sneja Gunew, this book considers the specific ways in which multicultural writing is undermining monolithic cultural myths – which were difficult enough to justify in 1901 when the population was 98 per cent English in background, but now impossible. Rosa Capiello is, with Polish-born Ania Walwicz, one of the very aggressively irreverent debunkers of Australian culture as it has been commonly constructed. This extract from *Oh Lucky Country* demonstrates:

> Together with the migrant masses I am contributing to the process of your civilization, to widening your horizon which doesn't extend any further than the point of your great ugly nose. I tear the weeds out of your ears. I give you a certain style. I teach you to eat, to dress, to behave and above all not to belch in restaurants, trains, buses, cinemas, schools. You probably don't know, but I'll tell you in confidence, for your information, that your country, which is now mine too, is based on a gigantic belch. Its flag flutters in the wind created by the toxic gases produced by your stomachs which are choked up like sewers. The myth about being happy and lucky is based on your drunken bouts. (192–3)

With path-clearers like Rosa Capiello giving courage to other immigrants, and with newly emerging confidence drawn from an increasing sense of solidarity as a transnational group, a 'Fifth World' of post-war immigrant experience claims attention not so much in terms of specific nationality (old or new) but in terms of the common history of displacement and diaspora. As this happens, it is likely that many new stories will emerge to change Australia's historical consciousness more radically. As I have argued elsewhere, the stories of many immigrants have not been told in the past because of fear. The fear takes many forms, but it often begins as political fear based on the experiences from the 'Old World' which originally forced them to become refugees. In the case of my own parents, Ukrainian refugees, whose stories I am gathering, I am aware how slow and painful the process of self-revelation is within a culture that has, for the most part, rejected all but the pleasantly exotic tourist or gourmet aspects of Fifth World culture and blocked off those aspects that might force a confrontation with pain or shame. One of the challenges urgently facing those who are writing these stories is that of form. How can the stories be told when they have, through constant re-editing *in memory*, already put up their defences against the hostile histories into which their tellers have been absorbed? And how can any literary form do justice to the multiple intersection of such stories with oppressive public texts and secret private texts, some of them still too painful to be spoken? If there is any example to follow in Australia, it is in the work of experimental women writers who are, more than anyone else, taking risks with structures that are capable of self-revelation and self-protection at the same time. In fact, the form becomes a powerful weapon against fear, the fear of other more authoritative stories and of the dark well of lived experience that it opens up. To quote Trinh T. Minh-ha again: 'We fear heights, we fear the headless, the bottomless, and the boundless ... This is why we keep on doing violence to words: to tame and cook the wild raw, to adopt the vertiginously infinite' (131).

Three women whose recent writing demonstrates three kinds of experimentation with narrative are Kate Grenville and Mary Fallon, whose work I have already mentioned, and Marion Campbell in *Not Being Miriam*. Kate Grenville's *Joan Makes History* specifically attacks heroic historicism by chopping up its own structure into intimate parallel narratives of women whose lives provide alternative vantage points and time frames for viewing Australian colonial history. It works by parody and carnivalesque inversions. Even more radically subversive of narrative process itself is Mary Fallon's *Working Hot*. In this remarkable book about women's social and sexual lives there is a narrative thread outlining an intense lesbian relationship; but it has to be drawn out from a jumble of quotations and virtuoso imitations of film, literature, opera, theatre, public notices, interviews, letters, puns, and jokes, including crazy games with names such as Toto Caelo, One Iota Smithereen, Shadow Box, Lexi Con, and E C R Saidthandone, who acts as a kind of narrator or chorus. It is simultaneously about women's lives within patriarchal social structures and women's speech and writing performing in relation to coercive canons and genres. In a chapter called 'Curse-evidence ' Fallon writes,

> they'll never stop using words strung into sentences
> wound around a knuckle-duster logic
> they pistol-whip you with words
> he said to me 'you know basically there's a certain
> amount of megalomania about you and I mean that in
> the broadest possible sense'
> he said this to me
> on and on
> about topics of interest
> stories from the army interesting medical cases

```
pedantic
ponderous
patronising
bore
men
bore
you
into
the
ground
are
great
weighty
things
on
top
of
you
must tell you
level you trying to make you explain to them just
precisely exactly what you mean in clear logical concise
terms with examples and 'could you define your terms
more satisfactorily please so there's no
misunderstanding in a less emotive way if you don't
mind.' (191–2)
```

Above all, Fallon's novel is about pain, pain inherent in everyday negotiation with worlds that *appear* to be safe and friendly but which constantly reduce women. Using different oppositional strategies, Marion
Campbell looks closely at the day-by-day impact on women's lives of
the abject roles they find themselves accepting and the degrading discourses by which they find themselves being defined, and with which
they often helplessly collude. While Mary Fallon works by direct attack
and violent satiric exposure, Marion Campbell explores similar problems by presenting the intersecting lives of her women in bits and
pieces, taking leaps through time and space, but nevertheless allowing
the reader to enter their most private worlds of dream, imagination,
and feeling and to become deeply involved with their lives. *Not Being
Miriam* is brilliant in its capacity to subvert the genre of the novel by
cut-and-paste methods of presenting parallel lives while at the same
time exploiting the novel's *realist* capacity to draw the reader into its

lifelike maze of 'experience.' In this Campbell is like Virginia Woolf:
she has the ability to create the illusion of the lived moment and of the
feelings and thoughts that fly through it, but she does not arrange the
moments into chronological lines, nor does she allow them to shape
coherent characters. As the title suggests, *Not Being Miriam* is about
fractured subjectivity and, more specifically, about the various ways in
which women find themselves negated or left out of desired worlds by
being defined in terms of *something else*, something they can never be
nor want to be. Miriam is the long-dead former wife whom one of the
women, Elsie, can never replace in the imagination of her husband,
and the book is, in part, a presentation of her intense suffering as a
result of this perpetual competition with an opposition that can never
be challenged, never be questioned. Elsie's humiliation in this situation becomes a metaphor for the way in which women are haunted by
impossible and *undesired* images which harass them daily – just as Miriam's portrait, with the help of the husband, constantly reminds Elsie of
her shortcomings in his eyes. In the house is a poster-sized blow-up of
an old photograph of Miriam, kept on a wall behind a rack of the husband's trousers. This is how the moment is described when Elsie is
drawn by fascination and anger to look, as she often does, at the hated
portrait:

> The scissors are in Elsie's hand. This time she has parted the trousers with
> a purpose. The scissor blade caresses, tracing loops on the glossy skin on
> the poster. It doesn't break the surface ... Now the scissor traces out loops
> on the skin of the photo. (106)

Bess, another of the women in Campbell's novel, is not so much concerned with attacking imposed definitions and formulae for her existence as with creating a means of her own for finding shape in the
chaos of lived experience: 'What she needs first is a single technique to
hold it still in her head, to find a centre of gravity, something to stop
the waves of chaos scrolling through' (82). To hold back chaos is to
hold back pain, and this Bess can sometimes do by inventing roles for
herself to act out, identities that temporarily hold together like a successful 'FIND THE GIRL IN THE TANGLE sort of exercise' (143).
    If there is anything that can draw together the diverse writers of the
post-bicentenary period in Australia, it is the way in which all grapple
with the problem of how much they can afford to cut themselves free
from the voices and structures and other controlling ties which have
silenced them or led them along prescribed paths in the past, and how

they can thereby control the chaos in *writing* while acknowledging its existence in life. Also, related to this challenge of *form*, there is a concern with expressing pain, but expressing it in such a way that they do not leave themselves open to further abuse. The contemporary Australian examples demonstrate some of the strategies, available to all post-colonial women, of exploring pain from positions of power.

Works Cited

Astley, Thea. *It's Raining in Mango*. Melbourne: Viking 1987
Baker, Candida. *Yacker 3: Australian Writers Talk about Their Work*. Sydney: Picador 1989.
Brock, Peggy, ed. *Women, Rites and Sites*. Sydney: Allen 1989
Brooks, David, and Brenda Walker, eds. *Poetry and Gender: Statements and Essays in Australian Women's Poetry and Poetics*. St Lucia: U of Queensland P 1989
Campbell, Marion. *Not Being Miriam*. Fremantle: Fremantle Arts Centre P 1988
Capiello, Rosa R. *Oh Lucky Country*. St Lucia: U of Queensland P 1984
Carter, Paul. *The Road to Botany Bay*. London: Faber 1987
Chatwin, Bruce. *The Song Lines*. London: Cape 1987
Ciccotosto, Emma, and Michael Bosworth. *Emma: A Translated Life*. Fremantle: Fremantle Arts Centre P 1990
Ellis, Adriana. *Cleared Spaces, Cleared Moments*. Fremantle: Fremantle Arts Centre P 1990
Fallon, Mary. *Working Hot*. Melbourne: Sybylla 1989
Fremd, Angelika. *Heartland*. St Lucia: U of Queensland P 1989
Gelder, Ken, and Paul Salzman. *The New Diversity: Australian Fiction, 1970–1988*. Melbourne: McPhee 1989
Goodwin, Ken. *A History of Australian Literature*. London: Macmillan 1986
Grenville, Kate. *Joan Makes History*. London: Heinemann 1989
Guerber, H.A. *The Myths of Greece and Rome: Their Stories, Signification and Origin*. London: Harrap 1907
Gunew, Sneja. *Displacements 2: Multicultural Storytellers*. Victoria: Deacon UP 1987
–, and Kateryna O. Longley. *Striking Chords: Multicultural Literary Interpretations*. Mebourne: Allen and Unwin 1992
Hergenhan, Laurie, ed. *The Penguin New Literary History of Australia*. Victoria: Penguin 1988
Jolley, Elizabeth. *The Sugar Mother*. Victoria: Penguin 1989
Labumore [Elsie Roughsey]. *An Aboriginal Mother Tells of the Old and the New*. Victoria: Penguin 1986

London, Joan. *Sister Ships and Other Stories.* Fremantle: Fremantle Arts Centre P 1986

Moorhead, Finola. *Remember the Tarantella.* Sydney: Primavera 1987

Morgan, Sally. *My Place.* Fremantle: Fremantle Arts Centre P 1987

– *Wanamurraganya: The Story of Jack McPhee.* Fremantle: Fremantle Arts Centre P 1989

Narogin, Mudrooroo [formerly Colin Johnson]. 'Sunlight Spreadeagles Perth in Blackness: A Bicentennial Gift Poem.' Printed in the external studies reader for Australian literature (H284). Coordinator Kateryna Olijnyk Longley. 1990

Neidjie, Bill. *Story about Feeling.* Broome: Magabala 1989

Polizzotto, Carolyn. *Approaching Elise.* Fremantle: Fremantle Arts Centre P 1988

Spender, Dale, ed. *The Penguin Anthology of Australian Women's Writing.* Victoria: Penguin 1988

Trinh T. Minh-ha. *Woman, Native, Other.* Bloomington: Indiana UP 1989

Ward, Glenyse. *Wandering Girl.* Broome: Magabala 1988

White, Terri-ann, et al. *No Substitute: Prose, Poems, Images.* Fremantle: Fremantle Arts Centre P 1990

Zwicky, Fay. *Ask Me.* St Lucia: U of Queensland P 1990

'touch the matrix': Native/Woman/Poet

JEANNE PERREAULT

Contemporary First Nations women's poetry exists in the contexts of ethical and aesthetic traditions of First Nations literatures, and of feminist consciousness. Negotiating these communities, some poets make their individual voices and values bear the weight of a poetry that is both 'representative' and which refuses 'representation' as a role. Wendy Rose indignantly asserts that 'if you are of a minority group and you are a writer, you are simply not allowed to do anything other than be a minority writer' ('The Bones' 254). In a similar vein Chrystos insists that she is not 'the "Voice" of Native women' (*Not Vanishing*, Introduction n. pag.). These First Nations women poets resist the position and role of representative minority writer, working against the force of the white reader's impulse to see any 'other' as necessarily the voice of her people. Yet both Chrystos and Wendy Rose, like most other First Nations writers, at times choose a collective voice, speaking from a 'we' that takes on some of the rights and responsibilities of being 'representative.' They take on this collective voice in the face of the dominant culture's assumption of the right to define what constitutes subjectivity or its absence, and universality or its demise. The First Nations woman writer is neither allowed the voice of an individual subjectivity – formed and informed by available discourses and articulating them in unique ways – nor perceived as speaking in a 'universal' voice, addressing a 'common' human condition. What she is left with then is a narrow frame in which she is perceived as the 'voice of her people.' Refusing this imposed role while claiming the right to speak from deeply rooted cultures, First Nations writers articulate a resistance to 'obliteration either of [their] cultures or [their] personhood' (Allen 2). This double task brings into play a range of 'subject-positions' from which the multivocal text can speak.[1] And resistance is a consistent and powerful choice in the writing of First Nations women. But 'resistance' carries the flavour of mere reaction, implying an inevitable dialectic of imposition/refusal. Many First Nations women's texts seem rather to participate in a practice explored by other writers of colour; in the words of Stuart Hall, 'We're now talking about resistance that is not a[n] enclosing but one that is open, dialogical' (25).

Going beyond resistance, the poet's 'representation' of her own voice as 'I' alongside her self-in-community as 'we' may be part of the creation of the 'new social subject' that Teresa de Lauretis promised (*Alice* 186). De Lauretis identifies the 'feminist mode of analysing self and reality' as a 'mode of acting politically' (*Alice* 185). At the same moment as they refuse every stable image of what 'self' must be, First Nations poets such as Joy Harjo, Wendy Rose, and Chrystos affirm both an individual reality and a speaking-on-behalf-of that is implicated in any 'we' representation. That written self, or subject, brings into discourse a presence that enacts 'a place of struggle' (hooks 16). As a textual being, that 'new social subject' engages readers who must themselves undertake deeply revisionist critical practices. This paper examines the challenges facing a (largely) white feminist critical community and reads some of the 'selves' presented and represented in some of the poems of Wendy Rose and Chrystos.

At a recent presentation to an academic audience Chrystos, a Menominee poet, forcefully asserted that 'when a white person writes about Native people, every bit of it is fantasy and lies.' This passionate declaration was followed by a request: 'actively support all Indigenous authors, of which there are many. Make sure we are published. Make sure we are read ... Order our books for your courses.'[2] Chrystos's request that whites read, teach, and write about First Nations authors, and her declaration that whatever we (whites) say is necessarily 'fantasy and lies,' place us in a peculiar dilemma. We can ignore her words (although they are a summary of what many First Nations women writers are saying); we can make the facile and now conventional response that *all* writing is 'fantasy and lies' and thereby dismiss her specific concerns; we can give up on First Nations literatures and turn our attention to the works of safely dead white writers; or, we can attempt to negotiate what Barbara Godard calls the 'impossible' project of whites working in racist structures (institutions, cultures, languages) against racism.[3]

It is an odd moment in literary time when people of some conscience fear that the critical act is potentially destructive or racist. This
readerly anxiety asks what assumptions, values, and interests do we
bring to our critical writing? When the critic is white and the writer is
of a First Nation, our questions are more than merely over-scrupulous
nervousness. Knowing that my critical acts are a manifestation of white
and class privilege, and will inevitably reinscribe at least some of the
values and powers of a dominant discourse, how can I speak? How can
my speaking not become an over-writing of texts fighting for voice?

Feminist critics, whatever our heritage, require a way to use language in which difference is not marked by domination. Françoise
Lionnet passionately believes that it is the 'foregrounding of our *differences* as women which can ultimately unite us as a powerful force of
resistance against all repressive systems of ideology' (xi). If we accept
Audre Lorde's view that difference does not harm us, but silence will
destroy us, we may also find hope in her assertion that the 'failure of
academic feminists to recognize difference as a crucial strength is a
failure to reach beyond the first patriarchal lesson. In our world, divide
and conquer must become define and empower' (112). The question
here must be, who is to have the power to define? Any 'reading' must
be interpretive and thus carry the conscious and unconscious ideological freight of its maker. Can interpretative discourse of the white
reader work *against* the authoritative power to define which by its
nature (that is, its habitual practice) *disempowers* the First Nations
writer? Can the white reader/critic affirm the 'crucial strength' she
finds in the different voice of the First Nations writer? Can she engage
in critical discourse that does *not* participate in what Trinh T. Minh-ha
asserts is inevitable: 'A conversation of "us" with "us" about "them" is a
conversation in which "them" is silenced' (67). Trinh offers a deconstructive 'solution' to this problem, believing that a '*suspension* of language' where a 'reign of codes yields to a state of constant non-
knowledge' is possible (76). This she defines as 'a practice of language
which remains, through its signifying operations, a process constantly
unsettling the identity of meaning and speaking/writing subject' (76).
The sovereign speaking subject, the being that Trinh refutes using 'I/i'
as first-person pronoun when she focuses on this issue, is neither possible nor desirable (37). The 'I/i' who writes *this* piece inevitably lives in
the indeterminate, fragmented, and perplexing condition of subjectivity that allows and requires ongoing provisional revisions of manner
and mode of selfhood. Moreover, the constitution of that selfhood/
subjectivity is in part a phenomenon of language and is thus available

for the 'constant unsettling' of deconstruction. Yet some other parts of *this* writing self wish (for once) to be quiet about its processes. The anxiety attending the issue of 'us' speaking about 'them' may be an issue only when 'they' have not yet got a public voice of their own. I am not alone in the feeling that the white writer's self-conscious concerns are not the most important thing. As Marlene Nourbese Philip said at a recent panel discussion on the issue of appropriation of voice, of whites constructing fictional characters of colour (I paraphrase), 'If we could get our own stuff published, we wouldn't give a damn what white writers are doing.'[4]

Yet the agonizing self-examination is necessary. The painstaking unbinding of cultural manacles is useful. But to displace discussion of First Nations women's texts with analysis of our own deliberations and our own dismantling would reinscribe a centred discourse – one that we are ostensibly working against. Obviously it is necessary to problematize the writer/speaker/seer. The voice of disembodied authority has become that of the Victrola record-player's ad for 'His Master's Voice' – with the record stuck. The significant and courteous gesture of asserting what everyone already knows, that this speaker is a limited speaker, a being caught in class, race, gender, time, and space – with no essential attributes credited to any of those categories, of course – may be unavoidable just now, but that gesture must not be allowed to distract our attention from the words of poets who are at last becoming more readily accessible.

Wendy Rose's poem 'If I Am Too Brown or Too White for You' offers us a way into the mediated selfhood of the First Nations woman unsettling expectations and affirming her right to define the boundaries from which she will be read. She images herself as a 'garnet woman' saying,

> and you touch the matrix
> shattered in winter
> and begin to piece together
> the shape of me. (52–3)

These words spoke to me, not as one of the brown or white people challenged in the title who hungers for 'purity,' but as one who wishes to understand, to read, the lives of women. Because I am a Western Canadian university-educated white woman, that desire cannot but participate in the will to know, the assumption of the value of 'knowledge,' and even the arrogance of assuming the 'right' to know that characterize Western (or European) culture. When Rose addresses the reader, naming the 'touch' of the 'matrix' that is herself, she attributes a will to power in the act: 'you are selecting me / from among polished stones / more definitely red or white'; and says [you] 'begin to piece together / the shape of me.' The reader of words is in a place of power, able to give shape to the 'she' who is a self, an 'I' in this poem. She names the desire of the reader for perfection, for clarity, for simplicity,

> wanting the curl in your palm
> to be perfect
> and the image less clouded,
> less mixed. (53)

Rose, however, resists surrender to the touch she has named:

> you always see
> just in time
> working me around
> the last hour of the day
>
> there is a small light
> in the smoke, a tiny sun
> in the blood, so deep
> it is there and not there,
>
> so pure
> it is singing. (53)

The possibility of violation, the threat of re-construction, the desires of those who 'touch the matrix' are inscribed here. Yet she affirms the inviolable, the elusive, the 'singing,' that is there and not there. For the white reader that seeing offers hope, as Rose makes a gesture of trust, here, in her reader ('you always see, just in time') and gives us what is there to see and not see.

This poem names the anxieties and dangers of the self-writing of a woman of colour, of mixed blood, who claims her own purity, her own mix of beingness. It further inscribes what Trinh T. Minh-ha suggests as a kind of ideal of reading and writing wherein differences exist. She disdains a theorizing that claims to pierce 'through the sediments of psychological and epistemological "depths"' (48). Articulating an alternative approach to coming to know, one that parallels the delicate turning in the palm, touching the matrix that Rose images, Trinh says, 'I may stubbornly turn around a foreign thing or turn it around to play with it, but I respect its realms of opaqueness' (48).

Françoise Lionnet finds at the cornerstone of 'the cultural aesthetics of many postcolonial writers' issues of 'transparency and obscurity' (4). The ambivalence that Wendy Rose demonstrates in this poem is precisely the question of how accessible she wishes to be, how much protection of silence or invisibility she is willing to surrender. The silenced, the erased, the unseen, the unheard (by whom?), are frequent presences in poems by First Nations women. But they are not simple or single, nor are they necessarily participants in the strategies and devices of assertion and evasion with which our 'persona'-voiced mainstream poetry is at ease.

To respect the 'realms of opaqueness' need not imply that understanding is abandoned or that we must give up all dreams of a common language, though the dreaming may be more realizable than the language. The 'tiny sun / in the blood, so deep' that 'it is there and not there, / so pure / it is singing' offers a vision and a sound, neither one definable, both representing Rose's matrix of selfhood.

That self is asserted in the ambiguous configurations of presences and absences. For Chrystos, too, the play upon what is 'there and not there' is part of her *strategy* of textualizing a highly diverse subjectivity. The title of Chrystos's collection of poems is *Not Vanishing*. Defiance is strong here, and the evocation of generations of anxious assertion that Indians are a 'vanishing' people. The title reminds us of what has come before and directly refuses white definition of what is true for First Nations peoples. Chrystos opens this collection with a note informing readers that she intends to refute the 'myths and misconceptions' about First Nations people (n. pag.). She makes a precise distinction between what she is willing to make available as written text and what is private to her. For Chrystos, that which is most private is not information about her personal history, but rather cultural or spiritual matters. Here we see Chrystos participate in the assertion of a secrecy, one that resists the greedy consumption of the dominant culture, whose encroachments will eventually anticipate, accommodate, and ultimately neutralize diversity (Lionnet 8). Each gesture of the introductory note, written, she says, to 'clarify' herself to the reader who does not know her, establishes her terms and her boundaries. In this note Chrystos refers to herself in quotation marks as part of a group called '"Urban Indians" by the government,' and in this double gesture asserts her independence from that naming. Further, she demarcates

by negation the parameters of this self-writing, denying the rights of
the dominant culture to certain kinds of knowledge.

In this list of negatives Chrystos posits an inversion of her stated
intention: she says, 'I am not a "Spiritual Leader"' and then asserts that
'while I am deeply spiritual, to share this with strangers would be a violation. Our ritual, stories & religious practices have been stolen &
abused ... I don't publish work which would encourage this – so you
will find no creation myths here.' Chrystos's precise articulation of the
responsibilities of a First Nations spiritual person towards her own history and traditions and beliefs carries with it, in this declaration, an
implicit criticism of those who do encourage cultural 'theft' by publishing 'creation myths.' In this judgment Chrystos does make herself
believable as a 'Spiritual Leader' – not of the 'many white women
[who] have tried to push [her] into that role' but of First Nations
women looking for a representative voice. Despite her insistence that
she is 'not the "Voice" of Native women, nor representative of Native
women in general,' she speaks of 'we' and 'us' and 'our' as firmly and
forcefully as possible; she wishes to make clear 'what the actual material conditions of our lives are' and warns whites not to admire 'what
you perceive as our stoicism or spirituality.' She makes a direct charge
upon the responsibility of whites: 'work for our lives to continue in our
own Ways.'

In itself this claim upon the energies of those who assert their concern or their shame for what whites have done to the First Nations is
simple. Yet it works from a monolithic stand that Chrystos herself has
disclaimed. The illusory nature of a secure 'we' and 'us' and 'our' in
any group is addressed by Gloria Anzaldúa: 'Colored feminists must
present a united front in front of whites and other groups. But the fact
is we are not united. I've come to suspect,' she says, 'that unity is
another Anglo invention like their one sole god' (15). First Nations
women's communities are no more uniform, no simpler, no easier
than white women's groups. Differences within groups may also work
towards silencing, towards negation. Cherríe Moraga, Chicana lesbian
feminist, insists that 'the danger lies in ranking the oppressions. *The
danger lies in failing to acknowledge the specificity of the oppression* ... Without
an emotional, heartfelt grappling with the source of our own oppression, without naming the enemy within ourselves and outside of us, no
authentic, non-hierarchical connection among oppressed groups can
take place' (29). In a terse poem in which two First Nations lesbians
overhear a Chippewa man and a gay white man, Chrystos makes the
difficulty of this ideal possibility of 'non-hierarchical connection'

immediate: 'YA DON WANNA EAT PUSSY / that Chippewa said to that gay white man who never has / *Ya don wanna eat pussy after eatin hot peppers* he laughed' (36). The women ignore this because 'Ya don wanna take offense at an Indian man's joke / no matter how crude / in front of a white man' (36). The poem ends with the bitterness of untenable and unresolvable allegiances:

> Much later that gay white man called that Chippewa a drunk
> we both stared at a different floor
> in a different silence   just as sharp
> & hot. (36)

Identity is part of community here, and as divergent loyalties are called upon (First Nations people among whites, gays among straights, women among men), the deeply felt anguish of conflicted subject-positions is evoked. The poem breaks the silence that the situation commanded, and the poem becomes the speaking agent of that multiply silenced self.

The self-censorship of divided loyalties to a complex community of identity is broken when Chrystos focuses on the 'Indian Princess' motif that plagues her. 'I Am Not Your Princess' speaks a selfhood of individual and cultural integrity. She outlines what she can and cannot do for her white companions: 'I'm not / a means by which you can reach spiritual understanding or even / learn to do beadwork' (66). She says,

> I won't chant for you
> I admit no spirituality to you
> I will not sweat with you or ease your guilt with fine turtle tales
> I will not wear dancing clothes to read poetry or
> explain hardly anything at all. (66)

These refusals to do or be what evidently has been required of her are further elaborated:

> If you tell me one more time that I'm wise I'll throw up on you
> ... If you ever
> again tell me
> how strong I am
> I'll lay down on the ground & moan so you'll see
> at last   my human weakness   like your own. (67)

Her refusals to perform her self as 'Princess' compose a kind of screen upon which the expectations of her audience dance before our eyes while the voice of the poet, the woman, cries out for recognition, for visibility: 'See that to pity me or to adore me / are the same.' She determines explicitly what she has to offer (a fry bread recipe), and even that is focused in its limitation:

> Remember   this is only my recipe   There are many others
> Let me rest
> here
> at least. (67)

This poem images a woman drained by the needy demands of white adorers, outfitting her with generations of 'noble savage' stereotypes, or expecting her to satisfy the Lynn Andrews brand of spiritual consumerism.

To accept the image that whites make of her is to be absent to herself, a form of vanishing that this whole collection opposes. The idea of 'Indianness' that whites hold, then, is a species of erasure. The articulation of selfhood as a cultural and personal reality is not something that Chrystos will give away:

> Scattered   they say we are vanishing
> leaves of autumn   red dust raked away so the snow
>   can fall flat
> They have our bundles split open in museums
>   our dresses & shirts at auctions
>   our languages on tape
>   our stories in locked rare book libraries
>   our dances on film
> The only part of us they can't steal
>   is what we know. (21)

In its emotional landscape Chrystos's poetry demonstrates de Lauretis's assertion that 'the stakes, for women, are rooted in the body – which is not to say that the body escapes representation, but quite the opposite' ('Issues' 12). Chrystos, in the voice of her heritage as a First Nations person, is walking, she says, 'in the history of [her] people.' She images herself thus:

> My knee is wounded so badly that I limp constantly

Anger is my crutch   I hold myself upright with it
My knee is wounded
see
How I Am Still Walking. (7)

The intertext of history and body, of crimes against the people visited upon the person, speaks here in the 'I' of the poet. This extended metaphor of physical suffering, cultural destruction, and historical crime coalesces and becomes representative of the body politic whose consistency is its endurance. Any racial misconceptions the reader may hold, any 'received representations' of the First Nations body, are eroded by the precision of Chrystos's visual and emotional figurations (de Lauretis, 'Issues' 12). These representations of body speak from places that have only rarely been 'received.'

The voice Chrystos uses speaking from her personal or erotic body, however, brings 'we' and 'you' away from the social, historical, and political into the most intimate of presences. The lesbian lyrics of desire, pleasure, passion, are all spoken here. We feel the sensual delight in this voice:

We could swallow desire whole
fingers caught in our sweet smell
We'd transform the air
O honey woman
won't you suckle me
Suckling
won't you let me
honey you. (6)

Or the celebration of her lover's diversely textured tongue:

O you rainy tongue   you amaryllis tongue   you early spring
tongue   you smooth blackleather tongue ... you feather
tongue   you take me all in tongue   you fill me up tongue
you butter tongue   you maple syrup tongue   you rising
wind tongue   you creamy silky tongue
you fine fine tongue
you knows the way
tongue. (45)

This body's joy, represented in its intimate conversation with the lover, must stand alongside the same body's anguish. In the poems that speak out of the violence and violation she has undergone, Chrystos demonstrates her power and range most profoundly. She makes us know the body's delight, as well as the child's terror and the woman's despair and rage. Cruelty, abandonment, brutality, come together as punches and blows fade into 'Lost Years' and time focuses upon the most particular of degradations:

> sticks
> at my head legs back   fists in the face   missing teeth
> Lost years   Lost home   dirty bread pissed on
> that white boys forced me to eat   cornered at seven
> my heart beating with terror I knew how much more they could do
> how little anyone would care. (54)

Through this writing, as through the experience, Chrystos becomes one of the 'edges that blur' to which Adrienne Rich alerts us: 'the body's pain   and the pain in the streets / are not the same   but you can learn / from the edges that blur' (111). Her poem 'Bitter Teeth' (with the epigraph 'about my uncle, Jean LeMaitre') extends the history of violence she endured and explicates the rage of her resistance. Anyone familiar with the manifestations of sexual abuse will recognize the patterns of exorcism Chrystos attempts:

> Praying for relief I've buried you therapied you
> talked you into blue streaks & scars   cut my arms
>   my breasts
> expelled a thousand seeds   Wet clay to your fist I
> couldn't drink enough   shoot up enough
>   spread my legs enough
>
> ...
>
> to wipe you out. (63)

The final poem in *Not Vanishing* is called 'Ceremony for Completing a Poetry Reading' (100). In this poem Chrystos brings together her gifts to make a celebration of images from her First Nations heritage, and from her female community: 'This is,' she says, 'a give away poem' (100). She speaks to her readers, or perhaps to only certain readers – the rest of us can overhear, can try to understand what is given, and of what the gifts have been formed: 'You've come gathering   made a circle with me of the places / I've wandered.' Taking and remaking what has been given, the poem reforms the gifts of earth and sea, and spirit and language: 'Within this basket is something you've been looking for / all of your life   Come take it   Take as much as you need.'

In this closing poem Chrystos seems to wish to teach us that ritual and ceremony are inexhaustible in the transformations of identity, of community, and of the life they allow. The subjectivity, the selfhood, that speaks has become one with(in) this poem, and the self written here is inseparable from its speaking.

In Chrystos the configurations of selfhood seem inexhaustible – perhaps because Chrystos participates in the ceremony of identity that Rayna Green describes:

> ... 'identity' is never simply a matter of genetic make-up or natural birth-right. Perhaps once, long ago, it was both. But not now. For people out on the edge, out on the road, identity is a matter of will, a matter of choice, a face to be shaped in a ceremonial act. (7)

Notes

1 Paul Smith elaborates the concept of 'the subject' in useful ways in *Discerning the Subject*. While my present discussion does not avail itself of the vocabulary of interpellation and agency, my underlying assumptions have been informed by the arguments attending those issues.
2 Chrystos, untitled paper presented at 'Native Women Writing the Self' panel at the Canadian Association of American Studies Conference, Toronto, 2–5 November 1989 (referred to with the writer's permission)
3 Personal conversation, Calgary, 1990
4 This view was expressed at a panel on appropriations and representations presented at the Canadian Association of American Studies Conference, Toronto, November 1989.

Works Cited

Allen, Paula Gunn. Introduction. *Spider Woman's Granddaughters: Traditional Tales and Contemporary Writing by Native American Women*. Boston: Beacon 1989
Anzaldúa, Gloria. '*En Rapport*, in Opposition: *Cobrando Ceuntas A Las Neustras*.' *Sinister Wisdom* 33 (Fall 1987), 11–17
Chrystos. *Not Vanishing*. Vancouver: Press Gang 1988

– Untitled paper. 'Native Women Writing the Self' panel. Canadian Association of American Studies Conference. Toronto, 2–5 Nov. 1989

de Lauretis, Teresa. *Alice Doesn't: Feminism, Semiotics, Cinema.* Bloomington: Indiana UP 1984

– 'Issues, Terms, and Contexts.' In *Feminist Studies/Critical Studies.* Ed. Teresa de Lauretis. Bloomington: Indiana UP 1986, 1–19

Green, Rayna. Introduction. *That's What She Said: Contemporary Poetry and Fiction by Native American Women.* Ed. Rayna Green. Bloomington: Indiana UP 1984, 1–12

Hall, Stuart. 'Morning Discussion,' in 'Third Scenario: Theory and the Politics of Location.' *Frameworks* 36 (1989), 24–8

hooks, bell. 'Choosing the Margin as Space of Radical Openness.' *Frameworks* 36 (1989), 15–23

Lionnet, Françoise. *Autobiographical Voices: Race, Gender, Self-Portraiture.* Ithaca: Cornell UP 1989

Lorde, Audre. 'The Master's Tools Will Never Dismantle the Master's House.' In her *Sister Outsider.* Trumansburg, NY: Crossing P 1984, 110–13

Moraga, Cherríe. 'La Güera.' In *This Bridge Called My Back: Writings by Radical Women of Color.* Ed. Cherríe Moraga and Gloria Anzaldúa. New York: Kitchen Table 1983, 111

Rich, Adrienne. '29' in 'Contradictions: Tracking Poems.' In her *Your Native Land, Your Life.* New York: Norton 1986

Rose, Wendy. 'If I Am Too Brown or Too White for You.' In her *The Halfbreed Chronicles and Other Poems.* Los Angeles: West End P 1985, 52–3

– 'The Bones Are Alive.' In *Survival This Way: Interviews with American Indian Poets.* Ed. Joseph Bruchac. Tucson: Sun Tracks and U of Arizona P 1987, 249–70

Smith, Paul. *Discerning the Subject.* Minneapolis: U of Minnesota P 1988

Trinh T. Minh-ha. *Woman, Native, Other: Writing, Postcoloniality and Feminism.* Bloomington: Indiana UP 1989

◎ 17 ◎

Imag(in)ing Racism: South Asian Canadian Women Writers

ARUNA SRIVASTAVA

Foreword, Afterword, Afterwards

Revising this paper for consumption by readers has proven to be a difficult task: the revisions requested and suggested were by no means major and would undoubtedly 'improve' the paper, but 'Imag(in)ing Racism' is so much a product and a process derived from its oral, conference context that I felt I had to come up with other ways of de- and re-forming that context so that it was still recognizable, recognizably different. What follows, then, is the paper as written/spoken with authoritative intrusions – *afterwords, afterwards* – afterthoughts, both mine and others', responses to the paper, post-paper elaborations, even re-visions, re-creations. As I suggest earlier, below, the academic convention of foot- or end-note postscripts violates my intention(s): fallacious as they might be, I choose to interrupt your reading with these *afterwords*, my hope being to re-create through re-writing, re-visioning, re-imagining (racism) (women), a conference that has been for me the most important, both personally and politically, that I have had the opportunity to attend.

Re-imag(in)ing Racism: South Asian Canadian Women Writers

Scene (appropriately enough): An Ethiopian restaurant in Vancouver. **Time**: Late evening. **Topic**: Being stuck halfway through the paper I'm to deliver in two days. We ruminate on the presence and absence of

racism, repression, displacement, academia, conferences, frames, contexts, language, and the imagination. I return to my computer the
next morning able to finish the paper, which I fully intend to be made
up of women's voices only, among them my own. The male voices who
intrude are my own creation: those mythical White Male Colleagues of
the story I have written and which you are here to hear. But I cannot
quite sustain that fiction, or relegate my intellectual and personal debt,
academically, to the feet and ends of my narrative. One doesn't read
out the footnotes, after all. And, as we postcolonials know, the margins
define, redefine, and undefine the centre ... *All writing is autobiography*,
someone said. Someone else said *all writing is plagiarism*. And yet
another someone said *this tale grew in the telling*. The tale I have written,
and have headed with this footnote before I tell it, would have been an
entirely different one if it were not underwritten and inhabited by the
voice of my friend and colleague Richard Cavell.

[**Afterwords**: The tale, re-taled, clamours with other voices, conference voices, voices from the past, afterword voices: four women, Linda
Hutcheon, Jamelie Hassan, Asha Varadharajan, and Anila Srivastava,
who ground this story; two men, Thomas Hastings and Ashok Mathur,
shifting the grounds. A question put to me after reading this paper on
male mentorship and feminist theorizing still haunts me, directed not
only to considering other feminists and the men in their theoretical
lives, but to myself as feminist as well. The problem of men-in-femi-
nism is not a subject of this paper but certainly (in)forms the sub-
ject(s) in this paper. My answer? Male mentorship and influence,
patriarchal theorizing, can be subverted, created anew, hybridized by
the feminist for her own strong theories. Does this weak answer necessarily elide the indisputable contributions of my male mentors to this
work, this process?]

The tale: Once upon a time there was a girl of seventeen, away from
home for the first time to start university in Sudbury, Ontario.
Entranced and enchanted by the perils of residence life and the cold,
lunar landscape of her surroundings (a far cry from the steamy sunni-
ness of southwestern Ontario), this girl came face to face for the first
time with the word *PAKI*. To her puzzlement, it referred to her and was
meant, she later discovered, all in good fun and the spirit of friendship. *What an odd word*, she remembers thinking, *I am/we are not from
Pakistan*. This girl had a lot to learn about words (she was just starting a
translator's degree, after all), about the power of words, the subtlety of
metaphor, about racism, both hers and others. *I am not from Pakistan*.
Perhaps it comes as a surprise that this literal-minded girl ended up
doing her doctorate in English literature.

Years later (I am under no constitutional obligation to specify how many, on the grounds that it may discriminate me), or twice upon a time, this woman is writing her PHD dissertation. (She is a woman now by virtue of years and her immersion, meanwhile, in feminism.) She has been asked – because she is a woman and a rapidly-becoming ethnic – to speak about women in Indo-Caribbean literature. She can't locate any, and is pondering, between thesis chapters on the British Raj, how she will write this absence, to be presented a week from now (our heroine's work habits are by now entrenched). It is a beautiful summer day in downtown Hamilton, Ontario, and, as she ambles homeward mulling over this difficulty, she encounters two men and a bulldog. *Don't get too close*, enjoins the dog owner, *to that PAKI broad*. She forgets the incident immediately, later to ruminate about her first encounter with that Freudian fiction, repression. What a perfect ending to the paper, though. So she relates the incident to conclude her ironic discourse about academic feminism, identity formation, First World arrogance, and postcoloniality. To her minimal surprise the published version of her paper has been substantially condensed, ironic musings and, most importantly, the story of the encounter with dog and Man editorially exorcised. What place for imagining racism in conference proceedings?

Thrice upon a time, roughly a year later. Interview time at the University of British Columbia (the ending of which chapter you can all guess). The same paper, re-ironized, over-theorized, focusing more resolutely on how we academics come up with our narratives. The racist incident unrelated, lesson learned, is displaced instead with Madeline Coopsammy's poem 'The Second Migration' by way of conclusion. But, before giving that reading, a comment on the responses of her colleagues-to-be to said poem: *not*, thought two of them, an appropriate ending to a fragmentary and unfocused paper; why in/con/clude with such polemical and, at that, poor poetry? Not to worry, they themselves answered their rhetorical question: *this is only the view of a woman* (said one), *and an immigrant* (added the other). Thus, 'The Second Migration':

> Whoever were those mocking gods
> who thought it fit to lead us
> from the green wastes of the Indo-Gangetic
> to the sweet swards of the Caroni
> then in a new migration
> to Manitoba's alien corn
> never thought to state

the price to be exacted
or how or where it would be paid.
Images of a just society dangled
harlot-like before our eyes
we thought that here at last and now at last
the spectres of colour
would never haunt
our work, our children's lives, our play
that in the many-faceted mosaic
we, angled and trimmed to fit
would find ourselves our corner of the earth.
How could we not know
that time, which heals
just as frequently destroys
and like the sixties flower darlings
we too, would soon become anachronisms
be reminders of a time
a time of joy and greening
We are the mistakes of a liberal time
you did not really court us, it is true
rather, purging us with sugar-coated pills of
medicals and points and two official languages
your tolerant humanity
festered woundings of 'brain drain'
while our leaders pleaded, impotent in agony
'Do not take our best!'
'We want your best,
No Notting Hills for us,' you warned.
And so again we crossed an ocean
convinced that little Notting Hills we'd never be.
Now lounging in our bite-sized backyards
and pretending that we do not see
the curling vapours of our neighbour's burger feast
(the third this week)
wafting across the picket fence
we know that careless of our birthright
we have sold it for
a mess of pottage. (72–3)

[**Afterwords**: An assault on my/self, this whitewashing reduction: *only an immigrant's*, **only** *a woman's perspective* – hers, Madeline's, and mine: partial, incomplete, unjustified ... images of a just society. So many migrations in the immigrant woman's life, from place to place, self to self, from whiteness to brownness, back and forth. This job interview is the start of a new migration for me, *South Asian Canadian woman*, into gainful academic employment. This paper, imagining racism, my second migration, a year later, not to Manitoba's, but to Alberta's alien corn, so that I can find myself a displaced voice – among imagining women – with/in the academy, that bastion of liberal values, my values? We are the mistakes of a liberal time ...]

If, as Gayatri Spivak would have it, the lesson of 'heroic liberal women' is 'to return to the third person with its grounds mined under' (89), the lesson of our less-than-heroic quester is now to return to the first person with *its* grounds similarly giving way under my feet. Besides, I can't get further than thrice upon a time, as convention would have it. And so to my latest encounter with the imagination of racism. March 1990. Term is ending and trees are blossoming at the University of British Columbia. The Engineering Undergraduate Society publishes their infamous newsletter with its usual dose of sexism, homophobia, and racism, a long-standing tradition. What particularly catches and horrifies the imagination of the university community this time, however, is a (native) 'Indian Job Application Form' covering almost an entire page, and containing almost every hateful stereotype directed against native people imaginable. [**Afterwords**: Resisting the temptation, here, to reproduce, and thus reinscribe examples from this not-so-blank page, marginalized on two sides by jokes directed against women, and against gays. A tale within: that this *funny* 'job application form' is proudly tacked up in a bank in the interior of our fair province. Another story, true: a proliferation of chapters in our fair province of the Ku Klux Klan, one of the largest and most active being in a town with the highest population concentration of Indo-Canadians.] The university administration acts quickly and punitively, to many people's surprise ... *There is a place for racism and sexism, you know, boys will be boys* intones a liberal (White) (Male) Colleague, angered at the furore, especially the threatened suspensions for the students involved. Naïve as always, I am entirely taken aback. [**Afterwords**: Freedom of speech, academic freedom, constantly brought forth as justification, explanation. These freedoms, as opposed to others? Thought to be absolute, inviolable, true.]

But my most pressing anxiety is *how am I to deal with this in class?* I am so enraged, so personally offended and involved, that my first instinct is not to mention it at all. But how, in good conscience, can I, who have attempted consistently to foreground the issues of racism, sexism, homophobia, and their direct relation to literature, avoid them now in my classes on Canadian and Commonwealth literature? I cannot be silent this time. Nevertheless, the issue raises for me an irresolvable pedagogical conflict – how to maintain decorum, distance, a level of analysis which I myself cannot muster? In the first class, a second-year Canadian literature course, I drop all pretence at dialogue and discussion, silence my students, preach at them, and, still barely able to keep myself professorially intact, make a grand exit after the sermon. *Racism*, I intone, *is a failure of the imagination.* I've had an effect, but not, I am certain, on those who chuckled appreciatively over the offending page with their First Nations classmate present and speechless. [**Afterword**: 'First Nations' is becoming among many a term preferred over 'native' and certainly over 'Indian.' In the Canadian context I suggest that the term is an ironic reinscription of the historical and cultural priority of the First Nations people, and more than an innocent political gesture pointing to the role of nationalism in the oppression of indigenous peoples.] I read with cynicism the predictable response in the student newspaper of an upset engineer: *I am not Native and don't know how it feels.*

In my fourth-year Commonwealth class I introduce the issue in the last twenty minutes of class, fully intending to pack up my briefcase and flee immediately. My cowardice doesn't protect me this time. Decorum abandoned, both I and my somewhat startled class voice our emotion and frustration and anger, our academically sanctioned inaction, our worried complicities and silences, our belated recognition that the university, especially in the eyes of its pupils, is not a sanctuary of higher education, but like the 'real world,' a place of fear and hate as well. Gay students (in)articulate their oppression, women talk about the Montreal murders, we wonder what we can learn in this institution of higher learning. We ask whether these graduates can take anything from the class. As a cynical observer later noted, we are testifying. Many of us are in tears. I don't preach or profess this time, and never as a (fledgling) professor have I felt more professionally threatened, undecorous, out of control, and full of doubt. Manabendra Bandyopadhyay's 'A Savage Aesthetic' seems a timely reminder, and a comfort:

> 'Remember, poetry too is architecture
> all else is redundant except the form, the style –
> what you call – texture ...'
> ...

... and so the poetry class unending.
Always the same. Sharp, academic
an exhibition of smug narcissism. Full of apt
and self-conscious quotations, allusions and message
in a voice that plays with a joke or two,
calculating, avoiding emotional excess.
So stands this hour of aesthetics, an exact reflection,
of the confidence of the glass and concrete phallus
that arises on an erased slum or broken shanty town. (46–7)

Imagining racism. The title for this paper is suggested not only by
the conference's title, but by encounters with students reading Bharati
Mukherjee's 'An Invisible Woman.' To a person, it seems, these students accuse Mukherjee of imagining things, of interpreting incor-
rectly, of not being fair, not looking at all sides of the question. None of
them close readers, they refuse the *once upon a time*ness of Mukherjee's
story of Canada, her claim that it is indeed 'a story of politics and para-
noia and bitter disappointment' (39). After reading her short story
'Tamurlane,' student opinion is confirmed: Mukherjee is *extremist; these
things don't happen. There is always another side to racism.* The racists' side,
I assume. [**Afterwords**: *Racism exists elsewhere, in the United States: how
dare she find sanctuary, there? Become American?*] And I begin to wonder,
quite seriously, about what racism is: I've heard it modified in so many
ways: *benign racism, benevolent racism, unconscious racism, institutional racism,* yes even *harmless, justified racism.* I am, for instance, tempted to say
that I myself encounter racism, but hastily qualify that to *overt racism.*
Himani Bannerji:

> And a grenade explodes
> in the sunless afternoon
> and words run down
> like frothy white spit
> down her bent head
> down the serene parting of her dark hair
> as she stands too visible
> from home to bus stop to home
> raucous, hyena laughter,
> 'Paki, Go home!' (15)

What, then, am I to make of those who make so much of my patro-
nym? Who accuse me of being a 'professional ethnic'? Who, benignly,

assume my automatic knowledge of and identification with a particular community? Which one, I want to ask? South Asia? Do any of us/them identify with that geographical fiction? India? Pakistan? Trinidad? Sri Lanka? The Phillipines? What really unites us/them, makes us cohere? Not any fictional nation. For we are all here now, for now, *Canadian South Asian women*, de-territorialized, unhoused in a country that has severe doubts about its own territory, its homeness – the myths of multiculturalism, even of biculturalism and bilingualism, unravelling as I speak. Our otherness – inessential, ephemeral, defined by – what?? – perceived gradations of colour, by accent, by name – is defined against our Canadianness, so that we 'not-quite Canadians,' to use Bharati Mukherjee's apt phrase, are always, already, continuously, continually, dispossessed, and displaced. [**Afterwords**: And I cannot do better, afterwards, than to cite the readerly marginalia of Ashok Mathur to the conference version of this paper: 'and ... invisible often, to use Mukherjee's terms. The consciously "othered" communities are so often gendered. (Thus: *All the Women are White, All the Blacks are Men, but Some of Us are Brave*).'] Suniti Namjoshi tell us

HOW TO BE A FOREIGNER
First,
> You take off your clothes,
> Your titles and name
> And put on a robe,
> Sterile and clean,
> With neat black letters,
> Marking THE STRANGER.
Then,
> You walk down the street,
> Alone in fancy dress. (14)

Sometimes, a stranger to myself, I imagine the matriline, the Scot in me, asserting it/myself, parading the fancy dress of kilt, not sari. But then I wouldn't be '*The* Stranger,' wouldn't be one of those immigrant once-children who is 'precluded by their skin colour from merging unobtrusively into the society at large' (A. Mukherjee 59); I have both chosen and been forced to assume and profess my ethnic identity. Am I therefore fuelling the imagination of racism? Surely not; surely I am conscious of the pitfalls and the pleasures of the 'politics of identity formation'; and situate myself as a *South Asian Canadian woman* in a rigorously '*strategic* use of positivist essentialism in a scrupulously visible political interest' (Spivak 205). I often turn, as I have just done, to Gayatri in times of need and theoretical self-doubt. And I cling to that notion of *strategy*, for it is empowering, just as strategically asserting my identity as a woman is. But ... it was strategy that sent me racism-hunting in Canadian South Asian women's writing, and a *scrupulously visible political interest* that found me wondering what to do with the amount of writing that is not *about racism*. Cultural displacement, yes, especially in children: many of these women write stories for children, encouraging them to celebrate their multiple identities, often in the face of ridicule; or, as in this poem by Parameswaran, they explore the poet's pain as she watches her children go through this process:

> Ma, you think you could change my name
> to Jim or David or something?
> ...
> When the snow comes, ma,
> I'll get less brown won't I?
> It would be nice to be white,
> more like everyone else
> you know? (quoted in A. Mukherjee 59).

Or question, like Lakshmi Gill, her own place in a new home:

> blue ice
> (O my Canada)
> can I call
> you mine
> foreign sad
> brown that I
> am (6)

I cannot argue, as I have of myself, that these writers repress racism, fail to imagine it. Their act of dis-placing racism, in their own political and personal interests, warns me of the signal failure in the imagination of a critic, especially a *Canadian South Asian woman*, who reduces writing to theme, to its *about*ness. I read with renewed interest, then, Surjeet Kalsey's poem of 'Farm Worker Women' in Vancouver:

> Women come and work
> in the broccoli fields
> smiling energetic they come

tired with aching feet and
hands sore they go home
Women women women
working working working

Women from the Punjab
come and work in the Canadian farms
brides wearing silk and gold
with soft henna colored palms
women with holding babies
women with pre-schoolers
women with grand parents ...
women with large families
women work for them
Women work in the blueberry
and raspberry fields
Women pick mushrooms, cut
broccoli and sprouts
Women work on the marshy land
their hands get blisters
their feet get swollen
their eyes and noses become
watery they breathe on [*sic*] fumes
and their arms, necks and faces
get infected with killer pesticides
women work round the clock
late at night after coming home
women cook food for their children
for their men, for their large families.
women wash every body's dirty clothes
women wash every body's dirty dishes
women take care of the crying hungry
or sick children in the house
women look after every body's needs.
They go to bed very late and get up very
early to go to the fields again.
In the fall when the season ends
and they get their stamps to live
through the winter, farm worker women
usually join English classes in their
neighbourhood to learn how to talk

to the strange world around who do not
understand their tongue.
Farm worker women are brave: ZINDABAD! (11-12)

[**Afterwords:** The un(literary)-critical contextualizing of my subject-
positions *vis à vis* these poems begins to break down here: we have
more poem than 'text.' I recall a question about the literary quality of
'ethnic' poetry: what do we do with the fact that we perceive some
poems to be, simply, 'better' than others? I answer, predictably, by
pointing out that notions of literary quality are inevitably ideological,
that we are, as readers and critics, resolutely historically situated, and
that, additionally, my reading of the above poem fails (in a way that
Surjeet's own readings don't) to capture the repetition, monotony,
drudgery, of the work these women are subject-ed to, and to capture
the celebration-through-repetition of their woman/women-ness. For
the moment, I leave the poem whole. To 'speak' for itself?]
    As I read (and type) this poem, however, I become increasingly con-
scious of how difficult it is going to be to (re)cite a poem like Nila Gupta's 'So She Could Walk,' visually dependent as it is on conventions of
typography [**Afterwords:** but reading it aloud is a searing experience,
conveying to me (the performer) the pain, the fragmentation of self
that accompanies the imagination of racism]:

and a man   is pushed   onto the subway tracks   and the train   go home
paki   is coming   the young men shout and laugh   the t.v. screams   a
young family on the elevator up   holds open the doors on the 10th   floor
to let some adolescents in who brandish broken beer bottles   in return
the parents must fall   on their children   to protect them   felled   spray of
glass   jagged blades   and   everywhere a stabbing   child developmental-
ists   say everything is   as it should be   everything is unfolding   according
to plan. (163)

    As if in answer to Bharati Mukherjee, who some years ago wrote, 'My
Indianness is fragile ... my ... use of English as a first language has cut
me off from my *desh* [homeland]' (*Calcutta* 170) and that 'to be a
Third World woman writer in North America, is to confine oneself to a
narrow, airless, tightly roofed arena' (285–6), some of these *Canadian
South Asian women writers* use English literary forms, and the language
'as she writ' against itself, trans-formatively. Gupta's 'poem' is, yes,
about racism but is not reducible to it.
    Jamila Ismail's 'poetry' 'From the DICTION AIR' continues in the femi-

nist project of rewriting and rethinking the words we use, of deconstructing that Great Book, the dictionary. An example: '*patriarchly* "am
I going to be a father," she wondered. patriarchly' (37). Or this re- and
de-finition of the word *serendipity:*

> about serendipity. *oxford & brittanica* hav it that sarandib, a former name
> of ceylon (now sri lanka), is an arabic 'corruption' of the sanskrit simhal-
> advipa ... & that an englishman hitched-*ity* onto serendip to make seren-
> dipity. well, that's one way to do it. english a word by romanizing an
> arabesque of sanskrit & grafting on a latin tail. it's a tail that wags the dog,
> for latin sends on its imperializing ways. but a colonizing onomatopoeia
> (ceylon became a crown colony in 1802) needn't be an onomatopooper.
> one could learn by it to resuffix paris-*ian* with an -*ite*, or decline 'british'
> to 'brutish.['] me, i like e.s.l. trips, such as 'united sates.'
>
> when serendipity was coined in the 1750s it meant 'the faculty of mak-
> ing happy & unexpected discoveries by accident.' a brutish example,
> from the 1750s might be, the takeover of bengal; which financed the
> english 'industrial revolution,' & so england went on to Empaaah. no of
> course i hadn't it figured this way when the word first buzzed me, testily,
> in the 1960s in hong kong. (42)

I want to continue this excursus on these writers' resolute attention to
the surfaces of language and form, the (to some) radical notion that
all language is metaphor, and that therein lies its power.

At the same time, I want to make connections, to point out part of
what underlies my narrative, to use Bharati's words again: 'Indianness
... [is not] a fragile identity to be preserved ... [but] a set of fluid identities to be celebrated ... Indianness is now a metaphor ... [for] partially
comprehending the world' ('Introduction' 3). I want to do this
because, comfortingly, it takes me back to Gayatri, to strategies – to
that simultaneous assertion of and undercutting of my identity, my
identities. It leads me forward to that optimistic ending of many of the
stories, poems, and plays I've read, to that space opened up by reading
elsewhere that 'the postcolonial inheritance [is that] of hybridization'
(Trinh 12). Strategic identities: I imagine wearing a kilt one day, a sari
the next, jeans the next. Hybridity: a costume of kiltsarijeans, parts
thereof, with holes, in tatters, unrecognizable.

[**Afterwords** of *South Asian American* 'immigrant' poet Meena Alexander:

> Appearance then was a problem: not just how to appear – saris, kurtas,

jeans, the choice of garment, women's issues, in the weak sense of the word – but the very fact of appearing, of existing for the eye. To what extent I might ask myself if I were to take a theoretical distance from all this, was my sense of self-identity invaded by the gaze, by the look of a world to which I was Other. But there was no way in which I could stand apart from this question. It was what I was and in many ways am, this perpetual reconstruction of identity. (80)]

Unimaginable.

At the same time ... at the same time, something buzzes me, testily, for there are those men (and women) who take up their positions, too, strategically situate themselves in scrupulously(?) visible political interests, some of which I, too-shifting – share. And they say *there is a place for racism and sexism*; they say *she's just a woman – and an immigrant*; they say *where's your sense of humor?* they say *I am free to speak: you are free to object*; they say *they're* just words; they say *PAKI go home*.

[**Afterwords**: A salutary warning to those of us (un)comfortable with our strategic identifications:

> I confess that I have become increasingly suspicious of the recurrent appeal to 'political strategy' or 'tactical necessity' in recent critical disputes ... for no matter how reactionary or dangerous a notion may be, it can always be salvaged and kept in circulation by an appeal to 'political strategy' ... Perhaps the question we must always keep before us is: 'politically strategic *for whom?*' (Fuss 106–7)]

Imagining racism. I said, I preached, you will remember, to my silent students that racism is a failure of the imagination. And in a certain way, I still believe that. I am a fan of literature, after all. But my imagination, too, failed. Failed to recognize that there is no such thing as racism. Racism is as inessential as race. It is a metaphor: not *just a word*, but a word nonetheless. Racism, in all of its forms, *is* an act of the imagination.

[**Afterwords**: my words *racism is a failure of the imagination* caught the imaginations of several people who heard or read the paper. But to stop there is an imaginative failure. Some resisted what they perceived to be the political implications of what I see as a crucial idea, worth repeating: that *racism is also an act of the imagination* depends on ways of imagining the world. Perhaps the conflict here lies in how we imagine the imagination: as individual, transcendent and transcending, unfettered, essentially free, independent, creative in all the best ways? A romantic view of the imagination which still has great power, indeed can be empowering. But those who create images of harm – racism, for example – however passively, do not lack imagination; they fail only to conform to a particularly limited and liberal image of the imagination. We must recognize the power of all manner of imagining.] Racism, as imagination, has a grammar and a syntax, a pervasive and almost impermeable narrative power, a power that makes a poet like Himani want to stop writing, stop using words, remain silent. This is her poem 'Doing Time,' which opens her collection of the same name:

> This is not a poem, nor the introduction to my poems, because I cannot write poetry anymore ... as I was saying I cannot write poems anymore because I don't know what language, what words, what metaphors or myths I could use to describe the world around me or express what I feel or think about it. And I am not sure that there should be any more of these metaphors around, or myths, or signs and symbols, or whatever they call them. In fact never more than now have I felt, things have been ever more of themselves. They are what they are. They are fully un-covered. All the bricks, barbed wires, concrete, chrome, glass, gasses, bombs, helicopters, dogs and Wallstreet Journals are there for us to see. (9)

Of course, her story, her poetry, does not end there; she does not fall silent: who among us can forget the image of those racist 'words run[ing] down / like frothy white spit'?

There is a series of discussions at my university called 'Hate Hurts.' This slogan seems almost trite, clichéd, and, of course, this cliché underwrites my rhetoric, my story here. As long as hatred exists in the form of racism, that imaginary and imagined concept, I can and will, if uncomfortably, inhabit the interstices and contradictions of my own – and others – imaginative theories. For me, there is a value – always to be questioned – in my trying to find homes in imagined communities and in participating in the fight against the power that racism holds over our imaginations.

I have felt the effects of racism's power and will continue to hunt for it, track it down, and wish to eradicate it. Contradictorily and finally, then, I claim the authority and the community of experience. [**Afterwords**: 'How are we to negotiate the gap between the conservative fiction of experience as the ground of all truth-knowledge and the immense power of this fiction to enable and encourage [us]?' (Fuss 118).] Theoretically, politically correct? Of course not; but I myself must be the first to criticize, question, shift my positions, both personal and political. It is this self-examination that I have attempted in this paper, and I have been informed by the context, the frame that this conference has provided. I will therefore not complete that other frame and end my story [even *afterwords*] with a 'happily ever after.' Instead, I begin again, imag(in)ing racism and imag(in)ing women with the help of Himani Bannerji:

> If we who are not white, and also women, have not yet seen that here we live in a prison, that we are doing time, then we are fools, playing unenjoyable games with ourselves. I won't go so far, however, as to say that we deserve what we get. ('Doing Time' 9)

Works Cited and Consulted

Alexander, Meena. 'The Poem's Second Life: Writing and Self-Identity.' *Toronto South Asian Review* 6, no. 2 (Fall 1987-Winter 88), 77–85

Bandyopadhyay, Manabendra. 'A Savage Aesthetic.' In *A Separate Sky*. Toronto: Domestic Bliss 1982, 46–7

Bannerji, Himani. 'Doing Time.' In *Doing Time: Poems*. Toronto: Sister Vision 1986, 9–11

– 'Paki Go Home.' In *Doing Time: Poems*. Toronto: Sister Vision 1986, 15

– trans. 'A Savage Aesthetic.' By Manabendra Bandyopadhyay. In *A Separate Sky*. Toronto: Domestic Bliss 1982, 46–7

Coopsammy, Madeline. 'The Second Migration.' *Kunapipi* 8, no. 2 (1986), 72–3

Fuss, Diana. *Essentially Speaking: Feminism, Nature and Difference*. New York: Routledge 1989

Gill, M. Lakshmi. 'Song.' In *First Clearing (an Immigrant's Tour of Life): Poems*. Manila: Estaniel P 1972, 6

Gupta, Nila. 'So She Could Walk.' In *Fireworks: The Best of Fireweed*. Toronto: Women's P 1986, 162–4

Ismail, Jam. 'from the DICTION AIR.' *Contemporary Verse* 2 11 (1988), 37–42

Kalsey, Surjeet. 'Farm Worker Women.' In *Foot Prints of Silence: Poems*. London: Third Eye 1988, 11–12

Mukherjee, Arun. 'South Asian Poetry in Canada: In Search of a Place.' In *Towards an Aesthetic of Opposition*. Stratford, Ont.: Williams-Wallace, 1988, 52–68

Mukherjee, Bharati. Introduction. *Darkness*. By Bharati Mukherjee. Markham, Ont.: Penguin 1985, 1–4

– 'An Invisible Woman.' In *Saturday Night* March 1981, 36–40
– 'Tamurlane.' In *Darkness*. Markham, Ont.: Penguin 1985, 117–25
–, and Clarke Blaise. *Days and Nights in Calcutta*. Garden City, NY: Doubleday
   1977
Namjoshi, Suniti. 'How to be a Foreigner.' In *More Poems*. Calcutta: Writers
   Workshop 1971, 14
Spivak, Gayatri Chakravorty. *In Other Worlds: Essay in Cultural Politics*. New York:
   Routledge 1988
Trinh T. Minh-ha. 'Introduction.' *Discourse* 11, no. 2 (Spring–Summer 1989),
   5–17

⊘ 18 ⊘

The Pure and the Impure, Again and Again and Again[1]

CATHARINE R. STIMPSON

I am writing in pain, ambivalence, and self-doubt. My subject is a cultural representation of the addicted mother. Only a fool or charlatan would speak of her without pain, ambivalence, and self-doubt. Given this, I need a fixed point with which to begin, an image. Perhaps trivially I have selected a pair of shoes. They look chunky and clunky, but they are elegantly Parisian, a Charles Jourdan design. Diamonds stud the heels. They were once in the closet of a politician and mathematician manqué, Elena Ceausescu, the powerful wife of the 'Genius of the Carpathians.' Both husband and wife are now dead, shot in 1989 in the Romania they tyrannized, on Christmas Day, the day on which Christians believe the perfect son was born to the perfect mother. As soldiers were tying her hands behind her back, Elena Ceausescu rebuked them, 'This is shameful. Why, why? I raised you all like a mother' ('Ceausescu Wept').

If I were tracing one pattern of the representation of women, I might place these glitzy pumps in the long tradition of images of women, their shoes, and their feet. Again risking trivialization, I might call it 'the podiatric tradition.' It would include the Old Woman Who Lived in a Shoe, Cinderella, the Red Shoes, Dorothy in *The Wizard of Oz*, Imelda Marcos, and, far more painfully, women with bound feet. I wish, however, to explore a related tradition: the association of women with the pure, a Cinderella or a Dorothy, and the impure, an Elena Ceausescu or Imelda Marcos.

Since the late-1960s feminist theory and scholarship have anatomized three associations of women with the pure and the impure. First, like deconstruction, feminist theory has shown how dependent hegemonic representations of gender and women are upon binary oppositions. Among the most entrenched are the polarizations between female and male, necessary for gender structures, and between pure and impure, necessary for absolute religious and moral judgments. Second, representations of women themselves are split and divided. Each half then floats towards one half of the opposition between the pure and the impure. Some women are pure, some impure. However, the meaning of purity and impurity is unstable, shifting in time, deliriously footloose if never fancy free. If the woman of little or no public power is pure, the woman of great public power, an Elena Ceausescu, is impure, sometimes deservedly so. Ceausescu, of course, presented herself at the moment of execution as the powerful *and* pure mother. If the white woman is pure, the woman of colour is impure. If the mistress is pure, the servant girl is impure. If the woman of controlled sexuality is pure, the woman of uncontrolled sexuality is impure. Perhaps most consistently, the good mother, who transforms sexual desire into reproductive bounty, is pure. The bad mother, whose libido is imperfectly restrained, whose maternity is erratic, is impure, even diabolically so. In May 1990 a New York City tabloid, the *New York Post*, headlined a series about addicted mothers and their babies 'The Crack Crisis: Children of the Damned.'[2]

Third, and finally, feminism has imagined and inscribed alternative linkages among women, purity, and impurity. They at once adapt, revise, and rebuke these cultural legacies. Now the pure woman has a body, robust, polymorphic, multiplicitous in desires and pleasures. This body might be maternal, lesbian, celibate, heterosexual – any, some, or all of these over time. The pure woman has a voice, as robust, polymorphic, and multiplicious. Post-structuralism has, however, fractured any consensus about the signifying capacities of this voice. For some, it is plain, authentic, the voice of a witness. For others, it is the rhythm of Kristevan semiotic or the lyric of *écriture féminine*, erupting before and beyond the symbolic order. The pure woman also has a moral code. She heals rather than damages other women, loves rather than spurns the female other. Only reluctantly did feminism recognize an Elena Ceausescu and the grinding sound of her footsteps.

Although unevenly, feminist scholarship has also influenced literature in the social sciences. Women have become a fit subject for serious research. Among them are unfit women, those, for example, who drink too much or take drugs (Harrison and Belille 574). Following a well-worn path, research on substance-abusing women has led to research on such women who are mothers, which in turn has led to research on the influence of maternal addiction on neonates and infants (see, for example, Householder). In part because of the rules of research and scholarship, the representation of women here lacks crude, overt bias. Suggestively, some of the most valuable work shows addicted women accepting maternal obligations. Indeed, losing this sense of responsibility is a sign, to themselves and to others, that they are overwhelmingly addicted. When their addiction becomes their identity, they lose self-respect and the respect of others as well (Pettiway 744). A study of women heroin addicts who sought methadone treatment concludes as follows:

> For women, parenting issues are foremost. Women often get on methadone in an effort to stabilize a chaotic life which is hurting their children. If they are pregnant, they most want to prevent their unborn children from withdrawal. If they have children, they want them away from the heroin world and also want to protect their own images and identities as mothers. (Rosenbaum 140)

In brief, internalizing the representation of the good mother as the pure mother, no matter how ideologically controversial, no matter how traditional, can be a conserving, preserving force for women and their children. In the 1980s, however, the representation of the good mother as the pure mother became conservative in a more harshly ideological sense. In Reaganesque rhetoric the substance abuser – be the substance alcohol or drugs – joined the lesbian, the tramp, and the slothful woman as necessarily *a priori* 'unfit' mothers. Indeed, I would guess that in the United States the substance abuser became the primary example of the unfit mother, a foot soldier in the enemy's army in the War on Drugs.[3] This negligent, wilful creature appears in the discourses of medicine, politics and law, the media, and literature. She joins the far more threatening pollutants of acid rain and oil spills, although some voices declare her to be a greater violation of the natural order than environmental disasters. As the frightful use of crack cocaine increased, figures who would not otherwise endorse Reaganism adopted this rhetoric.

The addictive mother signifies a terrible, double impurity. First, she craves and ingests noxious substances without restraint. She abandons herself totally to their seductive powers. Second, these substances corrupt her unborn child. She abandons the future to the pollutants that have seduced her. The placenta is not the passageway of nutrients but of physical and social corruption. The bad mother defiles, not only an ideal of health and hygiene, but the process of species renewal itself. In contrast, the non-addictive mother abjures impure substances. Controlling herself and her appetites, she takes only good food and drink into her body. Her placenta remains the passageway of nutrients. She respects, even reveres, an ideal of hygiene and the process of species renewal.

In contemporary discourse the impure mother is so dangerous that she must be deprived of ordinary rights: the right to privacy, the right to claim control over her own person and body. The state must intervene in order to clean her up and to rescue a baby from her filth. Such a justification for state action cuts across political lines. One example: Alan Dershowitz, the well-publicized Harvard Law School professor and defence lawyer, a self-labelled liberal. He calls for more state-sponsored prenatal care for pregnant women. Pro-choice in the abortion struggle, he explicitly distances himself from the doctrine of 'fetal rights.' Nevertheless, he warns his fellow pro-choicers to be careful; their arguments are such that they seem to preclude any state requirement for prenatal care. The choice to give birth, Dershowitz cautions, is not synonymous with 'the right to neglect or injure that child by abusing their collective body during pregnancy' (5). Retreating from the practical consequences of his theory of the collective body, he does not beat the drum for constant, aggressive state vigilance, only for a sensitive state vigilance when a pregnant woman's behaviour is sufficiently impure, obviously destructive. He claims that there is a 'principled distinction between totalitarian intrusions into the way a woman treats her body, and civil-libertarian concerns for the way a woman treats the body of the child she has decided to bear' (5). Muffle his drum though he will, Dershowitz deepens the only too popular confusion between the foetus and a person.

An extreme act of state intervention is the criminalization of impure behaviour, the metamorphosis of bad mother into law-breaker. By February 1990, in the United States, there were perhaps thirty-five cases in which various juridical units (a county, for example) charged a woman with a crime during or immediately after her pregnancy (Lewin).[4] The accounts of the arrests of the women extend the genre of the melodrama in which a knight/sheriff rides to the rescue of an innocent. Here, however, the innocent is not a fair maiden, but a baby. The fair maiden has disappeared. So has the male villain, to be replaced by a female villain, the addicted mother, impure enough to warrant cruel treatment. The knight/sheriff may not have legal theory on his side, but he has even better companions: his moral certainty that a mother's drug abuse is child abuse and the axiological imperative of translating moral certainties into legal and community action.

Ultimately, however, the state must test the knight/sheriff's legal theory. In part because of its shakiness, only one of the thirty-five arrested women has been convicted, a verdict under appeal as I write. A more typical case is that of Diane Pfannenstiel. A woman of twenty-nine, four months pregnant, she was arrested on 4 January 1990 and charged with 'felony child abuse.' Two months earlier, a judge had ordered her to remain alcohol-free in order to 'protect' the foetus. A second judge dismissed the felony complaint on the grounds that he lacked proof that the mother's drinking had harmed the foetus. These legal weaknesses have combined with moral and pragmatic questions to mark the criminalization of the addicted mother as a contested zone, which, like all contested zones, is both a symptom of immense social concerns and a deflection of attention from that immensity.

In a 1989 feature the *New York Times* attempted to demarcate this particular contested zone ('Ideas and Trends'). Neither supporters nor opponents of criminalization denied the existence of a *problem*: addicted women, especially crack-addicted women, are giving birth to addicted babies. Instead their quarrel was about a response to the problem, a solution. The arguments for criminalization were at once moral (society must prevent harm to children, in the uterus and out); financial (it is going to cost society vast sums of money to support addicted babies, who will grow up to be damaged children and adults); and socio-political (the problem of addicted mothers/damaged children is now so acute that we must bring in the law, as well as medicine and social work, in order to contain it).

The arguments against criminalization were far more sensitive to the situation of the mother, far more fearful of state power, far more dubious about criminalization's ability to stop unhealthy maternal behaviours, and far more sceptical about the fate of criminal charges in a court. How, they asked, could one prove in court that the impure mother *intended* to harm her child? These arguments, too, were at once moral (criminalization and the surveillance of women it entails is a violation of privacy); financial (it is bitterly ironic that a society will pay for criminal proceedings against women but not for adequate prenatal care); and socio-political (criminalization will increase state control for a questionable purpose, i.e., the punishment of women). The opponents of criminalization, however, seemed the shrewder social psychologists. Correctly, they saw that the discourse of criminalization serves two deeper purposes: first, it provides an outlet for the frustration over addiction and the reduction of helpless babies to helpless and hapless patients; second, it serves as a surrogate debate for that over abortion. The mother who is bad because her habits pollute the womb *represents* the mother who is bad because she wants to abort the foetus in the womb. The damaged foetus *represents* the aborted foetus. However, to grant that damaged foetus rights and 'personhood' would be to grant any foetus the rights, personhood, and legal standing that would label abortion murder.

Though criminalization is a contested zone, the figure of the addicted mother as impure, which provokes the arguments for criminalization, gains more and more cultural weight. Let me cite three recent examples from respectable publications that engineer the cultural middle-of-the road. Each is warmly responsive to the plight of bruised and aching children. Far less admirably, each isolates and censures women.

My first example is a *New York Times* major feature article published on 4 February 1990: 'When a Pregnant Woman Drinks' (Rosenthal). Ironically, but unsurprisingly, the magazine, which appears every Sunday, derives a great deal of its income from eroticized advertisements that spotlight desirable women for a spectrum of heterosexual tastes: pouty Lolitas in Guess jeans, sleek ladies of the ranch in Lauren jackets. The article's author is a doctor who specializes in emergency-room care, hard cases, nerve-wracking scenes. Accompanying the text is a large black-and-white painting. Although the style is soft-edged realism, the message is hard-edged and stark. A white woman stands, in profile, hair falling down her back, a doubled sign of both innocence and dishevelment. She is conspicuously pregnant. She is reaching for a bottle on an otherwise bare table. It contains alcohol, not formula.

The text begins with a vivid anecdote about a damaged child and then generalizes about her condition, moving from little victim to disease. She suffers from 'fetal alcohol syndrome,' first described, significantly, in 1973 as the change in modern gender roles became more and more obvious. This syndrome has a variant, 'fetal alcohol effect.' A number of drinking mothers now 'scar' their children through infecting them with these conditions – in the United States alone perhaps 2.7 babies for every one thousand live births (eight thousand babies a year); on Indian reservations perhaps 25 per cent of all children. The scar is deep and livid. The affected child will suffer from physical anomalies and abnormalities; unusual brain waves that show immature development; irritability, distractibility, and impulsiveness; abnormal levels of dopamine, a neurotransmitter; and such erratic growth that the child will have trouble in school. Simultaneously the scarred child can be too sociable, too trusting of others. Unwrapped, this package of difficulties of body and behaviour reveals the prophecy of a bad future: dropping out of school, criminality, prostitution.

The rhetoric that inscribes the impurities of foetal alcohol syndrome has several of the features of the rhetoric of pollution. Although we can sense the harm of the miasma, it is nevertheless mysterious, elusive, hard to diagnose precisely. The pollution floats around and through us, nameable and unnameable, presence and ghost: as the article admits, we cannot easily tell exactly when a drinking mother will hurt her baby. A 'major mystery' surrounds the moment when a mother will become a bad mother, a pure figure impure. Trying to pin the mystery to the mat of certainty, the text first biologizes the syndrome by suggesting that a genetic tendency towards it may exist. The text next sociologizes the syndrome by asserting that it is more common in African-Americans and native Americans. Unfortunately, neither biology nor sociology is a wholly victorious wrestler. For the genetic tendency 'may' only exist. Moreover, African-American women, like Hispanic women, are more abstinent as a group than are white women.

Because the syndrome is a modern pollutant, 'experts' must deal with it, despite the explanatory failures of the modern academic disciplines. Experts wave the silver cross of specialized knowledge before the werewolf of impurity. 'Most' of them recommend abstinence as the 'only prudent course' for a pregnant woman (Rosenthal 61). In order to be good a pure mother must reject impure substances. If she has a habit, she must purge herself through counselling or rehabilitation programs. Without much anger on behalf of women and their babies the article also notes that many in-patient alcohol rehabilitation programs exclude pregnant women. So do most drug rehabilitation programs in the United States, especially those that might be available to poor pregnant women. Without social supports the good mother must gain purity through self-control and self-reliance.

My second example comes from Joyce Johnson, a well-known writer, who published a book about the Steinberg case, *What Lisa Knew: The Truth and Lies about the Steinberg Case* (1990). The Steinberg case was the most famous murder trial in the United States in the 1980s. In November 1987 Lisa Steinberg, a first grader, was beaten and left to die in her home in New York City. A baby boy was lying in a urine-soaked playpen in the next room. Joel Steinberg and Hedda Nussbaum, who had wrongly claimed to have adopted them both, were charged with murder. Steinberg, a sleazy criminal lawyer, had also been battering Nussbaum for years. Nearly a year later, the prosecuting attorney's office dropped all charges against Nussbaum. She then became a witness against Steinberg. In January 1989, after days of deliberation, a jury convicted him of manslaughter.

Johnson's title is a promise to dig up the hidden realities of the Steinberg case, to expose the lies its participants told. Breaking that promise, Johnson deals instead in conjecture, possibilities, perhapses, maybes, and wanly imagined scenes from Lisa's mind. For the purpose of this angry whiplash of a book is to do what Johnson wishes the machinery of justice had done: try Nussbaum as well as Steinberg; and find her guilty, at the very least, of malignant child abuse, perhaps of murder. Johnson presents a vile, literally non-natural mother, a drug addict who keeps a recipe file, not of nourishing dishes for her family, but of ways in which to free-base cocaine.

After Lisa's death the media turned tragedy into mass melodrama, casting Steinberg as Monster and Nussbaum, the battered woman, as Victim. Johnson refuses to redeem Steinberg. However, she tongue-lashes Nussbaum, the bad mother who seems worse than the bad father. Nussbaum is no victim, but a shallow, literal-minded, angry, narcissistic masochist who played dangerous power games with Steinberg, got addicted to cocaine before he did, and jealously feared that he preferred Lisa to her. A typical passage: 'Hedda's injuries have damaged her vocal cords, but one wonders, Did that voice ever have any real music in it?' (81).

Obviously Johnson is submitting a brief in the ferocious trial of all battered women that the Steinberg case provoked. Because many pregnant addicts are battered women, I fear that people will stupidly apply Johnson's brief to them as well. For some people like me a battered woman gets broken psychologically as well as physically. By November 1987 Nussbaum was as capable as a corpse of helping Lisa. I need not elevate Nussbaum, or any battered woman, to the status of plaster saint in order to believe that the Steinberg/Nussbaum apartment housed three victims: one woman, two children. In Johnson's view no battered woman can cite her injuries as the reason why she did not act. She still has responsibilities, especially to her children. No matter how hurt she might have been, Nussbaum ought to have protected Lisa.

My last example is a glossily illustrated 1990 *Life Magazine* story: 'Did I Do the Right Thing?' (Capuzzo).[5] Its hero is a boy, Bradley O'Hara, born in 1980, who loves sports, cartoons, and his mother.

However, he suffers from tremendous guilt because of that love. When he was three, his parents got a divorce. The subject of joint custody, the boy divided his time between an affluent, remarried father and a working-class mother, a barmaid, and her male friend, a house painter. An unhappy child, who showed some signs of neglect, he was told in school that drugs were bad. However, he saw drugs in his mother's home. For some time no one would act on his reports of what he saw. Then, one afternoon, he tuned in to President George Bush on television telling children to enlist in the War on Drugs and help people who are on them. Immediately, playing protective adult to his mother's straying child, Bradley talked about his mother to a police lieutenant, by happenstance once his father's best man. One afternoon, while the child was at home with his mother, doing homework with her, the police crashed in to arrest her and her boyfriend in front of the child.

The aftermath of the police action sickeningly combines official muscularity and glee, official embarrassment, some adult compassion, and human misery. Discovering that the mother was a small-time marijuana user who did a little dealing, legal authorities downgraded the case. After plea bargaining she and her boyfriend were put on probation. They had also married after six days in jail, a signifier of their straightening up and flying right after the formal discovery of sin. Bradley's biological father was given full custody, the mother some visitation rights. Men rushed in to proclaim the child a hero in the War on Drugs, the smallest soldier, no less courageous for being less than ten. A player on his home-town professional football team, the Buffalo Bills, told the child that he was tougher than any football player. A retired army colonel wrote to praise him. The first picture in the story takes up a page and a half. Bradley rides an exercycle, a postmodern horse, and wears a T-shirt, printed with Nancy Reagan's slogan, 'Just Say No.' However, to join the male world of public authority, he must deny the female world of love and maternal authority. On his cycle he watches a videotape of his mother under arrest. Compulsively the boy also repeatedly enacts the arrest, often in front of his mother, justifying and defending himself. The last picture, a play on the Pietà, seems to endorse his self-justifications. His mother, now nicely groomed, is hugging her son, his cheek against her breast, the impure mother revivified and redeemed by the child's anguished love.

In part, the intensification of the representation of the addicted mother is coming to this pass because more women, for many reasons, are drinking and doing drugs. More babies, for many reasons, are getting hurt. In the United States one estimate suggests that perhaps 375,000 babies a year now suffer because their mothers take drugs. The National Institute on Drug Abuse suggests that possibly ten out of every one hundred pregnant women have used or are using cocaine (Teltsch). Theoretically we might picture and help these pregnant women without labelling them bad and impure. Influential operators of the machinery of culture choose not to do so.

The motives for our interpretations are complex. In part, we desperately fear any bad mother, the empty breast, the maternal fist. This may be especially true in societies, such as the contemporary United States, in which mothering is the prime and primal symbol of nurturance. Any woman who seems to deviate for an instant from the norms of self-sacrificial maternal goodness is immediately suspect. In part, the representation of the impure mother efficiently both screens out and encodes other cultural anxieties. It is powerful enough to seem to be seen only for itself even as it is expressing these other fears. Obviously such emotions take no monolithic form. They vary from community to community, place to place. Today, three of them may be especially pervasive.

There is the panic about AIDS. A significant portion of the women who have tested HIV positive either use intravenous drugs or tend to live with men who do. An infected, pregnant woman has as much as a 65 per cent chance of bearing a HIV-infected infant (Cohen 46). The reality of the AIDS baby is unbearably poignant. We search for a causal agent to punish for the infant's suffering.

Among 'majority' communities there is a related panic about race. In the United States many of the women who suffer from AIDS are African-Americans or Hispanics living in urban centres. Also poor, they are usually unable to pay for their treatment or for that of their children without recourse to public funds. They are 'drains,' a word linked to sanitation, on the economy.

Among gender traditionalists there is a panic about the independent woman who controls her own life, appetites, and reproductive capacities. Look, the representation of the impure mother shouts out, look at her. Let women go, and they go crazy. They booze, they shoot up, they have sex with men who shoot up. They romp in the wilderness of addiction. The substance-abusing mothers are the new Bacchae; the addicted baby, the baby with foetal alcohol syndrome, is the new, tiny Pentheus.

It is important for me now to confess my own ethical and emotional response to the figure of the addicted mother in the past. I did respond positively to the chaining of the pregnant, substance-abusing woman to the image of the impure woman. I did so for a number of reasons. My feminism insisted, and still insists, that women are active moral agents, capable of making informed choices and serving as plausible voices. I also believed, and still believe, that we judge a society by the way in which it treats children, an individual by the way in which he or she treats a child. I want babies to be born with the advantages of health, love, sustenance, education. I want pregnant women to treat their bodies conservatively; to abstain, as my mother did, from cigarettes, alcohol, and drugs; to maintain a healthy diet. More problematically, I was angry at women who did not seem abstinent. I blamed them for giving birth to sick babies and resented the social and fiscal cost of the babies' care. Simultaneously I did furiously criticize, blame, and resent the fathers of such babies. Although I have never supported criminalization, I have called, and still do call, for urgent, aggressive programs of intervention that would provide pre- and postnatal care for all women, no matter what the race, no matter what the class. My language eerily echoed that of an Alan Dershowitz.

As I struggled with the ardour of my verdicts against these pregnant women, I fortunately encountered a searing article by Katha Pollitt, the poet. I wish to paraphrase, cite, and interpret it in some detail. For Pollitt pulled me up short. She helped me examine my disciplinary and regulatory rage. I had to become far more self-conscious about my judgments of women in a society that is so brutally indifferent to women, especially poor and minority women, and to their children. Doing so compelled me to contextualize my belief in women as moral agents more finely. Pollitt also glances at the proponents of the theory of the 'duty to care,' a theory I find ethically attractive. They might be sympathetic to women's reproductive rights, but, like Dershowitz, they argue that a woman must care for the foetus if she carries it to full term. But what, Pollitt asks, is a significant risk? How do we know when a mother is harming, not caring for, the foetus?

Although Pollitt is most generally addressing the question of 'foetal rights,' she considers (although not always in my language) the representation of the bad, impure, substance-abusing mother. This question and this representation are inseparable. If the foetus has rights, law and society may have to value this little person above anyone else. The mother, then, has a self-contradictory place in the birth process. On the one hand, she is reduced to the status of a container, a hold for a cargo more precious than she. She is no longer a rich, creative matrix, a shaper, whose placenta is a lifeline that she sustains with her effort, will, imagination, and blood. On the other hand, she is potentially a menace, an actively dangerous force.

Pollitt suggests that the control of the substance-abusing pregnant woman is a first step towards the control of any pregnant woman. Taking care of the bad girls will set a precedent that will enable public authorities to take care of bad and good girls alike. Not coincidentally, the debate about the bad mother is a response to women's new strength, a reaction to 'legalized abortion and contraception, which have given women, for the first time in history, real reproductive power' (416).

Pollitt offers a number of other reasons why we should fear the admonitory measures designed to control the drinkers and druggies. First, she writes, with great persuasiveness, it is at best ironic to punish addicted women when most treatment programs refuse to admit them if they want to enroll. Next, punitive approaches will drive women away from the prenatal care they need. The stigmatizing of abortion also makes it hard for an addicted woman, especially if she is poor or ill, to choose an abortion. If she could do so, she might get well and then have her babies. Next, our concern for the 'innocent' foetus is now a substitute for, not a supplement to, any concern for the health and well-being of women. Moreover, it is patently easier and cheaper to blame the 'bad mother' than to provide women with good social services and health care. Next, the representational practices that generate the picture of the bad/impure mother are careless. They both assume that we know how substances actually affect pregnant women and the foetus and refuse to distinguish among various kinds and levels of substance abuse. 'A joint on the weekend is the moral equivalent of a twenty-four-hour-a-day crack habit; wine with meals is next door to a daily quart of rotgut' (411).

Pollitt is equally sardonic about the professional responses to the substance-using and abusing pregnant woman. The history of medicine, she notes, is not reassuring. In the early 1970s doctors put pregnant women on tranquilizers. In the late 1980s they put pregnant women off everything except a Rocky Mountain high. Some of the research designs and methods of current studies of women, pregnancy, and substance-abuse are flawed. Yet the media, the great furnace that heats up cultural representations, headline the studies that show the bad effects of maternal behaviour and under-report the studies that show the bad effects of paternal behaviour. I must emphasize this point. For such a dangerous habit, which pollutes public consciousness, not only pictures women as stupid, selfish, and bad. It makes the mother assume every risk of pregnancy and exculpates the father from everything. In Tennessee, Pollitt writes, a husband got a court order that forbade his wife to drink or take drugs. He had, however, lost his driver's licence for drunken driving. This is a nasty example of a trend: the expansion of a father's rights movement without any real commitment to a father's fulfilment of his responsibilities, especially if a father does not live with his child. As reproduction is reduced to a unisexual act, men are literally home free.

After such knowledge, what resistance? It will be no shoo-in to dislodge this image of the impure mother, the late-twentieth-century version of the gin-soaked slum mum that haunted earlier cultural imaginations. It will be even more difficult to reform the social and psychological practices (for example, the devaluation of women) that such a heavily interpreted image permits and perpetuates. Wondering about the terms of such a resistance, I met, in late March 1990, a graduate student in the school of education at a major Canadian university, a strong-tongued, feisty birth-child of Ireland. She was telling me about some outrageous efforts to silence her in the classroom, especially when she was analysing the ways in which a classroom replicates larger structures of power. The instructor warned her that she was 'intimidating' the other students. 'Intimidating?' she said scornfully, 'Intimidating? If they're going to go into education, they'd better not be so easily scared by the likes of me. Besides,' she went on, 'I have a theory about conversations. Everybody talks, and you just get your spoke in.'

The woman's pun shows how speech, speaking, the spoken, serves the double, contradictory function of a spoke in the wheel of discourse. A spoke can either prevent a wheel from turning *or* connect the hub of a wheel to its rim. As a preventive, resisting act our speech can sever the linkage of the substance-using mother and the impure woman. We can expose the tawdry meanness and cruel limitations of this representational coupling, its denial of the probability of a woman being in pain and projection of the probability of a woman administering pain to an innocent victim, her own child.

As an act that connects the hub and rim of discourse, our speech can nurture an abundance of alternative representations of women. They will not deny the historical realities of the bad woman. Elena Ceausescu did order those shoes from Paris. She did support policies that forced women into botched abortion after botched abortion, that pushed tainted blood into the veins of babies who now die of AIDS. These alternative inscriptions and scripts will, however, spin out fresh images of goodness. In them, women will have power over themselves and use it freely. They will have power over others and use it sparingly. Though women will manage their own lives, they will help and counsel others. From time to time, they will need help and counsel, as many pregnant women now do. They will call out for a care from society, family, lovers, and friends who must be there. Women will no longer be pure or impure, but pure and impure at once, struggling for small decencies and against the temptations of indecencies.

What will these women wear on their feet? Anything and everything but boots that kick out hurtfully. These women will put on sandals and pumps; slingbacks and loafers; nothing and nothing but rings. The point, however, is not the shoe, but the direction in which the feet can go.

Notes

1 I am indebted to Judith Allen, Shirley Neuman, and Elizabeth Wood for comments. This paper is not meant to be an exhaustive review of the various literatures about the substance-using and abusing mother, but an intervention at a cultural moment. It draws heavily on articles and reports in the *New York Times*, because the *Times* is a paper of record and a barometer of the concerns of the middle, upper-middle, and professional classes. Because my research for this piece ended in 1990, it does not refer to developments since then.

2 *Signs* 15, no. 3 (Spring 1990) is devoted to the analysis of 'a largely white, Western, middle-class ideal of mothering ... this patriarchal story of mothering is of a woman, entirely nurturant and provident, whose shadow side – potential or realized – is entirely wicked and withholding' (441).

3 With her customary incisiveness, Barbara Ehrenreich points out that the 'experts' in the current debate about drugs tend to be male, even though women are 'criminals and crusaders, abusers and enforcers,' as well as researchers (52). She speculates that if more female voices were heard, the rhetoric of war would decrease; there would be more emphasis on treatment and less on punishment; and that a more rational, case-by-case approach to a social response to drugs would emerge.

4 On 29 May 1990, in a less drastic move, a New York State Appeals Court ruled that New York City could ask for a Family Court hearing about child neglect if a child had been born with cocaine in her/his system and if the mother had admitted to drug use. About five thousand such hearings now take place in New York City each year. The biological mother has retained custody in about 25 per cent of these cases. Other children,

the remaining 75 per cent, go into foster care or with relatives ('Hearings on Neglect').
5 I am grateful to John McDowell for bringing this article to my attention.

Works Cited

Capuzzo, Mike. 'Did I Do the Right Thing?' *Life Magazine,* April 1990, 28–34
'Ceausescu Wept As He Faced Firing Squad, Footage Shows.' *New York Times,* April 1990, A10
Cohen, Judith B., Laurie B. Hauer, Constance B. Wofsy. 'Women and IV Drugs: Parenteral and Heterosexual Transmission of Human Immunodeficiency Virus.' *Journal of Drug Issues* 19, no. 1 (1989), 39–56
Dershowitz, Alan. 'Drawing the Line on Prenatal Rights: When a Pregnant Woman Abuses Her Health, Should the State Intervene on Behalf of Baby?' *Los Angeles Times,* 14 May 1989, sec. 5, 5
Ehrenreich, Barbara. 'Sounds of Silence.' *Savvy,* June 1990, 50–3
Harrison, Patricia Ann, and Carol A. Belille. 'Women in Treatment: Beyond the Stereotype.' *Journal of Studies on Alcohol* 48, no. 6 (1987), 574–8
'Hearings on Neglect Upheld in Newborn Cocaine Cases.' *New York Times,* 30 May 1990, B3
Householder, Joanne, et al. 'Infants Born to Narcotic-Addicted Mothers.' *Psychological Bulletin* 92, no. 2 (1982), 453–68
'Ideas and Trends: Punishing Pregnant Addicts: Debate, Dismay, No Solution.' *New York Times,* 10 Sept. 1989, sec. 4, E5
Johnson, Joyce. *What Lisa Knew: The Truth and Lies about the Steinberg Case.* New York: Putnam's 1990
Lewin, Tamar. 'Drug Use in Pregnancy: New Issue for the Courts.' *New York Times,* 5 Feb. 1990, A14
Pettiway, Leon E. 'Participation in Crime Partnerships by Female Drug Users: The Effects of Domestic Arrangements, Drug Use, and Criminal Involvement.' *Criminology* 25, no. 3 (1987), 741–66
Pollitt, Katha. '"Fetal Rights": A New Assault on Feminism.' *Nation* 250, no. 12 26 March 1990, 409–18
Rosenbaum, Marsha. 'Getting on Methadone: The Experience of the Woman Addict.' *Contemporary Drug Problems* 11 (Spring 1982), 113–43
Rosenthal, Elizabeth. 'When a Pregnant Woman Drinks.' *New York Times Magazine,* 4 Feb. 1990, 30–1, 49, 61
Teltsch, Kathleen. 'In Detroit, a Drug Recovery Center That Welcomes the Pregnant Addict.' *New York Times,* 20 March 1990, A8

Notes on Contributors

PAMELA BANTING is assistant professor of English at the University of Western Ontario. She has published articles on postmodern poetry and poetics, feminist and critical theory, translation poetics, and pleasure. Together with the author, she edited Sharon Thesen's *The Pangs of Sunday* (1990). She is currently working on a book on writing the body.

DIANNE CHISHOLM is assistant professor of English at the University of Alberta. She is author of *H.D.'s Freudian Poetics: Psychoanalysis in Translation* (Cornell 1991), and co-editor (with Elizabeth Wright, Margaret Whitford, and Juliet Flower MacCanuell) of *Feminism and Psychoanalysis: A Critical Dictionary* (Blackwell 1992).

PATRICIA DEMERS is professor of English at the University of Alberta, where she teaches Renaissance literature, the Bible, and children's literature. She has edited two anthologies of children's literature, *From Instruction to Delight* (with R.G. Moyles) and *A Garland from the Golden Age*, and published three books: *P.L. Travers, Introducing Louis Hémon's 'Maria Chapdelaine,'* and *Women as Interpreters of the Bible*.

NICOLE DUBREUIL-BLONDIN is professor of art history at the Université de Montréal. She specializes in nineteenth- and twentieth-century art and in art theory and criticism, and has published in Canada and in France. Her dissertation, *La Fonction critique dans le Pop Art américain*, was published by the Presses de l'Université de Montréal in 1980. She is interested in the relationship between feminism and art history.

BRIDGET ELLIOTT teaches nineteenth- and twentieth-century art history in the Department of Art and Design at the University of Alberta. She is co-author with Jo-Ann Wallace of *Modernist (Im)Positionings: Representations of and by Women in Culture, 1900–1939* (Routledge 1993).

UZOMA ESONWANNE is currently assistant professor of English and African studies and a member of the Michigan Society of Fellows at the University of Michigan, Ann Arbor. The essay 'Feminist Theory and the Discourse of Colonialism' is part of an on-going project entitled 'Difference, Interpretation, and Referentiality.'

ELIZABETH GROSZ is director of the Institute of Critical Theory and Cultural Studies at Monash University, Australia. She is the author of *Sexual Subversions: Three French Feminists* and *Jacques Lacan: A Feminist Introduction* and has edited a number of anthologies on contemporary feminist theory.

ISOBEL GRUNDY has just left Queen Mary and Westfield College, University of London, to become Henry Marshall Tory Professor at the University of Alberta. She is the author-editor (with Virginia Blain and Patricia Clements) of *The Feminist Companion to Literature in English: Women Writers from the Middle Ages to the Present* (Yale 1990), and the editor, with Susan Wiseman, of *Women, Writing, History* (1992). She has published chiefly on eighteenth-century women writers and on Samuel Johnson; she is now working on a biography of Lady Mary Wortley Montagu.

LINDA HUTCHEON is professor of English and comparative literature at the University of Toronto. She is the author of *Narcissistic Narrative* (1980; 1984); *Formalism and the Freudian Aesthetic* (1984); *A Theory of Parody* (1985); and *A Poetics of Postmodernism* (1989); and has co-edited *Other Solitudes: Canadian Multicultural Fiction and Interviews* (1990).

KATERYNA OLIJNYK LONGLEY is a senior lecturer in English and comparative literature and dean of humanities at Murdoch University in Western Australia. She is the co-editor of *Striking Chords: Multicultural Literary Criticism* (1991) and *Beckett's Later Fiction and Drama: Texts for Company* (1988). She has also published in the areas of Australian and Canadian literature, in particular on Aboriginal, immigrant, and women's writing.

SHIRLEY NEUMAN, professor and chair of English at the University of Alberta, is the author of monographs and articles on Gertrude Stein, W.B. Yeats, autobiography, women's writing, and Canadian literature. She is co-editor (with Smaro Kamboureli) of the first collection of essays about Canadian women writers, *A Mazing Space: Writing Canadian Women Writing* (1986); (with Ira B. Nadel) of *Gertrude Stein and the Making of Literature* (1988); and editor of *Autobiography and Questions of Gender* (1992). She is at work on a book tentatively titled 'Autobiographies, Bodies, Gender.'

MARY NYQUIST teaches in the women's studies and the literary studies programs at the University of Toronto, where she is also a member of the Department of English. She is the author of articles on feminist theory, Anglo-American realist fiction, and seventeenth-century sexual politics. Co-editor with Margaret Ferguson of *Re-Membering Milton*, she has just written *Joyning Causes: Genesis, Feminism, Milton* (forthcoming: Cornell UP and Methuen).

JEANNE PERREAULT is assistant professor in the Department of English, University of Calgary. She has published on James Joyce, Sharon Riis, and Audre Lorde; is a contributor to *The Feminist Companion to Literature in English*; and, with Sylvia Vance, has compiled and edited *Writing the Circle: Native Women Writers of Western Canada, an Anthology* (1990). She is currently working on a manuscript that examines autography in the writings of contemporary U.S. feminists.

PATRICIA E. PRESTWICH is professor of history at the University of Alberta. She specializes in the history of modern France and in the history of European women in the nineteenth and twentieth centuries. She has recently published a book on alcoholism and the temperance movement in France, *Drink and the Politics of Social Reform: Antialcoholism in France since 1870*. She is currently working on a book-length study of the Parisian psychiatric hospital Saint-Anne.

ROSE MARIE SAN JUAN, assistant professor in the Fine Arts Department at the University of British Columbia, has published in the field of Renaissance studies on fresco decoration and its audiences, gender and collecting practices, and the role of mythology in defining social spaces. Currently she is completing a study on conflicting representations of seventeenth-century urban Rome, particularly in relation to different forms of street spectacle and a diversifying tourist population.

ARUNA SRIVASTAVA is assistant professor at the University of Calgary, where she teaches postcolonial literature. She has published and spoken on South African, Caribbean, Indian, and Canadian South Asian literature, and on pedagog-ical theory. Other areas of interest include writing by aboriginal peoples, African-American literature, writing by women of colour, and feminist theory.

GLENNIS STEPHENSON is lecturer in the Department of English Studies, Univer-sity of Stirling. Her publications include *Elizabeth Barrett Browning and the Poetry of Love* (1989) and *Nineteenth-Century Stories by Women* (1992).

CATHARINE R. STIMPSON is university professor and dean of the graduate school at Rutgers University, New Brunswick, NJ.

JO-ANN WALLACE teaches in the areas of children's literature, women's literary modernism, and women and film at the University of Alberta. She has pub-lished on children's literature, Virginia Woolf, Laura Riding, and film theory, and is the co-author of *Modernist (Im)Positionings: Representations of and by Women in Culture, 1900–1939* (Routledge 1993) with Bridget Elliott. She is cur-rently completing *Feminist Theories of the Body* (forthcoming: Routledge).

PATRICIA YAEGER is associate professor of English at the University of Michigan, Ann Arbor. She is the author of *Honey-Mad Women: Emancipatory Strategies in Women's Writing* and numerous essays, including 'Toward a Female Sublime' in *Gender and Theory: Dialogues on Feminist Criticism*, edited by Linda Kauffman. She has edited *Refiguring the Father: New Feminist Readings of Patriarchy* with Beth Kowalski Wallace, and is working on a new book, 'The Poetics of Birth.'